A FEDERAL RIGHT TO EDUCATION

A Federal Right to Education

Fundamental Questions for Our Democracy

Edited by Kimberly Jenkins Robinson

With a Foreword by Martha Minow and an
Afterword by Congressman Robert C. "Bobby" Scott

NEW YORK UNIVERSITY PRESS
New York

NEW YORK UNIVERSITY PRESS

New York
www.nyupress.org

Library of Congress Cataloging-in-Publication Data
Names: Robinson, Kimberly Jenkins, editor. | Minow, Martha, 1954–   writer of foreword. |
Scott, Bobby, 1947–   writer of afterword.
Title: A federal right to education : fundamental questions for our democracy /
[edited by] Kimberly Jenkins Robinson ; with a foreword by Martha Minow.
Description: New York : New York University Press, [2019] |
Includes bibliographical references and index.
Identifiers: LCCN 2019004715| ISBN 9781479893287 (cl : acid-free paper)
| ISBN 1479893285 (cl : acid-free paper) | ISBN 9781479825899 (pb :
acid-free paper) | ISBN 9781479872770 (library ebook) | 9781479890743
(consumer ebook)
Subjects: LCSH: Right to education—United States. | Educational equalization—Law and
legislation—United States. | LCGFT: Essays.
Classification: LCC KF4155 .F43 2019 | DDC 344.73/079—dc23
LC record available at https://lccn.loc.gov/2019004715

This book is printed on acid-free paper, and its binding materials are chosen for strength and durability. We strive to use environmentally responsible suppliers and materials to the greatest extent possible in publishing our books.

Manufactured in the United States of America

10 9 8 7 6 5 4 3 2

Also available as an ebook

CONTENTS

FOREWORD

"The Whole People Must Take Upon Themselves the Education of the Whole People"

MARTHA MINOW

The whole people must take upon themselves the education of the whole people, and must be willing to bear the expenses of it. There should not be a district of one mile square, without a school in it, not founded by a charitable individual, but maintained at the expense of the people themselves.
—John Adams

What could be more important than preparing the next generation to take up the duties of work, family, and community? Passing on knowledge, culture, and skills is how human societies survive and improve. Education affords individuals chances to develop their capacities, become economically self-sufficient, and grow into adults able to help the next generation following their own. In a constitutional democracy, this crucial task also includes preparation for the responsibilities and opportunities of self-governance. The founders of the United States understood that "[a]n ignorant people can never remain a free people" and that "democracy cannot survive too much ignorance."[1] John Adams, a participant in the Constitutional Convention, the nation's first vice president, and its second president, emphasized the centrality of education to the new nation and the duty of all the people to support education for all the people, as quoted in the epigraph above.

It is difficult to sustain a constitutional democracy committed to protecting fundamental rights and to governance by the people. Doing so requires the engagement and vigilance of people in local communities and across the nation.[2] And in a society committed to individual freedom and equal protection of the law—a society also deeply marked by historical, social, political, and economic inequalities—education is the hope for justice. This vibrant and timely collection of essays explores whether the project of educating the next generation should be recognized as a right established and implemented by the United States government, rather than left to individual states and localities.

From the start, schooling in America excluded many people on the basis of gender, race, disability, ethnicity, and economic resources. The movement for "common schools" that was initiated in the 1830s sought to promote political stability, equip more people to earn a living in a changing economy, and enable people to follow the law and transcend differences in religion and background.[3] State constitutions and statutes embraced these commitments but, in practice, distributed resources unequally and continued to exclude many people. Constitutional amendments after the Civil War laid the predicate for overcoming unequal protection of the law and governmental deprivations of liberty, but public school systems by law, custom, or governmental convenience divided students by race and class. The sustained legal strategy attacking legally mandated racial segregation in schools yielded official victory in 1954 but triggered resistance, and despite some successes, massive racial and economic separation persists in US schools.[4] Disparities in per-pupil expenditures reflect sharp differences in local wealth because most of the country funds schools in significant part on the basis of local property taxes. One commentator reports that we now live in an era of hoarding by upper-middle-class families—those in the top 20 percent of income—that have used zoning laws, local control of schooling, college application procedures, and unpaid internships to pass their opportunities onto their children while making it harder for others to break in.[5]

Policy arguments for sturdier and more fairly shared investments in education are overwhelming. The economic case is compelling; researchers report ongoing shortages of people with skills needed for good jobs.[6] Consider also the civic needs: only 36 percent of Americans can name the three branches of government.[7] People with more education feel more efficacious and participate more in government than others, and low voter turnout contributes to the mismatch between what people report they want from government and the policies that ensue. At a time when political and cultural polarization generates instability and possible violence, schools could cultivate habits and skills of initiative, respect, listening, and controlling emotions in the face of disagreement.

Less clear are whether the US Constitution authorizes a federal right to education, whether there is a viable path toward judicial recognition of this right, and what judicial recognition of such a right would entail.[8] This volume astutely tackles these challenging issues. There are plenty of plausible and even powerful constitutional arguments for a federal right to education, as demonstrated by some of the chapters in this book. The federal constitutional right to education could be implicit in "ordered liberty" or anticipated by the guarantee of a republican form of government or in the conception of the people as sovereign. It could be found as the next step in the line of established and well-regarded judicial opinions. *Brown v. Board of Education* held that educational opportunity, "where the state has undertaken to provide it," is "a right which must be made available to all on equal terms."[9] Each state has chosen to provide public schooling for minors; the federal guarantee of equal protection ensures equal provision, with attention to both tangible and intangible elements, including the potentially stigmatizing effects of legally mandated racial segregation.[10] The Supreme Court reached this judgment after emphasizing the foundational role of education in citizenship, service in the armed forces, the operation of democracy, and preparation for success in life.[11] Other courts have relied on *Brown* to reject exclusion of children with disabilities from public schooling, and the decision laid the foundation for the federal statutory guarantee of a free and appropriate education for all students with disabilities.[12] A political movement supporting litigation and legislative efforts similarly could expand the federal right to effective education for all children.

Equal protection also supplied the basis for the Supreme Court's decision in *Plyler v. Doe* to strike down a state statute denying funding for schooling for undocumented minors and also charging the immigrant children for the loss of state funding.[13] Besides interpreting the Constitution to bar the imposition of a discriminatory burden on children who had little or no control over their movement into the country, the Court rejected defenses by the state and instead stressed that denying the children a proper education would probably lead to "the creation and perpetuation of a subclass of illiterates within our boundaries, surely adding to the problems and costs of unemployment, welfare, and crime."[14] The

Court acknowledged that the Constitution does not specify an individual right to education but also emphasized that education is not merely "some governmental 'benefit' indistinguishable from other forms of social welfare legislation."[15] As the Court continued, it reviewed how often it had hovered on the brink of articulating a fundamental right to education:

> Both the importance of education in maintaining our basic institutions, and the lasting impact of its deprivation on the life of the child, mark the distinction. The "American people have always regarded education and [the] acquisition of knowledge as matters of supreme importance." We have recognized "the public schools as a most vital civic institution for the preservation of a democratic system of government," and as the primary vehicle for transmitting "the values on which our society rests." . . . "[S]ome degree of education is necessary to prepare citizens to participate effectively and intelligently in our open political system if we are to preserve freedom and independence."[16]

When presented with questions about education as a fundamental right, the US Supreme Court has consistently shied away from a declaration while also repeatedly using language of support unlike any other area lacking fundamental right status.

Alternative constitutional bases for a federal right to education include finding a quid pro quo in due process for the constraint on individual liberty enacted by state governments and finding no rational basis for compulsory schooling that fails to provide a minimally adequate education. Nationally authorized education rights could produce more equal opportunities across the country and more protection for vulnerable individuals and groups from neglect or mistreatment in local or state settings. Arguments for a federal right to education could well persuade voters and might even persuade some judges.

Exploring legal and policy arguments for a federal right to education is an important and worthwhile undertaking given the widespread disparities and inadequacies in educational opportunity and achievement—and the crucial role of education to the economy, to the development of knowledge, and to the viability of democracy. Constitutional claims, in particular, can help elevate attention and assist the mobilization of hopes and actions that translate into political and legal change.[17] Yet realistic chances for judicial recognition of such a right diminish with the changing composition of the federal judiciary and the rise of varied versions of originalist interpretation methods for constitutional adjudication, although originalist arguments, stemming from the history of the Fourteenth Amendment, can also be mounted for a federal right, as Derek Black explains in his chapter in this volume.

Serious arguments against a federal right to education are explored by contributors to this volume. Historical, functional, and political defenses call for reserving control over education to state and local governments, and constitutional arguments underscore limitations on the power of Congress and difficulties associated with judicially announced rights that have not been recognized in the past. Even if Congress were to enact a federal right by statute, problems of scope, content, enforcement, and control would arise, as would political and constitutional claims of state and local prerogatives. Equal protection jurisprudence permits leveling down, not just leveling up; deriving rights from due process can be a vexed effort analytically and also may unleash judicial powers that hurt people, even the most vulnerable people.[18] Even courts willing to recognize a federal right might be hard-pressed to articulate its scope and enforceability. State constitutional litigation over school finance gives a taste of these challenges: Is the right standard the same dollar expenditure per pupil, regardless of each pupil's individual needs? Is it the same tax effort by community, reinforcing the wealth differences across local tax bases? Some more substantive definition of a minimally adequate education—defined by whom, measured by inputs or outputs, and at risk of growing outdated—is needed. Some reassurance comes with the durability of the landmark Kentucky Supreme Court decision in *Rose v. Council for Better Education*, but the link to state constitutional language and state economic and political values provides crucial elements that are difficult to duplicate at the federal level.[19]

Justiciability, limits on judicial capacity to craft remedies, and under-enforcement of even a declared right have already hampered efforts in the school desegregation context and would no doubt arise in response to litigation regarding a federal right to education. Conceptual debates over crucial elements of education and practical implementation problems compound the difficulties. Federal legislation seeking to improve educational quality has already triggered backlash against the focus on testing or other measurable results—where the particular prescription may end up uniting both those who seek and those who oppose more federal involvement.

Pursuing discrete pieces of federal legislation could advance educational equity and quality, although definitional and political obstacles remain substantial for this path as well. The political obstacles arise from gridlock in general and from the conservative tilt of the Congress. Definitional and conceptual problems mirror those connected with a constitutional predicate for a federal right to education.

These may be distinctively American problems. International law repeatedly has recognized and advanced a right to education. The Universal Declaration of Human Rights (Article 26), the International Covenant on Economic, Social and Cultural Rights (Articles 13 and 14), the Convention on the Elimination of All Forms of Racial Discrimination (Article 5), the Convention on the Elimination of All Forms of Discrimination against Women (Articles 10 and 14), and the Convention on the Rights of the Child (Article 28) each declare a right to education, embraced by the signatory nations. Until recently, the United States has been a driving force in the development of international human rights, but it has long been reluctant to commit to the laws and institutions designed to implement them.[20] In part, the United States may claim that its own Constitution and laws cover the same territory as international human rights while ensuring enforceability and also protecting national sovereignty. Yet it is striking that a majority of nations around the globe agree that every child must have equal access to a quality education adapted to meet the individual's needs, to develop the individual's potential, and to prepare the individual to participate in society, the economy, and ongoing learning and expression.[21] Alongside the analyses in this book's chapters, Americans might do well to pay attention to these global developments.

A national and indeed a global right to education is in fact more within reach now than ever before, in no small measure due to the resources of this digital age. The Internet, social media, and search engines bring much of the world's knowledge within reach of more people than ever in human history. These resources are no substitute for face-to-face relationships that motivate children to learn and provide support and memorable models, but the digital opportunities offer genuine chances for access not only to knowledge but also to outstanding and personally tailored instruction from peers and teachers who would otherwise not be within reach.[22] The very architecture of the digital age also makes a new educational task urgent: the development of critical thinking about the information and other materials developed by digital tools. Information and disinformation are plentiful and a few keystrokes away. Web tools and social media also enable people to find others with similar interests, to share and spread information and views, and to recruit others because they facilitate one-to-many communication with little cost.[23] And now, the very existence of digital resources creates opportunities and obligations that are urgent if education is to equip succeeding generations to be responsible and savvy recipients of and contributors to the global education and communications of digital worlds.

Founding father John Adams wrote his wife, Abigail Adams, in a 1775 letter, "It should be your care, therefore, and mine, to elevate the minds of our children and exalt their courage; to accelerate and animate their industry and activity; to excite in them an habitual contempt of meanness, abhorrence of injustice and inhumanity, and an ambition to excel in every capacity, faculty, and virtue. If we suffer their minds to grovel and creep in infancy, they will grovel all their lives."[24] Will these sentiments extend as a duty, as Adams thought they should, beyond each parent, in each local community, to the nation as a whole? That is the focus of this entire book, orchestrated by Kimberly Robinson, who carries on here the crucial work of her own teacher, Charles Ogletree, Jr. May this book engender lively debates and vital actions.

NOTES

Epigraph: JOHN ADAMS, THE WORKS OF JOHN ADAMS, SECOND PRESI- DENT OF THE UNITED STATES, Vol. IX, 540 (Little, Brown ed. 1854). Thanks to Mira Singer for the sources on John Adams.

1. Justice David Souter, referring to Thomas Jefferson, in *How to Teach Citizenship in Schools*, ECONOMIST, Feb. 2, 2017, https://www.economist.com.
2. *See* Martha Minow, *Education and Democracy*, HARV. L. REV. BLOG, Oct. 17, 2017, https://blog.harvardlawreview.org. After the Constitutional Convention of 1787, when citizens gathered outside Independence Hall to learn what the delegates had drafted, "[a] Mrs. Powel of Philadelphia reportedly asked Benjamin Franklin, 'Well, Doctor, what have we got, a republic or a monarchy?' With no hesitation whatsoever, Franklin responded, 'A republic, if you can keep it.'" John F. McManus, *"A Republic, If You Can Keep It,"* NEW AM., Nov. 6, 2000, https://www. thenewamerican.com (quoting diary of James McHenry). Significantly, Franklin

said not "a democracy"—which would imply simply majority rule—but "a republic," embracing fundamental rights as well as participatory governance. *Id.*

3. MARTHA MINOW, IN *BROWN'S WAKE: LEGACIES OF AMERICA'S EDUCATIONAL LANDMARK* 115 (2010).

4. Of the fifty-three hundred communities with fewer than one hundred thousand people in this country, at least 90 percent are white, and in large urban districts, upward of 70 percent of the public students are nonwhite and over half are poor or nearly poor. JENNIFER L. HOCHSCHILD & NATHAN SCOVRONICK, THE AMERICAN DREAM AND THE PUBLIC SCHOOLS 25, 37 (2003).

5. RICHARD V. REEVES, DREAM HOARDERS: HOW THE AMERICAN UPPER MIDDLE CLASS IS LEAVING EVERYONE ELSE IN THE DUST, WHY THAT IS A PROBLEM, AND WHAT TO DO ABOUT IT (2017); Richard V. Reeves, *The Dream Hoarders: How America's Top 20 Percent Perpetuates Inequality,* BOSTON REV., Sept. 26, 2017.

6. Allie Bidwell, *Report: Economy Will Face Shortage of 5 Million Workers in 2020,* US NEWS, (July 8, 2013), https://www.usnews.com (estimate that by the year 2020, the US economy will face a shortage of five million educated workers).

7. Reid Wilson, *Only 36 Percent of Americans Can Name the Three Branches of Government,* WASH. POST, Sept. 18, 2014, https://www.washingtonpost.com.

8. *See* Gary B. v. Snyder, No. 2:16-cv-13292, 2018 WL3609491 at *17 (E.D. Mich. July 27, 2018) (dismissing complaint arguing for a federal right to literacy, despite observing, "The conditions and outcomes of Plaintiffs' schools, as alleged, are nothing short of devastating. When a child who could be taught to read goes untaught, the child suffers a lasting injury—and so does society.") *See* Jacey Fortin, *"Access to Literacy" Is Not a Constitutional Right, Judge in Detroit Rules,* N.Y. TIMES, July 4, 2018, https://www.nytimes.com. At the time of this writing, the case is on appeal to the Court of Appeals for the Sixth Circuit.

9. Brown v. Bd. of Educ., 347 U.S. 483, 493 (1954).

10. *Id.* at 495.

11. *Id.* at 493.

12. *See* Individuals with Disabilities Education Act, 20 U.S.C. § 1400 et seq. (building on *PARC v. Commonwealth of Pennsylvania* and *Mills v. Board of Education*).

13. Plyler v. Doe, 457 U.S. 202 (1982).

14. *Id.* at 230.

15. *Id.* at 221 (pointing to *San Antonio Indep. Sch. Dist. v. Rodriguez*, 411 U.S. 1, 35 (1973)).

16. *Id.* (internal citations omitted).

17. *See* JACK M. BALKIN, CONSTITUTIONAL REDEMPTION: POLITICAL FAITH IN AN UNJUST WORLD (2011); ROGER C. HARTLEY, HOW FAILED ATTEMPTS TO AMEND THE CONSTITUTION MOBILIZE POLITICAL CHANGE (2018); Reva B. Siegel, *Text in Contest: Gender and the Constitution from a Social Movement Perspective,* 150 U. PA. L. REV. 297 (2001); Mark Tushnet, *Social Movements and the Constitution, in* THE OXFORD HANDBOOK OF THE U.S. CONSTITUTION (Mark Tushnet, Mark A. Graber & Sanford Levinson eds., 2015).

18. Mark Joseph Stern, *A New Lochner Era*, SLATE, June 29, 2018, https://slate.com.
19. David K. Karem & Debbie Wesslund, *Rose Decision Defines Ky. Education Goals*, COURIER-JOURNAL, Feb. 16, 2017, https://www.courier-journal.com. The Kentucky Supreme Court interpreted the state constitutional language ("The General Assembly shall, by appropriate legislation, provide for an efficient system of common schools throughout the State") to require the state schools to ensure students sufficiently develop seven capacities:

    1. Oral and written communication skills to enable students to function in a complex and rapidly changing civilization;

    2. Knowledge of economic, social and political systems to enable them to make informed choices;

    3. Understanding of governmental processes to enable the student to understand the issues that affect his or her community, state and nation;

    4. Self-knowledge and knowledge of his or her mental and physical wellness;

    5. Grounding in the arts to enable each student to appreciate his or her cultural and historical heritage;

    6. Training or preparation for advanced training in either academic or vocational fields so as to enable each child to choose and pursue life work intelligently; and,

    7. Academic or vocational skills to enable public school students to compete favorably with their counterparts in surrounding states, in academics or in the job market.

    Id. The legislature enacted implementing legislation, and the state is still working under this framework. *Id.*
20. *See* G. John Ikenberry, *Review of Michael Ignatieff, "American Exceptionalism and Human Rights,"* FOREIGN AFF., Nov. 1, 2005, https://www.foreignaffairs.com.
21. *See* NAT'L ECON. & SOC. RIGHTS INITIATIVE, WHAT IS THE HUMAN RIGHT TO EDUCATION?, https://www.nesri.org.
22. Valerie Strauss, *Blended Learning: The Great New Thing or the Great New Hype*, WASH. POST, June 21, 2015, https://www.washingtonpost.com. *See also* MONICA R. MARTINEZ & DENNIS MCGRATH, DEEPER LEARNING: HOW EIGHT INNOVATIVE PUBLIC SCHOOLS ARE TRANSFORMING EDUCATION IN THE TWENTY-FIRST CENTURY (2018).
23. Mary C. Joyce, *The Democratic Power Shift on the Internet*, INTERNET & DEMOCRACY BLOG, BERKMAN CTR., May 14, 2008, http://blogs.harvard.edu; J. M. Berger, *How Terrorists Recruit Online (and How to Stop It)*, BROOKINGS INST. BLOG, Nov. 9, 2015, https://www.brookings.edu; HAL ABELSON, KEN LEDEEN & HARRY LEWIS, BLOWN TO BITS: YOUR LIFE, LIBERTY, AND HAPPINESS AFTER THE DIGITAL EXPLOSION 229–230 (2008).
24. Letter from John Adams to Abigail Adams (Oct. 29, 1775), https://founders.archives.gov.

Introduction

The Essential Questions Regarding a Federal Right to Education

KIMBERLY JENKINS ROBINSON

What the best and wisest parent wants for his own child, that must the community want for all of its children. Any other ideal for our schools is narrow and unlovely; acted upon, it destroys our democracy.
—John Dewey

Although the United States has often been called the land of opportunity, its history reveals that too often opportunities have been unequally distributed. Education serves as a primary example of this inequality in US society, despite the importance of education to an effective democracy, a robust economy, and a just society. Race, class, ethnicity, zip code, and school district boundaries oftentimes mark sharp disparities in educational opportunities, such as in funding, the quality of teachers, the rigor of the curriculum, and the adequacy of facilities, among other differences.

These disparities are tolerated by all levels of government because the United States has never fulfilled its 1954 promise made in *Brown v. Board of Education* that the opportunity to receive an education "where the state has undertaken to provide it, is a right which must be made available to all on equal terms." The United States Supreme Court's decision in *San Antonio Independent School District v. Rodriguez* foreclosed federal challenges to long-standing educational opportunity gaps. In *Rodriguez*, the Court held that the federal Constitution neither explicitly nor implicitly guaranteed a right to education. This decision left remedies for disparities in educational opportunities to the primary province of states and localities.[1]

Reformers, litigators, scholars, policy makers, and educators have proposed an array of reforms to reduce disparities in and raise the quality of educational opportunities. State school finance litigation and reform has served as one of the leading efforts to reduce inequitable disparities.[2] Other reform efforts to reduce disparities in educational opportunities and outcomes include reauthorizations of the Elementary and Secondary Education Act, socioeconomic integration, and school choice, to name only a few.[3] Furthermore, given that the largest disparities in educational opportunity exist between, rather than within, states, many scholars and reformers have noted the need for increased federal intervention to level the playing field between states.[4]

Yet, despite some gains from state school finance litigation and other reforms, disparities in educational opportunity and achievement endure today in substantial part because state and local efforts to close educational opportunity gaps—in the states and localities that have actually worked to reduce them—too often have not been sufficiently powerful and sustained long enough to eradicate them. Instead, success can sometimes be short-lived and superficial such that long-standing commitments to local control, neighborhood schools, and suburban interests remain unchanged impediments to reform. Other states have simply turned a blind eye to these disparities and have imposed high standards on students despite inequitable disparities in educational opportunity that disadvantage many low-income, minority, rural, and other children from reaching those standards.[5] In addition, many federal efforts to incentivize states to reduce opportunity gaps have been weak and ineffective.[6] As a result, generations of schoolchildren, as well as our nation, bear the costs of the national failure to guarantee all children equal access to an excellent education.

The absence of an effective vehicle to achieve equitable and excellent educational opportunities that can consistently be employed throughout the United States has led numerous scholars and advocates to call for recognition of a federal right to education.[7] However, recognizing a federal right to education raises an array of questions that should be examined if such calls are to be taken seriously. This volume brings together numerous leading scholars to consider three critical questions about a federal right to education. First, should the United States recognize a federal right to education? Second, if yes, how should the United States recognize a federal right to education? Finally, what should a federal right to education guarantee?

Before turning to how this book addresses these questions, the nature and scope of educational disparities—in both inputs and outputs—must be understood as one considers the arguments for and against a federal right to education. In addition, this chapter presents the federal legal landscape as an essential context for considering potential answers to these questions. The benefits and limitations of state school finance litigation and reform also inform why reformers and advocates recommend recognition of a federal right to education. The chapter also considers why it matters whether education is recognized as a right by considering what the language of rights can convey. Finally, a brief synopsis of each chapter follows.

This volume builds on *The Enduring Legacy of* Rodriguez: *Creating New Pathways to Equal Educational Opportunity*. In that book, Charles Ogletree, Jr., and I gathered together leading school finance and education scholars to examine how *San Antonio Independent School District v. Rodriguez* had impacted educational opportunities. After several chapters analyzed the impact of *Rodriguez*, most of the book offered novel law and policy solutions at the federal, state, and local levels that could assist in efforts to close opportunity and achievement gaps. The proposals offered a fresh infusion of new ideas that could advance the unfinished work that the *Rodriguez* plaintiffs initiated more than forty years ago.

Enduring Disparities in Educational Opportunities and Outcomes

Research confirms that the scope and depth of the opportunity and achievement gaps are substantial. Deeply entrenched disparities drive the persistent nature of the achievement gaps along lines of race, ethnicity, and poverty, among other disparities. Both the opportunity and achievement gaps have led scholars, lawmakers, and policy makers to contend that the United States should recognize a federal right to education that would help to close these gaps.[8]

The Long-Standing Opportunity Gaps

Although educational opportunity gaps exist within plain view in US society, it is important to understand the nature and scope of the disparities in educational opportunity along lines of race and class because many people remain unaware of their existence, and perceptions of the disparities vary by demographic. A recent poll provides evidence of both this lack of awareness and the variations in the perceptions of these disparities along racial, ethnic, and class lines. A nationwide survey asked parents throughout the United States, "Do you feel that students of color are afforded the same education opportunities as their peers?" The overwhelming majority of whites—81 percent—replied yes, while only 43 percent of African American respondents replied yes, which was considerably less than the 72 percent of Hispanic respondents who replied yes. Only 30 percent of African American parents indicated that schools provide sufficient support to students from low socioeconomic backgrounds, while 66 percent of white parents and 59 percent of Hispanic parents responded that such students receive sufficient support. Parents from low-income households also are significantly less likely than other parents to agree that schools provide adequate support to low-income students.[9] This survey data reveals that parental demographics drive perceptions of opportunity gaps, with parents from minority groups and low-income households being more likely to perceive inferior educational opportunities and support.

Research and data confirm that minority and low-income children receive inferior educational opportunities. The disparities are present in funding, teachers, course offerings, resources, and facilities, among others. For instance, three 2018 reports and a 2019 report on funding gaps found that minority and low-income children receive substantially less state and local funding. The Education Trust recently found that nationally districts that serve the highest number of students of color receive approximately $1,800, or 13 percent, less in state and local per-pupil funds than do districts serving the fewest students of color. The districts serving the highest concentrations of poverty receive approximately $1,000, or 7 percent, less in state and local funds than do districts serving the lowest poverty concentrations. In addition, Ed Build found in its 2019 report that "despite decades of lawsuits throughout the country, there remains a $23 billion gap between white and nonwhite school districts, even though they serve the same number of children."[10] The Education Law Center confirmed that a majority of states fail to supply high-poverty districts with more state and local funding: seventeen states supply less and twenty states supply the same state and local funding to high-poverty districts. Only eleven states provide more state and local funding.[11] These funding disparities persist despite a clear consensus that children living in poverty need more resources—not the same or fewer resources—to compete successfully with their peers. The United States Commission on Civil Rights confirmed these funding gaps and their harmful consequences in its 2018 report on funding inequities.[12]

These funding disparities translate to tangible inequities in resources in schools and classrooms across the United States. Schools that are segregated by race, ethnicity, and class continue to offer inferior educational opportunities. The United States Commission on Civil Rights noted, "Low-income students and students of color are often relegated to low-quality school facilities that lack equitable access to teachers, instructional materials, technology and technology support, critical facilities, and physical maintenance," and these inequities harm student outcomes as well as their health.[13] For instance, research confirms that on every measure of teacher qualifications, low-income and minority students receive less effective teachers when compared to their more affluent and white peers. Districts that educate more low-income and minority students employ a disproportionate number of teachers who are inexperienced and are teaching subjects they are not trained to teach.[14] These challenges encourage a frequent turnover of teachers that disrupts the continuity of the instructional program. The funding disparities noted earlier drive disparities in teacher salaries as well as the quality of the teaching environment. The United States tolerates these disparities in teacher quality despite the fact that "[t]eachers, together with principals, are the single most important in-school factor affecting student achievement."[15]

Schools in low-income and minority communities often lack access to the full complement of honors, Advanced Placement, music, and arts classes, to name a few of the disparities. For example, while 50 percent of all high schools offer calculus, only 38 percent of high schools with high concentrations of African American and Hispanic students offer calculus. Similarly, 60 percent of all high schools offer physics, but 51 percent of high schools with high concentrations of African American and Hispanic students offer physics.[16] Schools that serve more economically disadvantaged students and minorities also experienced a narrowing of the curriculum after test-based accountability was implemented because these schools are more likely to receive lower scores on standardized tests.

These schools have increased instructional time for math and language arts while sacrificing time for other subjects, such as science, social studies, the arts, and physical education. They also are more likely to employ teachers who teach to the test, including teachers who focus only on material that is likely to be tested and who require students to spend a significant amount of time on practice tests. Narrowing the curriculum prevents schools from serving one of the equalizing functions of schools: providing the opportunities that disadvantaged communities cannot.[17]

Schools with high concentrations of minority and economically disadvantaged students also have access to fewer resources within classrooms and schools, and their schools are too often poorly maintained. For instance, many majority-minority urban schools have outdated textbooks in substandard condition, inadequate libraries, and scarce materials, as well as facilities that are both overcrowded and poorly maintained.[18] Further, the National Center for Education Statistics found that the likelihood that survey respondents rate indoor environmental factors such as lighting, heating, water quality, and acoustics as either unsatisfactory or very unsatisfactory increased as the percentage of low-income students increased, while more mixed results were found on these factors as the percentage of minority students increased.[19]

School facilities affect both students' performance and their health, yet disadvantaged communities oftentimes lack the resources they need to maintain high-quality facilities. Local districts bear the greatest burden for making capital investments that districts use to improve, as opposed to simply maintain, their facilities, which results in wealth-based disparities in the ability of districts to invest in new construction or renewals. A study of more than 146,559 school improvement projects across the nation revealed that "projects in schools located in high-wealth zip code areas had more than three times more capital investment than the schools in the lowest-wealth zip code areas."[20] The funding of facilities construction exacerbates the wealth disparities because only five states provide nearly full support for capital investments, twelve states provide no support, and the remaining thirty-three states "vary greatly" in their levels of support.[21] This inequitable funding structure undermines any chance of reducing the facilities gap in the absence of systemic change.

Opportunity gaps remain entrenched because of the deep economic and racial segregation in US schools that both causes and reinforces the inequities in the schools. These opportunity gaps are influential not only annually but also over time because even relatively small deficits compound over the entirety of a child's education to create significant differences in experiences and outcomes.[22]

The Persistent Achievement Gaps

These disparities in educational opportunity substantially contribute to the enduring achievement gaps along lines of race and class, and they converge with other contributing factors to low achievement such as housing, nutrition, health, safety, and out-of-school experiences.[23] Nationally, student achievement has shown some modest gains followed by consistently flat student achievement for schoolchildren since the early 2000s.[24] The achievement gaps between African Americans and whites as well as between Hispanics and whites have declined, although not steadily, over the past forty years. For instance, since 2003, the gaps between the achievement of African Americans and Hispanics when compared to whites have declined by approximately the gains made in half a school year of instruction. Despite this reduction, the gaps remain "very large."[25]

The 2017 results of the National Assessment for Educational Progress (NAEP) confirm these large gaps persist even when modest or significant narrowing occurs. For instance, fourth-grade scores are particularly important because they measure if students have transitioned "from learning to read to reading to learn." This time frame also predicts future successes, such as graduating from high school, attending college, and maintaining employment.[26] African American students on average scored substantially (thirty-two points) below proficient at this grade and also were significantly (twenty-six points) behind their white peers, despite some improvement since 1992 (when the score gap was thirty-two points). This reveals that many fourth-grade African American students are not on track for college and career success.[27] African American eighth and twelfth graders also scored well below their white peers in reading, with the largest gap in twelfth grade at thirty points, and this twelfth-grade reading gap has increased since 1992.[28] Whites also substantially outperform African Americans in math. Despite a decline in the fourth-grade math achievement gap between African Americans and whites, this gap also remained large, at twenty-five points for fourth grade in 2017, and the gap increased in higher grades to thirty-two and thirty points in eighth and twelfth grade, respectively.[29]

A large achievement gap also persists between Hispanics and whites in math and reading. In reading, the largest gap in 2017 was in fourth grade, at twenty-three points, with eighth- and twelfth-grade Hispanics and whites showing a gap of nineteen points and twenty points, respectively. Only the eighth-grade reading score has significantly improved since 1992. In math, the smallest Hispanic and white achievement gap was nineteen points in fourth grade, and, like African Americans, it was higher in eighth and twelfth grades, at twenty-four and twenty-two points, respectively. This Hispanic-white math gap has remained steady over time since 1990.[30]

Whites and Asians also have a significant achievement gap that favors Asians. Asians outperformed other racial groups on NAEP in reading in fourth and eighth grade and performed similar to whites in twelfth-grade reading. In math, Asians outperformed whites in fourth, eighth, and twelfth grades.[31]

A large achievement gap also endures between students of a lower socioeconomic status and their more affluent peers. Students living in poverty, as measured by participation in the National School Lunch Program, consistently performed worse than their peers in reading and math in the results reported in 2017. In reading, the gap declined from twenty-eight to twenty-four points between fourth and eighth grade, while in math the gap increased between fourth and eighth grade from twenty-four to twenty-nine points.[32] Furthermore, research that compares the achievement of students in the top ninetieth percentile in household income versus those in the bottom 10 percent of household income shows a consistent increase in the achievement gap for half a century. This socioeconomic-based gap is twice the size of the very large African American–white achievement gap.[33]

Children from most minority and socioeconomically disadvantaged households also graduate at lower rates than do their peers. According to the National Center for Education Statistics' most recent data, the national average graduation rate for public high school students is 84 percent. However, American Indian / Alaska Native, African American, and Hispanic students all graduate at below-average rates (72 percent,

76 percent, and 79 percent, respectively, in 2015–16). By contrast, white students (88 percent) and Asian students (91 percent) routinely outperform the national average.[34] Moreover, students in tenth through twelfth grades in the lowest socioeconomic quartile drop out between school years at almost twice the rate of students in the highest quartile (7.2 percent versus 3.9 percent).[35]

The persistence of long-standing opportunity and achievement gaps raises the inevitable question: What should the United States do about these gaps? The next section explores how federal and state litigation over disparities in funding and other educational opportunities has attempted to address these gaps.

The Path to Litigation Regarding a Federal Right to Education

Those who are disadvantaged by educational inequality in the United States have sought redress through the courts for more than a century. In 1849, the Supreme Judicial Court of Massachusetts rejected five-year-old Sarah Roberts's challenge of the state law that required her to pass five white elementary schools on her way to a dilapidated and outdated school for African American children. In *Roberts v. City of Boston*, the court held that although colored schoolchildren were entitled to equal rights under state law, the separate provision of education for African American children by the City of Boston was lawful. Yet this defeat did not deter the Roberts family, who worked with attorney Charles Sumner to convince the legislature of the Commonwealth of Massachusetts to be the first state to outlaw segregated schools in the United States in 1855.[36]

School desegregation litigation served as the primary weapon to challenge inequality for much of the middle of the twentieth century. Begun as litigation that attempted to enforce the "equal" portion of "separate but equal" in higher-education institutions, school desegregation efforts ultimately succeeded in convincing the Supreme Court to strike down the odious "separate but equal" doctrine that, despite its name, had consistently relegated African American schoolchildren to inferior educational opportunities. Yet the Court's invitation of protracted compliance, its failure to clarify the required nature and scope of desegregation remedies, and its rush to return districts to local control ultimately undermined the ability of school desegregation to achieve lasting integration or the sought-after reduction in the opportunity gap for African American and other minority schoolchildren.[37]

As advocates began to question whether school desegregation litigation could or would provide equal educational opportunity, they turned to state and federal litigation that challenged funding disparities to close educational opportunity gaps. These efforts achieved an initial much-celebrated victory from the California Supreme Court in *Serrano v. Priest*, in which the court held that the federal Equal Protection Clause both prohibited the wealth discrimination that resulted from the California funding system and protected education as a fundamental interest. The court struck down the California funding system because it was not necessary to advance a compelling state interest. In response to the state's argument that it needed the system to promote local control, the court noted that California could allow localities to control how funds are spent even if all of the funds are not locally raised.[38]

The Legacy of *San Antonio Independent School District v. Rodriguez*

Federal school finance litigation proved short-lived. In *San Antonio Independent School District v. Rodriguez*, the Supreme Court, in a 5–4 decision written by Justice Powell, rejected a challenge of the Texas school funding system under the Equal Protection Clause.[39] In rejecting education as a fundamental right, the Court noted the absence of protection for education in the federal Constitution and expressed its unwillingness to recognize it as an implied constitutional right. The Court explained that neither education's importance nor its close connection to exercising the rights to free speech and to vote would lead the Court to elevate the constitutional scrutiny of disparities in education to strict scrutiny, which is the highest level of judicial scrutiny.[40]

The Court upheld the Texas funding scheme as rationally related to a legitimate state interest, the most lenient standard for constitutional review. The Court provided several reasons for its decision to apply rational basis review. First, it questioned how education could be distinguished from other important personal interests, such as access to shelter and food, for heightened constitutional protection. Second, the Court observed that it lacked expertise to question the state's decision to allow localities to tax local property to fund schools and to second guess the educational policy decisions made by state and local officials. Third, the Court rejected the invitation to disturb the balance of federalism that would occur if it accepted the invitation to overturn the funding system that existed in almost every state. The Court concluded that the Texas system was rationally related to a legitimate state interest in local control of schools and thus constitutional under the federal Equal Protection Clause.[41] Justices Stewart, Brennan, White, and Marshall each filed a separate dissent.[42]

Although the *Rodriguez* Court held that the Constitution did not guarantee a right to education, it also did not foreclose a future claim that a state had not provided a minimally adequate education. The Court commented that if it assumed that the Constitution protects some minimum amount of education that enables individuals to exercise the right to vote and free speech, "no charge fairly could be made that the system fails to provide each child with an opportunity to acquire the basic minimal skills necessary for the enjoyment of the rights of speech and of full participation in the political process." Instead, the plaintiffs had failed to make such a claim and instead had only challenged "relative differences in spending levels."[43] Thus, the Court upheld the constitutionality of spending differences but did not address whether the federal Constitution guarantees a minimally adequate education.

Since *Rodriguez*, the Court has acknowledged its holding that education is not a fundamental right, but it also has noted that it has not foreclosed future federal recognition of a minimally adequate education while also trumpeting the importance of education.[44] Indeed, it appeared to give some special protection to education in the *Plyler v. Doe* decision when it overturned a Texas law that permitted districts to exclude children who had not been legally admitted to live in the state. The *Plyler* Court stated that it applied rational basis review to overturn the Texas law, while subjecting the rationale offered by the state of Texas to rigorous scrutiny. The *Plyler* Court also heralded the importance of education in stating, "[N]either is [public education] merely some governmental 'benefit' indistinguishable from other forms of social welfare legislation. Both the importance of education in maintaining our basic institutions, and the lasting impact of its deprivation on the life of the child, mark the distinction. The 'American people have always regarded education and [the] acquisition of knowledge as matters of supreme importance.' . . . We have recognized 'the public schools as a most vital civic institution for the preservation of a democratic system of government' . . . and as the primary vehicle for transmitting 'the values on which our society rests.'"[45] These and other statements by the Court regarding education and the door left open by *Rodriguez* to recognize a right to an adequate education provide the Court latitude to recognize a federal right to education if it so chooses.

The *Rodriguez* decision drove litigation on school funding disparities out of federal court and into state court, where it has mostly remained until quite recently.[46] The next section describes both the benefits of school finance litigation and reform and also their limitations. The limitations of state litigation and reform have led advocates and scholars to advance new cases and theories in federal court that might provide a more consistent and widely available forum to address educational inequities and inadequacies. The subsequent section describes recent federal litigation.

The Benefits and Limitations of State School Finance Litigation and Reform

Following *Rodriguez*, state school finance litigation advanced two converging theories that sought to define states' constitutional obligation for education, as discussed in greater detail by Joshua Weishart in chapter 12. Litigation has sought greater equity of funding, greater adequacy of funding to enable students to learn the content of state standards, or some combination of both.[47] Plaintiffs have prevailed in a state's highest court in twenty-three states and have never prevailed in the state's highest court in twenty states.[48]

One important benefit of this litigation has been the emergence of a consensus that money spent well matters in education, a consensus that is based in part on expert testimony in numerous state courts that established a link between educational resources, opportunities, and outcomes. This consensus supplies an answer to one of the key questions that the *Rodriguez* Court noted remained open to debate as it highlighted its lack of expertise to resolve education policy debates.[49]

Research also has confirmed several important benefits from successful litigation. For instance, a 2016 comprehensive study of adequacy litigation found that successful litigation led states to drive additional resources to low-income districts and that these "reforms increased the absolute and relative achievement of students in low-income districts."[50] Research also indicates that sustained school funding reform can provide such benefits as an increase in the number of years of school completed, an increase in adult earnings, and a reduction in adult poverty. Successful litigation followed by comprehensive reform also can help to improve student achievement.[51] A 2017 study analyzed the impact of court-ordered finance reform from 1989 to 2010 and found that seven years after the system was reformed, funding and graduation rates increased by approximately 11 percent for the students in the highest poverty quartile in a state. This study also found that additional money spent in high-poverty districts had a greater impact than did any additional money spent in districts that were not poor.[52]

However, even when plaintiffs prevail, they face formidable obstacles to securing relief. For instance, the New Jersey litigation is celebrated as some of the most successful school finance litigation in the country; but it took numerous decades to secure, and even then the legislature has underfunded the revised funding formula since 2011. This has left many schoolchildren in New Jersey without the benefits that additional, sustained funding could bring.[53] The obstacles to the New Jersey reform are not unique to the Garden State. Instead, resistance to successful school finance litigation is often fierce, protracted, and effective in limiting the scope of reforms. Additionally, research by the education scholar and University of Virginia President James Ryan found that urban, minority districts rarely prevail in court and meet more prolonged and intense legislative resistance when they do succeed.[54]

Furthermore, with some notable exceptions, even where state litigation has succeeded and reform has occurred, the changes too often tinker at the margins of school funding while leaving the expectations of middle-class suburbanites untouched.[55] For instance, funding schools through local property taxes remains the prevailing method for raising the local contribution to schools,[56] despite the fact that this guarantees disparate contributions to education that are tied to the wealth of a community rather than a community's appetite for investment in education. Similarly, courts also have not redrawn school district lines, which would help to redistribute wealth. As a result, the funding increases that do occur and that help to raise student achievement are occurring within systems that are fundamentally flawed in ways that hinder comprehensive reform.[57]

Most importantly, the benefits of successful school finance reform are limited to those states where plaintiffs have found a sympathetic state supreme court or where coalitions have prevailed on legislatures to upend the expectations of the more privileged families within the state. Children who had the misfortune to be born in states where litigation or reform has not occurred remain stuck in schools that too often are funded irrationally, inequitably, and inadequately. These flaws remain because school finance systems reveal "the absence of any concrete relationship between school funding and the actual cost of meeting substantive state standards and performance goals, along with turning a blind eye toward the manner in which funding is used by districts and in schools and classrooms."[58]

Given the deeply entrenched and long-standing shortcomings of many state finance systems, many scholars and advocates, including those who have prevailed in state court, agree that state forums are inadequate to accomplish the full scope of reform that is needed to end inequitable and insufficient educational opportunities and to transform schools into the high-quality institutions that students need today to be college and career ready. For instance, Michael Rebell, who successfully led the New York litigation *Campaign for Fiscal Equity v. State*, commented in his chapter in *The Enduring Legacy of* Rodriguez that despite the gains of state school finance litigation, state litigation wins lack "the power and the sustained impact of a federal constitutional right." Therefore, he contends that *Rodriguez* should be overturned because providing all children "meaningful educational opportunities . . . simply cannot be accomplished on a state-by-state basis."[59] David Sciarra successfully litigated much of the New Jersey *Abbott* litigation that has required the New Jersey legislature to tailor its funding of schools to the disparate needs of students and the state standards that guide instruction. Yet he and his coauthor, Danielle Farrie, endorse in their chapter in *The Enduring Legacy of* Rodriguez a greater federal role in education to strengthen the link between standards-based education and school funding.[60]

An array of scholars also has called for federal reforms that address the failure of states to provide equitable and excellent schools. For instance, Areto Imoukhuede has contended that the federal Due Process Clause requires the government to provide a high-quality education. The education scholar and current California Supreme Court Justice Goodwin Liu has argued that the Fourteenth Amendment affords and requires Congress to provide "a meaningful floor of educational opportunity" that enforces national citizenship rights. I also have called for a gradual and incremental increase in federal involvement in school funding that would incentivize states to provide funding that ensures equal access to an excellent education.[61]

Two federal commissions also have both highlighted the inequitable nature of state funding of schools and have called for greater federal involvement in education to address these inequities. The Equity and Excellence Commission was the first federal commission to examine state funding since President Nixon's 1972 review noted that a heavy reliance on property taxes caused large inequities. The 2013 report notes a laundry list of flaws of school funding that burdens schoolchildren, their families, and communities. For example, the Equity and Excellence Commission noted that states continue to fund education through methods that are not linked to the cost of providing students with the content of robust standards and ensuring high academic performance for all students, including students who live in poverty, English-language learners, and students with disabilities. These broken systems endure in part because only a few states have measured the cost of delivering the knowledge in content standards, particularly across diverse groups of students. States also fail to ensure the efficient allocation of resources. Therefore, the commission calls for "bold" reform by both states and the federal government that, among other things, includes federal incentives to ensure all students receive a "meaningful educational opportunity," as well as "'equity and excellence' legislation" that directs additional federal funding to schools with high concentrations of poverty, that incentivizes states to invest in schools with the greatest needs, and that monitors federal investments to ensure that they help to improve student achievement.[62]

The United States Commission on Civil Rights issued a report in 2018 that identified similar flaws in state funding of schools and recommended federal and state action to remedy these flaws. The commission found that "vast funding inequities in our state public education systems render the education available to millions of American public school students profoundly unequal."[63] The commission endorsed the recommendations of the Equity and Excellence Commission while it offered several recommendations of its own. It acknowledged that a quality education has become even more essential since *Rodriguez* and thus recommended that "Congress should make clear that there is a federal right to education." It also urged federal, state, and local governments to promote communities that are integrated racially and socioeconomically because integration benefits the opportunities provided in public schools.[64]

The next section explores the recent return to federal court to address disparities in educational opportunities.

The Recent Return to Federal Court

Litigants recently have returned to federal court to attempt to secure redress for inadequate learning conditions in three cases. This litigation is noteworthy for its attempt to seek federal redress for these conditions because these issues have primarily been litigated in state court since *Rodriguez*. In the fall of 2016, schoolchildren in Detroit filed *Gary B. v. Snyder*, a case that alleged that the state of Michigan has denied them the access to literacy that is protected by the federal constitutional Due Process and Equal Protection Clauses. The plaintiffs argue that they have been functionally excluded from the state education system through such conditions as insufficient access to qualified teachers, "inadequate instructional materials," and unsafe physical conditions, "includ[ing] vermin infestation, extreme temperatures, insufficient or inappropriate facilities, and overcrowding." The plaintiffs allege that the right to literacy "means not only the ability to recognize or pronounce a written word, but the ability to use language to engage with the world—to understand, analyze, synthesize, reflect, and critique"—and that to receive this right to literacy, the schools must offer such basics as "appropriately trained teaching staff, basic instructional materials and safe physical conditions that do not impede learning." The complaint also alleges that the state has engaged in intentional race discrimination against the Detroit schoolchildren through this functional exclusion.[65]

The federal court in the Eastern District of Michigan rejected the plaintiffs' claims. The court acknowledged, "The conditions and outcomes of Plaintiffs' schools, as alleged, are nothing short of devastating. When a child who could be taught to read goes untaught, the child suffers a lasting injury—and so does society."[66] The court also recognized the importance of education to voting, access to justice, meaningful participation in civic life, obtaining a job and a home, and securing government benefits. Yet the court held that access to literacy was not a fundamental right under the Due Process Clause because to recognize a fundamental right the Supreme Court requires that both justice and liberty would not exist without state-provided access to literacy. Although the history of the United States demonstrates a long-standing commitment to education, this history "runs counter to the notion that ordered society demands that a state provide one." The court concluded that the Due Process Clause does not require the state to offer each child "a defined, minimum level of education by which the child can attain literacy." The court also rejected the plaintiffs' claims of intentional race discrimination because they could not show disparate treatment of the Detroit schoolchildren when compared with children at other Michigan schools that were controlled by emergency managers and the plaintiffs failed to show that the state's decisions lacked a rational basis.[67] The plaintiffs' appeal of the decision is currently pending before the United States Court of Appeals for the Sixth Circuit.

A second lawsuit also seeks relief in federal court from substandard educational opportunities. In *Martinez v. Malloy*, schoolchildren and parents in Bridgeport and Hartford have sued the governor of Connecticut and other state officials in the federal court in Connecticut. They allege that the students' rights under the Equal Protection and Due Process Clauses of the Fourteenth Amendment are being violated because trapping students in schools that have been failing for decades imposes a long-lasting stigma on the children and discriminates against them in ways that undermine their dignity and liberty. Plaintiffs seek an injunction against enforcement of Connecticut laws that limit the opening of new magnet schools, hinder charter schools, and penalize interdistrict transfer. A federal court also rejected these claims. The court noted that the federal Constitution does not guarantee a right to education. The court also noted that Connecticut made a rational decision to remedy the shortcomings in failing schools, rather than create a new system of magnet and charter schools.[68]

A.C. ex rel. Waithe v. Raimondo represents a third attempt by advocates to invite a federal court to recognize a federal right to education.

Filed in late fall 2018, the case asks the federal court in Rhode Island to find that Rhode Island has violated the federal Constitution's Fourteenth Amendment by failing "to provide all students a meaningful opportunity to obtain an education adequate to prepare them to be capable citizens." The complaint notes that in *Rodriguez* the Supreme Court left open the question of whether the Fourteenth Amendment provides students a fundamental right to "the basic minimal skills necessary for the enjoyment of the rights of speech and of full participation in the political process." The complaint charges Rhode Island with decades of neglect of the civic aims of education and provides evidence of a profound lack of knowledge of the foundations of our democracy among students. No ruling has been issued in the case.[69]

Despite the initial lower-court losses in *Gary B.* and *Martinez*, the return of litigants to federal court to challenge disparities in educational opportunity remains noteworthy for at least two reasons. First, these cases signal that advocates may develop additional theories for relief in federal court that could spark further litigation (although some reformers might strategically delay such lawsuits until a more favorable majority sits on the United States Supreme Court). This is particularly likely given that these federal cases were brought by distinct groups of attorneys.[70] Second, given the deplorable conditions and outcomes described in the Detroit, Bridgeport, Hartford, and Rhode Island schools, the return to federal court confirms what scholars and advocates have contended for some time: state courts should not remain the sole arbiters of claims regarding the inadequacies and inequities of public schools.[71] In the many states where state school finance litigation and legislative reform have been unsuccessful or ineffective, communities need another forum to secure the educational opportunities that will enable their children to be engaged and productive citizens as well as college and career ready.

This recent litigation, as well as the work of federal commissions, advocates, and scholars, reveals the growing groundswell of support for federal involvement in education broadly as well as a federal right to education specifically. The next section considers why this volume frames its analysis around a right to education protected by the federal government, rather than analyzing other options for closing opportunity and achievement gaps. In *The Enduring Legacy of* Rodriguez, Charles Ogletree Jr. and I included in parts 2 and 3 of the book an array of innovative state and federal approaches to achieve this goal. This volume asks the tough questions regarding a federal right to education as a reform strategy.

Why an Education Right?

A variety of education advocates are employing the language of rights as they push for reform.[72] The discourse of rights, as Ronald Dworkin famously argued, arises because rights can serve as "political trumps" that enable an individual to make a claim against the people in power that must be privileged above other collective goals.[73] Rights can help to shift the balance of power toward those who are disadvantaged by the current system and public officials.[74] A wide-scale reform effort typically relies on the creation and enforcement of a right because in the United States, rights language, particularly federal rights, conveys a national priority.[75]

Rights also can influence both the internal mind-set and external actions of rights-holders. The language of rights empowers individuals to seek the attention, resources, and actions required to protect the right.[76] In this way, rights can encourage individuals to "name . . . a long-experienced injustice" and to identify an entitlement to better treatment.[77] With this newfound understanding, rights encourage individuals to engage in political organizing and mobilization that capitalize on the new balance of power.[78] Individuals will rally around a right to demand change[79] far more often than they rally around a singular government program.

An education right can help to move education away from the haves and have-nots paradigm and toward a common understanding of the education to which all children are entitled.[80] In our majoritarian democracy, the interests of the minority can too often be neglected.[81] Such a right also can limit what the majority may do and serve as a counterbalance to the tradition of state and local control that too often can neglect equity issues.[82] A right to education can help to provide citizens the education they need to participate in democratic governance. Furthermore, a right to education can inform those who receive a substandard education that their inferior education is neither inevitable nor deserved.[83]

It is important to acknowledge that a right to education, just like any right, may fall short of attaining its aims. For example, Mary Ann Glendon offers a comprehensive critique of rights language as one that "promotes unrealistic expectations, heightens social conflict, and inhibits dialogue that might lead toward consensus, accommodation, or at least the discovery of common ground."[84] In many ways, some of Eloise Pasachoff's arguments in chapter 3 of this volume echo these sentiments when she argues that a right might undermine the ability of Congress to reach consensus on specific programs and reforms.

Rights also have been criticized as ineffectual at accomplishing systemic reform and failing to target the economic inequality that lies at the root of the need for rights. Thus, rights require an individual to identify discrimination and claim one's right, but these claims do not remedy deep structural inequities.[85] Richard Ford provides compelling arguments in support of this critique in contending, "Rights can offer limited improvements in a narrow set of circumstances, but the effectiveness of the civil rights approach diminishes and its costs increase as they are applied to more novel, complex, and elusive social problems."[86] The cautionary tales regarding rights that these and other scholars tell must be acknowledged and accounted for as a federal right to education is contemplated, contested, and endorsed.

In pushing for a national dialogue about a federal right to education, the scholars in this volume who support a federal right to education are under no illusion that a federal right to education would be a cure-all for the nation's education ills. Instead, this volume explores the critical questions surrounding a federal right to education because such a right warrants serious deliberation among the array of options that education reformers and advocates are considering to advance equity and excellence in education. Simply put, the privileged place that rights enjoy in US law and society and their conveyance of political and moral urgency given their potential to trump majority interests offers an important but imperfect vehicle to achieve these aims. Such a right would not guarantee equal access to an excellent education. Achieving that goal will require a broad demand for reform by the public, a realignment of political pressures to support equity rather than elitism, and an array of education and social programs. Nevertheless, a federal right to education has the potential to ignite these actions in a way that other reforms do not. Therefore, this volume builds on the current dialogue—both political and scholarly—that contends that education is a critical civil rights issue of our time.[87]

The Structure of a Federal Right to Education

This volume examines the why, how, and what questions that surround recognition of a federal right to education. Part 1 considers the arguments for and against a federal right to education. Part 2 assumes that a federal right to education would reap important benefits and considers how such a right could be implied, enacted, or adopted. Part 3 analyzes what a federal right to education should guarantee.

The exploration of why the United States should or should not recognize a right to education begins with chapter 1 by Jason P. Nance. Nance offers the rationales for the federal government to address the current inequalities and inadequacies within the education system, including economic, criminal justice, health, democratic, and fairness rationales. He also critiques past and current federal legislation designed to address these disparities and concludes that such legislation has been inadequate to remedy these shortcomings. In fact, federal legislation has established conditions for such disparities to continue and perhaps widen. Nance concludes by arguing that further federal intervention is needed and that the time is ripe for the creation of a federal right to a high-quality education for all children that can be enforced by both federal agencies and courts.

Kristine L. Bowman continues this volume's exploration of why a federal right to education would be beneficial in chapter 2. She explores state-level obstacles to closing educational opportunity gaps that explain why the United States should not solely rely on state courts or legislatures to remedy inequitable and inadequate state education systems. At the state level, weak or unenforceable rights to education, limited fiscal capacity, and the absence of sufficient political will too often intersect in ways that undermine educational opportunities and leave many schoolchildren without an effective avenue for relief. Bowman focuses on Michigan as a case study to understand these dynamics and also situates Michigan's experience in the national context to shed light on the limitations of state reform.

Eloise Pasachoff then offers an array of arguments against a federal right to education in chapter 3. She argues that a federal constitutional right to education is both unnecessary and insufficient, regardless of whether that right is developed through constitutional amendment by Congress and the states or through constitutional interpretation by federal courts. She contends that it is unnecessary because the goals that advocates have for a constitutional right to education can already be accomplished through ordinary legislation using Congress's powers under the Constitution's Spending Clause. She argues that it is insufficient because having a constitutional right to education would not remove practical limits on Congress and federal courts in ensuring its implementation. While there is an argument that building a movement for a constitutional right to education would itself create change, Pasachoff highlights the downsides to that work, from breeding cynicism about government (if the constitutional right is declared but fails to achieve its goals in practice) to furthering destructive politics (if, as is more likely, the movement to achieve a constitutional right fails while creating conflict and reducing the possibility of finding common ground on smaller reform projects). She concludes that advocates instead should focus their energy on reforms that have a greater likelihood of success.

In chapter 4, Kevin R. Johnson argues that Latina/os would benefit from a federal right to education as a means to supplement an array of litigation strategies that have failed to ensure equal educational opportunity for Latina/os. He argues the growth in the Latina/o population has been accompanied by widespread segregation of Latina/o students in schools across the country. Heavily Latina/o schools on the average are funded at significantly lower levels than predominantly white schools are, and educational outcomes for Latina/os on average lag behind those of all other racial groups. Johnson concludes that Latina/os, suffering from stark educational inequalities, would benefit from a federal right to education.

Part 2 explores three avenues for creating or acknowledging a federal right to education: a judicially implied right, a congressionally created right, and a constitutional amendment. In chapter 5, Derek W. Black surveys the various litigation, judicial, and scholarly theories through which courts might recognize a right to education under the United States Constitution. He begins by sorting those theories into their major doctrinal categories and subcategories and explaining their basic arguments, including substantive due process, equal protection, privileges and immunities, citizenship, and originalism. Black then critically evaluates those theories, examining both their strengths and weaknesses. He concludes that while a number of theories are plausible, scholarly theories have tended toward originalism in recent years and are the most likely to be successful before the courts.

In chapter 6, Peggy Cooper Davis notes that in a democratic republic, the people are sovereign and must be free and educated to exercise that sovereignty. She contends that the history of chattel slavery's denial of human sovereignty in the United States, slavery's overthrow in the Civil War, and the Constitution's reconstruction to restore human sovereignty demonstrate this truth. Davis argues that the sovereignty of the American people provides a basis for recognizing that the personal rights protected by the United States Constitution, as amended upon the demise of slavery, include a fundamental right to education that is adequate to enable every person to participate meaningfully as one among equal and sovereign people.

I identify the challenges and benefits of Congress adopting a federal right to education in chapter 7. I note that the current backlash against the federal role in education and the lack of political will for greater federal involvement in education will forestall calls for a congressional right to education in the near future. Nevertheless, Congress possesses numerous strengths to recognizing a federal right to education over the courts that make it a forum worthy of serious consideration. I contend that Congress should adopt an incremental approach to recognizing a federal right to education that begins with incentives that set the stage for a federal right and that culminate with a federal law that requires states to provide equal access to an excellent education.

The Southern Education Foundation (SEF) makes the case for an Education Amendment to the United States Constitution in chapter 8. SEF begins with an examination of why a high-quality education is vital to the United States' national interests and contends that it is time for a fundamental change that embraces a federal guarantee of a high-quality education. SEF acknowledges the positive impacts of equity and adequacy litigation, while also noting that this litigation is unable to address radical inequality in the willingness or capacity of states to provide equitable and adequate resources for a high-quality education. SEF argues that an Education Amendment is the best approach for reducing radical disparities in the opportunity to learn and for ratifying public support for national leadership in education. An Education Amendment also would help to build public consensus for effective reform. SEF concludes by explaining why an effort to pass such an amendment would have a positive impact even if the effort was unsuccessful.

Part 3 analyzes what a federal right to education should guarantee. In chapter 9, Linda Darling-Hammond confronts the question of what floor of educational opportunity a federal right to education should guarantee. Darling-Hammond considers research regarding the resources that students need to receive an excellent and equitable educational opportunity, including high-quality teachers and principals as well as access to a rigorous curriculum and the course materials and technology needed for a modern education. She argues that a federal right to education should guarantee these resources for all children as the nation strives to eliminate educational opportunity and achievement gaps.

In chapter 10, Rachel F. Moran explains that equal educational opportunity is essential to prepare students for civic duties, but significant inequalities inevitably result from sorting students for jobs. In recent years, efficiency has become a driving force behind school reform, one that subordinates equal citizenship to the demands of a global economy. These tensions are most evident in school finance reform as calls for equal education devolve into demands for adequate education. Despite state court victories, disparities in per-pupil resources remain severe, threatening to deprive disadvantaged children of any meaningful opportunity to approximate the accomplishments of their privileged peers. In Moran's view, reformers must craft a right to education that guarantees every child a fair opportunity to compete. Only then will disadvantaged students have authentic pathways to civic participation and upward mobility, pathways that can make the American dream feel like a real promise rather than a remote possibility.

In chapter 11, Carmel Martin and Ulrich Boser, along with their associates Meg Benner and Perpetual Baffour, examine five decades of state fiscal-equity cases and determine what lessons can be used to inform the development—and enforcement of—a federal right to education. They conclude that the federal government will need to go beyond simply requiring that education be a right. In other words, the federal government also will need to ensure that all schools have adequate levels of funding and address fiscal accountability and enforcement.

In chapter 12, Joshua E. Weishart concludes part 3 by noting that courts have resolved lawsuits invoking state constitutional rights to education in ways that have subdued the tension between two principles of justice: equality and liberty. The equality-versus-adequacy debate in school funding challenges at first stoked that tension, until court decisions gradually demonstrated their potential interrelation. State constitutions, however, do not fix standards for the mutual enforcement of educational equality and adequacy, and thus, courts have struggled with remedies that serve both aims. Weishart contends that reconciliation ultimately must come through reconceptualizing children's equality and liberty interests as an integral demand for equal liberty, one that treats differently situated children according to their needs so as to cultivate positive freedoms for equal citizenship. A federal right to education can elucidate this demand and facilitate its enforcement, aligning with the newly professed synergy between equal protection and substantive due process.

In the volume's conclusion, I highlight the lessons and themes that emerge from the chapters. I also explore the characteristics and benefits of a "right" that justify a rights-based response to disparities in educational opportunities and outcomes. I acknowledge that a federal right to education is far from a perfect vehicle to close educational opportunity and achievement gaps but assert that it remains superior to the other reforms that have been tried and have failed to disrupt long-standing opportunity and achievement gaps and to ensure that all children receive equal access to an excellent education. In the afterword, Congressman Robert C. "Bobby" Scott of Virginia notes the shortcomings of federal education law and policy and calls for recognition of a federal right to education to fulfill *Brown*'s promise of equal educational opportunity.

NOTES

Epigraph: John Dewey, *The School and Social Progress, in* THE SCHOOL AND SOCIETY 19 (1907).

1. Brown v. Bd. of Educ., 347 U.S. 483, 493 (1954); Charles J. Ogletree, Jr. & Kimberly Jenkins Robinson, *Creating New Pathways to Equal Educational Opportunity, in* THE ENDURING LEGACY OF *RODRIGUEZ*: CREATING NEW PATHWAYS TO EQUAL EDUCATIONAL OPPORTUNITY 263, 264 (Charles J. Ogletree, Jr. & Kimberly Jenkins Robinson eds., 2015).

2. For an overview of some of the gains from state funding litigation, *see* Michael A. Rebell, Rodriguez *Past, Present, and Future, in* THE ENDURING LEGACY OF *RODRIGUEZ, supra* note 1, at 65, 68–75 (summarizing trends in state school funding litigation); David G. Sciarra & Danielle Farrie, *From* Rodriguez *to* Abbott: *New Jersey's Standards-Linked School Funding Reform, in* THE ENDURING LEGACY

OF *RODRIGUEZ, supra* note 1, at 119, 125–33 (detailing the successful *Abbott* litigation in New Jersey).

3. *See, e.g.*, Richard D. Kahlenberg, *Introduction: Socioeconomic School Integration*, *in* THE FUTURE OF SCHOOL INTEGRATION: SOCIOECONOMIC DIVERSITY AS AN EDUCATION REFORM STRATEGY 1, 2–3 (2012) (noting that some districts are increasingly considering economic integration as a strategy to improve student achievement); Kimberly Jenkins Robinson, *Disrupting the Elementary and Secondary Education Act's Approach to Equity*, 103 U. MINN. L. REV. 915, 974–97 (2018) (proposing how the Elementary and Secondary Education Act should be reformed to promote greater equity and excellence in educational opportunity); Gerard T. Robinson, *Can the Spirit of* Brown *Survive in the Era of Choice? A Legal and Policy Perspective*, 45 HOW. L.J. 281, 335 (2002) ("[O]ur nation can use school choice as a tool to keep the spirit of *Brown* alive.").

4. *See, e.g.*, LINDA DARLING-HAMMOND, THE FLAT WORLD AND EDUCATION: HOW AMERICA'S COMMITMENT TO EQUITY WILL DETERMINE OUR FUTURE 280 (2010); Rebell, *supra* note 2, at 72–85; Kimberly Jenkins Robinson, *Disrupting Education Federalism*, 92 WASH. U. L. REV. 959, 961, 1002–05 (2015).

5. Darling-Hammond, *supra* note 4, at 73–74; JAMES E. RYAN, FIVE MILES AWAY, A WORLD APART: ONE CITY, TWO SCHOOLS, AND THE STORY OF EDUCATIONAL OPPORTUNITY IN MODERN AMERICA 153 (2010).

6. Derek W. Black, *Leveraging Federal Funding for Equity and Integration*, *in* THE ENDURING LEGACY OF *RODRIGUEZ, supra* note 1, at 227, 229–41; Kimberly Jenkins Robinson, *The High Cost of Education Federalism*, 48 WAKE FOREST L. REV. 287, 293–330 (2013); Kimberly Jenkins Robinson, *Resurrecting the Promise of* Brown: *Understanding and Remedying How the Supreme Court Reconstitutionalized Segregated Schools*, 88 N.C. L. REV. 787, 811–39 (2010).

7. *See, e.g.*, QUALITY EDUCATION AS A CONSTITUTIONAL RIGHT: CREATING A GRASSROOTS MOVEMENT TO TRANSFORM PUBLIC SCHOOLS (Theresa Perry et al. eds. 2008); Susan H. Bitensky, *Theoretical Foundations for a Right to Education under the U.S. Constitution: A Beginning to the End of the National Education Crisis*, 86 NW. U. L. REV. 550, 632 (1992); Julius Chambers, *Adequate Education for All: A Right, an Achievable Goal*, 22 HARV. C.R.-C.L. L. REV. 55, 69–72 (1987); Barry Friedman & Sara Solow, *The Federal Right to an Adequate Education*, 81 GEO. WASH. L. REV. 92, 110–48 (2013); Goodwin Liu, *Education, Equality and National Citizenship*, 116 YALE L.J. 330, 399–406 (2006); Ogletree & Robinson, *supra* note 1, at 264; Rebell, *supra* note 2, at 80–85; Kimberly Jenkins Robinson, *The Case for a Collaborative Enforcement Model for a Federal Right to Education*, 40 U.C. DAVIS L. REV. 1653, 1712–16 (2007).

8. For examples of scholars recommending recognition of a federal right to education, see note 7 above. For examples of lawmakers recommending legislation that would protect a federal right to education, see chapter 7 text and accompanying notes 5 to 9. For examples of policy makers recommending a federal right to

education, see US COMM'N ON CIVIL RTS., PUBLIC EDUCATION FUNDING INEQUITY IN AN ERA OF INCREASING CONCENTRATION OF POVERTY AND RESEGREGATION 10 (2018) ("Congress should make clear there is a federal right to a public education."); Catherine E. Lhamon, Children Can't Wait: Why Congress Should Declare a Federal Right to Public Education (March 21, 2018), https://www.youtube.com (remarks by Catherine Lhamon, Chair, US Commission on Civil Rights).

9. PATHWAYS IN EDUCATION & YOUGOV, PARENT VIEWS ON EDUCATION, EQUALITY (2015), www.educationsurveyresults.org; Gerard Robinson, *A Tale of Two Disparity Gaps*, BROOKINGS INST.: BROWN CTR. CHALKBOARD, (June 20, 2016), https://www.brookings.edu.

10. IVY MORGAN & ARY AMERIKANER, EDUC. TR., FUNDING GAPS 2018: AN ANALYSIS OF FUNDING EQUITY ACROSS THE U.S. AND WITHIN EACH STATE 6, 10 (2018); EDBUILD, 23 BILLION 2 (2019), https://edbuild.org. EdBuild defines a nonwhite district as one that is 75 percent or more nonwhite students and a white district as one that is 75 percent or more white students.

11. BRUCE D. BAKER, DANIELLE FARRIE & DAVID SCIARRA, EDUC. LAW CTR., IS SCHOOL FUNDING FAIR? A NATIONAL REPORT CARD 9 (7th ed. 2018).

12. U.S. COMM'N ON CIVIL RIGHTS, PUBLIC EDUCATION FUNDING INEQUITY IN AN ERA OF INCREASING CONCENTRATION OF POVERTY AND RESEGREGATION 9 (2018).

13. *Id.* at 5, 9–10.

14. *See* Linda Darling-Hammond, *Inequality and School Resources: What It Will Take to Close the Opportunity Gap, in* CLOSING THE OPPORTUNITY GAP: WHAT AMERICA MUST DO TO GIVE EVERY CHILD AN EVEN CHANCE 77, 84–87 (Prudence L. Carter & Kevin G. Welner eds., 2013) [hereinafter CLOSING THE OPPORTUNITY GAP]; THE SAGUARO SEMINAR, HARVARD KENNEDY SCHOOL, CLOSING THE OPPORTUNITY GAP 36 (2016) (noting the teacher quality gap between low-income students and their peers) [hereinafter SAGUARO SEMINAR]; US DEP'T OF EDUC., EQUITY & EXCELLENCE COMM'N, FOR EACH AND EVERY CHILD: A STRATEGY FOR EDUCATION EQUITY AND EXCELLENCE 21 (2013).

15. US DEP'T OF EDUC., EQUITY & EXCELLENCE COMM'N, *supra* note 14, at 21.

16. *Id.* at 27; US DEP'T OF EDUC., OFFICE FOR CIVIL RIGHTS, 2015–2016 CIVIL RIGHTS DATA COLLECTION: STEM COURSE TAKING 5 (2018).

17. Christopher H. Tienken & Yong Zhao, *How Common Standards and Standardized Testing Widen the Opportunity Gap, in* CLOSING THE OPPORTUNITY GAP, *supra* note 14, at 111, 114–56.

18. Darling-Hammond, *supra* note 14, at 83.

19. DEBBIE ALEXANDER & LAURIE LEWIS, NAT'L CTR. FOR EDUC. STATISTICS, CONDITION OF AMERICA'S PUBLIC SCHOOL FACILITIES: 2012–13, at 11, Table 6 (2014).

20. 21ST CENTURY SCH. FUND, NAT'L COUNCIL ON SCH. FACILITIES & CTR. FOR GREEN SCH., STATE OF OUR SCHOOLS: AMERICA'S K–12 PUBLIC SCHOOL FACILITIES 4, 7, 18 (2016).

21. *Id.* at 4.

22. Darling-Hammond, *supra* note 14, at 82–83; SAGUARO SEMINAR, *supra* note 14, at 37–38.

23. Prudence L. Carter & Kevin Welner, *Achievement Gaps Arise from Opportunity Gaps, in* CLOSING THE OPPORTUNITY GAP, *supra* note 14, at 1, 3.

24. Michael Hansen et al., *Have We Made Progress on Achievement Gaps? Looking at Evidence from the New NAEP Results,* BROOKINGS INST.: BROWN CTR. CHALKBOARD (blog), (Apr. 17, 2018), https://www.brookings.edu.

25. EDUCATIONAL OPPORTUNITY MONITORING PROJECT, STAN. CTR. FOR EDUC. POLICY ANALYSIS, RACIAL AND ETHNIC ACHIEVEMENT GAPS, http://cepa.stanford.edu (last visited Apr. 30, 2018); Hansen et al., *supra* note 24.

26. Haley Ast, *Nation's Report Card Begs Us to Get Back to Basics,* U.S. CHAMBER OF COMMERCE FOUNDATION, (Apr. 19, 2018), https://uschamberfoundation.org.

27. NAT'L CTR. FOR EDUC. STATISTICS, U.S. DEP'T OF EDUC., THE NATION'S REPORT CARD, NAEP READING REPORT CARD: NATIONAL STUDENT GROUP SCORES AND SCORE GAPS (2018), https://www.nationsreportcard.gov [hereinafter NCES GRADE 4 READING]; CTR. FOR PUB. EDUC., LEARNING TO READ, READING TO LEARN: WHY THIRD-GRADE IS A PIVOTAL YEAR FOR MASTERING LITERACY 1–6 (2015).

28. NAT'L CTR. FOR EDUC. STATISTICS, U.S. DEP'T OF EDUC., THE NATION'S REPORT CARD, NAEP READING REPORT CARD: NATIONAL STUDENT GROUP SCORES AND SCORE GAPS (2018), https://www.nationsreportcard.gov [hereinafter NCES GRADE 8 READING]; NAT'L CTR. FOR EDUC. STATISTICS, U.S. DEP'T OF EDUC., THE NATION'S REPORT CARD, 2015 MATHEMATICS AND READING AT GRADE 12, NATIONAL SCORE GAPS (2015), https://www.nationsreportcard.gov [hereinafter NCES GRADE 12 GAPS].

29. NAT'L CTR. FOR EDUC. STATISTICS, U.S. DEP'T OF EDUC., THE NATION'S REPORT CARD, NAEP MATHEMATICS REPORT CARD, NATIONAL STUDENT GROUP SCORES AND SCORE GAPS (2018), https://www.nationsreportcard.gov [hereinafter NCES GRADE 4 MATH]; NAT'L CTR. FOR EDUC. STATISTICS, U.S. DEP'T OF EDUC., THE NATION'S REPORT CARD, NAEP MATHEMATICS REPORT CARD: NATIONAL STUDENT GROUP SCORES AND SCORE GAPS (2018), https://www.nationsreportcard.gov [hereinafter NCES GRADE 8 MATH]; NCES GRADE 12 GAPS, *supra* note 28.

30. *See* Hansen et al., *supra* note 24; NCES GRADE 4 READING, *supra* note 27; NCES GRADE 8 READING, *supra* note 28; NCES GRADE 12 GAPS, *supra* note 28; NCES GRADE 4 MATH, *supra* note 29; NCES GRADE 8 MATH, *supra* note 29.

31. *See* NCES GRADE 4 READING, *supra* note 27; NCES GRADE 8 READING, *supra* note 28; NCES GRADE 12 GAPS, *supra* note 28; NCES GRADE 4 MATH, *supra* note 29; NCES GRADE 8 MATH, *supra* note 29.

32. *See* NCES GRADE 4 READING, *supra* note 27; NCES GRADE 8 READING, *supra* note 28; NCES GRADE 4 MATH, *supra* note 29; NCES GRADE 8 MATH, *supra* note 29.

33. Sean Reardon, *The Widening Academic Achievement Gap between the Rich and the Poor: New Evidence and Possible Explanations, in* WHITHER OPPORTUNITY? RISING INEQUALITY, SCHOOLS, AND CHILDREN'S LIFE CHANCES 91, 91 (Greg J. Duncan & Richard J. Murnane eds., 2011).

34. NAT'L CTR. FOR EDUC. STATISTICS, THE CONDITION OF EDUCATION 2018: PUBLIC HIGH SCHOOL GRADUATION RATES 3–5 (2018), https://nces. ed.gov.

35. NAT'L CTR. FOR EDUC. STATISTICS, TRENDS IN HIGH SCHOOL DROP-OUT AND COMPLETION RATES IN THE UNITED STATES (2016), https://nces. ed.gov.

36. Roberts v. City of Boston, 59 Mass. 198, 209 (1849); RICHARD KLUGER, SIMPLE JUSTICE: THE HISTORY OF *BROWN V. BOARD OF EDUCATION* AND BLACK AMERICA'S STRUGGLE FOR EQUALITY 74–76 (Vintage Books ed. 2004).

37. Brown v. Bd. of Educ., 347 U.S. 483, 495 (1954) (holding that separate schools are "inherently unequal" and thus unconstitutional for public school systems); Sweatt v. Painter, 339 U.S. 629, 635–36 (1950) (holding that the University of Texas at Austin must admit Mr. Sweatt because the separate African American law school that it required him to attend was not equal to the law school at the University of Texas at Austin); McLaurin v. Okla. State Regents, 339 U.S. 637, 642 (1950) (holding that the disparate treatment at a state graduate school for education violated the plaintiff's right to equal protection of the law); Missouri ex rel. Gaines v. Canada, 305 U.S. 337, 351–52 (1938) (holding that a state that offers an in-state law school to white students must provide an in-state law school to African American students); Robinson, *Resurrecting the Promise of* Brown, *supra* note 6, at 811–35.

38. Serrano v. Priest, 487 P.2d 1241, 1258–63 (Cal. 1971); RYAN, *supra* note 5, 121–22 (noting that litigators turned to school-finance litigation when it appeared that desegregation failed to provide African American students with equal resources).

39. San Antonio Indep. Sch. Dist. v. Rodriguez, 411 U.S. 1, 35 (1973).

40. *See id.* at 35–37.

41. *See id.* at 37, 40–42, 44, 49–50, 55.

42. For a summary of most of the dissenting opinions, *see* Charles J. Ogletree, Jr. & Kimberly Jenkins Robinson, *Introduction, in* THE ENDURING LEGACY OF *RODRIGUEZ, supra* note 1, at 7–9.

43. *See Rodriguez,* 411 U.S. at 37.

44. *Compare* Papasan v. Allain, 478 U.S. 265, 285 (1986) ("As *Rodriguez* and *Plyler* indicate, this Court has not yet definitively settled the questions whether a minimally adequate education is a fundamental right and whether a statute alleged to discriminatorily infringe that right should be accorded heightened equal protection review.") *with* Kadrmas v. Dickinson Pub. Sch., 487 U.S. 450, 458 (1988) ("Nor have we accepted the proposition that education is a 'fundamental right,' like

equality of the franchise, which should trigger strict scrutiny when government interferes with an individual's access to it."); Plyler v. Doe, 457 U.S. 202, 221 (1982) ("Public education is not a 'right' granted to individuals by the Constitution.").

45. *Plyler*, 457 U.S. at 221 (internal citations omitted).

46. One exception to school-funding litigation being filed in state court is *Powell v. Ridge*, in which the United States Court of Appeals for the Third Circuit rejected a motion to dismiss a complaint that alleged that the disparate impact regulations of Title VI of the Civil Rights Act of 1964 prohibited a funding system that had a disparate impact on the basis of race. *See* Powell v. Ridge, 189 F.3d 387, 394, 397–403 (3rd Cir. 1999). The United States Supreme Court's rejection of a private cause of action under the disparate impact regulations prevented this litigation from moving forward. *See* Alexander v. Sandoval, 532 U.S. 275, 288–93 (2001).

47. Ogletree & Robinson, *supra* note 42, at 12.

48. *School Finance Litigation Cases, in* THE ENDURING LEGACY OF *RODRIGUEZ*, *supra* note 1, at 275, 277. Since the publication of *The Enduring Legacy of* Rodriguez, school finance plaintiffs lost in the highest state court in Mississippi. This loss raises the number of states in which plaintiffs have lost and never prevailed in the state's highest court from nineteen to twenty. *See* Clarksdale Mun. Sch. Dist. v. State, 233 So. 3d 299, 304–05 (Miss. 2017).

49. *Rodriguez*, 411 U.S. at 43; Ogletree & Robinson, *supra* note 1, at 266–68 (summarizing some of the research that shows that money spent well matters); Rebell, *supra* note 2, at 71.

50. Julien Lafortune et al., *School Finance Reform and the Distribution of Student Achievement* 31 (Nat'l Bureau of Econ. Research, Working Paper No. 22011, 2016). The study noted the caveat that the average low-income student does not live in a generally low-income district, and thus reforms targeted at low-income students might need to focus on reform within districts rather than between districts. *See id.* at 33–34.

51. ANNE NEWMAN, REALIZING EDUCATIONAL RIGHTS: ADVANCING SCHOOL REFORM THROUGH COURTS AND COMMUNITIES 82 (2013) (noting the improved student achievement after the successful *Rose* litigation in Kentucky); C. Kirabo Jackson et al., *The Effects of School Spending on Educational and Economic Outcomes: Evidence from School Finance Reforms*, 131 Q.J. ECON. 157, 160 (2016); Sciarra & Farrie, *supra* note 2, at 121–22 (summarizing research showing improved student outcomes from funding increases and reductions in funding inequities).

52. Christopher A. Candelaria & Kenneth A. Shores, *Court-Ordered Finance Reforms in the Adequacy Era: Heterogeneous Causal Effects and Sensitivity* 15–16, 30 (2017) (Stan. Ctr. for Educ. Policy Analysis Working Paper).

53. Sciarra & Farrie, *supra* note 2, at 125–33.

54. *See* RYAN, *supra* note 5, at 153, 171.

55. *See id.* at 153–54, 177.

56. BETTY COX ET AL., THE COSTS OF EDUCATION: REVENUE AND SPENDING IN PUBLIC, PRIVATE AND CHARTER SCHOOLS 34 (2013); US DEP'T OF EDUC., EQUITY & EXCELLENCE COMM'N, *supra* note 14, at 17.

57. RYAN, *supra* note 5, at 153. *See also id.* at 177–78 ("Unless and until the basic politics of educational opportunity change, attempts to secure increased funding and to translate that funding into real improvement on the ground will meet with halting success at best. By working within the current political reality, rather than trying to change it, courts and school finance lawyers are working at the margins of educational opportunity. Indeed, at the end of the day, they may unintentionally be doing as much as anyone to entrench the current politics and structure of educational opportunity, where poor and minority students remain largely separate from their wealthier and white peers, and where most disparities in opportunity and result follow from that basic fact.").

58. Sciarra & Farrie, *supra* note 2, at 142.

59. Rebell, *supra* note 2, at 72–73.

60. Sciarra & Farrie, *supra* note 2, at 135–41.

61. Areto A. Imoukhuede, *Education Rights and the New Due Process*, 47 IND. L. REV. 467, 467 (2014); Goodwin Liu, *Education, Equality and National Citizenship*, 116 YALE L.J. 330, 334–35, 357 (2006); Kimberly Jenkins Robinson, *No Quick Fix for Equity and Excellence: The Virtues of Incremental Shifts in Education Federalism*, 27 STAN. L. & POL'Y REV. 201, 220–37 (2016).

62. US DEP'T OF EDUC., EQUITY & EXCELLENCE COMM'N, *supra* note 14, at 17, 19.

63. US COMM'N ON CIVIL RIGHTS, *supra* note 8, at 5, 9.

64. *See id.* at 10.

65. Complaint at 3–4, 77–78, 125–27, Gary B. v. Snyder, No. 2:16-cv-13292, 2018 WL 3609491 (E.D. Mich. July 27, 2018).

66. *Gary B.*, 2018 WL 3609491, at *16–19 (emphasis added).

67. *See id.*

68. Complaint at 3–4, Prayer for Relief, Martinez v. Malloy, No. 3:16-cv-01439 (D. Conn. Aug. 23, 2016); Martinez v. Malloy, No. 3:16-cv-1439, slip op. at 29–32, 36–37 (D. Conn. Sept. 28, 2018).

69. Complaint at 2, 4, A.C. ex rel. Waithe v. Raimondo, No. 18-cv-00645 (D.R.I. Nov. 28, 2018) (quoting San Antonio Independent School District v. Rodriguez, 411 U.S. 1, 37 (1973)). The case alleges violations of the Equal Protection, Due Process, and Privileges and Immunities Clauses of the Fourteenth Amendment. It also alleges violations of the Republican Guarantee Clause of Article IV, Section 4, of the United States Constitution for failing to prepare students to be effective civic participants. *See id.* at 41–45.

70. Derek W. Black, *The Constitutional Compromise to Guarantee Education*, 70 STAN. L. REV. 735, 763 (2018).

71. *See, e.g.*, Rebell, *supra* note 2, at 72–73, 85; Robinson, *supra* note 7, at 1671–73, 1686–89.

72. NEWMAN, *supra* note 51, at 1. A robust body of scholarship examines the benefits and shortcomings of "rights." A thorough review of this literature is beyond the

scope of this chapter; however, some of the most prominent arguments are noted here.

73. RONALD DWORKIN, TAKING RIGHTS SERIOUSLY xi (1977).

74. NEWMAN, *supra* note 51, at 95.

75. Michael A. Rebell, *The Right to Comprehensive Educational Opportunity*, 47 HARV. C.R.-C.L. L. REV. 47, 52 (2012).

76. *See* NEWMAN, *supra* note 51, at 1; Rebell, *supra* note 75, at 52–53; Martha Minow, *Interpreting Rights*, 96 YALE. L.J. 1860, 1879–80 (1987).

77. MICHAEL W. MCCANN, RIGHTS AT WORK: PAY EQUITY REFORM AND THE POLITICS OF LEGAL MOBILIZATION 88 (1994) (internal quotation omitted). *See also* Minow, *supra* note 76, at 1867.

78. STUART A. SCHEINGOLD, THE POLITICS OF RIGHTS: LAWYERS, PUBLIC POLICY AND POLITICAL CHANGE 131 (2d ed. 2004); MCCANN, *supra* note 77, at 11.

79. *See* MCCANN, *supra* note 77, at 88; Rebell, *supra* note 75, at 52. *See also* Robinson, *The High Cost of Education Federalism*, *supra* note 6, at 293–305, 307–14, 322–30 (explaining how efforts to advance equal educational opportunity were hindered by an insistence on state and local control of education).

80. Barry Friedman & Sara Solow, *The Federal Right to an Adequate Education*, 81 GEO. WASH. L. REV. 92, 151 (2013).

81. *See* NEWMAN, *supra* note 51, at 12.

82. *See id.* at 1; Cynthia G. Brown, *From ESEA to ESSA: Progress or Regress?*, *in* THE EVERY STUDENT SUCCEEDS ACT: WHAT IT MEANS FOR SCHOOLS, SYSTEMS AND STATES 153, 164–65 (Frederick M. Hess & Max Eden eds., 2017).

83. NEWMAN, *supra* note 51, at 93, 116.

84. MARY ANN GLENDON, RIGHTS TALK 14 (1991).

85. Sally Engle Merry, *Inequality and Rights*, 48 LAW & SOC'Y REV. 285, 285 (2014).

86. Richard Thompson Ford, *Rethinking Rights after the Second Reconstruction*, 123 YALE L.J. 2942, 2944 (2014). *See also generally* RICHARD THOMPSON FORD, RIGHTS GONE WRONG: HOW LAW CORRUPTS THE STRUGGLE FOR EQUALITY (2011).

87. Among others, Presidents George W. Bush and Barack Obama have characterized education as an important civil rights issue. Former US secretary of education Arne Duncan has similarly characterized education. *See* JACK JENNINGS, PRESIDENTS, CONGRESS, AND THE PUBLIC SCHOOLS: THE POLITICS OF EDUCATION REFORM 205–06 (2015). *See also* Catherine Rice, *Two Decades of Presidents Have Called America's Schools a "Civil Rights Issue"—Here's Why That's Troubling*, BUS. INSIDER, Mar. 16, 2017, https://www.businessinsider.com; Valerie Strauss, *Why It's Worth Re-reading George W. Bush's 2002 No Child Left Behind Speech*, WASH. POST, Dec. 9, 2015, https://www.washingtonpost.com; US DEP'T OF EDUC., STATEMENT BY US SECRETARY OF EDUCATION ARNE DUNCAN ON THE 50TH ANNIVERSARY OF THE CIVIL RIGHTS ACT OF 1964 (2014), https://www.ed.gov.

PART I

Why the United States Should (or Should Not) Consider
Recognizing a Federal Right to Education

1

The Justifications for a Stronger Federal Response to Address Educational Inequalities

JASON P. NANCE

Introduction

Inequalities within our nation's public education system stubbornly persist on multiple levels with respect to several student groups but particularly with respect to race and poverty. These inequalities are present in both access to educational resources and educational results. Research confirms that students of color and low-income students are more likely to attend schools in deplorable physical conditions;[1] to have less access to higher-level courses, counselors, gifted and talented programs, and music and art programs;[2] to be taught by teachers who are less credentialed, less experienced, and lower paid;[3] and, to attend racially segregated schools where there are lower levels of peer competition and support.[4] For example, in Livingston Junior High School, a school in Alabama where most of the students are from low-income families and all of them are African Americans, there are several broken windows, the bathrooms have broken stalls, tiles fall from the ceiling, the roof leaks, and there is mold, peeling paint, and cracked floors throughout the school.[5] In William Penn School District, a school district in Philadelphia where most of the students are African Americans, students run to arrive early to class during the winter months in order to receive the best blankets because they attend a school with uninsulated metal walls.[6]

Many disparities in educational opportunity can be traced to funding inequalities. Per-pupil spending varies significantly on many levels, thereby limiting the educational opportunities and achievement for many children. For example, a recent study reveals that in the majority of states the difference between the highest and lowest spending district is over $10,000 per student (and over $20,000 in some states).[7] Furthermore, funding disparities too often do not correspond to differences in student needs. In almost half the states, school districts serving more affluent students on average receive more money per student than do school districts serving impoverished students.[8] In those states that do provide on average more funding to high-poverty school districts, only a handful provide substantially more funding to higher-poverty school districts.[9] One empirical study found that on average the highest poverty school districts in the nation spend approximately $1,200 less per student than do the lowest poverty school districts.[10] That same study also found that on average school districts serving the highest concentrations of students of color spend approximately $2,000 less per student than school districts with the highest concentrations of white students do.[11] These funding inequalities are particularly concerning because economists document that increases in funding for low-income school districts lead to increases in student achievement.[12]

As important as adequate funding is for providing a meaningful educational opportunity, student integration is just as important, if not more important. Poor students attending predominantly middle-class schools benefit from (1) attending schools where parents are more involved in the school community and know how to hold the school accountable for shortcomings, (2) having more highly skilled teachers who have higher expectations for their students, and (3) being surrounded by peers who are more academically engaged and less likely to misbehave.[13] Indeed, several empirical studies confirm that student integration along socioeconomic status (SES) lines (which is highly correlative to integration along racial lines) is a critical component for student achievement.[14] To be clear, none of these studies suggest that simply going to school with poor children directly impacts a student's ability to achieve. Rather, the level of student poverty in a school turns out to be a proxy for other school characteristics that do directly affect student achievement.[15]

Heather Schwartz studied seven years of performance data from 850 low-income students in Montgomery County, Maryland. These students were randomly assigned to public housing apartments that were zoned for either moderate-poverty schools or low-poverty schools. The school district made a series of educational investments to support the students who attended the moderate-poverty schools, such as full-day kindergarten, reduced class sizes, increased professional development for teachers, and specialized instruction for high-needs students, but did not make these investments in the low-poverty schools. After five to seven years, students assigned to low-poverty schools outperformed their peers who attended moderate-poverty schools in both reading and math. In addition, by the time the low-income children who attended the low-poverty schools graduated from elementary school, the gap existing between the low-income children and the other children was cut by one-third for reading and one-half for math. These findings underscore that the opportunity to attend a predominantly middle-class school may be more critical to closing the achievement gap than providing additional resources to high-poverty schools.[16]

Unsurprisingly, we also find stark inequalities in educational outcomes for minority and low-income students. Recent data show that 48 percent of fourth-grade, 42 percent of eighth-grade, and 48 percent of twelfth-grade African American students read below grade level, compared to 21 percent, 15 percent, and 21 percent of white students, respectively.[17] These wide achievement gaps were also present with respect to Hispanic students, American Indian / Alaska Native students, and low-income students generally.[18] Sean Reardon recently analyzed roughly forty million state achievement-test scores in grades three through eight during 2009–13 in every public school district in the country.[19] He found that, on average, African American students score roughly two grade levels lower than white students in the same district, and Hispanic students score roughly one and a half grade levels lower.[20] One also observes academic achievement disparities with respect to student wealth, except that, notably, these achievement gaps have widened over the past few decades, not narrowed.[21] Alarmingly, Reardon's massive study revealed that differences in the average student achievement levels between school districts serving the most and least socioeconomically advantaged students nationally exceeded four grade levels.[22]

Inequalities within the public education system hurt our children and nation in dramatic ways. Our children's future employment and income opportunities, as well as their overall levels of happiness, are severely limited when they do not reach their full potential.[23] There are also staggering economic and social costs associated with undereducating a significant proportion of our children.[24] Not only does our nation lose the opportunity to achieve higher economic growth, to increase tax revenues, and to fortify our democracy, but poor education also is associated with bad health and a high mortality rate, increased reliance on public assistance, and increased involvement in the criminal justice system.[25] Strikingly, economists estimate that increasing graduation rates even by one-third would result in an aggregate annual savings of approximately $250 billion for our nation.[26]

While there are strong rationales for the federal government to rectify current education inequalities, past and current federal legislation has largely failed and, in fact, in some ways has created conditions for disparities to widen. For example, the No Child Left Behind Act's test-based accountability approach did not sufficiently narrow achievement gaps and, instead, had several unintended consequences for all children, particularly marginalized children. The Every Student Succeeds Act (ESSA) also fails to adequately address these inequalities. ESSA provides tremendous discretion to states to devise accountability structures, many of which have shown no signs in the past or present of rectifying education inequalities. Furthermore, Title I of the Elementary and Secondary Education Act, which was enacted to create more education opportunities for impoverished children, does not provide nearly enough resources to address current inequalities. In addition, the rules governing disbursement of Title I funds severely limit Title I's reach to adequately narrow education inequalities. It is time for the federal government to enact stronger legislation to narrow education inequalities and create equal education opportunities for all children. Not only would this benefit marginalized students and families, but it would benefit all students and our nation as a whole.

Why the Federal Government Should Address Inequalities in Education

Although inequalities in education deserve immediate attention, the vast majority of states do not appear to be addressing them in a meaningful way.[27] In fact, from 2008 to 2012, almost every state cut spending to public education, and, as of 2015, the majority of states still provided less funding to public education than they did prior to the recession.[28] While that in and of itself might justify a stronger response by the federal government, there are other compelling rationales for the federal government to address our nation's stark educational inequalities, including economic, criminal justice, health, democratic, and fairness rationales.

Economic Rationale

Lower educational attainment imposes significant economic costs on our nation. Education is fundamental to our nation's economic growth because economic growth depends in part on the ability of our workforce to efficiently accomplish complex tasks, understand and solve problems, and adapt to change.[29] Employers are rapidly replacing unskilled laborers with lower levels of education with machines or are outsourcing lower-level work to laborers in other countries who are willing to work for lower wages.[30] To accomplish complex tasks and earn high wages, workers must have strong literacy, numeracy, analytical, technical, and problem-solving skills.[31]

Historically, the US education system has helped create an educated workforce that sustained a high level of economic growth.[32] However, education inequalities threaten to stand in the way of our continued economic growth and ability to compete internationally.[33] Our school-age population has and will increasingly become more racially and ethnically diverse.[34] If we fail to properly educate and prepare such a sizeable portion of our youth to enter the workforce, our nation will lose a valuable economic growth opportunity.[35] As Marta Tienda and Sigal Alon observe, "The opportunity costs of not closing achievement and graduation gaps will continue to grow as global market integration continues apace. Rising to this monumental challenge requires a highly skilled labor force. The window of opportunity to harness the demographic dividend is closing, but unlike developing countries with high youth dependency rates, the United States has the economic resources to make the necessary investments. Whether it has sufficient political will is the real question."[36]

Henry Levin and Clive Belfield attempted to quantify the cumulative costs to our nation of inequalities within our education system in terms of real dollars. They observe that workers with more education earn significantly more wages over their lifetimes than do workers with less education. Workers who graduated from high school earn over $300,000 more over their lifetimes than high school dropouts; workers who attended some college earn over $400,000 more than high school drop-outs; and, workers who attained a college degree earn over $1.2 million more than high school dropouts. Thus, increasing the education level of workers could provide significant additional sources of tax revenue for federal, state, and local governments.[37]

Not only do Levin and Belfield demonstrate that higher levels of education are associated with higher earnings and more tax revenue, but they also show that higher levels of education are associated with less involvement in the criminal justice system, less dependence on public welfare programs, and better health. Thus, reducing education inequalities also can lead to tremendous savings in government expenditures in these areas. Strikingly, these economists estimate that providing schools with the resources to help close the current high school dropout rate by one-third would result in an annual savings of approximately $250 billion for our nation.[38] For the sake of comparison, the total public elementary-secondary school system expenditure for the fiscal year of 2015 was $639.5 billion.[39]

Criminal Justice Rationale

The federal government also should address our nation's educational inequalities because of the strong association between a weak education and increased levels of involvement in the criminal justice system and the costs that crime imposes on the federal government and society. Scholars explain this connection by pointing out that education levels are associated with higher earnings, and higher earnings increase the opportunity cost of serving time in prison and spending time engaging in criminal acts.[40] Furthermore, education may help individuals to become more risk-averse and less impatient, causing individuals to more deeply consider the possibility of future punishment for breaking laws.[41] Education may also help individuals develop a greater distaste for criminal behavior, improve social habits, and better understand the societal benefits of obeying the law.[42]

Several empirical studies show a strong connection between dropping out of school and eventually becoming incarcerated.[43] For example, 40 percent of all institutionalized persons in 2009 had failed to graduate from high school, compared to 8 percent of noninstitutionalized persons.[44] Examining several sources of data, Lance Lochner and Enrico Moretti found that higher education levels were strongly associated with reduced criminal activity and that "the estimated effects of education on crime cannot easily be explained away by unobserved characteristics of criminals [or] unobserved state policies that affect both crime and schooling."[45]

Just as we observe racial disparities relating to education, racial disparities relating to incarceration rates are also well documented.[46] Nationally, African Americans are incarcerated at a rate over five times higher than whites, and Hispanics are incarcerated at a rate 1.4 times that of whites.[47]

It is also important to recognize the connection between inadequate educational resources, student misbehavior, and increased student involvement in the criminal justice system.[48] Educators working in schools with high concentrations of low-income and minority students often teach large groups of students with acute needs but many times lack the experience and resources to meet those needs. As a result, too many schools turn to extreme forms of exclusionary discipline—such as suspensions, expulsions, and referring students to law enforcement officers—to handle routine student behavior problems, many of which could be handled or prevented using more effective methods.[49] Empirical evidence has repeatedly confirmed that excluding a student from school substantially increases the likelihood that this student will not graduate from high school, will become immediately involved in the juvenile justice system, and will eventually become involved in the justice system as an adult.[50]

As intimated earlier, public expenditures associated with the criminal justice system are enormous. Direct annual expenditures on the criminal justice system as a whole amount to over $270 billion.[51] Lowering crime would reduce pressure to spend tax dollars on police, prison systems, and the criminal justice system generally.[52] In addition, involvement in the criminal justice system affects one's ability to find employment, enter the military, find housing, and pursue postsecondary education,[53] all of which lead to decreases in tax revenue and increases in expenditures for government welfare programs.[54]

Furthermore, the social benefits associated with reduced crime would be tremendous. Not only do members of our society pay high costs trying to avoid becoming victims of crime, but actual victims of crime suffer both economically and psychologically. Victims of crimes (as well as the victims' friends and family members) often miss time at work, suffer physical and emotional injuries, experience loss of property, and have a lower quality of life.[55] Clive Belfield and Henry Levin estimate that each high school graduate saves our nation on average approximately $70,000 in criminal justice expenses over that individual's lifetime, and each college graduate saves our nation an average of $175,000 on criminal justice expenses.[56] Lance Lochner and Enrico Moretti estimate that even a 1 percent increase in the graduation rate of all men between twenty and sixty years old would amount to an annual savings of $1.4 billion in costs from victims of crimes and society at large, or a 14–26 percent return on investment in our education system.[57]

Health Rationale

The federal government should also address our nation's educational inequalities because of the high health costs that lower educational attainment imposes on the federal government and society. Individuals with higher education levels on average have better health and live longer.[58] High school dropouts are more likely than those who graduated from high school to die prematurely from cardiovascular disease, cancer, infection, injury, lung disease, and diabetes.[59] They are more likely to suffer from disabilities or illness.[60] Because education is positively related to income levels, those who have more education tend to live in areas that offer more opportunities for exercise and are less exposed to environmental hazards.[61] They are also more likely to obtain jobs that provide better health insurance.[62] Individuals who are educated are also more likely to avoid risky behavior, eat more healthily, exercise more, engage in health-promoting social activities, better comprehend medical information and doctors' instructions, better deal with stressors, and better navigate the complex health care system.[63]

Research confirms the significant health costs of failing to graduate from high school and college. Peter Muennig found that each high school graduate gains 1.7 years of perfect health, valued at approximately $183,000, and each graduate saves the government approximately $39,000 in costs related to health care. Accordingly, he found that the net present value of each cohort of high school dropouts amounts to approximately $110 billion in forfeited health and $23 billion in government expenditures.[64] Clive Belfield and Henry Levin estimated that each high school graduate saves our nation on average approximately $50,300 in public health expenses over that individual's lifetime, and each college graduate saves our nation $86,560 in public health expenses.[65]

Democratic Rationale

The federal government also should address our nation's educational inequalities because a strong educational system for all our nation's citizens is essential for the effectiveness of our democratic government. Education fosters a commitment to and capacity for deliberating issues, serving on a jury, exercising the right to vote, serving in a public office, and serving in the armed forces.[66] In *Brown v. Board of Education*, the US Supreme Court observed, "Compulsory attendance laws and the great expenditures for education both demonstrate our recognition of the importance of education to our democratic society. It is required in the performance of our most basic public responsibilities, even service in the armed forces. It is the very foundation of good citizenship."[67] Justice Byron White, in his dissent in *San Antonio Independent School District v. Rodriguez*, cogently explained that education is critical for assisting youth to understand and appreciate "the principles and operation of our governmental processes," to instill "political consciousness and participation," and to generate "the interest and provide the tools necessary for political discourse and debate."[68] In *Campaign for Fiscal Equity v. New York*, the New York Court of Appeals reasoned that a "sound basic education" consisted of "the basic literacy, calculating, and verbal skills necessary to enable children to eventually function productively as civic participants capable of voting and serving on a jury."[69] Indeed, to effectively serve on a jury, vote, or serve in a public office, individuals must have the capacity to weigh evidence, listen well, communicate effectively, and rethink one's own beliefs and positions.[70]

Critically, empirical studies have repeatedly confirmed the positive relationship between better-educated citizens and political participation, including the increased likelihood of voting, donating to a political campaign, belonging to a civic organization, and participating in political protest activities.[71] Thus, education inequalities can and do lead to different levels of political participation along the lines of race and social class.[72] According to the American Political Science Task Force on Inequality and American Democracy, such inequalities reinforce current social inequalities. It concludes, "The privileged participate more than others and are increasingly well organized to press their demands on government. Public officials, in turn, are much more responsive to the privileged than to average citizens and the least affluent. Citizens with lower or moderate incomes speak with a whisper that is lost on the ears of inattentive government officials, while the advantaged roar with a clarity and consistency that policy-makers readily hear and routinely follow."[73]

The current growing wealth divide also determines who does and does not wield political influence. As Michele Moses and John Rogers observe, since the 1970s, growth in real income has favored the wealthiest Americans, amounting to the largest income inequalities in the United States since the Great Depression.[74] Wealth increases the ability of Americans to voice their opinions and be heard.[75] Research shows that lawmakers respond to the voices of wealthy Americans by passing laws that favor wealthy Americans.[76] Larry Bartels's empirical study shows that, from 1989 to 1995, US senators' votes were most closely aligned with the interests of the affluent and not at all aligned with the interests of the constituents in the bottom third of income levels.[77] Bartels further reports regarding low-income constituents that from 2011 to 2013 "it is highly implausible to suppose that their views had even half as much effect on senators' voting behavior as those of high-income constituents. The statistical results strongly suggest that their opinions were of little or no consequence."[78]

Fairness Rationale

Finally, the federal government should address educational inequalities because doing so is fair and just. That a child's access to a quality education is determined by factors completely outside that child's control, such as where a child happens to live or the income levels of that child's parents, is strikingly inequitable and nonsensical.[79] This is especially true because of the lifelong impact that access to a quality education has on that child's development and future opportunities.[80]

Furthermore, one should deeply consider the harmful psychological messages that inequalities in education send to our children. Catherine Lhamon, former Assistant Secretary for Civil Rights at the US Department of Education, observed that many minority and low-income students' self-perceptions today are strikingly similar to those held by students involved in the "doll test" more than seventy years ago. She illustrated this point by describing an experience she had when she was litigating a case about resource equity in schools. Her team hired several experts to conduct focus-group discussions among minority students in high-poverty schools to better understand these students' experiences. The experts displayed photos of well-resourced schools and classrooms to these students and asked them to share their thoughts about what they saw. The students consistently responded with comments such as, "Those must be schools for white kids. They wouldn't give those materials to us."[81] Students who participated in focus groups conducted by Martha Fine in the *Williams v. California* education-funding litigation also doubted their self-worth because of the inequalities they witnessed. One student, Alondra Jones, shared the following:

> It make you feel less about yourself, you know, like you sitting here in a class where you have to stand up because there's not enough chairs and you see rats in the buildings, the bathrooms is nasty, you got to pay. And then you, like I said, I visited Mann Academy, and these students, if they want to sit on the floor, that's because they choose to. And that just makes me feel real less about myself because it's like State don't care about public schools. If I have to . . . stand in the class, they can't care about me.[82]

Lhamon concludes that many of our minority students in high-poverty schools are hearing the nation's message "loud and clear"—that we do not believe in them, that we do not value their civic engagement, and that there is no point in participating productively in their schools and communities. She concludes that this is exactly the wrong message to be sending to our children; in fact, it is exactly contrary to our vision of what public education should stand for and the opportunities it should afford all children.[83]

Equally disturbing, education inequalities also send a powerful, wrongful message to white students: that they are more privileged and deserve a greater share of our nation's resources. That harmful message contributes to the racial divide and fuels racial tensions, creating a less desirable nation for all of us.[84] As Sharon Rush explains, "Our children are watching us. They learn about race and race relations from us. As adults, we must be careful not to promote a vision of social reality that teaches nonwhite children that they are racially inferior or that teaches white children that they are racially superior."[85]

Federal Responses to Address Educational Inequalities Have Been Inadequate

As the foregoing evidence and rationales demonstrate, there are several compelling reasons for the federal government to rectify educational inequalities in our nation. The federal government has responded to these inequalities to some degree by passing several legislative acts under its spending power, including Title I of the Elementary and Secondary Education of 1965, the No Child Left Behind Act, and the Every Student Succeeds Act. However, all of these acts have largely failed and, in fact, in some ways have created conditions for disparities to widen.[86]

Title I of the Elementary and Secondary Education Act of 1965

The US Congress passed Title I of the Elementary and Secondary Education Act of 1965 to expand educational opportunities for impoverished and marginalized students by providing additional funds to schools for these children.[87] Although this is a laudable goal, there are several reasons why Title I and its subsequent reauthorizations have not narrowed the education equality gap in a more meaningful way.

As an initial matter, the overall amount that the federal government provides to cash-strapped schools to help impoverished children is insufficient. The federal government provided approximately $15.4 billion for schools for the fiscal year 2018 under Title I of the ESEA.[88] While this is not an insignificant amount of money, it amounted to only around 2.4 percent of the total expenditures for public elementary and secondary schools in the United States (approximately $639.5 billion in the fiscal year of 2015),[89] which already was woefully inadequate to properly educate all children in the United States. Nevertheless, this amount has been sufficient to induce all states to accept the money in exchange for their agreement to comply with various federal mandates.[90]

Furthermore, as Derek Black and Goodwin Liu point out, the rules governing disbursement of Title I funds severely limits Title I's ability to sufficiently narrow current inequalities in our education system.[91] There are several examples of this. First, when Congress originally enacted Title I, the federal government dispersed Title I funds to a limited number of schools serving high concentrations of poor students.[92] Presently, however, the eligibility requirements for receiving Title I funds are not at all difficult to meet. For instance, through the Basic Grant formula, school districts are entitled to receive Title I funds by demonstrating that a mere 2 percent of their students are poor.[93] Because of this low threshold, almost all school districts, even very affluent ones, receive Title I funding.[94] During the 2016 fiscal year, the federal government awarded about 43 percent of the total Title I funding through the Basic Grant formula.[95] While allocating more federal funds to educating students generally is praiseworthy, the practical effect of such a low threshold is the dilution of Title I funds to the poorest schools and school districts, which is where the funds are most needed.[96] Many people estimate that poor students require at least 40 percent more resources (or much more) than other students to obtain an equal education opportunity,[97] yet federal resources account for only around 10 percent of the neediest school districts' budgets.[98]

Second, Title I funding formulas do not adequately account for the deleterious effects of concentrated poverty.[99] This can be seen in at least two ways. The first is that Title I funding formulas do not adequately address the fact that as the percentage of poor children in a school increases, the student's chances for success—regardless of that student's own socioeconomic status—decreases.[100] The second is that Title I funding formulas do not adequately account for the deleterious effects of multigenerational poverty. Multigenerational poverty often multiplies the negative effects of poverty on children, meaning that those children often require even more sustained attention and resources to attain levels of academic achievement reached by other students.[101] For example, Charles Sharkey found that children from families who lived in poverty for two generations scored significantly lower on reading and language comprehension tests than did children living in poverty for one generation, even after controlling for other factors that explain variations associated with children's cognitive development.[102]

Title I contains two formulas, the "Concentration Grants" and the "Targeted Grants," both of which Congress designed to address the effects of concentrated poverty, but neither of which adequately does so. A district is eligible for a Concentration Grant if it serves at least sixty-five hundred poor children or if at least 15 percent of the district's children live in poverty.[103] Yet, despite clear evidence that schools serving higher concentrations of impoverished children need more resources to educate students, all school districts receive the same amount of money per student under this formula once the district meets the eligibility requirement, irrespective of whether a district has 15 percent of its students living in poverty or 99 percent.[104] Further, the Concentration Grant (or any of the other formulas) does not take into account the fact that students from families that have lived in poverty for two or more generations require even more resources than do students whose families have lived in poverty for one generation.

The Targeted Grant formula, on the other hand, does account for concentrated poverty to a greater extent than the Concentration Grant does, but it still falls short. A school district is eligible to receive a Targeted Grant if it serves at least ten poor students or if at least 5 percent of its students are living in poverty.[105] Once a district meets this eligibility requirement, the federal government distributes funds using weighted child counts.[106] For example, a district in which .01 percent to approximately 16 percent of its students live in poverty receives a weighted child count of 1.0, whereas a district in which approximately 38 percent or more of its students live in poverty receives a weighted child count of 4.0.[107] Stated another way, districts in which 40 percent of the students live in poverty receive four times as much funding per student as a district in which 15 percent of the students live in poverty. While this is better than the Concentration Grant, the federal government only appropriated 24 percent of all of the Title I funds through the Targeted Grant formula during the 2016 fiscal year.[108] This amount simply is not enough to address the severe inequalities that plague our nation.

Further, the Targeted Grant also inexplicably awards higher funding weights for the total number of poor students a district serves.[109] That is, the final weighted child count under the Targeted Grant results from the larger of two weights determined under two different rubrics.[110] Under the first rubric, as explained earlier, school districts receive a weighted child count for the total percentage of students they serve who are poor.[111] But under the second rubric, school districts receive a weighted child count for the total number of poor students they serve.[112] Thus, large, wealthy school districts that serve a sufficient number of poor students but still have an overall low percentage of poor students benefit from the weighted child count, diluting the overall number of funds available for poor children, even though the empirical evidence suggests that it is the percentage of poor students in the school that affects student achievement, not the total number of students.[113]

Third, all of the Title I formulas take into consideration a state's average per-pupil expenditure to determine the amounts of the awards that states and school districts receive.[114] Congress may have decided to take into account the states' expenditures for at least two possible reasons. First, Congress may have wanted to identify a figure that would accurately reflect the cost of educating students in that geographic area.[115] Nevertheless, as the United States General Accounting Office and scholars have noted, actual state education expenditures are not strongly associated with geographic costs.[116] Second, Congress may have sought to provide an incentive for states to spend more on public education.[117] Realistically, however, Title I probably does very little to motivate states to spend more on education because federal funds account for only a small portion of a state's total education budget, and states would have to spend a great deal more to receive meaningful increases in Title I funds.[118] Thus, because poorer states tend to spend less on public education, scholars conclude that the end result of awarding Title I funds in proportion to a state's average per-pupil expenditure is to penalize poor states and reward wealthy states, further exacerbating per-pupil spending inequalities across states.[119]

Fourth, Title I does not do enough to ensure that states avoid the practice of using federal funds to supplant instead of supplement their current expenditures on education.[120] While "supplement, not supplant" provisions were included for the first time in the 1970 ESEA amendments,[121] over the years Congress has changed the standards or refused to enforce them, making it easy for states to simply replace their education expenditures with federal funds, thereby reducing their own expenditures on education and defeating the purpose of Title I funding.[122] Recognizing this problem, ESSA, for the first time, requires districts to "demonstrate compliance" with the "supplement, not supplant" provision.[123] However, both prior to and after the passage of ESSA, Title I has not identified a specific methodology or standard to determine whether school districts are violating the "supplement, not supplant" provision or how districts should "demonstrate compliance."[124] In addition, Title I includes a maintenance of effort (MOE) requirement so that states and/or school districts must provide a level of funding that is at least 90 percent of the funding in the second preceding year.[125] However, because federal funds account for less than 10 percent of total education expenditures, it is not difficult for most states and districts to replace their expenditures with federal funds over time and still meet the MOE requirement.[126] And while Title I expressly prohibits states and school districts from supplanting their own funds with federal funds,[127] the US Department of Education has done very little to enforce this prohibition.[128]

Fifth, Title I does not do enough to motivate states and school districts to equalize per-pupil spending. It contains no provisions aimed at motivating states to address unequal spending between districts, where huge disparities exist.[129] Furthermore, Title I falls short in addressing spending disparities within school districts. Under the current "comparability" requirements, before qualifying for Title I funds, recipients must provide "substantially comparable services" to Title I schools and non–Title I schools.[130] Yet Title I also contains a provision expressly stating, "Nothing in this title shall be construed to mandate equalized spending per pupil for a State, local educational agency, or school,"[131] making it difficult for the US Department of Education to craft regulations to promote more equitable spending among schools within a district.[132] In addition, Title I does not require a school district to include "staff salary differentials for years of employment" in its comparability analysis if it files a written assurance that it has implemented a district-wide salary schedule.[133] This exemption permits school districts receiving Title I funds to exclude teacher salaries, which make up a high percentage of each school's per-pupil expenditures, from the comparability analysis.[134]

No Child Left Behind Act

In 2001, Congress reauthorized the Elementary and Secondary Education Act by passing the No Child Left Behind Act (NCLB).[135] The central feature of NCLB was that all schools receiving federal funds were required to test all K–12 students at various stages in math, science, reading, and language arts.[136] To avoid certain sanctions, such as a negative label or being taken over by the state, schools had to demonstrate improvement in student test scores across all student subgroups and, by 2014, demonstrate that all students were "proficient" in these subject areas.[137] The federal government hoped that NCLB would raise educators' expectations of students, hold schools accountable for failing to help their students meet curricular standards, narrow the academic achievement gap between student groups, and bring all students up to a predetermined academic standard.[138]

However, this test-based, high-stakes accountability approach largely did not achieve its desired effect and, in fact, had several perverse effects on all children but particularly on marginalized children.[139] First, NCLB did not do enough to provide children with the resources that empirical research confirms most influence academic achievement, which includes having effective teachers, adequate instructional resources, appropriate class sizes, a culturally relevant and challenging curriculum, sufficient support, adequate facilities, sufficient tools and training to enhance the school climate, and an opportunity to attend a middle-class school.[140] Rather, NCLB largely only increased levels of accountability.

Second, NCLB caused many of our nation's schools to suffer from a problem called goal displacement.[141] That is, instead of focusing on appropriate learning outcomes such as developing critical thinking skills, preparing for higher-education opportunities and the workforce in a global economy, and creating lifelong learners, educators were compelled to narrow their focus to helping students achieve a "proficient" score on a standardized exam.[142] Thus, NCLB led to several unintended results, particularly in poor districts serving underachieving students, such as a narrowing of the curriculum; an intense focus on multiple-choice test-taking skills; less creative and engaging classes; fewer project-based learning activities; less time on or the elimination of arts, music, drama, social studies, and other important subjects that are not tested;

and, less time spent on developing important values and skills, such as cooperative learning, creative problem-solving, and good citizenship.[143]

Third, many scholars fear that school officials began pushing low-performing students out of their schools, in an effort to avoid having their low scores count against them, by suspending, expelling, or referring them to law enforcement for certain infractions they commit on school grounds.[144] David Figlio found evidence of this worrisome trend by examining data from Florida school districts on student suspensions and standardized test scores. Figlio found that schools tended to give harsher punishments for the same offense to low-performing students than to high-performing students. Figlio also found that the differences in punishment for similar offenses grew wider during testing windows for students enrolled in grades that administered high-stakes tests.[145]

Fourth, even assuming that focusing so much attention on a state-wide achievement test is beneficial for our students, it appears that the high-stakes accountability approach did little to improve student test scores or reduce achievement gaps.[146] Empirical research shows at best small gains and at worst no gains or even declines in student achievement scores.[147] But even if there were some small gains, one questions whether the significant costs merit these small benefits.[148]

Finally, NCLB did almost nothing at all to promote student integration.[149] NCLB did compel school districts to develop intradistrict transfer policies for Title I students in failing schools.[150] However, these policies did not promote meaningful student integration for two reasons. First, most student poverty and racial segregation exist between districts instead of within districts, making meaningful integration very difficult under that policy.[151] Second, the burden of transferring schools fell on students and parents, and there were no incentives for nonfailing schools to accept or recruit these students.[152] Thus, it was far more likely for students from more advantaged families to find ways to transfer to better schools than for students from disadvantaged families to do so.[153]

Every Student Succeeds Act

On December 10, 2015, the newest reauthorization of the ESEA, embodied in the Every Student Succeeds Act (ESSA), was signed into law.[154] At its core, ESSA remains a test-based accountability system, requiring the

same testing schedule, development, student demographic disaggregation, and subject matter to be tested as NCLB,[155] but it is distinctive
from NCLB in important ways. As with NCLB, states are permitted
to develop their own "challenging" academic standards.[156] However,
states are now also permitted to devise their own goals and accountability structures that must include the following indicators: "academic
achievement, as measured by proficiency on the annual assessments";
another measure of student growth "that allows for meaningful differentiation in school performance," such as graduation rates for high schools;
"progress in achieving English language proficiency"; and, "not less than
one indicator of school quality and student success," such as "student
engagement," "educator engagement," "student access to and completion
of advanced coursework," "postsecondary readiness," or "school climate
and safety."[157] Thus, whereas under NCLB the annual assessments were
the primary means to evaluate schools, under ESSA annual assessments
now represent one of four factors to which states can assign any evaluative weight, as long as that weight is "substantial" (although "substantial"
is undefined), and, in the aggregate, states give greater evaluative weight
to the first three factors than the fourth factor.[158]

Another primary difference between NCLB and ESSA is the accountability structure. Under NCLB, all schools had to make annual
yearly progress toward proficiency in student assessments in order to
avoid negative labels and sanctions set forth in the statute.[159] ESSA requires state intervention only for "the lowest-performing 5 percent of
all schools" and "high schools in the State failing to graduate one third
or more of their students."[160] Thus, for the vast majority of schools in
the United States, ESSA does not impose federal consequences for failing to make annual progress toward state-determined goals, requiring
only that states and schools devise their own improvement plans when
schools fail to meet the state's assigned criteria.[161] Thus, as Michael Heise
observes, while "standards-setting and accountability mechanisms . . .
under NCLB was among NCLB's hallmarks[,] ESSA, in contrast, affords
states greater autonomy, both in terms of control over substantive standards setting and the consequences for states that fail to achieve their
own self-defined achievement goals."[162]

ESSA on its face contains some provisions that are aimed at narrowing educational inequalities. For example, it authorizes a small increase

to support English-language learning programs,[163] mandates more educational opportunities for students involved in the juvenile justice system,[164] and provides certain protections, including school placement stability, to students who are homeless or involved in the foster-care system.[165] It also requires each state to develop a plan that describes how low-income and minority children will not be disproportionately served by teachers who are inexperienced, out of field, or ineffective.[166] In addition, it permits school districts to enter into an experimental program that consolidates federal, state, and local funds to create a single funding system using a weighted per-pupil allocation that accounts for poverty and other disadvantages for students.[167] It also provides grants for consortiums of districts to expand interdistrict and regional magnet programs to promote integration.[168]

While it is too early to fully understand the effect that ESSA will have on our public education system, there are serious concerns that its current structure will not adequately address the educational inequalities that are so deeply embedded within our nation. First, and most importantly, ESSA kept Title I funds largely flat. In 2018, Title I funding for disadvantaged students was $15.4 billion, which amounts to only approximately 2.4 percent of the total expenditures for public elementary and secondary education.[169] As explained earlier, many people estimate that poor students require at least 40 percent more resources (or much more) than other students to achieve comparable academic levels.[170] $15.4 billion simply is not enough to close the educational inequalities gaps that plague our nation. Second, ESSA does not address the problems associated with the rules governing the disbursements of Title I funds discussed earlier, which also severely limit Title I's ability to narrow inequalities.

Third, ESSA transfers the power over education accountability back to the states. While it is still too early to tell, we should not be surprised at all if states accomplish very little to close education inequality gaps given the states' general refusal to promote equal educational opportunity on their own in the past,[171] especially when they have not been given more resources to do so. Indeed, in exchange for federal funds, ESSA does not require states to create more equitable school funding systems across districts or to ensure that every student will have an opportunity to attend a middle-class school.

Finally, ESSA, similar to its predecessor, still requires states that receive federal education funds to conduct student academic assessments in public schools for accountability purposes, even if it prohibits the federal government from determining how to weigh those assessment tests.[172] Having a continued emphasis on high-stakes testing most likely will continue to put students at risk of being subjected to the perverse effects of the high-stakes accountability movement described earlier.

Conclusion

Under our current public education system, inequalities in educational opportunities for students of color and students who live in poverty are severe and harm our children and nation in serious ways. The rationales for the federal government to address these education inequalities are straightforward, especially because most states do not appear to be addressing these inequalities in a meaningful way, as this volume's introduction persuasively explains. Education inequalities threaten the sustainability of our democracy and decrease the quality of life for millions of individuals. Inequalities also pose severe economic harm to our nation in two major forms. First, governments lose billions of dollars in lost tax revenue that would accompany increased earnings by a more educated workforce. Second, poor education systems lead to billions of dollars in increased government expenditures by putting more individuals on a pathway that leads to incarceration, poor health, and increased dependency on government welfare programs.

Furthermore, not only would addressing the inequalities of our public education system put our nation on a more secure path democratically, economically, and socially, but addressing these inequalities is more consistent with the moral values to which our nation ought to adhere. Limits to a child's future should not be determined by factors that are completely outside a child's control, such as in what neighborhood a child lives or the income levels of the child's parents. Rather, as the wise philosopher and reformer John Dewey astutely observed over one hundred years ago, "What the best and wisest parent wants for his own child, that must the community want for all of its children. Any other ideal for our schools is narrow and unlovely; acted upon, it destroys our democracy."[173]

Although the federal government has passed several legislative acts under its spending powers with the intent to improve the quality of K–12 education, this legislation thus far has failed to close the opportunity and achievement gaps and, in some ways, has created conditions for these inequalities to expand. The time has come for a much-stronger response by the federal government to ensure that all children have access to a quality education.[174] As Marta Tienda and Sigal Alon remind us, clearly we have the justifications and resources to make the necessary corrections and put our nation on a more secure path. Whether we have sufficient political will to do so is an entirely different question altogether.[175]

NOTES

The author thanks Sara L. Salem for the assistance she provided for this book chapter.

1. *See, e.g.,* Meredith Phillips & Tiffani Chin, *School Inequality: What Do We Know?*, *in* SOCIAL INEQUALITY 467, 500 (Kathryn M. Neckerman ed. 2004).

2. *See* OFFICE OF CIVIL RIGHTS, US DEP'T OF EDUC., 2013–2014 CIVIL RIGHTS DATA COLLECTION: A FIRST LOOK 6–7 (2016); OFFICE OF CIVIL RIGHTS, US DEP'T OF EDUC., PROTECTING CIVIL RIGHTS, ADVANCING EQUITY 16–17 (2015); US GOV'T ACCOUNTABILITY OFFICE, GAO-16-345, K–12 EDUCATION: BETTER USE OF INFORMATION COULD HELP AGENCIES IDENTIFY DISPARITIES AND ADDRESS RACIAL DISCRIMINATION 21–22 (2016) [hereinafter GAO EDUCATION REPORT].

3. FRANK ADAMSON & LINDA DARLING-HAMMOND, CTR. FOR AM. PROGRESS, SPEAKING OF SALARIES: WHAT IT WILL TAKE TO GET QUALIFIED, EFFECTIVE TEACHERS IN ALL COMMUNITIES 15–22 (2011); Linda Darling-Hammond, *Inequality and School Resources: What It Will Take to Close the Opportunity Gap,* *in* CLOSING THE OPPORTUNITY GAP: WHAT AMERICA MUST DO TO GIVE EVERY CHILD AN EVEN CHANCE 77, 87 (Prudence L. Carter & Kevin G. Welner eds., 2013).

4. *See* GAO EDUCATION REPORT, *supra* note 2, at 10; GARY ORFIELD ET AL., *BROWN AT 60: GREAT PROGRESS, A LONG RETREAT, AND AN UNCERTAIN FUTURE* 15 (2014).

5. *See* Cory Turner et al., *Why America's Schools Have a Money Problem,* NPR, Apr. 18, 2016, www.npr.org.

6. *See* Kevin McCorry, *Struggling School Districts Find Little Help in Pennsylvania,* NPR, Apr. 27, 2016, www.npr.org.

7. Cory Turner et al., *Is There a Better Way to Pay for America's Schools?,* NPR, May 1, 2016, www.npr.org.

8. *See* BRUCE BAKER ET AL., EDUC. LAW CTR., IS SCHOOL FUNDING FAIR? A NATIONAL REPORT CARD 5–6 (5th ed. 2016).

9. *Id.*

10. NATASHA USHOMIRSKY & DAVID WILLIAMS, FUNDING GAPS 2015: TOO MANY STATES SPEND LESS ON EDUCATING STUDENTS WHO NEED THE MOST 1 (2015), http://edtrust.org.

11. *Id.*

12. *See* Julien Lafortune et al., *School Finance Reform and the Distribution of Student Achievement* 33 (Nat'l Bureau of Econ. Research, Working Paper No. 22011, 2016).

13. *See* Richard D. Kahlenberg, *From All Walks of Life: New Hope for School Integration*, AM. EDUCATOR, Winter 2012–13, at 3.

14. *See* Roslyn Arlin Mickelson & Martha Bottia, *Integrated Education and Mathematics Outcomes: A Synthesis of Social Science Research*, 88 N.C. L. REV. 993, 1028–29 (2010); Sean F. Reardon, *School Segregation and Racial Academic Achievement Gaps* 1, 10, 19–20 (Stanford Ctr. for Educ. Policy Analysis, Working Paper No. 15–12, 2016); Russell W. Rumberger & Gregory J. Palardy, *Does Segregation Still Matter? The Impact of Student Composition on Academic Achievement in High School*, 107 TCHRS. C. REC. 1999, 2002, 2008–09 (2005).

15. *See* Reardon, *supra* note 14, at 21.

16. *See* HEATHER SCHWARTZ, CENTURY FOUND., HOUSING POLICY IS SCHOOL POLICY: ECONOMICALLY INTEGRATIVE HOUSING PROMOTES ACADEMIC SUCCESS IN MONTGOMERY COUNTY, MARYLAND 5–13 (2010).

17. *See* NAT'L CTR. FOR EDUC. STAT., DIGEST OF EDUCATION STATISTICS, table 221.20, https://nces.ed.gov (last visited May 9, 2018).

18. *Id.* One observes similar gaps for mathematic achievement among these student groups. *See id. at* table 222.20.

19. *See* Jonathan Rabinovitz, *Local Education Inequities across U.S. Revealed in New Stanford Data Set*, STANFORD NEWS, Apr. 29, 2016, https://news.stanford.edu.

20. *Id.*

21. *See* Sean F. Reardon, *The Widening Academic Achievement Gap between the Rich and the Poor*, 24 COMMUNITY INV. 19, 20 (2012).

22. *See* Rabinovitz, *supra* note 19.

23. *See* Kevin G. Welner & Prudence L. Carter, *Achievement Gaps Arise from Opportunity Gaps*, *in* CLOSING THE OPPORTUNITY GAP, *supra* note 3, at 1, 3.

24. *See* Clive Belfield & Henry M. Levin, *The Cumulative Costs of the Opportunity Gap*, *in* CLOSING THE OPPORTUNITY GAP, *supra* note 3, at 195; JOHN M. BRIDGELAND ET AL., CIVIC ENTERS., THE SILENT EPIDEMIC: PERSPECTIVES OF HIGH SCHOOL DROPOUTS 2 (2006).

25. *See* HENRY LEVIN ET AL., THE COSTS AND BENEFITS OF AN EXCELLENT EDUCATION FOR ALL OF AMERICA'S CHILDREN 9–16 (2007); Jason P. Nance, *Dismantling the School-to-Prison Pipeline: Tools for Change*, 48 ARIZ. ST. L.J. 313, 322–23 (2016).

26. *See* Belfield & Levin, *supra* note 24, at 205.

27. *See* Derek W. Black, *Averting Educational Crisis: Funding Cuts, Teacher Shortages, and the Dwindling Commitment to Public Education*, 94 WASH. U. L. REV. 423, 424–26 (2016).

28. *Id.* at 424.

29. *See* Thomas Bailey, *Implications of Educational Inequality in a Global Economy*, *in* THE PRICE WE PAY 74, 74 (Clive R. Belfield & Henry M. Levin eds., 2007); Belfield & Levin, *supra* note 24, at 196.

30. Belfield & Levin, *supra* note 24, at 196.

31. *Id.*

32. Bailey, *supra* note 29, at 74.

33. *Id.* at 75.

34. *See id.* at 75; Marta Tienda & Sigal Alon, *Diversity and the Demographic Dividend: Achieving Educational Equity in an Aging White Society*, in THE PRICE WE PAY, *supra* note 29, at 48, 50–58.

35. *See id.* at 49.

36. Tienda & Alon, *supra* note 34, at 70–71.

37. *See* Belfield & Levin, *supra* note 24, at 195–200.

38. *Id.* at 200–05.

39. US CENSUS BUREAU, PUBLIC EDUCATION FINANCES: 2015, at 8 (2017).

40. *See* Enrico Moretti, *Crime and the Costs of Criminal Justice*, *in* THE PRICE WE PAY, *supra* note 29, at 142, 144.

41. *Id.* at 145.

42. *Id.*

43. *See* Nance, *supra* note 25, at 322–23.

44. NAT'L CTR. FOR JUVENILE JUSTICE, JUVENILE OFFENDERS AND VICTIMS: 2014 NATIONAL REPORT 15 (Melissa Sickmund & Charles Puzzanchera eds., 2014).

45. Moretti, *supra* note 40, at 157; *see also* Lance Lochner & Enrico Moretti, *The Effect of Education on Crime: Evidence from Prison Inmates, Arrests, and Self-Reports*, 94 AM. ECON. REV. 155, 156 (2004).

46. *See generally* MICHELLE ALEXANDER, THE NEW JIM CROW (2012).

47. *See* ASHLEY NELLIS, THE SENTENCING PROJECT, THE COLOR OF JUSTICE: RACIAL AND ETHNIC DISPARITY IN STATE PRISONS 3 (2016).

48. For a thorough analysis of this alarming trend, *see* Nance, *supra* note 25, at 324–31.

49. *Id.*

50. *Id.* at 319–24.

51. *See* EXEC. OFFICE OF THE PRESIDENT OF THE US, ECONOMIC PERSPECTIVES ON INCARCERATION AND THE CRIMINAL JUSTICE SYSTEM 7 (2016).

52. *See* Belfield & Levin, *supra* note 24, at 201.

53. *See* EXEC. OFFICE OF THE PRESIDENT OF THE US, *supra* note 51, at 5; FED. ADVISORY COMM. ON JUVENILE JUSTICE, ANNUAL REPORT 10 (2010).

54. Belfield & Levin, *supra* note 24, at 200–01.

55. *Id.* at 203.

56. *Id.* at 204, table 14.6.
57. Lochner & Moretti, *supra* note 45, at 157; Moretti, *supra* note 40, at 155–57.
58. *See* Peter Muennig, *Consequences in Health Status and Costs, in* THE PRICE WE PAY, *supra* note 29, at 125.
59. *See id.* at 127.
60. *Id.*
61. *Id.* at 130.
62. *Id.*
63. Belfield & Levin, *supra* note 24, at 200–01; Muennig, *supra* note 58, at 130–31.
64. *See* Muennig, *supra* note 58, at 136–37.
65. Belfield & Levin, *supra* note 24, at 204, table 14.6.
66. *See* Michele S. Moses & John Rogers, *Enhancing a Nation's Democracy through Equitable Schools, in* CLOSING THE OPPORTUNITY GAP, *supra* note 3, at 207, 209.
67. Brown v. Bd. of Educ., 347 U.S. 483, 493 (1954).
68. San Antonio Indep. Sch. Dist. v. Rodriguez, 411 U.S. 1, 113 (1973).
69. Campaign for Fiscal Equity v. State, 86 N.Y.2d 307, 316 (1995).
70. *See* Moses & Rogers, *supra* note 66, at 209, 213; Testimony of Dr. Linda Darling-Hammond, Campaign for Fiscal Equity, Inc. v. State, 1, 17 (Dec. 14, 1999), http://finance.tc-library.org.
71. *See* Ronald La Due Lake & Robert Huckfeldt, *Social Capital, Social Networks, and Political Participation,* 19 POL. PSYCHOL. 567, 567 (1998); Moses & Rogers, *supra* note 66, at 210–11.
72. *See* Moses & Rogers, *supra* note 66, at 210.
73. TASK FORCE ON INEQ. & AM. DEMOCRACY, AM. POLITICAL SCI. ASS'N, AMERICAN DEMOCRACY IN AN AGE OF RISING INEQUALITY 1 (2004).
74. Moses & Rogers, *supra* note 66, at 210.
75. *Id.*
76. *Id.*
77. LARRY M. BARTELS, UNEQUAL DEMOCRACY: THE POLITICAL ECONOMY OF THE NEW GILDED AGE 246 (2d ed. 2016).
78. *Id.* at 243.
79. Belfield & Levin, *supra* note 24, at 195.
80. *Id.*
81. Catherine Lhamon, *2015 Allen Chair Symposium—School Inequality: Challenges and Solutions* (Part 2 of 6), YOUTUBE (Oct. 12, 2017), http://youtube.com.
82. Michelle Fine et al., *Civic Lessons: The Color and Class Betrayal,* 106 TCHRS. C. REC. 2193, 2199 (2004).
83. *Id.*
84. *Cf.* Jason P. Nance, *Student Surveillance, Racial Inequalities, and Implicit Racial Bias,* 66 EMORY L.J. 765, 800 (2017).
85. Sharon Elizabeth Rush, *The Heart of Equal Protection: Education and Race,* 23 N.Y.U. REV. L. & SOC. CHANGE 1, 33, 42 (1997).

86. Some of that legislation that will not be discussed in detail here includes the Individuals with Disabilities Education Act, Pub. L. No. 101-476, 104 Stat. 1142 (1990) and the Bilingual Education Act as part of the ESEA, Pub. L. No. 90-247, § 701, 81 Stat. 816 (1968).

87. *See* OFFICE OF EDUC., US DEP'T OF HEALTH, EDUC. & WELFARE, HISTORY OF TITLE I ESEA 1, 19 (1969).

88. *See* US DEP'T OF EDUC., FISCAL YEAR 2019 BUDGET: SUMMARY AND BACKGROUND INFORMATION 9 (2018).

89. US CENSUS BUREAU, *supra* note 39, at 8.

90. *See* DEREK W. BLACK, EDUCATION LAW: EQUALITY, FAIRNESS, AND REFORM 276 (2013).

91. *See* Derek W. Black, *Leveraging Federal Funding for Equity and Integration, in* THE ENDURING LEGACY OF *RODRIGUEZ*: CREATING NEW PATHWAYS TO EQUAL EDUCATIONAL OPPORTUNITY 227, 229–41 (Charles J. Ogletree, Jr. & Kimberly Jenkins Robinson eds., 2015); Goodwin Liu, *Improving Title I Funding Equity across States, Districts, and Schools*, 93 IOWA L. REV. 973, 981–1011 (2008).

92. Black, *supra* note 91, at 232.

93. *See* 20 U.S.C. § 6333(b) (2012); 34 C.F.R. § 200.71 (2017).

94. *See NCLB Title I Distribution Formulas*, NEW AM., http://atlas.newamerica.org (last visited May 9, 2018). Approximately fifty-six thousand schools received Title I funding in 2009–10. *See* US DEP'T OF EDUC., IMPROVING BASIC PROGRAMS OPERATED BY LOCAL EDUCATION AGENCIES (TITLE I, PART A) (2015), www2.ed.gov.

95. *See* REBECCA R. SKINNER, CONG. RESEARCH SERV., R44164, ESEA TITLE I-A FORMULAS: IN BRIEF 1 (2016).

96. *See* Black, *supra* note 91, at 232.

97. *See* BLACK, *supra* note 90, at 278; William D. Duncombe & John Yinger, *How Much More Does a Disadvantaged Student Cost?* (Ctr. for Policy Research, Working Paper No. 60, 2004), http://surface.syr.edu.

98. BLACK, *supra* note 90, at 278.

99. *See* Black, *supra* note 91, at 232.

100. *See id.* at 234; RICHARD D. KAHLENBERG, ALL TOGETHER NOW: CREATING MIDDLE-CLASS SCHOOLS THROUGH PUBLIC SCHOOL CHOICE 49–50 (2001).

101. *See* Patrick Sharkey, STUCK IN PLACE: URBAN NEIGHBORHOODS AND THE END OF PROGRESS TOWARD RACIAL EQUALITY 46 (2013).

102. *Id.* at 129.

103. 34 C.F.R. § 200.71 (2017).

104. *See Grant Distribution Formulas*, NEW AM., https://www.newamerica.org (last visited June 15, 2018).

105. 34 C.F.R. § 200.71 (2017).

106. *See* 20 U.S.C. § 6335(c)(2)(B) (2012); *see also* CONG. RESEARCH SERV., R44219, ALLOCATION OF FUNDS UNDER TITLE 1-A OF THE ELEMENTARY AND

SECONDARY EDUCATION ACT: FORMULA CHANGES UNDER S. 1177 AND
H.R. 5, at 9 (2015).

107. 20 U.S.C. § 6335(c)(2)(B); *see also* NAT'L CTR. FOR EDUC. STATISTICS, ALLO-
CATING GRANTS FOR TITLE I, at 8 (2016). Districts in which 15.58–22.11 percent live in poverty receive a weight of 1.75; 22.11–30.16 percent receive a weight of
2.5; and 30.16–38.24 percent receive a weight of 3.25. 20 U.S.C. § 6335(c)(2)(B); *see
also* NAT'L CTR. FOR EDUC. STATISTICS, *supra*.

108. *See* SKINNER, *supra* note 95, at 1.

109. 20 U.S.C. § 6335(c)(2)(C); *see also* Black, *supra* note 91, at 236–37.

110. 20 U.S.C. § 6335(c)(2)(A).

111. *Id.* § 6335(c)(2)(B).

112. 20 U.S.C. § 6335(c)(2)(C) (2012).

113. *See* Black, *supra* note 91, at 236–37; Liu, *supra* note 91, at 1007–08.

114. *See* 20 U.S.C. §§ 6333(a)(1)(B) (2012), 6334(a)(2)(B) (2012), 6335(b)(1)(B) (2012), &
6337(b)(1)(A)(i) (2012 & Supp. IV 2016).

115. *See* Black, *supra* note 91, at 234–35; Liu, *supra* note 91, at 1001; US GOV'T AC-
COUNTABILITY OFFICE, GAO-02-242, TITLE I FUNDING: POOR CHIL-
DREN BENEFIT THOUGH FUNDING PER POOR CHILD DIFFERS 33 (2002)
[hereinafter GAO TITLE I FUNDING].

116. Black, *supra* note 91, at 234; GAO TITLE I FUNDING, *supra* note 115, at 33.

117. Black, *supra* note 91, at 235; Liu, *supra* note 91, at 985.

118. Black, *supra* note 91, at 235; Liu, *supra* note 91, at 985.

119. *See* Black, *supra* note 91, at 235; Liu, *supra* note 91, at 985–86.

120. *See* Black, *supra* note 91, at 238.

121. *See* JODY FEDER & REBECCA SKINNER, CONG. RESEARCH SERV., 7-5700,
MEMORANDUM: PROPOSED REGULATIONS ON THE SUPPLEMENT, NOT
SUPPLANT PROVISION THAT APPLIES TO THE TITLE I-A PROGRAM AUTHO-
RIZED BY THE ELEMENTARY AND SECONDARY EDUCATION ACT 2 (2016).

122. *See* Black, *supra* note 91, at 238.

123. 20 U.S.C. § 6321(b)(2) (Supp. IV 2016); *see also* James S. Liebman & Michael
Mbikiwa, *Every Dollar Counts: In Defense of the Obama Department of Education's
"Supplement Not Supplant" Proposal*, 117 COLUM. L. REV. ONLINE 36, 41–42
(2017).

124. *See* Liebman & Mbikiwa, *supra* note 123, at 42; FEDER & SKINNER, *supra* note
121, at 3, 4.

125. 20 U.S.C. §§ 6321(a) (2012), 7901 (2012 & Supp. IV 2016); FEDER & SKINNER,
supra note 121, at 2.

126. *See* Black, *supra* note 91, at 238.

127. *See* 20 U.S.C. § 6825 (Supp. IV 2016).

128. *See* Black, *supra* note 91, at 239.

129. *See id.*

130. *See* 20 U.S.C. §§ 6321(c)(1)(A)–(B) (2012); *see also* FEDER & SKINNER, *supra* note
121, at 4.

131. 20 U.S.C. § 7372 (Supp. IV 2016).

132. In fact, because of this provision, the Congressional Research Service recently opined that a proposed regulation by the US Department of Education that seeks to require school districts to spend equal amounts of state and local funds per pupil in each school exceeded its statutory authority. FEDER & SKINNER, *supra* note 121, at 5–9.

133. 20 U.S.C. §§ 6321(c)(2)(A)–(B) (2012).

134. *See* Black, *supra* note 91, at 240.

135. No Child Left Behind Act of 2001, Pub. L. No. 107-110, 115 Stat. 1425 (codified as amended in scattered sections of 20 U.S.C.).

136. *See* Jason P. Nance, *School Surveillance and the Fourth Amendment*, 2014 WIS. L. REV. 79, 94–95.

137. *Id.; see also* KEVIN G. WELNER & WILLIAM J. MATHIS, REAUTHORIZATION OF THE ELEMENTARY AND SECONDARY EDUCATION ACT: TIME TO MOVE BEYOND TEST-FOCUSED POLICIES 2–3 (2015).

138. *See* WELNER & MATHIS, *supra* note 137.

139. *See* JENNIFER KING RICE, INVESTING IN EQUAL OPPORTUNITY: WHAT WOULD IT TAKE TO BUILD THE BALANCE WHEEL? 4–5 (2015).

140. *See id.*

141. *See* WELNER & MATHIS, *supra* note 137, at 4.

142. *See id.*

143. *Id.* at 5; John Gilliom, *Lying, Cheating, and Teaching to the Test, in* SCHOOLS UNDER SURVEILLANCE: CULTURES OF CONTROL IN PUBLIC EDUCATION 194, 197–99 (Torin Monahan & Rodolfo D. Torres eds., 2010); Christopher H. Tienken & Yong Zhao, *How Common Standards and Standardized Testing Widen the Opportunity Gap, in* CLOSING THE OPPORTUNITY GAP, *supra* note 3, at 111, 114–16.

144. *See* Deborah Gordon Klehr, *Addressing the Unintended Consequences of No Child Left Behind and Zero Tolerance: Better Strategies for Safe Schools and Successful Students,* 16 GEO. J. ON POVERTY L. & POL'Y 585, 602–03 (2009); Jason P. Nance, *Students, Security, and Race,* 63 EMORY L.J. 1, 15–16 (2013); *see also* Linda Darling-Hammond, *Race, Inequality, and Educational Accountability: The Irony of "No Child Left Behind,"* 10 RACE ETHNICITY & EDUC., 245, 252–55 (2007); James E. Ryan, *The Perverse Incentives of the No Child Left Behind Act,* 79 N.Y.U. L. REV. 932, 969–70 (2004).

145. *See* David N. Figlio, *Testing, Crime, and Punishment,* 90 J. PUB. ECON. 837, 839 (2006).

146. *See* WELNER & MATHIS, *supra* note 137, at 4.

147. *See* Thomas S. Dee & Brian A. Jacob, *The Impact of No Child Left Behind on Students, Teachers, and Schools,* BROOKINGS PAPERS ON ECON. ACTIVITY 149, 190 (Fall 2010); Jaekyung Lee & Todd Reeves, *Revisiting the Impact of NCLB High-Stakes School Accountability, Capacity, and Resources: State NAEP 1990–2009*

Reading and Math Achievement Gaps and Trends, 34 EDUC. EVALUATION & POL'Y ANALYSIS 209, 224 (2012).

148. *See* WELNER & MATHIS, *supra* note 137, at 4.

149. *See* Black, *supra* note 91, at 229.

150. *See* HALLEY POTTER ET AL., CENTURY FOUND., A NEW WAVE OF SCHOOL INTEGRATION: DISTRICTS AND CHARTERS PURSUING SOCIOECONOMIC DIVERSITY 16 (2016).

151. *Id.*

152. *See id.*; Jennifer Jellison Holme & Amy Stuart Wells, *School Choice beyond District Borders: Lessons for the Reauthorization of NCLB from Interdistrict Desegregation and Open Enrollment Plans, in* IMPROVING ON NO CHILD LEFT BEHIND: GETTING EDUCATION REFORM BACK ON TRACK 156 (Richard D. Kahlenberg ed., 2008).

153. *See* Holme & Wells, *supra* note 152; POTTER ET AL., *supra* note 150, at 16–17.

154. Every Student Succeeds Act, Pub. L. No. 114-95, 129 Stat. 1802 (2015) (codified as amended in scattered sections of 20 U.S.C.).

155. *See* 20 U.S.C. § 6311(b)(2) (Supp. IV 2016); Derek W. Black, *Abandoning the Federal Role in Education: The Every Student Succeeds Act*, 105 CALIF. L. REV. 1309, 1333 (2017); WILLIAM PENUEL ET AL., MAKING THE MOST OF THE EVERY STUDY SUCCEEDS ACT (ESSA)—HELPING STATES FOCUS ON SCHOOL EQUITY, QUALITY AND CLIMATE 2 (2016).

156. Distinct from NCLB, however, is that the ESSA defines "challenging State academic standards" as being "aligned with entrance requirements for credit-bearing coursework in the system of public higher education in the State and relevant State career and technical education standards." 20 U.S.C. § 6311(b)(1)(D)(i) (Supp. IV 2016).

157. 20 U.S.C. § 6311(c)(4) (Supp. IV 2016).

158. 20 U.S.C. § 6311(c)(4)(C) (Supp. IV 2016).

159. *See* Michael Heise, *From No Child Left Behind to Every Student Succeeds: Back to a Future for Education Federalism*, 117 COLUM. L. REV. 1859, 1872 (2017).

160. 20 U.S.C. § 6311(c)(4)(D) (Supp. IV 2016).

161. 20 U.S.C. § 6311(d) (Supp. IV 2016); *see also* Black, *supra* note 155, at 1334; Heise, *supra* note 159, at 1873.

162. Heise, *supra* note 159, at 1873.

163. 20 U.S.C. § 6821 (2012 & Supp. V 2017).

164. 20 U.S.C. § 6434 (Supp. IV 2016).

165. 20 U.S.C. § 6311(g)(1)(E) (Supp. IV 2016).

166. 20 U.S.C. § 6311(g)(1)(B) (Supp. IV 2016).

167. 20 U.S.C. § 6491 (Supp. IV 2016).

168. 20 U.S.C. § 7231f(a) (2012 & Supp. V 2017).

169. *See supra* notes 88–89.

170. *See supra* note 97.

171. *See* Black, *supra* note 155, at 1342–46; Emily Hodge et al., *Lessons from the Past, Model for the Future: A Return to Promoting Integration through a Reauthorized ESEA*, 3 EDUC. L. & POL'Y REV. 58, 59 (2016); Charles J. Ogletree Jr. & Kimberly Jenkins Robinson, *The K–12 Funding Crisis*, EDUC. WK., May 17, 2016, www.edweek.org.

172. *See* 20 U.S.C. §§ 6311(b)(2), 6311(e)(1)(B)(iii) (Supp. IV 2016).

173. JOHN DEWEY, THE SCHOOL AND SOCIETY 3 (1915).

174. *See* Kimberly Jenkins Robinson's introduction and conclusion to this volume.

175. *See* Tienda & Alon, *supra* note 34, at 70–71.

2

The Inadequate Right to Education

A Case Study of Obstacles to State Protection

KRISTINE L. BOWMAN

Introduction

Since the Great Recession of 2007–09, states have devoted less and less money to public education, and state courts have become even more hostile to structural reform litigation that has sought to challenge education funding and quality. Yet the current model of education federalism (cooperative federalism) still leaves these matters largely to the states even as federal influence over education has increased in recent years. As a result, state-level legislative inaction, executive acquiescence, and judicial abdication can combine to create a situation in which the quality of traditional public schools sharply declines. This is the case in Michigan, which is an important state to study because the dynamics that are mature in Michigan are taking root in other states across the country. Thus, studying that state lets us understand a reality that may become more widespread if significant federal protection of education rights remains unavailable.

Who is to say that a more extensive federal role is a better option though? Not everyone thinks it would be, in part because, admittedly, the federal government has a mixed record on education reform issues (which some observers would characterize in even less favorable terms).[1] As one scholar notes, "Unless state courts prove themselves unwilling and unable to deal with the structural problems created by educational policies, the federal government should assume a role that leaves sufficient space for state courts to operate."[2] So are state governments able and willing to perform these functions? Numerous scholars answer this question in the negative.[3] This chapter concurs and adds detail to that response.

I first discuss what the right to education actually means at the state level and illustrate that despite state constitutional language, a right to education sometimes is a weak or unenforceable right. Then I analyze how school funding debates intersect with the right to education, including the question of lack of political will to engage challenging issues of finance and equity, and I question the capacity of states to create a meaningful floor of educational quality. Throughout the chapter, I engage the national context and also provide depth by focusing on the state of Michigan. To make a long story short, Michigan, at least, is nowhere near holding up its end of the deal of cooperative federalism, and many other states have followed a similar pattern or are primed to do so.

The Right to Education Is Not What You Think It Is

All fifty states have a right to education in their state constitutions. However, the language of the right varies significantly, and the interpretation of that language varies even more. In total, forty-four states across the country have experienced litigation about these provisions via school finance disputes, but litigation is the last resort, not the beginning of a quality or funding dispute.[4] Additionally, litigation in many states, including Michigan, illustrates that constitutional language does not mean that a robust right exists.

Before discussing states' rights to education and related litigation, it is important to remember that each branch of state government plays a role in school finance. The executive branch is involved through the state's department of education and on occasion through the advocacy of the state's governor and the attorney general.[5] The legislature determines the amount of the state per-pupil grant and the amount of supplemental funding available to districts.[6] (On average, state funding constitutes slightly less than half of a school district's budget, and sometimes the budget is not finalized until school districts have already started a new fiscal year.)[7] The judiciary functions as a check on the legislature and the executive, hearing claims of funding inequality and insufficiency under the state's constitutional provisions when courts interpret these provisions to provide legal redress for such claims.[8]

School finance litigation generally is based on two types of provisions: those that establish a positive right to education and those that guarantee equal protection of the laws more generally.[9] Although some scholars have divided school finance litigation into phases described by a focus on adequacy of funds provided or equity of opportunities available, the reality of the claims is more complex than that.[10] School finance litigation began in earnest in the late 1960s and early 1970s. By 1972, courts across the country had issued decisions in only ten school finance cases.[11] The first such decision was issued in 1968 in Illinois,[12] and soon thereafter, what would become the famous *Rodriguez v. San Antonio Independent School District* litigation was on its way from Texas to the US Supreme Court.[13]

At this same time, another one of the early school finance cases arose in Michigan, where Governor William Milliken and Attorney General Frank Kelley joined together to initiate a school funding case that moved forward with astonishing speed. They were inspired by school finance plaintiffs' 1971 watershed victory via the California Supreme Court's *Serrano v. Priest* decision and intrigued by the political popularity of school finance reform efforts.[14] As a result of the case they initiated, on December 29, 1972, the Michigan Supreme Court struck down the state's school finance system.[15] The facts in the Michigan case told a now-familiar story that has since been echoed in school finance litigation all across the country. The majority summarized school districts' disparities as follows:

[A]mong approximately one eighth of Michigan School districts, the 48 richest districts had at least 4 times or more the property tax ability to support their students as 32 of the poorest districts. . . . [A]mong approximately two-thirds of Michigan school districts serving about two-thirds of Michigan school children the property tax power favors the richer half of the districts by a ratio of at least 3 to 2. . . . [T]he inequalities between school districts in their ability to finance an education for their school children are sufficiently common and severe to conclude that even with the equalizing efforts of the Michigan school aid formula, the inherent differences in the property tax bases of the school districts prevent equal resources for the education of Michigan school children in a substantial number of school districts.[16]

The plaintiffs' victory was short-lived. Unlike in *Serrano* and *Rodriguez*, the Michigan justices' internal decision process was somewhat unusual, and the influence of judicial elections was significant. In short, correctly anticipating that the November 1972 elections had shifted the majority, the court issued the 4–3 decision just two days before the new justices took office.[17] The two outgoing justices were split between the majority and the dissent, but the incoming justices both aligned with the dissenters.[18] In January 1973, the new court lost no time granting a rehearing.[19]

Roughly two months later, in March 1973, the US Supreme Court decided *San Antonio Independent School District v. Rodriguez*.[20] The facts in *Rodriguez* were similar in many ways to the facts in the Michigan litigation just described, and both reflected norms in school finance across the country: vast disparities in districts' taxable property values resulted in substantially different revenues among school districts in a system heavily reliant on local property taxes.[21] As the introduction to this volume explains, *Rodriguez* is perhaps best known for bringing an end to school finance litigation in federal courts.[22] After *Rodriguez*, advocates across the nation refocused on state courts and legislatures. Back in Michigan, at the end of 1973, the state Supreme Court issued a vague one-paragraph amended order dismissing the school finance case and vacating the prior decision on arguably unpersuasive procedural grounds.[23]

Although the early Michigan litigation pitted the executive against the legislature and judiciary, since the time the decision was vacated, the three branches have been aligned. In the early 1980s, twenty Michigan school districts again brought a school finance claim against the state, and the Michigan Court of Appeals affirmed the trial court's grant of summary judgment in favor of the state, holding that the question presented was essentially the same as in the prior litigation.[24] In 1985, the long-serving and still-revered Michigan Attorney General Frank Kelley issued an Opinion Letter concluding that school districts did not need to provide alternative education for a student facing a long-term suspension or expulsion because "public education is not a fundamental right under either the United States or Michigan Constitutions."[25] The Opinion Letter significantly overstated the support for its conclusion, and yet that letter is part of the conventional wisdom about what education rights mean in Michigan.

For most of the past fifty years, state courts have been the place to challenge the legislative decisions that have contributed to educational disparities, but that does not mean this option remains even as modestly effective as it has been in the past. The story in Michigan is not unique. Courts in Florida, Illinois, Louisiana, Pennsylvania, and Rhode Island also have declined to review legislative decisions about school finance, citing concerns about separation of powers, justiciability, and other issues[26]—and these states' constitutional language about education varies substantially. Additionally, it appears that the 2008 recession marked a sea change. In fact, courts have been more hostile to school finance claims after the recession, and even when plaintiffs have prevailed, legislatures have resisted sometimes to the point of defiance.[27]

State courts' growing lack of receptivity to school funding claims is especially frustrating for educational quality advocates because scholars increasingly are coming to understand that the impact of these state-level decisions can be far-reaching. In 2016, the University of California–Berkeley and Northwestern University economists Julien Lafortune, Jesse Rothstein, and Diane Whitmore Schanzenbach determined that funding reforms "lead to sharp, immediate, and sustained increases in mean school spending and in relative spending in low-income school districts." They found a relationship between spending and achievement and concluded that "[f]inance reforms are arguably the most important policy for promoting equality of educational opportunity since the turn away from school desegregation in the 1980s."[28] Two years earlier, in 2014, the economists C. Kirabo Jackson, Rucker Johnson, and graduate student Claudia Persico, also from Northwestern University and the University of California–Berkeley, similarly determined that "court-mandated reforms were effective . . . [and] legislative reforms were somewhat effective at reducing spending gaps" between high- and low-income districts. Furthermore, they found that increasing per-pupil spending 20 percent can eliminate at least two-thirds, if not all, of the gaps between adults raised in poor and nonpoor families when measuring education completed, adult earnings, and adult poverty.[29]

These findings are consistent with earlier work and analysis by the leading school finance expert Michael Rebell and others concluding that decisions by courts and legislatures are critically important in equalizing school funding and also that school funding increases are especially significant if education is to be anything close to a great equalizer.[30] Ideally, state legislatures would fund schools at a level that is both adequate and equitable, but in at least thirty states, total funding for public schools was less in fiscal year 2014 than prior to the recession in fiscal year 2008.[31] Furthermore, a 2018 report by the Education Law Center documents that states continue to vary radically in their level of funding fairness within the state.[32]

Although this is a new dynamic in many states, Michigan has a longer history of judicial abdication dovetailing with legislative inertia and executive inaction regarding school funding levels as well as educational quality. The result, as Education Trust reported in 2016, is a "systemic failure . . . [in which] Michigan ranks an abysmal 42nd of 47 states in the fairness of its funding system."[33] Furthermore, student achievement in Michigan, regardless of race, ethnicity, poverty, and wealth, "in early reading and middle school math [is] not keeping up with the rest of the U.S., much less . . . international competitors."[34] It is tempting to view the situation in Michigan as idiosyncratic, but doing so would be a mistake. Rather, we should view Michigan as the canary in the coal mine showing us how far a state judiciary can go to avoid engaging the merits of educational quality claims and what can happen when all three branches of government endorse or acquiesce in the "new minimal state"[35] approach to public education.

School Funding and Educational Opportunities: States' Finance Schemes, the Policy Web, Political Will, and States' Capacity

In any state, the lack of a robust right with a meaningful judicial remedy would be a theoretical but not practical concern if public education were delivered at an acceptable level of quality across the state; however, educational inequality and lack of quality both run rampant throughout the nation.

For more than twenty years, *Education Week* has generated what it describes as an annual "report card" regarding education across the nation and in each state.[36] The key criteria are K–12 achievement, school finance (both spending patterns and equity), and the chance for successful child and adult outcomes. In January 2018, the nation on the whole earned a grade of C: divided into a C for K–12 achievement, a C for school finance, and a C+ for chance of success.[37] Michigan ranked on the low side of average, earning an overall grade of C; just eighteen states ranked lower. It earned a D+ on K–12 achievement, a C on school finance, and a C+ on chance for success.[38]

There are multiple issues to consider here, and this section engages three with a focus on Michigan: first, how a state chooses to fund education matters; second, a state's school finance scheme is one aspect of the policy web in each state that influences the health of the public school system and also demonstrates where the state's citizens and interest groups demonstrate and lack political will; and, third, questions of states' contributions to these crises and capacity to intervene are important.

School Finance Schemes

As discussed earlier, each state legislature determines its school finance scheme. Of all the revenues available to local school districts across the country, roughly 9 percent come from the federal government, with local governments contributing 46 percent and state governments contributing 46 percent.[39] This breakdown has been fairly consistent for decades. That said, there can be significant variation from one state to another.

For example, from around the time of Michigan's ill-fated school finance litigation in the early 1970s through the mid-1990s, Michigan had a school finance system that was heavily reliant on local property taxes, so much so that Michigan's property taxes were among the highest in the nation.[40] Michigan made national headlines when, in 1994, it enacted its current school finance system and lowered local property-tax rates substantially.[41] The new system offset school districts' reduction in local tax revenues by increasing state support via the state's per-pupil foundation grant significantly and supplementing this with equalization funding to school districts that are especially property poor.[42] Soon after this modified foundation grant system was implemented in 1994, the amount of school funding received by Michigan's most property-poor districts increased noticeably.[43] Over time, several demographic and statutory changes combined to complicate this school finance system, creating direct and substantial fiscal hardship for districts across the state and contributing to a decline in the quality of education provided to the many children who live and attend school in those districts.[44]

The overlay of various factors exposed the system's flaws and eventually pushed it to the breaking point. From fiscal year 2011 through fiscal year 2014, roughly fifty of Michigan's school districts were in deficit, and even though the number was down to fourteen in June 2017,[45] for most of the post-recession period Michigan had the largest number of deficit districts of any state in the country including California,[46] where the statewide school system has been in financial trouble and where it educates roughly four times as many students as Michigan (the number of deficit districts in California surpassed Michigan in mid-2017). The heterogeneity of Michigan's deficit districts demonstrates that the system's flaws run deep.[47] These districts are urban, suburban, and rural. They have varying levels of students with disabilities and students who are English-language learners. While the deficit districts are disproportionately poor and minority, not all are so. They range from very small districts to the state's largest and many in between.[48]

The Policy Web and Political Will

School finance statutes and regulations are not the only aspect of state law that influence school districts' financial and thus academic health. State laws regulating school choice, public school employees' pension systems, and the source of financial support for capital improvements are key aspects of a web of policies that interact with school finance. Again, Michigan provides an illustration of the interaction of these variables.

Between 2002–03 and 2012–13, enrollment in Michigan's traditional public schools dropped by more than 13 percent.[49] In part this is due to a decline in the state's school-age population, some of which is because Michigan, a former titan of industry, has been in an economic nosedive and was the only state in the nation with a smaller population in 2010 than in 2000.[50] However, the other key variable is that Michigan has some of the most permissive school choice statutes in the country, an approach supported by US Secretary of Education Betsy DeVos, a long-time Michigan philanthropist.[51] Michigan's school choice statutes enact two policies: charter schools and open enrollment.

The first charter school in the country opened in Minnesota in 1992, and since that time, charter schools have grown rapidly—by 2015–16, they educated 5.1 percent of children nationally.[52] In 1994, Michigan authorized charter schools as part of the statewide school finance overhaul[53] and created the state's current cross-district, open-enrollment policy (known as "schools of choice") in 1996.[54] In Michigan, charters now educate nearly 10 percent of school-age children, and the state has three of the eleven school districts nationally with the highest percentage of students enrolled in charter schools.[55] Due to the lack of oversight and the permissive nature of the charter-school-enabling statute, many of Michigan's charters are academically quite weak; thus, a significant number of charters perform worse than the home schools that the students leave to attend them.[56] Many Michiganders have taken advantage of the state's unusually permissive open-enrollment policy as well; in 2015–16, 13 percent of Michigan public school students attended school in a district other than the one in which they lived.[57]

As a result, enrollment levels at the district level can be quite volatile from year to year, which is troubling for a district that is losing students because school funding in Michigan is unusually centralized at the state level. When a student leaves a district, roughly $7,500 of state per-pupil funding follows that student out of a particular district and often entirely out of the traditional public school system.[58] Thus, a major drop in enrollment district-wide can trigger a sort of death spiral because school districts have substantial fixed costs and cannot simply reduce their expenditures in proportion to the number of students they lose. Yet school districts with precipitously declining enrollments (and thus falling revenue) must close schools and cut services for the students who remain, even though doing so often encourages those students to consider leaving as well.[59]

The next piece in the web, the state teachers' pension system, is significant enough to stand alone and yet also part and parcel of the prior piece. Many states' pension systems for teachers and other public employees are severely underfunded, and the legacy costs continue to grow because the total number of retirees is growing and many of them are former school district employees.[60] This is even more of a challenge in states such as Michigan because of the way the pension system can interact with charter schools. Specifically, the high and growing number of employees in Michigan charter schools do not contribute to the pension system, and because of the declining enrollment in traditional public schools, the growing legacy costs are borne by a public school system across the state that is getting smaller and smaller.[61]

Not surprisingly, Michigan's increases in education funding in recent years often have been dwarfed by districts' growing mandatory contributions to the pension system (rising from 13 percent of employee salaries in 2004 to almost 25 percent in 2012),[62] resulting in a net per-pupil loss to districts when calculated in terms of classroom dollars.[63] A 2016 costing-out study determined that the base level of funding the state should provide per student is $8,667.[64] However, in fiscal year 2010, $6,350 of the state of Michigan's $7,316 foundation grant remained after districts met retirement obligations, but by fiscal year 2014, only $5,882 of the $7,409 foundation grant was available to districts.[65]

The final major piece in this web is that only fifteen states (including Michigan) require that each school district fully fund capital improvements rather than the state and the local district sharing these costs.[66] The greatest facility needs often are in property-poor districts, which are often also districts that lose an unusually high portion of their students to charter schools and to other districts through the schools of choice program, suggesting limited support for a local referendum. The shrinking districts are often the least able to raise the needed funds, though they may be the ones that need to invest in facilities the most.[67]

Michigan's school finance system has remained largely unchanged for the past twenty years.[68] This stagnation is unusual, as school funding reform efforts have remained active across the country during this time.[69] Even so, in some states preserving the status quo may be acceptable, but in Michigan the status quo is that of a broken system. In addition to the nationally record-setting number of school districts that have operated in deficit, student achievement levels and physical conditions of school buildings in many parts of Michigan are abysmal.[70] Michigan students' scores have been below national averages in all National Assessment for Educational Progress (NAEP) categories for many years, and for the past decade, the state's largest district—Detroit—has had lower math and reading scores than any other major urban district in the country.[71]

State Capacity and Responsibility

When a school district is in fiscal or academic crisis (or both), it is difficult to imagine how that district can provide its students an adequate education. This has been the case often in Michigan and also around the country. In these circumstances, the state has a moral if not a practical or constitutional obligation to assist—after all, even if a state closes a particular school district, the children who were attending those schools will need to go to school somewhere, and the state is the parent of education at the end of the day. States have enacted various policies in response to school districts' fiscal and academic crises, and although takeovers have been shown to create financial stability in many districts, community responses as well as districts' academic results have not been so positive.

The most extreme form of state intervention is a comprehensive takeover of a local school district. These takeovers are controversial for multiple reasons, and in Michigan they have come under fire for dissolving democracy. Additionally, takeovers do not have a record of producing academic gains, and while takeovers have a moderate record of success with regard to righting the ship financially, the water crisis in Flint, Michigan, has demonstrated the very real risks of state takeovers. The state of Michigan applied the same takeover policy to school districts that it applied to Flint, and between 2009 and 2016, four Michigan school districts were taken over by emergency managers who effectively displaced the superintendent and school board.[72] Also during this time, two districts were liquidated and their students channeled into surrounding districts (it still is not entirely clear who owns the liquidated districts' debt).[73] Additionally, the emergency managers in Detroit's public schools were eventually phased out via a radical reconfiguration of the district inspired by private-sector bankruptcy in late 2016.[74] Michigan continues to try to figure out how to best assist districts in anticipating, averting, and managing fiscal crises.[75] Not surprisingly, school districts in fiscal crisis are hardly places of educational achievement and innovation.[76]

Although a limited amount of school districts' fiscal troubles may be due to local mismanagement or malfeasance, the fiscal crisis in Michigan districts is largely the natural result of state policies enacted through statute and executive action.[77] In many states—and indeed in other states with constitutional language similar to Michigan's—plaintiffs could challenge the state action through what would probably be protracted school finance litigation.[78] As recent research by the economists Lafortune, Rothstein, Schanzenbach and Jackson, Johnson, and Persico demonstrates, a judicial remedy could reduce school finance inequality across the state and improve educational quality for some students,[79] and as the philosopher Anne Newman suggests, a judicial remedy coupled with community support could lead to long-lasting, positive, far-reaching change.[80] But that has not happened in Michigan because the conventional wisdom is that the right to education in the state constitution is not a fundamental right and at most constitutes a thin access right. The legislature, the executive, and the judiciary have not been willing and able to create a higher floor.

In 1986, the US Supreme Court noted when deciding *Papasan v. Allain* that *Rodriguez* and *Plyler* left open the question of whether there was a federal right to an education of a minimum quality.[81] If so, even a thin federal quality right would exceed the contours of the right to education, such as it is, in a state like Michigan. State law in Michigan has not established the floor that we have assumed exists. If this failure is happening in a state ranked on the low side of average by many indicators, it is troubling to think about what must be happening in states ranked even closer to the bottom.

Conclusion

Unlike in many countries around the world, in the United States there is no positive right to education in federal law.[82] Such a right exists only at the state level, and it varies from one state to another. Part of this variation occurs because similar language in state constitutions has been interpreted as creating moderate to robust education rights in one state and weak to nonexistent education rights in another.[83] The blame is not entirely at the feet of state courts though—in a state with a failing level of educational quality, all three branches of government are complicit. Michigan shows us precisely what it looks like when the proverbial floor rots and children fall through: in one small district, a native English speaker without a learning disability matriculates to seventh grade while reading only at a first-grade level and sometimes misspelling his or her own name, and in a neighboring major district, the percentage of eighth graders proficient in reading is in the single digits.[84]

Early in this chapter, a commentator's question was raised as something to be answered before making the case for a greater federal role in education: simply put, are states "unwilling and unable to deal with the structural problems created by educational policies"?[85] If they are willing and able, the commentator's argument continued, then a larger federal role is not needed. Although an exhaustive state-by-state analysis is far beyond the scope of this chapter, this chapter has demonstrated that at least in the case of Michigan the answer is clear.

Under the current model of education federalism, though, these glaring gaps in educational quality are not the federal government's problem, and in some ways the federal government's hands are tied when it comes to being part of the solution. This must change. The present reality of public education in Michigan shows us what is likely to occur in a growing number of states unless at least one branch of the federal government intervenes. Recognizing a federal right to education built on a more effective approach to federalism would enable us to avoid a dystopian future by establishing a federal floor of minimal educational quality.[86] The children of this country deserve no less.

NOTES

I am grateful to the *University of Michigan Journal on Law Reform* for granting permission to adapt "The Failure of Education Federalism" and publish it here. Additionally, I appreciate the exceptional research assistance provided by MSU law librarians Jane Meland, Daryl Thompson, and Barbara Bean and MSU Law alumnae Adrienne Anderson and Janieasha Freelove-Sewel. My education law seminar students also have my gratitude for influencing my thinking on these issues. Colleagues at MSU and across the country graciously provided thoughtful and insightful comments on the piece at various stages—thank you to David Arsen, Joyce Baugh, Scott Bauries, Derek Black, Robert Garda Jr., Mary Mason, Rachel Moran, Jason Nance, Eloise Pasachoff, Sarah Reckhow, Aaron Saiger, Michael Sant'Ambrogio, and of course Kimberly Jenkins Robinson.

1. *See* Aaron Lawson, *Educational Federalism: A New Case for Reduced Federal Involvement in K–12 Education*, 2013 BYU EDUC. & L.J. 281, 302 (2013).

2. *Id.* at 286.

3. *See, e.g.*, Charles Barone and Elizabeth DeBray, *Education Policy in Congress: Perspectives from Inside and Out*, *in* CARROTS, STICKS, AND THE BULLY PULPIT (Frederick M. Hess & Andrew P. Kelly eds., 2011); Kimberly Jenkins Robinson, *Disrupting Education Federalism*, 92 WASH. U. L. REV. 959, 1005 (2015) (quoting Barone and DeBray).

4. SCHOOLFUNDING.INFO, http://schoolfunding.info/ (last visited June 28, 2018) (showing six states—Delaware, Hawaii, Iowa, Mississippi, Nevada, and Utah— that have not had important education-finance litigation court decisions); *see also*

Derek Black, *Unlocking the Power of State Constitutions with Equal Protection: The First Step toward Education as a Federally Protected Right*, 51 WM. & MARY L. REV. 1343, 1360–73 (2010).

5. Kristi L. Bowman, *The Failure of Education Federalism*, 51 U. MICH. J.L. REFORM 1, 49–52 (2017).

6. FAITH E. CRAMPTON, DAVID C. THOMPSON & R. CRAIG WOOD, MONEY AND SCHOOLS 51–53 (6th ed. 2015).

7. *Id.* at 56–57.

8. *Id.* at 57–68, 86–101.

9. *Id.*

10. *See* James E. Ryan, *Standards, Testing, and School Finance Litigation*, 86 TEX. L. REV. 1223, 1229–30 (2008).

11. *See, e.g.*, Milliken v. Green (*Governor I*), 203 N.W.2d 457, 476 n.1 (Mich. 1972) (Brennan, J., dissenting) (listing similar actions in other state courts). This case is known as "*Governor*," in contrast to the well-known school desegregation litigation proceeding at the same time and also bearing Governor Milliken's name, Milliken v. Bradley, 418 U.S. 717 (1974), which is known as "*Milliken.*"

12. McInnis v. Shapiro, 293 F. Supp. 327 (N.D. Ill. 1968); *Governor I*, 203 N.W. 2d at 484–85.

13. 337 F. Supp. 280 (W.D. Tex. 1971), *rev'd*, San Antonio Indep. Sch. Dist. v. Rodriguez, 411 U.S. 1 (1973).

14. 487 P.2d 1241 (Cal. 1971); Elwood Hain, Milliken v. Green: *Breaking the Legislative Deadlock*, 38 LAW & CONTEMP. PROBS. 350, 351 (1974).

15. *Governor I*, 203 N.W.2d at 474.

16. *Id.* at 463, 467 (majority opinion).

17. *Id.* at 474–75 (Brennan, J. addendum). *See* Elizabeth Wheat & Mark S. Hurwitz, *The Politics of Judicial Selection: The Case of the Michigan Supreme Court*, JUDICATURE, Jan.–Feb. 2013, at 8.

18. Hain, *supra* note 14, at 354.

19. Milliken v. Green (*Governor II*), 212 N.W.2d 711, 712 (Mich. 1973) (the rehearing was granted on January 30, 1973).

20. 411 U.S. 1 (1973).

21. *See* Kimberly Jenkins Robinson, *The High Cost of Education Federalism*, 48 WAKE FOREST L. REV. 287, 309 (2013).

22. *See, e.g.*, Kristi L. Bowman, *A New Strategy for Pursuing Racial and Ethnic Equality in Public Schools*, 1 DUKE F. FOR L. & SOC. CHANGE 47, 57 (2009); MARK G. YUDOF ET AL., EDUCATIONAL POLICY AND THE LAW 813 (5th ed. 2012).

23. *Governor II*, 212 N.W.2d at 711; Hain, *supra* note 14, at 359.

24. E. Jackson Pub. Sch. v. State, 348 N.W.2d 304 (Mich. Ct. App. 1984). Thus, noting its agreement with the two concurring justices in *Governor II*, the appellate court affirmed the grant of summary judgment in favor of the state and closed the case. *Id.* at 305–06. Additionally, the appellate court held that because school districts are "creations of the state," the districts themselves have no authority to contest the school finance framework created by state statute. *Id.* at 306–07.

25. Mich. Att'y Gen., Opinion Letter No. 6271 (Feb. 7, 1985). To support the statement about the absence of a fundamental right to education in state law, the Opinion Letter relied on Michigan appellate courts' then-recent decisions in *East Jackson Public Schools*, discussed earlier, and in *Sutton*. In *Sutton*, a state appellate court held that the state constitution's education provision did not require districts to provide resident students with free transportation to and from school—the case did not engage fundamental finance or educational quality issues. Sutton v. Cadillac Area Pub. Sch., 323 N.W.2d 582, 583–85 (Mich. Ct. App. 1982) (quoting Bond v. Pub. Sch. of Ann Arbor, 178 N.W.2d 484 (Mich. 1970)). The attorney general's Opinion Letter does not mention the *Governor* litigation, but such an omission is in part understandable—it is not clear what one should make of the court's cryptic one-sentence reversal of *Governor I*.

26. *See* Lawson, *supra* note 1, at 314 n.166 (citing the Louisiana and Pennsylvania courts' reactions); Robinson, *supra* note 21, at 298, 315 (discussing the Florida, Illinois, Michigan, and Rhode Island courts' reactions); *see also* Milliken v. Green (*Governor I*), 203 N.W.2d 457 (Mich. 1972), *vacated*, 212 N.W.2d 711 (Mich. 1973) (*Governor II*), and Milliken v. Bradley, 418 U.S. 717 (1974).

27. Derek W. Black, *Averting Educational Crisis: Funding Cuts, Teacher Shortages, and the Dwindling Commitment to Public Education*, 94 WASH. U. L. REV. 423, 427 (2016); *see also* Madeline Davis, *Off the Constitutional Map: Breaking the Endless Cycle of School Finance Litigation*, 2016 B.Y.U. EDUC. & L.J. 117, 118 (2016). Since Black's article was published, the Kansas Supreme Court struck down the legislature's finance scheme, and the Kansas decision may fit within the trend that Black identifies.

28. Julien Lafortune, Jesse Rothstein & Diane Whitmore Schanzenbach, *School Finance Reform and the Distribution of Student Achievement* 1, 3 (Northwestern Inst. for Policy Research, Working Paper No. WP-16-04, 2016).

29. C. Kirabo Jackson, Rucker Johnson & Claudia Persico, *The Effect of School Finance Reforms on the Distribution of Spending, Academic Achievement, and Adult Outcomes* 43 (Nat'l Bureau of Econ. Research, Working Paper No. 20118, 2014).

30. *See generally* BRUCE BAKER, ALBERT SHANKER INST., REVISITING THAT AGE-OLD QUESTION: DOES MONEY MATTER IN EDUCATION? (2012); Rob Greenwald et al., *The Effect of School Resources on Student Achievement*, 66 REV. EDUC. RES. 361, 362, 368 (1996); Michael Rebell, *Poverty, "Meaningful" Educational Opportunity, and the Necessary Role of the Courts*, 85 N.C. L. REV. 1467 (2007); Robinson, *supra* note 21, at 317–18 (summarizing research).

31. MICHAEL LEACHMAN ET AL., CTR. ON BUDGET POLICY & PRIORITIES, MOST STATES HAVE CUT SCHOOL FUNDING, AND SOME CONTINUE CUTTING 1 (2016).

32. BRUCE D. BAKER, DANIELLE FARRIE & DAVID SCIARRA, EDUC. LAW CTR., IS SCHOOL FUNDING FAIR? A NATIONAL REPORT CARD iv (7th ed. 2018); *see also* Robinson, *supra* note 21 at 320.

33. AMBER ARELLANO, SUNEET BEDI & TERRY GALLAGHER, EDUC. TR.-MIDWEST, MICHIGAN'S TALENT CRISIS: THE ECONOMIC CASE FOR RE-BUILDING MICHIGAN'S BROKEN PUBLIC EDUCATION SYSTEM 8, 21 (2016).

34. *Id.* at 4.

35. *See* Michelle Wilde Anderson, *The New Minimal Cities*, 123 YALE L.J. 1118, 1181 (2014).

36. Educ. Week, For Quality Counts, A Renewed Focus on the Value of Data (Jan. 17, 2018).

37. *Id.*

38. *Id.* Hawaii and the District of Columbia were excluded from the school finance evaluation because they are single-district jurisdictions; thus, it is impossible to evaluate equity across school districts when the jurisdiction has only one school district. *Id.*

39. National Public Education Financial Survey Data, 2013–14 (data and calculations on file with author), https://nces.ed.gov/ccd/stfis.asp; Documentation for the NCES Common Core of Data National Public Education Financial Survey (NPEFS), School Year 2013–14 (Fiscal Year 2014), Sept. 2016.

40. William Celis III, *Michigan Votes for Revolution in Financing Its Public Schools*, N.Y. TIMES, Mar. 17, 1994. Not surprisingly, this caused significant dissatisfaction among property-owning taxpayers and eventually prompted legislative reform. *See* DAVID ARSEN & DAVID N. PLANCK, EDUC. POLICY CTR. AT MICH. STATE UNIV., MICHIGAN SCHOOL FINANCE UNDER PROPOSAL A: STATE CONTROL, LOCAL CONSEQUENCES 3–5 (2003).

41. *E.g.*, Celis, *supra* note 40.

42. ARSEN & PLANCK, *supra* note 40, at 7; Marya Sieminski, *Michigan's Constitutional Protection for Public Education: Legal Rights or Empty Promises*, 40 WAYNE L. REV. 1309, 1314–15, 1314 n.36 (1994).

43. ARSEN & PLANCK, *supra* note 40, at 9–11; Leslie E. Papke, *The Effects of Changes in Michigan's School Finance System*, 36 PUB. FIN. REV. 456, 456–57 (2008).

44. *See generally* Papke, *supra* note 43, at 456–57.

45. Michigan enrolls 1.5 million children in 900 school districts (601 districts not including public school academies). MICH. DEP'T OF EDUC., MDE FAST FACTS 2016–2017: STATISTICS FOR MICHIGAN SCHOOLS (June 2017), https://www.michigan.gov. As of June 2017, fourteen school districts were in deficit; one year earlier, that number was twenty-nine; two years earlier, the number was forty-one; and three years earlier, it was over fifty. Memorandum from Brian Whiston, State Superintendent, to the Mich. House and Senate K–12 Appropriations Comm. Attach. B (June 14, 2017); *see also* Citizens Research Council of Mich., *Managing School District Finances in an Era of Declining Enrollment*, CRC MEMORANDUM (Jan. 2015), at 3.

46. California schools enroll 6.2 million children in about one thousand school districts. *California Public K–12 Graded Enrollment and High School Graduate Projections by County—2017 Series*, CAL. DEP'T FIN. (2017), www.dof.ca.gov; *Fingertip*

Facts on Education in California, CAL. DEP'T EDUC. (2016), https://www.cde.
ca.gov/ds/sd/cb/ceffingertipfacts.asp. The state's approximately twelve hundred
charter schools, which educate over six hundred thousand children, are not designated as independent school districts. CAL. DEP'T OF EDUC., QUICKQUEST
(2017). Forty-three of the state's districts are in or projected to be in deficit. *Second
Interim Status Report, FY 2016–17*, CAL. DEP'T EDUC. (2017) https://www.cde.
ca.gov.

47. In mid-2015, forty-one Michigan districts were in deficit. In December 2016, only
twenty-two districts remained in deficit. Memorandum from Brian Whiston,
supra note 45, Attach. B; Nicquel Terry, *Mich. School District Deficit List Cut to 23*,
DET. NEWS (June 19, 2016), www.detroitnews.com/.

48. *See* Kristi L. Bowman, MI School Districts in Fiscal Crisis, Sept. 2014 (FY2014)
(on file with author); Memorandum from Mike Flanagan, State Superintendent,
to Mich. House and Senate K–12 Appropriations Comm. (Sept. 11, 2014).

49. An examination of the NCES data reveals the following: In the 2012–13 school
year, Michigan's student enrollment was 1,555,370. In the 2002–03 school year,
Michigan's total student enrollment was 1,785,160. *State Nonfiscal Public Elemen-
tary/Secondary Education Survey Data*, NAT'L CTR. FOR EDUC. STATISTICS
(2017), https://nces.ed.gov/ccd/stnfis.asp.

50. Matt Pearce, *Why Michigan Has Been Lurching from Crisis to Crisis*, L.A. TIMES,
May 4, 2016.

51. Allie Gross, *Betsy DeVos's Accountability Problem*, ATLANTIC, Jan. 13, 2017; *How
Betsy DeVos and Her Money Has Shaped Education in Michigan*, MLIVE (Nov. 29,
2016), www.mlive.com.

52. NAT'L CTR. FOR EDUC. STATISTICS, TABLE 216.90: PUBLIC ELEMENTARY
AND SECONDARY CHARTER SCHOOLS AND ENROLLMENT, BY STATE (Sept.
2015); *see also* Julie Mack, *23% of Michigan Public School Students Opt for School
Choice*, MLIVE (Aug. 29, 2016); Kate Zernike, *A Sea of Charter Schools in Detroit
Leaves Students Adrift*, N.Y. TIMES, June 28, 2016.

53. Dustin Dwyer, *The Day Michigan Killed Public Schools (and Then Created the
System We Have Today)*, MICH. PUB. RADIO: ST. OPPORTUNITY BLOG (June
9, 2014), http://stateofopportunity.michiganradio.org.

54. 1996 Mich. Pub. Acts 876.

55. NAT'L ALL. FOR PUB. CHARTER SCH., A GROWING MOVEMENT: AMERI-
CA'S LARGEST CHARTER SCHOOL COMMUNITIES 3 (10th ed. 2015); *See* Black,
supra note 27, at 435; Mack, *supra* note 52; Zernike, *supra* note 52.

56. *See generally* SUNIL JOY & AMBER ARELLANO, EDUC. TR.-MIDWEST, AC-
COUNTABILITY FOR ALL: 2016: THE BROKEN PROMISE OF MICHIGAN'S
CHARTER SECTOR (2016).

57. Mack, *supra* note 52.

58. David Arsen et al., *Which Districts Get into Financial Trouble and Why: Michigan's
Story* 6 (Educ. Policy Ctr. at Mich. State Univ., Working Paper, No. 51, 2015). Not
surprisingly, the decline in student enrollment and thus the drop in per-pupil

funding are not felt evenly across districts. Joshua M. Cowen, *A Look at Michigan's Schools of Choice*, GREEN & WRITE (Apr. 6, 2016), http://edwp.educ.msu.edu.

59. Arsen et al., *supra* note 58, at 12–13, 26; Citizens Research Council of Mich., *supra* note 45, at 6.

60. *See* RACHEL WHITE ET AL., KNOWLEDGEABLE NAVIGATION TO AVOID THE ICEBERG: CONSIDERATIONS IN PROACTIVELY ADDRESSING SCHOOL DISTRICT FISCAL STRESS IN MICHIGAN 2–6 (2015).

61. Lauren Camera, *America's Bankrupt Schools—Pension Plans Could Be the Culprit behind Broke Big-City School Districts*, U.S. NEWS, Mar. 18, 2016.

62. MICH. HOUSE FISCAL AGENCY, MICHIGAN PUBLIC SCHOOL EMPLOYEES' RETIREMENT SYSTEM 36 (2015). A system that used to look like a triangle right side up (a limited amount of legacy costs at the top supported by a much larger base of revenue) is on its way to looking more like a triangle inverted. School districts' and the state's inability to financially grapple with these challenges, too, connect back to the precipitous decline of the manufacturing industry in Michigan. Pearce, *supra* note 50.

63. Citizens Research Council of Mich., *Making Sense of K-12 Funding*, CRC MEMORANDUM, Oct. 2014, at 5, Chart 4 (2014); *see also* Citizens Research Council of Mich., *Detroit Public Schools' Legacy Costs and Indebtedness*, CRC MEMORANDUM, Jan. 2016.

64. Michael Addonizio & David Arsen, *Study a Step to Getting Michigan School Funding Right*, DET. FREE PRESS, July 21, 2016.

65. These figures account for additional state funds intended to offset the growing mandatory contributions and adjust for inflation. Citizens Research Council of Mich., *School District Fiscal Health Improves, but Some Long-Term Challenges Remain*, CRC MEMORANDUM, June 2014, at 6–7.

66. CTR. FOR CITIES & SCH., UNIV. OF CAL. BERKELEY, STATE FUNDING FOR K-12 SCHOOL FACILITIES: A SURVEY OF THE STATES 5 (2014).

67. *See, e.g.*, Arsen et al., *supra* note 58, at 20–22; David Arsen & Mary Mason, *The Role of State Courts in Securing School Facility Adequacy and Equity* (Educ. Policy Ctr. at Mich. State Univ., Working Paper No. 31, 2010); Sarah Dewees, *Improving Rural School Facilities for Teaching and Learning*, ERIC DIG., ED438153 (1999); Beth Hawkins, *Detroit's Educational Catastrophe*, ATLANTIC, May 10, 2016. The fiscal year 2017 minimum foundation grant was $7,511. STATE BUDGET OFFICE, STATE OF MICH., SCHOOL AID HIGHLIGHTS EXECUTIVE BUDGET FISCAL YEARS 2017 AND 2018 1 (2016). It may also be that Michigan's graying population plays a role in this, with older adults potentially less willing to vote for a local referendum and subsidize the cost of public education when their children are grown and thus their families receive no direct benefit. *Michigan Population Trends, 1990–2015*, MICH. DEPT. HEALTH & HUM. SERV., www.mdch.state.mi.us (last updated July 24, 2017); *see* RACHEL WHITE ET AL., *supra* note 60, at 2–3.

68. *See* MICH. CONST. art. IX, § 11 (the text of proposal A was amended to the Michigan constitution in 1994 and has not been modified since); Arsen et al., *supra* note 58, at 25.

69. *See, e.g.*, Daniel G. Thatcher, *School Finance Litigation Citations*, NAT'L CONF. ST. LEGISLATORS, https://docs.google.com (last visited June 17, 2018) (providing an online spreadsheet listing over 170 major school finance decisions from state courts the 1970s through 2017).

70. *See, e.g.*, Julie Bosman, *Crumbling, Destitute Schools Threaten Detroit's Recovery*, N.Y. TIMES, Jan. 20, 2016; Press Release, Educ. Tr.—Midwest, Michigan Students Fall Further behind Nation in Early Literacy (Oct. 28, 2015).

71. Jennifer Chambers, *Michigan Test Scores Lag Nationally Despite Increase*, DET. NEWS, Apr. 10, 2018.

72. *See* Kristi L. Bowman, *State Takeovers of School Districts and Related Litigation: Michigan as a Case Study*, 45 URB. LAW. 1, 7–8 (2013); MICH. DEP'T TREASURY, EMERGENCY FINANCIAL MANAGER/EMERGENCY MANAGER APPOINT-MENT HISTORY (2017).

73. Jake Neher, *Buena Vista, Inkster School Districts to Be Dissolved*, MICH. RADIO, July 22, 2013.

74. Associated Press, *Rhodes Could Exit School System Post Early If Legislation Stalls*, CRAIN'S DET. BUS., Mar. 3, 2016; Curt Guyette, *After Six Years and Four State-Appointed Managers, Detroit Public Schools' Debt Has Grown Even Deeper*, DET. METRO TIMES, Feb. 25, 2015; *see also* Kathleen Gray, *Legislature OKs $617M Detroit Public Schools Rescue Plan*, DET. FREE PRESS, June 9, 2016.

75. *See* Kyle Feldscher, *Gov. Snyder Signs Early Warning Bills That Could Increase State's Role in Fixing Districts' Finances*, MLIVE (July 7, 2015), www.mlive.com. *See generally* WHITE ET AL., *supra* note 60.

76. Del Stover, *Take It to the Limit*, AM. SCH. BOARD J., Nov. 2007, at 33.

77. Arsen et al., *supra* note 58, at 24.

78. *See generally Litigation*, EDUC. FIN. STATISTICS CTR., https://nces.ed.gov (last visited Aug. 16, 2017); SCHOOLFUNDING.INFO, *supra* note 4.

79. *See generally* Jackson, Johnson & Persico, *supra* note 29, at 15–17; Lafortune, Rothstein & Schanzenbach, *supra* note 28.

80. *See* ANNE NEWMAN, REALIZING EDUCATIONAL RIGHTS 69–70 (2013).

81. Papasan v. Allain, 478 U.S. 265, 283–85 (1986); *see also* Plyler v. Doe, 457 U.S. 202, 221–23 (1982); San Antonio Indep. Sch. Dist. v. Rodriguez, 411 U.S. 1, 36–37 (1973).

82. *See* Scott R. Bauries, *The Education Duty*, 47 WAKE FOREST L. REV. 705, 708–09 (2012).

83. *See id.* at 738–40, 738–40 nn.165–73.

84. *See* Bowman, *supra* note 5, at 15–40.

85. Lawson, *supra* note 1, at 286.

86. Robinson, *supra* note 3.

3

Doctrine, Politics, and the Limits of a Federal Right to Education

ELOISE PASACHOFF

Introduction

A deep strand of progressive legal thought holds that securing a federal right to education in the United States Constitution would help solve the problems of inequality and inadequacy that plague schooling in the United States.

At least five rationales animate this thinking. The federalism rationale suggests that a federal constitutional right to education would usefully reorder the balance of federal and state power in education, strengthening the federal government's ability to combat inequality in funding, standards, and outcomes nationwide.[1] The definitional rationale holds that a federal constitutional right to education would result in a stronger and more equal version of the right than the one that state courts and legislatures have provided through state constitutions.[2] The financial rationale provides that a federal constitutional right to education would result in a necessary and large influx of federal dollars.[3] The enforcement rationale explains that the federal constitution is enforceable in federal court, and federal court review is necessary to ensure nationwide compliance.[4] The moral rationale states that the Constitution sets forth our nation's core values, and securing a federal constitutional right to education would therefore serve an important expressive purpose.[5]

Appealing as these rationales sound, it does not follow that amending or interpreting the Constitution to provide a right to education is either a necessary or sufficient response to the problems of US education. While I am deeply sympathetic to the project of remedying educational inequality and inadequacy, I do not think that developing a federal constitutional right to education is a valuable approach. In this chapter, I explain why.

The first section of the chapter illustrates that an Education Amendment is both doctrinally unnecessary, in light of Congress's expansive powers under the Spending Clause, and insufficient, in light of political and institutional limitations that an Education Amendment would not cure. The second section of the chapter explains why judicial reinterpretation of the existing Constitution as already providing a right to education is no more likely to transform the US education system, given both doctrinal and institutional limitations. The third section of the chapter identifies significant risks associated with a movement to constitutionalize a federal right to education, risks that seriously jeopardize the progressive vision that animates advocates of such a constitutional right.

Proponents of a federal constitutional right to education do not suggest that their path forward is easy, and I do not mean to indicate that they do. Instead, my point is that no matter how hard they try, the path on which they wish to embark is not likely to produce the ultimate outcome they seek. There is no doubt that our current system to improve education is deeply flawed. But it may be, like Churchill's democracy, better than all the alternatives.

An Education Amendment: The Powers and Limits of Congress

This section explains that an Education Amendment would not meaningfully expand on Congress's existing powers to make education law under the Constitution's Spending Clause. The political limits that make an expanded federal role in education difficult in practice are the same limits that will likely keep an Education Amendment from being passed and ratified. Moreover, even if an Education Amendment were added to the Constitution, it would not have the effect its proponents want, because of inherent limits to congressional action.

The Power of the Spending Clause in Education Legislation

The Spending Clause, part of the powers given to Congress in Article I, Section 8, of the Constitution, grants Congress the authority to "provide for the common Defense and general Welfare of the United States."[6]

What Congress enacts under this power does not need to be otherwise enumerated in the Constitution.[7] In other words, education need not be explicitly mentioned in the Constitution in order for Congress to pass education legislation under the Spending Clause. All federal education law is a form of Spending Clause legislation; states agree to accept federal funds in exchange for implementing the basic contours of federal policy, in a relationship of "cooperative federalism."[8]

There are few limitations on Congress's power under the Spending Clause. In 1986, in *South Dakota v. Dole*, the Supreme Court set forth five basic requirements: Spending Clause legislation must be in pursuit of the "general welfare"; it must provide states with unambiguous notice of its requirements; its conditions must be related to the federal interest in the program being funded; it must not be unconstitutional under some other provision; and, it must not be "so coercive as to pass the point at which 'pressure turns into compulsion.'"[9]

In 2012, in *NFIB v. Sebelius*, the Supreme Court controversially complicated these factors by elevating the last prong.[10] But initial predictions that the new coercion doctrine might seriously limit federal legislation under Congress's spending powers have proved unfounded. There have been few lawsuits challenging Spending Clause legislation as unconstitutionally coercive, and the ones that have been brought have seen little success.[11] That is because the law the Supreme Court found problematic in *NFIB* was sui generis: it took the largest and most deeply entrenched cooperative federalism program, Medicaid, and tied the states' future receipt of Medicaid dollars to their agreement to accept the conditions of what the Court called a new and independent program under the Affordable Care Act. In contrast, most federal spending programs simply provide money in exchange for states agreeing to use that money to effectuate the program's terms, which *NFIB* approved as permissible.[12]

Effectively, then, the Spending Clause provides a way for Congress to pass legislation on almost any topic, as long as Congress provides federal money to support the legislation's requirements and—at least in cooperative federalism programs—as long as states want to accept the money.

In this light, it is clear that the rationales for a constitutional right to education articulated earlier could all be satisfied through Spending Clause legislation with no Education Amendment whatsoever. For example, consider the federalism rationale. Federal legislators of both parties supporting the previous reauthorization of the Elementary and Secondary Education Act—No Child Left Behind—saw themselves as making a stronger federal commitment to education than had ever existed in previous federal law.[13] Further legislation would be possible. Spending Clause doctrine would also permit Congress to create a federally implemented education program, akin to Social Security or Medicare, instead of giving money to the states for education.[14]

Similarly, as for the definitional rationale, Congress could use the Spending Clause to articulate a strong right to education. The Individuals with Disabilities Education Act (IDEA), for example, creates such a right for children with disabilities.[15] Advocates have called for similar kinds of educational rights through Spending Clause legislation.[16]

As for the financial rationale, Congress could simply use its spending power to appropriate significantly more money to support education. Congress could further make federal education spending "mandatory" rather than "discretionary," meaning that it would no longer be subject to the annual appropriations process and instead would issue automatically.[17]

As for the enforcement rationale, some Spending Clause legislation permits federal court review. The IDEA, for example, contains a provision permitting private lawsuits to enforce its terms.[18] The Supreme Court has read some other statutes to allow such lawsuits implicitly.[19]

Finally, it is not only through the Constitution that the nation expresses significant values. For example, some laws, including Spending Clause statutes, take on "super-statute" status and become even more strongly embedded in our cultural and legal order than some constitutional rights are.[20]

To be sure, one might not want to be too sanguine about the current permissiveness of Spending Clause doctrine. The Supreme Court might seize on the opening created by NFIB's new coercion doctrine and limit Congress's ability to pass legislation using its spending power. If the Court were to tie Congress's hands in this way, a constitutional amendment authorizing "appropriate legislation" to effectuate a right to education would be the only hook for federal education law.

Under those circumstances, an Education Amendment would add value. But even then, it would not have as powerful an effect as its proponents hope. If the Court were to restrict spending legislation, much more would be at stake than Congress's ability to affect education. The web of federal social and economic programs that support children and families would be similarly jeopardized. The contraction of these laws would be disastrous for would-be beneficiaries of an Education Amendment, as education is only one aspect of what children need to thrive.[21]

It is not sufficient to say that an Education Amendment would at least protect the federal role in education if the coercion doctrine limited other Spending Clause statutes. As Katherine Baicker and Nora Gordon have demonstrated through their research on the economic effects of rights to education embedded in state constitutions, states finance their constitutional commitments to education in part by cutting back on other critical services. As the authors explain, "a decline in programs such as community policing, summer camps, and vaccination campaigns" could well limit educational outcomes even if financial commitments to education are increased.[22] From this perspective, more important than securing a constitutional amendment for education is cementing a robust Spending Clause as well as robust legislation under it across all dimensions that affect children and families.

Even if current Spending Clause doctrine remains, however, one might also suggest that the opt-in nature of cooperative federalism statutes makes an Education Amendment necessary. That is, states need not accept federal funds if they do not want to participate in the program, so a strong Spending Clause statute could still be ineffective if states refused to join along. In contrast, states cannot opt out of the Constitution.

The problem with this argument is that, as David Strauss has argued, constitutional amendments are most effective when they are "suppressing outliers" and "bringing the stragglers into line," not when they are attempting to transform the "core" of the constitutional order; otherwise, an amendment "is likely to be evaded, or interpreted in a way that blunts its effectiveness."[23] It can in no way be said that an Education Amendment would merely bring a few outlier states into compliance with an almost-unanimous national consensus in support of a strong federal role. In fact, to the extent there is any national consensus on the federal role in education, the most recent statement of that consensus—the 2015 reauthorization of the Elementary and Secondary Education Act as the Every Student Succeeds Act—would be in favor of devolution.[24]

Of course, the federal role in education has ebbed and flowed over time. Although we are in a period of devolution now, there will likely come a time when the national consensus once more supports a stronger federal role. However, if there is enough consensus for a stronger federal role, then ordinary legislation rather than a constitutional amendment would be sufficient. As Strauss explains, "[W]hen society has changed enough to produce a supermajority in favor of a formal amendment, the amendment is probably unnecessary."[25]

To be sure, Strauss's theory of the irrelevance of constitutional amendments has detractors.[26] But one does not have to take the strongest view that amendments are irrelevant in order to accept the narrower point that given the difficulty of obtaining state buy-in through the Article V amendment process,[27] it is not likely that an amendment will completely transform the status quo. The states that would choose to opt out of spending legislation with a strong federal role in education would likely be the same states that would refuse to ratify an Education Amendment. Assuming that an Education Amendment would pass nonetheless, it is likely that over time, courts would interpret the amendment to be within the willingness and capacity of the nonratifiers, just as the Supreme Court's initial holding in *Brown v. Board of Education* has over time been watered down to align with divergent state and local acceptance and capacity.[28]

Political Limitations: The "Here to There" Problem

The main limits on Congress's authority to enact federal education legislation are thus not doctrinal but political, rooted in different normative visions of (among other things) the proper balance of the federal government, states, and localities. These political realities will prevent Congress from adopting and three-quarters of the states from ratifying such an amendment.[29]

This is what Heather Gerken calls the "here to there" problem in the context of a voting rights amendment.[30] There may be agreement that where we are, "here," is deeply troublesome, and there may be great ideas about how to fix the system visible over "there." But we should take seriously the difficulty of getting from here to there in evaluating whether to try.

Even assuming a shared sense that an Education Amendment over "there" would be a good fix, however, there are competing visions for what that Education Amendment should look like. In the past two decades, for example, there have been at least eight proposals offered in Congress for a constitutional amendment to secure a general right to high-quality and equal education,[31] the kind of amendment that progressive proponents envision. But during this same time period, members of Congress have proposed twenty-five amendments to make it easier for children to pray in school[32] and twelve amendments to guarantee the right of parents to direct the upbringing and education of their children,[33] both of which run counter to progressive proponents' goals. A great deal in politics would have to change before the former proposal would have any chance of superseding the latter two proposals either in Congress or in the states.

Limitations of Congressional Action

Of course, part of the point of a movement for a constitutional right to education would be to change these politics. If the benefits of the Education Amendment envisioned by the Left were big enough, the political battles to secure it might be worthwhile. Let us therefore imagine that politics somehow changed enough so that we have amended the Constitution to provide a right to an equal high-quality education.

Such an amendment would still not solve the problems plaguing US education. Congress would continue to face a number of practical impediments in achieving the reform envisioned by the amendment's proponents.

FEDERALISM OBSTACLES. An Education Amendment might put a thumb on the scale in favor of increased federal power in education, but strategic realities about federalism would not disappear. Congress would continue to be enmeshed in a multi-issue game with state actors. Even if Congress wanted to increase federal mandates in education because of that issue's importance, it would likely limit itself because of sensitivity to federalism in other important policy areas that Congress needs state buy-in for, such as Medicaid or the Clean Air Act—important items that would nonetheless lie outside any legislation to implement an Education Amendment.

In addition to strategic realities, normative arguments in favor of laboratories of democracy, state autonomy, and the value of dissent have an appeal that an Education Amendment on its own would not undo.[34] While some scholars have contended that solicitude for federalism has been harmful for the would-be beneficiaries of an Education Amendment,[35] proponents of a constitutional right to education are often careful to explain that they are not seeking to diminish the positive aspects of federalism but rather to permit them to flourish against the floor of a federal right to a high-quality education. Either way, an Education Amendment would hardly lay this dispute to rest once and for all. Even with an Education Amendment, most education decisions would likely remain at the state and local levels. Congress would have no more incentive to impose heightened requirements on states and school districts than it already has.

DEFINITIONAL OBSTACLES. A second obstacle lies in continuing disagreements about what the substance of an equal high-quality education would look like and what would be needed to implement it. Advocates have conflicting goals about what the purpose of education is. There is conflicting evidence about what works. Advocates read the evidence that is there differently. Further, these questions are value-laden rather than simply technocratic, and those debates about values are not going to dissipate even with an Education Amendment.[36] Even where there are shared commitments, there remain conflicts about how to operationalize those commitments. An Education Amendment would provide no clarity to Congress about how to resolve these complicated questions.

FINANCIAL OBSTACLES. A third obstacle lies in the limits of the public fisc. Nothing about a constitutional right guarantees its ultimate funding. Even though a balanced budget is not a constitutional requirement at the federal level the way it is in the states, there are both practical and political barriers to a dramatic increase in federal funding for education. Think of the ongoing battles over the past decade over sequester, government shutdowns, continuing resolutions, the debt limit, the deficit, and so on. Against this backdrop, it is implausible to imagine that significantly more federal education funding would be forthcoming.

This is especially so because discretionary spending—what Congress appropriates annually—is a much smaller part of the overall federal budget than is mandatory spending.[37] As unlikely as a huge influx of federal dollars for legislation implementing an Education Amendment is, it is even more politically implausible that any associated funding would be implemented as mandatory spending. Moreover, even if Congress were to devote increased resources to education, that money would likely come from some other policy priority, and that shifting of resources could limit the impact of any increase to education spending.

Evidence from the international context supports the conclusion that an Education Amendment would not be likely to lead to increased funding. A recent study of social spending in 196 countries with written constitutions across almost fifty years found that "the constitutionaliza-tion of the rights to education and healthcare . . . is not associated with increases in government spending in these areas."[38]

CAPACITY OBSTACLES AND THE LIMITS OF THE MORAL RA-TIONALE. A fourth obstacle lies in the limits of state and local capacity to deliver education, which they would continue to do even under an Education Amendment. There are practical limits on the states' ability to cofinance education, given both state balanced-budget requirements and the total taxable resources available for each state to collect.[39]

There are also organizational limitations. Calling something a constitutional right does not change the difficulty of implementing high-quality education in fourteen thousand school districts. In addi-tion, there are closely related human-capital limitations. For example, granting a right to high-quality teachers as an essential component of a general right to education does not automatically make high-quality teachers appear.

Here, too, an international comparison is instructive. A recent study of the relationship between constitutional rights to education and edu-cational outcomes found "no evidence supporting the view that coun-tries that enshrine the right to education in the constitution have higher quality educational systems than countries that do not."[40]

In these ways, changing the politics enough to obtain an Education Amendment would be insufficient to achieve the ends that the amend-ment's proponents want.[41]

A Judicially Implied Right to Education: The Powers and Limits of Courts

If Congress cannot realistically provide the kind of federal right to edu-cation that the proponents of such a right envision, perhaps federal courts can. This section first considers why proponents of a federal right to education might place their hope in courts. It then argues that such hope is misplaced.

Why Turn to Courts?

Federal courts are appealing in this context in a number of ways. In principle, they can provide countermajoritarian protection where the political process fails minorities. They can serve as neutral arbiters of justice rather than as politicians beholden to voters whose support they need for reelection. Because many state court judges—including those who rule in school finance cases under state constitutions—are elected rather than appointed, they are subject to this kind of pressure, whereas federal judges are not.

Federal courts can also reinterpret errant constitutional principles. *Brown v. Board of Education* is a foundational illustration, rejecting the "separate but equal" doctrine of *Plessy v. Ferguson*.[42] On this theory, the holding of *San Antonio Independent School District v. Rodriguez* that there is no constitutional right to education is not insurmountable.[43]

The Supreme Court can also issue commands to state and local officials. In *Cooper v. Aaron*,[44] for example, the Court ordered the Arkansas legislature and governor and the Little Rock school board to desegregate its schools instead of resisting the mandates of *Brown*. The Court would therefore have the power to order unwilling state education agencies and local school districts to comply with its constitutional holdings.

There are also a number of doctrinal paths readily available from which federal courts might find a constitutional right to education, including due process, equal protection, privileges and immunities, and national citizenship principles, as discussed in chapters 5 and 6 in this volume. Advocates would therefore not be starting from scratch in turning to the federal courts.

The Limitations of Judicial Action

But courts are not the answer either. To see why, consider again the five rationales that animate proponents' hopes for a constitutional right to education against the backdrop of judicial limits.

THE FEDERALISM RATIONALE. In order to get the stronger federal role in education that proponents of a federal constitutional right to education want, the Supreme Court would first have to get around the federalism limits it has imposed in its education cases.[45] It is possible that some of the Court's solicitude for federalism is a cover for a lack of institutional interest—rather than federalism limiting the Court's ability to declare a federal right to education, it is the Court's lack of interest in declaring a federal right to education that sends it to federalism arguments[46]—but federalism's entrenchment in the case law poses a high barrier.

Moreover, federalism limits run throughout broader doctrines in constitutional law far outside the education law context.[47] This is true even with respect to the Court's interpretation of the Reconstruction Amendments, which it has taken to have revised the traditional relationship between the states and federal government in the Bill of Rights and original body of the Constitution.[48] In finding a constitutional right to education, then, the Court would no doubt move narrowly without disrupting its other more general doctrines.

Nor would a more liberal court necessarily produce decisions less rooted in federalism. Recent Roberts Court decisions involving federalism have featured "some or all of the liberal justices (all of whom are also living constitutionalists) endors[ing] propositions about judicial review of federalism that have been traditionally associated with the political right."[49] Because federalism can give rise to progressive arguments just as well as it can conservative ones,[50] this trend is likely to continue, especially as progressives come to terms with what federal control means in the Trump era.

THE DEFINITIONAL RATIONALE. Let us imagine, nevertheless, that the Supreme Court was able to get past the initial federalism barrier to declare a federal constitutional right to education. Definitional challenges would remain. For example, at what level of generality would the Court announce the right? The most institutionally plausible path would be for the Court to announce the right at a high level of generality— say, an "equal right to a high-quality education." In so doing, however, Congress and the states would be left to fill in the details. Nothing about the judicial enunciation of the right would eliminate these institutions' capacity challenges.

For this reason, litigants may be tempted to push the Court to adopt a more thorough definition, something like the detailed description of the seven capacities that the Kentucky Supreme Court identified in its constitution's right to education.[51] Yet it is difficult to imagine, from a realist separation-of-powers perspective, the Court going down that path. The Kentucky construction goes far beyond even something as expansive as the *Miranda* warnings that the Court developed in a very different constitutional era.[52]

Moreover, even if the Court were inclined to define the right so broadly, it would likely want some indication that such a broad interpretation would have some impact on the ground. Why risk the institution's reputation otherwise? Instead, the evidence suggests that lofty commands often remain more precatory than effective.[53] Notwithstanding the demands of the Kentucky Supreme Court, for example, Kentucky's schoolchildren remain firmly in the middle of the pack with regard to nationwide educational outcomes and school finance.[54] In a similar vein, recall that Congress's exhortation in No Child Left Behind that all children achieve proficiency on state tests in reading and math by 2014 was a resounding failure.[55] This is because the command is less important on the ground than the difficulty with actualizing it. The key problem is operational. This truth is likely to keep the Supreme Court from acting expansively.

THE FINANCIAL RATIONALE. If the Court were able to get past these difficulties and issued a decision identifying a thick constitutional right to education, greater financial investment would not necessarily ensue. The battles between state supreme courts and state legislatures about adequate funding for school systems long after judicial declarations that more funding is necessary make this fact clear.[56]

Nor do those unresolved battles indicate the necessity for federal, as opposed to state, courts to tell the state legislatures what to do. Federal courts do not have a strong track record of requiring state funding to effectuate federal constitutional rights. Consider, for example, the lack of judicial response to state underfunding of counsel for indigent criminal defendants, despite the declaration in *Gideon v. Wainwright* that states must provide lawyers free of charge to effectuate the Sixth Amendment's right to counsel.[57] In fact, the Supreme Court has developed transsubstantive doctrine limiting the availability of remedies in federal court that would affect state treasuries.[58] Even if the Court were able to expand its view of federalism enough to allow for a federal constitutional right to education, it would likely have a hard time maintaining that expansive view as specific challenges presented institutional reasons to back off.

Nor is it any more likely that a federal constitutional right to education would lead the Supreme Court to require Congress to provide more funding than it already does. General separation-of-powers principles, as well as the more specific political question doctrine, make that idea implausible.[59] The Court would not order Congress to do something it would have no realistic chance of getting a recalcitrant Congress to do, for prudential reasons.[60] The hope that a judicially implied constitutional right to education would result in more funding is therefore unfounded.

THE ENFORCEMENT RATIONALE. It is true that a federal constitutional right permits enforcement of that right in federal court. But it is unlikely that federal court enforcement of a constitutional right to education will provide the outcomes that proponents want. Nothing about an initial constitutional victory cements that victory over time. Consider, for example, the way the Court pulled back on the principles enunciated in *Brown v. Board of Education*, such that schools have become more racially isolated over time and yet no constitutional violation exists under current doctrine.[61]

In addition to cutting back on substantive rights, the Supreme Court has crafted a wide variety of procedural doctrines that limit access to federal courts.[62] Courts can also craft remedial orders in a way that provides individual rather than systemic relief. For example, in the early years after *Brown v. Board of Education*, some district courts refused to grant black students' requests for class-wide desegregation, ordering only that the individual plaintiffs be admitted to previously all-white schools.[63] More recently, plaintiffs have attempted to use the right to education granted by state constitutions to secure vouchers for individual students, rather than to transform the state education system.[64] One can easily imagine that the kind of individual-focused remedies now provided to students with disabilities under the IDEA could be a model for incrementalist courts seeking some resolution to a challenge under a new Education Amendment without striking down entire school systems.[65] To use Robin West's distinction, even a more liberal Supreme Court might treat a federal constitutional right to education as a "right to exit," to "'opt out' of some central public or civic project" such as public education, instead of as a "right to enter civic society, or some civil project close to its core."[66]

There are further limits on judicial capacity for systemic reform. To take IDEA class actions as an example, Samuel Bagenstos has argued that the more wide ranging and detailed the scope of the litigation and the remedy, the less successful judicial oversight has been.[67] This conclusion might suggest that court oversight of school systems in general would be promising if narrow and targeted. Yet this suggestion is in tension with the argument that a constitutional right to education is necessary to achieve large-scale reform throughout the US educational system.

THE MORAL RATIONALE. Progressives and conservatives alike can agree that there is a moral value in courts' recognizing a fundamental constitutional right, whether gay marriage or gun ownership.[68] At the same time, courts are not the only institution with the power to establish the morality of rights. Congress and the executive branch alike make pronouncements as well as laws that communicate moral choices.

More to the point, however, sometimes a practical social program is needed to solve a problem rather than a morally rooted judicial declaration of a right. Contrast, for example, contemporary battles over health care with those over gay marriage. The Affordable Care Act is a complex law governing insurance markets, standards for health insurance plans, taxes, and more. Those who desired to reduce health disparities and ensure affordable health care sought a regulatory program rather than a declaration of an abstract right to health care in the Constitution. In contrast, advocates for gay marriage sought a declaration of the right in court because the moral imprimatur was part and parcel of what they were seeking: access to the same legal benefits of marriage already provided to heterosexual couples.[69]

Rights are useful where appropriate, but some issues "would be better reframed as public policy questions that involve difficult technical and administrative complexities and tricky questions of distributive justice."[70] Because education bears more similarity to health care, with all its programmatic complexity, than it does to the on/off switch of who has access to marriage, education advocates would do better to focus on the details of a regulatory program than on the judicial declaration of a right.

Moreover, obtaining the imprimatur of the Supreme Court about the justness of a cause does not end debate. *Brown* did not resolve contested arguments about segregation, nor did *Roe* for abortion,[71] *Heller* for gun rights,[72] or *Windsor* for gay marriage.[73] And claims about the morality of rights are not necessarily as effective as proponents want them to be. For example, advocates of gay marriage learned to reshape their messaging away from claims about rights and discrimination in favor of claims about human love and commitment.[74] To the extent that courts find popular sentiment relevant in determining how far to go in declaring constitutional rights,[75] advocates of a constitutional right to education may end up getting further by changing political views rather than making moral claims.

Finally, as the country becomes increasingly polarized, fewer people treat courts as neutral arbiters of justice,[76] making the moral rationale for judicial declaration of a right less effective. It is simply less likely to convince anyone who was not already primed to believe it. Advocates may hope to constitutionalize a federal right to education in order to remove decisions about that field from "workaday politics."[77] But constitutional politics—battles over the allocation of power in our constitutional democracy—will remain.[78]

For all of these reasons, a judicial declaration of a constitutional right to education cannot have the effect that its proponents want.

The Downside of a Battle for a Constitutional Right to Education

Might there be an argument that a movement for a federal right to education is worth building nonetheless? As Reva Siegel sets forth in her pathbreaking work on the "de facto" Equal Rights Amendment that exists even though the formal efforts for the ERA failed, "Debate over whether to amend the Constitution changed the meaning of the Constitution—in the process forging modern understandings of discrimination 'on account of sex.'"[79] And as Douglas NeJaime has demonstrated in the related context of litigation losses, social movements can end up "winning by losing" when "savvy advocates lose in court" yet "nonetheless configure the loss in ways that result in productive social movement effects and lead to more effective reform strategies."[80] Keeping with the apparent lessons of this work, one might imagine that it would make strategic sense to shoot for the moon of a federal right to education.

There are significant potential downsides to following this logic, however. Achieving the rights sought by the movements analyzed in Siegel's and NeJaime's work would actually have resulted in changes that met the movements' respective goals. In contrast, a constitutional right to education would not produce the systemic change that its proponents want. It would therefore be deceptive to use a constitutional right to education as a rallying ground. The nominal existence of the right in the absence of real change on the ground could also lead to demoralization and disenchantment with continuing efforts toward education reform. In turn, disrespect for government's empty promises might have broader effects, destabilizing government's role more generally. Providing a right to education that is facially equalizing while nonetheless ineffective in practice could further legitimate the status quo without moving the needle at all.

If, as I think is more likely, the movement is unsuccessful at securing a constitutional right to education, other problems arise, particularly in the context of efforts to amend the Constitution. There will likely have been a bruising battle over, among other things, which version of a right to education should prevail.[81] This battle could be so polarizing that it reduces the chance for agreement on issues that might permit agreement across the political spectrum.[82] It could also distract us from finding those issues and working toward common ground.

More generally, the prospect of amending the Constitution ought to trouble progressives more than intrigue them. It is conservative organizations such as ALEC, the American Legislative Exchange Council, that are at the forefront of the movement for a new constitutional convention. Indeed, ALEC is close to achieving its goal, with perhaps as many as thirty of the thirty-four necessary states on board. While the stated goal of that convention is to amend the Constitution to require a federal balanced budget, there is no guarantee that the convention would not expand beyond this initial goal, just as the framers in 1787 rejected their initial mandate simply to propose amendments to the Articles of Confederation.[83] The idea of adding a range of conservative amendments and constricting existing constitutional protections ought to worry liberal proponents of a federal right to education.[84]

To be sure, there are prominent liberals who disagree, arguing that the chances of a convention running amok are slim and that the upside of fixing what is wrong with our constitution is greater.[85] But I am among the skeptics who find it hard to believe that is true. Given the politics that have created and sustained what is wrong with our current

educational system, it is difficult to see how those politics would produce constitutional change that would be an improvement.

Advocates do not have unlimited time, energy, and money. It makes
sense to direct those resources where the potential outcomes are greatest and potential danger the least. Against this backdrop, calling for a
federal constitutional right to education does not make sense.

Conclusion

"When people try to amend the Constitution," Strauss observes, "they
are not ultimately concerned about the document; they are concerned
about the institutional arrangements that the document is supposed to
control."[86] The same point is true about judicial interpretation of constitutional rights; as Justice Thurgood Marshall once explained, "True
justice requires that the ideals expressed in [the Reconstruction Amend-
ments] be translated into economic and social progress for all of our
people."[87]

Despite the lofty and appealing goals of a constitutional right to
education—regardless of whether it is secured through constitutional
amendment or through judicial interpretation—it would not meaningfully change the facts on the ground. For that reason, pursuit of a constitutional right to education is not a good use of reformers' efforts.

Rather than engaging in endless second-order arguments about what
the Constitution does or should say about education, we should be focusing on first-order debates about the substantive merits of specific
education policies and practices at all levels—in individual classrooms
and schools, in school districts and states, and across the branches of the
federal government.[88] In other words, we should keep on doing what we
are already doing in the absence of a constitutional right to education.
Constitutional argumentation will not provide any way out.

NOTES

I am grateful to Claire Saba, Jennifer Safstrom, and Michelle Willauer for
excellent research assistance. Thanks also to Lilian Faulhaber, Nora Gordon,
Greg Klass, and David Super for discussing this project at different stages; to
participants in faculty workshops at the Georgetown University Law Center
and at Temple University Beasley School of Law for helpful comments; and,
to participants in a roundtable for junior faculty members held in connection

with the 2013 American Constitution Society annual meeting, at which I first shared the ideas in this chapter.

1. *See, e.g.*, Susan H. Bitensky, *Theoretical Foundations for a Right to Education under the U.S. Constitution: A Beginning to the End of the National Education Crisis*, 86 NW. U. L. REV. 550 (1992) (a federal constitutional right to education would constitute "a restructuring of the constitutional architecture [that] would institutionalize greater flexibility in allocating education responsibilities between the state and federal governments, thereby creating the potential for a national approach more immediately responsive to the crisis' exigencies"); Barry Friedman & Sara Solow, *The Federal Right to an Adequate Education*, 81 GEO. WASH. L. REV. 92, 110 (2013) (arguing that under a federal constitutional right to education, "states must provide the right in a way that meets minimal federal requisites"); Goodwin Liu, *Education, Equality, and National Citizenship*, 116 YALE L. J. 330, 404 (2006) (envisioning Congress as implementing a constitutional right to education under the Fourteenth Amendment's National Citizenship Clause, providing "a stronger role for the federal government" as "the ultimate guarantor of educational adequacy"); SOUTHERN EDUCATION FOUNDATION, NO TIME TO LOSE: WHY AMERICA NEEDS AN EDUCATION AMENDMENT TO THE US CONSTITUTION TO IMPROVE PUBLIC EDUCATION 30 (2009) ("There ought be nothing sacrosanct about the current vesting of primary responsibility for public education in the states"); *cf.* Kimberly Jenkins Robinson, *The Case for a Collaborative Enforcement Model for a Federal Right to Education*, 40 U.C. DAVIS L. REV. 1653 (2007) (arguing for an expanded federal role in education by statute, rather than by constitutional change); Kimberly Jenkins Robinson, *Disrupting Education Federalism*, 92 WASH. U. L. REV. 959, 963 (2015) (arguing for "restructuring and strengthening the federal role in education in the United States to establish the necessary foundation for a national effort to ensure equal access to an excellent education").

2. *See, e.g.*, Bitensky, *supra* note 1, at 639 (arguing that a federal constitutional right should guarantee "the minimum quantum of education necessary to enable the development of children's mental abilities to their fullest potential"); Liu, *supra* note 1, at 400–01 ("If educational adequacy for equal citizenship has constitutional stature, then legislative enactment of its essential substance must reflect something more than pedestrian political bargaining," avoiding "fashioning educational policy based on political or budgetary compromises rather than educationally relevant factors.").

3. *See, e.g.*, Bitensky, *supra* note 1, at 552–53 (explaining that one advantage of a federal constitutional right would be access to greater resources than the states have); Friedman & Solow, *supra* note 1, at 154–55 (describing how "enshrinement" of education as a constitutional right would help "safeguard it from shifts in economic currents"); Liu, *supra* note 1, at 402–04 (arguing for an expanded "federal role in school finance" to provide the "resources [that] are needed to ensure educational adequacy for equal citizenship"); SOUTHERN EDUCATION FOUNDATION,

supra note 1, at 30 (a federal constitutional amendment would "oblige the federal government itself to provide resources and guidance to ensure that gross inequality in the opportunity to learn is addressed"); *cf.* Derek Black, *Unlocking the Power of State Constitutions with Equal Protection: The First Step toward Education as a Federally Protected Right*, 51 WM. & MARY L. REV. 1343, 1394 (2010) (arguing that federal courts would do a better job of getting state legislatures to "force state legislatures into action" with respect to guaranteeing educational rights than do state courts, in part because of "the power and purse of the federal government").

4. *See, e.g.*, Robinson, *Collaborative Enforcement*, *supra* note 1, at 1684 (stating that "[s]cholars who contend that there should be a federal right to education typically presume that the judiciary would recognize, define, and enforce the right" and collecting citations).

5. *See, e.g.*, Bitensky, *supra* note 1, at 552 ("Were education to be recognized as an affirmative right under the Constitution, those doing battle against the crisis would be armed with a potent pedagogical message that education is a national priority of the first magnitude and that, as such, children, parents, teachers, administrators, and policymakers must treat their respective responsibilities vis-à-vis education with commensurate dedication and activity"); Eric Lerum et al., *Strengthening America's Foundation: Why Securing the Right to an Education at Home Is Fundamental to the United States' Efforts to Spread Democracy Abroad*, 12 HUM. RTS. BRIEF 13, 16 (2005) ("guaranteeing the right to an education will send the message to policymakers, parents, and students that education is as important as the right to speak, the right to worship, and the right to a fair trial"); ANNE NEW-MAN, REALIZING EDUCATIONAL RIGHTS: ADVANCING SCHOOL REFORM THROUGH COURTS AND COMMUNITIES 116 (2013) ("Rights give us a moral vocabulary with which to express our aspirations for education for democratic citizenship and, by extension, for a more just society"); SOUTHERN EDUCA-TION FOUNDATION, *supra* note 1, at 31 (An Education Amendment "would help to ensure that patterns of education opportunity stratification do not become permanently calcified at a time when the nation is becoming more diverse and maintenance of healthy intergroup relations and unity are vitally important to the country's future.").

6. U.S. CONST. art. I, § 8, cl. 1.

7. United States v. Butler, 297 U.S. 1 (1937).

8. *See, e.g.*, Robinson, *Collaborative Enforcement*, *supra* note 1, at 1726.

9. South Dakota v. Dole, 483 U.S. 203 (1987).

10. Nat'l Fed'n of Indep. Bus. v. Sebelius, 567 U.S. 519, 575–85 (2012).

11. *See, e.g.*, Mayhew v. Burwell, 772 F.3d 80, 88 (1st Cir. 2014); Jindal v. U.S. Dep't of Educ., 2015 WL 5474290, *10–*13, (M.D. La. Sept. 15, 2015).

12. *See* Samuel R. Bagenstos, *The Anti-leveraging Principle and the Spending Clause after NFIB*, 101 GEO. L. J. 861, 906, 909–10 (2013); Eloise Pasachoff, *Conditional Spending after NFIB v. Sebelius: The Example of Federal Education Law*, 62 AM. U. L. REV. 577, 582, 617–21 (2013).

13. Friedman & Solow, *supra* note 1, at 143–45.

14. Pasachoff, *supra* note 12, at 656 n.499.

15. 20 U.S.C. § 1412(a)(1)–(5) (2012 & Supp. IV 2016).

16. Robinson, *Collaborative Enforcement, supra* note 1, at 1689–1726; ROSEMARY C. SALOMONE, TRUE AMERICAN: LANGUAGE, IDENTITY, AND THE EDUCA-TION OF IMMIGRANT CHILDREN 179 (2010).

17. *See, e.g.,* MINDY R. LEVIT ET AL., CONG. RESEARCH SERV., MANDATORY SPENDING SINCE 1962, RL33074 (2015).

18. 20 U.S.C. § 1415(i)(2) (2004).

19. *See, e.g.,* Cannon v. Univ. of Chi., 441 U.S. 677 (1979) (holding that Title IX in-cludes an implied private right of action).

20. WILLIAM N. ESKRIDGE JR. & JOHN FEREJOHN, A REPUBLIC OF STAT-UTES: THE NEW AMERICAN CONSTITUTION 165–66 (2013). For a discus-sion of constitutional rights that are not deeply entrenched, *see* Richard Primus, *Unbundling Constitutionality,* 80 U. CHI. L. REV. 1079, 1105–13 (2013).

21. *See generally, e.g.,* WHITHER OPPORTUNITY? RISING INEQUALITY, SCHOOLS, AND CHILDREN'S LIFE CHANCES (Greg J. Duncan & Richard J. Murnane eds., 2011); Heather Schwartz, *Housing Policy Is School Policy: Economi-cally Integrative Housing Promotes Academic Success in Montgomery County, Maryland, in* THE FUTURE OF SCHOOL INTEGRATION: SOCIOECONOMIC DIVERSITY AS AN EDUCATION REFORM STRATEGY 27–65 (Richard D. Kahlenberg ed., 2012).

22. Katherine Baicker & Nora Gordon, *The Effect of State Education Finance Reform on Total Local Resources,* 90 J. PUB. ECON. 1519, 1533–34 (2006).

23. David Strauss, *The Irrelevance of Constitutional Amendments,* 114 HARV. L. REV. 1457, 1461, 1463 (2001).

24. Every Student Succeeds Act, Pub. L. No. 114-95, 129 Stat. 1802 (2015); *see also* Derek W. Black, *Abandoning the Federal Role in Education,* 105 CALIF. L. REV. 1309 (2017).

25. Strauss, *supra* note 23, at 1462–63.

26. *See, e.g.,* Brannon P. Denning & John R. Vile, *The Relevance of Constitutional Amendments: A Response to David Strauss,* 77 TUL. L. REV. 247 (2002).

27. U.S. CONST. art. V. No constitutional amendment is valid until it has been rati-fied by three-quarters of the states.

28. *See, e.g.,* Erwin Chemerinsky, *The Segregation and Resegregation of American Public Education: The Courts' Role,* 81 N.C. L. REV. 1597 (2003).

29. All twenty-seven amendments to the Constitution have originated in Congress rather than state constitutional conventions. *See The Constitutional Amendment Process,* NAT'L ARCHIVES, https://www.archives.gov (last visited June 13, 2018).

30. Heather K. Gerken, *The Right to Vote: Is the Amendment Game Worth the Candle?,* 23 WM. & MARY BILL RTS. J. 11, 13 (2014).

31. A search conducted at Congress.gov for constitutional amendments offered from the 106th through the 114th Congress identified the following such proposals:

H.R. J. Res. 29, 112th Cong. (2011); H.R. J. Res. 29, 111th Cong. (2009); H.R. J. Res. 29, 110th Cong. (2007); H.R. J. Res. 92, 109th Cong. (2006); H.R. J. Res. 29, 109th Cong. (2005); H.R. J. Res. 29, 108th Cong. (2003); H.R. J. Res. 31, 107th Cong. (2001); H.R. J. Res. 97, 106th Cong. (2000).

32. A search conducted at Congress.gov for constitutional amendments offered from the 106th through the 114th Congress identified the following such proposals: H.J. Res. 42, 113th Cong. (2013); H.J. Res. 127, 112th Cong. (2011); H.J. Res. 6, 111th Cong. (2009); H.J. Res. 41, 110th Cong. (2007); S.J. Res. 11, 110th Cong. (2007); H.J. Res. 13, 110th Cong. (2007); H.J. Res. 11, 110th Cong. (2007); H.J. Res. 85, 109th Cong. (2006); S.J. Res. 35, 109th Cong. (2006); H.J. Res. 57, 109th Cong. (2005); H.J. Res. 21, 109th Cong. (2005); H.J. Res. 7, 109th Cong. (2005); H.J. Res. 68, 108th Cong. (2003); H.J. Res. 46, 108th Cong. (2003); H.J. Res. 7, 108th Cong. (2003); H.J. Res. 81, 107th Cong. (2001); H.J. Res. 54, 107th Cong. (2001); H.J. Res. 52, 107th Cong. (2001); H.J. Res. 12, 107th Cong. (2001); S.J. Res. 1, 107th Cong. (2001); H.J. Res. 108, 106th Cong. (2000); H.J. Res. 66, 106th Cong. (1999); H.J. Res. 52, 106th Cong. (1999); S.J. Res. 1, 106th Cong. (1999); H.J. Res. 7, 106th Cong. (1999).

33. A search conducted at Congress.gov for constitutional amendments offered from the 106th through the 114th Congress identified the following such proposals: S.J. Res. 36, 114th Cong. (2016); H.J. Res. 91, 114th Cong. (2016); S.J. Res. 37, 113th Cong. (2014); H.J. Res. 50, 113th Cong. (2013); H.J. Res. 110, 112th Cong. (2012); S.J. Res. 42, 112th Cong. (2012); H.J. Res. 107, 112th Cong. (2012); H.J. Res. 3, 112th Cong. (2011); S.J. Res. 16, 111th Cong. (2009); H.J. Res. 42, 111th Cong. (2009); S.J. Res. 13, 111th Cong. (2009); H.J. Res. 97, 110th Cong. (2008).

34. *See, e.g.*, Jessica Bulman-Pozen & Heather K. Gerken, *Uncooperative Federalism*, 118 YALE L. J. 1256 (2009); Heather K. Gerken, *A New Progressive Federalism*, 24 DEMOCRACY (2012), http://democracyjournal.org.

35. *See generally, e.g.*, Kimberly Jenkins Robinson, *The High Cost of Education Federalism*, 48 WAKE FOREST L. REV. 287 (2013); David A. Super, *Laboratories of Destitution: Democratic Experimentalism and the Failure of Antipoverty Law*, 157 PENN. L. REV. 541 (2008).

36. Eloise Pasachoff, *Two Cheers for Evidence: Law, Research, and Values in Education Policymaking and Beyond*, 117 COLUM. L. REV. 1933 (2017).

37. *See* LEVIT ET AL., *supra* note 17, at 7 (explaining that mandatory spending accounts for 60 percent of federal spending). Moreover, even mandatory spending was subject to the sequester. *Id.* at 12.

38. Adam Chilton & Mila Versteeg, *Rights without Resources: The Impact of Constitutional Social Rights on Social Spending*, 60 J. L. & ECON. 713, 715 (2017).

39. Goodwin Liu, *Interstate Inequality in Educational Opportunity*, 81 N.Y.U. L. REV. 2044, 2084–89 (2006); David A. Super, *Rethinking Fiscal Federalism*, 118 HARV. L. REV. 2544, 2627 (2005).

40. Sebastian Edwards & Alvaro Garcia Marin, *Constitutional Rights and Education: An International Comparative Study*, 43 J. COMP. ECON. 938, 951 (2015).

41. It is for these reasons that I am also skeptical about the value of either a federal *statutory* right to education or the role of the federal Department of Education in implementing a federal constitutional right to education. As to the former, these same political and capacity limitations will limit the efficacy of any statutory right Congress would create. As to the latter, whatever the benefits of administrative constitutionalism in general, a brief reflection on how the Trump administration might interpret a constitutional right to education should end progressive reformers' hope that a such a right would lead the federal Department of Education to make the change those reformers think is needed. *See, e.g.,* Gillian Metzger, *Administrative Constitutionalism,* 91 TEX. L. REV. 1897, 1907, 1929 (2013) (discussing connection between agency interpretation of the Constitution and the political environment in which agencies are embedded).

42. Brown v. Bd. of Educ., 347 U.S. 483 (1954) (rejecting Plessy v. Ferguson, 163 U.S. 537 (1896)).

43. 411 U.S. 1 (1973).

44. 358 U.S. 1 (1958).

45. *See, e.g.,* Robinson, *supra* note 35, at 293–314.

46. *See, e.g., id.* at 306 (suggesting that "the Court's prior interest in preserving local control may have simply represented a convenient cover for its lack of willingness to ensure effective school desegregation"); Louis Michael Seidman, *Depoliticizing Federalism,* 35 HARV. J. L. & PUB. POL'Y 121, 122–23 (2012) (arguing that legal and political actors use the language of federalism inconsistently to advance different substantive positions).

47. *See, e.g.,* SUSAN LOW BLOCH & VICKI C. JACKSON, FEDERALISM: A REFERENCE GUIDE TO THE UNITED STATES CONSTITUTION 182–211 (2013).

48. *See, e.g., id.* at 195–99.

49. Ilya Somin, *Federalism and the Roberts Court,* 46 PUBLIUS: J. FEDERALISM 441, 452 (2016).

50. *See generally* Heather K. Gerken, *A User's Guide to Progressive Federalism,* 45 HOFSTRA L. REV. 1087 (2017).

51. Rose v. Council for Better Educ., 790 S.W.2d 186, 212 (Ky. Sup. Ct. 1989) (holding that "an efficient system of education must have as its goal to provide each and every child with at least the seven following capacities: (i) sufficient oral and written communication skills to enable students to function in a complex and rapidly changing civilization; (ii) sufficient knowledge of economic, social, and political systems to enable the student to make informed choices; (iii) sufficient understanding of governmental processes to enable the student to understand the issues that affect his or her community, state, and nation; (iv) sufficient self-knowledge and knowledge of his or her mental and physical wellness; (v) sufficient grounding in the arts to enable each student to appreciate his or her cultural and historical heritage; (vi) sufficient training or preparation for advanced training in either academic or vocational fields so as to enable each child to choose and pursue life work intelligently; and (vii) sufficient levels of academic or vocational skills to

enable public school students to compete favorably with their counterparts in surrounding states, in academics or in the job market").

52. Miranda v. Arizona, 384 U.S. 436, 467–73 (1966).

53. Education is not unique in this regard. For example, *Miranda* warnings have not stopped the problem of coercive police interrogation. Erwin Chemerinsky, *Why Have Miranda Rights Failed?*, DEMOCRACY (June 27, 2016), https://democracyjournal.org.

54. *See, e.g.*, *Kentucky Earns a C on State Report Card, Ranks 28th in Nation*, EDUC. WK. (Jan. 17, 2018), https://www.edweek.org (naming Kentucky twenty-eighth in the nation by averaging the state's scores in K–12 achievement, school finance, and overall "chance for success").

55. *See, e.g.*, Editorial Projects in Education Research Center, *Issues A–Z: No Child Left Behind*, EDUC. WK. (Sept. 19, 2011), www.edweek.org (explaining that by 2011, as many as 50 percent of schools were unable to meet the proficiency requirements outlined in 20 U.S.C. § 6311(a)(2) (2002)).

56. Robinson, *Disrupting Education Federalism, supra* note 1, at 1012.

57. *See, e.g.*, Erwin Chemerinsky, *Lessons from* Gideon, 122 YALE L. J. 2676 (2013) (calling the right to counsel set forth in *Gideon v. Wainwright* an "unfunded mandate").

58. *See, e.g.*, Edelman v. Jordan, 415 U.S. 651 (1974) (holding that sovereign immunity principles under the Eleventh Amendment prohibit federal courts from ordering states to provide retrospective monetary relief for violations of a plaintiff's federal constitutional rights).

59. *See, e.g.*, Baker v. Carr, 369 U.S. 186, 217 (1962) (discussing political question doctrine); CHARLES F. ABERNATHY, CIVIL RIGHTS AND CONSTITUTIONAL LITIGATION: CASES AND MATERIALS 582 (5th ed. 2012) (discussing the development of sovereign immunity defenses "created to protect the federal treasury").

60. *See, e.g.*, Marbury v. Madison, 5 U.S. (1 Cranch) 137 (1803).

61. *See, e.g.*, Chemerinsky, *supra* note 28.

62. *See, e.g.*, Pamela Karlan, *Disarming the Private Attorney General*, 2003 UNIV. ILL. L. REV. 183, 185–86.

63. JAMES E. RYAN, FIVE MILES AWAY, A WORLD APART: ONE CITY, TWO SCHOOLS, AND THE STORY OF EDUCATIONAL OPPORTUNITY IN MODERN AMERICA 52–53 (2010).

64. *Id.* at 237.

65. *See* Bitensky, *supra* note 1, at 639–41; *see also generally* CASS R. SUNSTEIN, ONE CASE AT A TIME: JUDICIAL MINIMALISM ON THE SUPREME COURT (2001).

66. Robin West, *A Tale of Two Rights*, 94 B.U. L. REV. 893, 894–95, 903–04 (2014).

67. Samuel R. Bagenstos, *The Judiciary's Now-Limited Role in Special Education*, *in* FROM SCHOOLHOUSE TO COURTHOUSE: THE JUDICIARY'S ROLE IN AMERICAN EDUCATION 130–36 (Joshua M. Dunn & Martin R. West eds., 2009).

68. *See, e.g.*, DAVID COLE, ENGINES OF LIBERTY: THE POWER OF CITIZEN ACTIVISTS TO MAKE CONSTITUTIONAL LAW 10–11 (2016).

69. To be sure, LGBT advocates also sought legislative change. *See, e.g.*, COLE, *supra* note 68, at 55. But the legislative change they sought was parallel to what they sought in court, not anything that would regulate the quality of marriage or the equal distribution of marriage or the funding of marriage or anything like what education law provides.

70. RICHARD THOMPSON FORD, RIGHTS GONE WRONG: HOW LAW CORRUPTS THE STRUGGLE FOR EQUALITY 230, 235 (2011).

71. Roe v. Wade, 410 U.S. 113 (1973).

72. District of Columbia v. Heller, 554 U.S. 570 (2008).

73. Windsor v. United States, 570 U.S. 744 (2013).

74. COLE, *supra* note 68, at 73–75.

75. *See generally, e.g., id.*

76. *See, e.g.*, SARAH A. BINDER & FORREST MALTZMAN, ADVICE AND DISSENT: THE STRUGGLE TO SHAPE THE FEDERAL JUDICIARY 11 (2009) (suggesting that "partisan differences over judicial nominees may be undermining the perceived legitimacy of the federal judiciary").

77. Liu, *supra* note 1, at 400.

78. *See, e.g.*, JOSH CHAFETZ, CONGRESS'S CONSTITUTION: LEGISLATIVE AUTHORITY AND THE SEPARATION OF POWERS 16–18 (2017) (discussing how "constitutional politics" sets the parameters for what constitutional text means). Moreover, as David Cole has illustrated, "the vitality of a constitutional right turns in significant part on the extent to which the people, or at least a significant portion of the people, view the right as fundamental and as warranting their attention, support, and political action." COLE, *supra* note 68, at 147–48. Far from avoiding "workaday politics," then, constitutional change demands it.

79. Reva B. Siegel, *Constitutional Culture, Social Movement Conflict and Constitutional Change: The Case of the de facto ERA*, 94 CALIF. L. REV. 1323, 1324 (2006).

80. Douglas NeJaime, *Winning through Losing*, 96 IOWA L. REV. 941, 945 (2011).

81. *See supra* notes 31–33 and accompanying text.

82. Publicly funded, nonmandatory preschool might be one of these matters. *See, e.g.*, Educ. Comm'n of the States, *State Pre-K Funding 2016–17 Fiscal Year: Trends and Opportunities* 1 (Jan. 2017), https://www.ecs.org (discussing "continuing support from both Republican and Democratic governors, legislators and state boards of education").

83. David A. Super, *A Constitutional Convention Is the Last Thing America Needs*, L.A. TIMES, March 16, 2017; Michael Wines, *Inside the Conservative Push for States to Amend the Constitution*, N.Y. TIMES, Aug. 22, 2016.

84. *See generally* Kathleen M. Sullivan, *Constitutional Amendmentitis*, AM. PROSPECT, Fall 1995.

85. *See, e.g.*, SANFORD LEVINSON, OUR UNDEMOCRATIC CONSTITUTION: WHERE THE CONSTITUTION GOES WRONG (AND HOW WE THE PEOPLE CAN CORRECT IT) 174–76 (2006); Lawrence Lessig, *A Real Step to Fix Democracy*, ATLANTIC, May 30, 2014.

86. Strauss, *supra* note 23, at 1459–60.

87. Sheryll Cashin, *Civil Rights for the Twenty-First Century: Lessons from Justice Thurgood Marshall's Race-Transcending Jurisprudence*, 17 LEWIS & CLARK L. REV. 973, 977 (2013) (alteration in original).

88. *Cf.* Louis Michael Seidman, *Substitute Arguments in Constitutional Law*, 31 J. L. & POL. 237, 295–96 (2016) (suggesting that all arguments about constitutional doctrine function as substitutes for substantive debates and arguing that other arguments—"from tradition, from inertia, from commonly held intermediate premises, from instrumental rationality, or from practical reason"—would be less "pernicious" than cover arguments about what the Constitution means).

4

Latina/os and a Federal Right to Education

KEVIN R. JOHNSON

Introduction

Despite *Brown v. Board of Education*'s[1] famous endorsement of educational equality, deep racial inequalities persist in school systems across the United States. Unfortunately, "[i]n a nation that professes a strong belief in equal opportunity, many of America's public schools still fail to offer children a high-quality education."[2]

Racial inequality in the US educational system extends well beyond African Americans. Classified as "Hispanic"[3] by the US Census, Latina/os have emerged as the largest minority group in US public schools. Similar to African Americans, Latina/os historically have been—and continue to be—denied the educational opportunities afforded to white students. That denial, in turn, significantly hinders Latina/os' social mobility and full membership in US society.

The growth in the Latina/o population has been accompanied by widespread segregation of Latina/o students, which currently is among the highest of all minority groups. Due to a variety of factors, heavily Latina/o schools on the average are funded at significantly lower levels than predominantly white schools. Not surprisingly, although improving in certain respects, educational outcomes for Latina/os lag behind those of all other racial groups. For example, Latina/os for years have had among the lowest high school graduation rates of all racial groups.[4]

After sketching the current disparities in Latina/o educational opportunities as well as the failure of efforts to reduce the disparities, this chapter outlines how a federal right to education could strengthen the efforts to assist Latina/os in the fight against segregation, school funding disparities, and unequal educational outcomes. A federal right could provide a national baseline for educational quality, with states allowed to provide more—but not fewer—protections for students. A federal right also would represent a positive step toward ensuring that Latina/os in all states have a formidable weapon in the struggle for equal educational opportunity.

Latina/os in US Public Schools

Latina/os today are the nation's largest minority group and, not coincidentally, the largest minority group in the US public schools. Latina/os in 2016 hit a new population high of 57.5 million, amounting to 18 percent of the nation's total population.[5] Segregation has accompanied this population growth. Because Latina/os are disproportionately poorer than other US residents, they experience racial and income segregation.[6] In a significant change from historical settlement patterns, Latina/os seeking economic opportunities have increasingly moved to regions outside the US Southwest.

The growing Latina/o population, combined with the greater dispersion of Latina/os across the entire United States, has dramatically transformed the racial demographics of the nation's public schools. These developments also have made Latina/o educational opportunity a national, not simply a regional, concern.

The Growth in Latina/o Students

In just a few decades, a surging Latina/o population has transformed minority K–12 enrollment in the nation's public schools. Minority enrollment grew from 36.6 percent in 1997 to more than 50 percent by 2014.[7] Latina/o public school enrollment in K–12 alone is projected to grow to 30 percent nationwide by 2023.[8]

The increase in the Latina/o composition of the student bodies of the nation's public schools is likely to continue. Nearly half of US-born Latina/os are younger than eighteen, making them by far the nation's youngest racial group.[9] Latina/os now account for more than 22 percent of all pre-K–12 public school students in the United States. Between 1996 and 2016, the share of Latina/os enrolled in kindergarten rose from 14.9 percent to 25.7 percent.[10] Now representing one in four kindergarten students, Latina/os will likely continue to fuel an increase in the percent-age of Latina/os in K–12 classes for years to come. Put simply, Latina/os for the foreseeable future will be heavily represented in the nation's public schools, and thus their educational success will greatly influence the ultimate success of the nation's public schools.

The Latina/o Diaspora

For much of US history, the settlement of immigrants from Mexico and Central America was largely concentrated in the Southwest region of the United States, much of which, until 1848, was part of Mexico. The geographic distribution of Latina/os in the United States has changed dramatically over the past twenty years.

In pursuit of economic opportunity (namely, jobs), Latina/os in re-cent years have settled in significant numbers in the South and Mid-west, which previously had relatively small Latina/o populations.[11] The Latina/o population in Georgia, for example, doubled from 2000 to 2015, which was the fastest growth in the ten states with the largest Latina/o populations.[12] The number of Latina/os also has grown substantially in Alabama, Arkansas, Iowa, North Carolina, North Dakota, Oklahoma, South Carolina, and Virginia, to name a few states. African Americans and Latina/os today represent a growing presence in all regions of the United States.

Besides growing in numbers, Latina/os today have a national, not sim-ply a regional, presence in the United States. With the increasing disper-sion of Latina/os across the entire country, their civil rights struggles today literally extend from coast to coast, including across the nation's heart-land, even while many states and localities continue to adjust to—and, at times, resist—the changing racial demographics.[13] Moreover, Latina/os have pressed for equal access to educational opportunity as well as for equal opportunity in other aspects of US social life to remedy the inferior educational opportunities and outcomes experienced by many Latina/os.

Unequal Latina/o Educational Inputs and Outcomes

As the introduction and chapter 1 of this book document, fundamental educational inequalities remain firmly entrenched in US social life. These chapters along with chapter 2 describe how efforts to challenge segregation, school funding disparities, and disparate educational outcomes have fallen short of their intended aims. As Latina/os have increased as a percentage of the overall public school population in the United States, they increasingly attend predominantly Latina/o public schools, which on average are more poorly funded than majority-white schools. Indeed, the gap may well be widening between the quality of the elementary and secondary education provided by the public schools to Latina/os (as well as to African Americans) and whites. Consequently, Latina/o educational outcomes lag far behind those of other racial groups.

A 2018 US Commission on Civil Rights Report succinctly summarizes the increasing segregation of students of color and glaring school funding disparities at predominantly minority schools:

> While the demographics of public school enrollment have shifted over the decades since *Brown* [*v. Board of Education*] due to desegregation efforts and population shifts, among other factors, racial, ethnic, and economic segregation remain a reality all across the U.S. Residential segregation exacerbates school inequalities. Students who live in high-poverty neighborhoods often attend schools that lack the financial resources to provide them with quality education opportunities, as school resources are so closely tied to the wealth of the surrounding community. An achievement gap has resulted and persisted, largely between students who attend well-funded schools in low-poverty neighborhoods and the most disadvantaged students—often students of color and students from poor households—who attend poorly-funded schools in high-poverty neighborhoods.
>
> Decades of social science research reflects that schools that remain segregated by income and race tend also to remain extremely unequal in the educational opportunities that they afford students of different racial, ethnic, and economic backgrounds. There is an emerging body of research that finds significant positive educational outcomes for students—particularly students of color—who attend integrated schools. Such outcomes include the development of critical thinking skills, higher graduation rates, more prominent educational and career goals, greater earnings in the workforce, and even more positive health outcomes. Despite these proven outcomes, educational inequity still persists across the U.S.[14]

Thus, many Latina/os experience inferior educational opportunities and segregation but lack an effective tool to remedy these harms.

Disparate School Funding and Educational Opportunities

Racial disparities in educational outcomes flow from disparate funding for predominantly minority schools. "[S]tudies have shown that districts serving the most students of color . . . tend to receive less state and local funding than districts serving the fewest. . . . Nationally, districts serving the most students of color receive about $1,800, or 13 percent, less per student than districts serving the fewest students of color."[15] Due in large part to funding disparities, Latina/os experience inferior educational opportunities compared to whites. For example, as will be discussed shortly, Latina/os on the average have fewer qualified teachers than whites do in the classroom, inferior school facilities than white students do, higher discipline rates than white students do, and less access than white students do to Advanced Placement courses that help secure admission to colleges and universities.[16]

In addition, despite a number of successful state court challenges over several decades,[17] school financing disparities—and stark educational inequalities—persist throughout the entire United States. The result is that "[w]hile migrant, low income, and inner city urban families are entrapped in lower funded schools because of low property values in those areas, the demographic of students becomes increasingly homogeneous, and more affluent families move to better communities with better schools and more resources."[18] Moreover, a global recession at the tail end of the first decade of the new millennium resulted in sharp declines in state and local tax revenues that necessitated significant reductions in state and local school budgets.[19] Even though tax revenues to a certain extent have rebounded, many school district budgets continue to lag behind prerecession levels.[20] Reduced budgets have meant dwindling educational opportunities for students of color.

Latina/o School Segregation

In a pattern similar to that of other minority groups, Latina/os, especially newly arrived immigrants, tend to settle in predominantly Latina/o enclaves. With neighborhood schools the norm in the United States, residential concentration directly translates into many predominantly Latina/o schools. As a result, schools with large Latina/o enrollments are now found across the country.

The segregation of Latina/os in school districts is remarkably similar to that of African Americans.[21] Just a few years ago, "a third of all black and Latino children attend[ed] schools where the classrooms [were] 90 to 100 percent black and Latino."[22] As of 2011–12, nearly 45 percent of Latina/o students in the western United States attended schools with 90–100 percent minority students, compared to 44 percent in the Northeast and 42 percent in the South.[23] By 2013–14, in California, Texas, and New York, three of the nation's most populous states, more than half of the Latina/o students attended schools with 90–100 percent minority enrollment.[24] The South also has seen an increase in segregation of African American and Latina/o students.[25] With Latina/o migration to the South likely to continue, African American and Latina/o school segregation likely will increase as well.

The widespread modern racial segregation of African Americans and Latina/os has been summarized as follows: "In seventy of the one hundred largest districts, whites comprise less than fifty percent of the student population. In more than one-third of these districts, seventy-five percent of the student membership is non-white. Seven of the ten largest school districts are comprised of student populations that are more than seventy-five percent non-white. This data reveals a striking trend toward re-segregation in school districts across the country."[26]

In the post-*Brown* era, racial segregation stems not from laws expressly requiring segregation. Rather, it is accomplished primarily through the persistence of housing segregation combined with the enduring commitment of local school districts to have students attend neighborhood schools.[27]

As a result, more than six decades after *Brown v. Board of Education*, segregation continues to be deeply entrenched, with few signs of change. Although segregation is on the rise in the South, Latina/o school segregation is particularly dramatic in the West, where the Latina/o population remains concentrated.[28] For many reasons, including the persistent consideration of the history of civil rights in the United States in black/white terms, the long history of Latina/o resistance to school segregation is less well-known than that of African Americans. However, Latina/os, like other minorities, traditionally have relied on the courts as a tool in the fight to promote integration of the public schools.

In an important step forward on the road culminating in *Brown v. Board of Education*, a federal court of appeals in 1947 ruled in *Westminster School District v. Mendez*[29] that it was unlawful for a California school district to segregate students of Mexican ancestry. Similar desegregation cases brought on behalf of Latina/o students have been pursued for generations. Some school districts found to have discriminated against Latina/os continue to this day to operate under judicial supervision.[30]

Commentators contend that, although the Supreme Court has prohibited legally enforced segregation since 1954, the federal courts bear significant responsibility for the persistent segregation of minority students.[31] In the intervening years, the courts, including the Supreme Court, have grown increasingly unsympathetic to school desegregation lawsuits.[32] For example, in *Milliken v. Bradley*,[33] the Court limited desegregation efforts across district lines to instances in which a court determined that a state actor had intentionally segregated students on the basis of race between districts, a requirement substantially restricting the ability of courts to order desegregation of the public schools.[34]

Judicial efforts have failed to moderate, much less reverse, the accelerating segregation of Latina/o students in the public schools. Although recognizing the complexities of the school segregation of African Americans, Latina/os, and whites, the courts have simply been unable to integrate the schools. For example, in one of the series of school desegregation cases decided in the wake of *Brown v. Board of Education*, the Supreme Court in 1973 in *Keyes v. School District No. 1*[35] held that a substantial portion of the Denver school system, "a tri-ethnic, as distinguished from a bi-racial, community," was unlawfully segregated. Although plaintiffs secured an order to remedy the segregation, the lawsuit failed to integrate the Denver schools. The *Keyes* litigation also failed to cure the academic challenges of the Denver public schools. The achievement of Latina/o and African American students generally improved when white enrollment increased; however, graduation rates and achievement test scores for African American and Latina/o students in the Denver schools continue to lag behind whites.[36]

The Supreme Court in fact has stifled innovative strategies to integrate the public schools. A Seattle, Washington, school district, for example, allowed students to choose among high schools; one of the "tiebreakers" in assignments for overenrolled schools was the student's race and the racial makeup of the school.[37] Similarly, the public school system in Louisville, Kentucky, sought to promote integration by considering race as one factor in elementary school assignments to attempt to avoid assigning a student to a school if the student's race would contribute to a racial imbalance.[38] Both school districts modeled these modest race-conscious plans after admissions programs employed by universities to enroll diverse student bodies, programs that the Supreme Court has found to be constitutionally permissible.[39]

Nonetheless, Chief Justice John Roberts, writing for a majority of the Court in *Parents Involved in Community Schools v. Seattle School District No. 1*, struck down both of these race-conscious plans because the Court found that they were not narrowly tailored to achieve a compelling governmental interest given the failure of the districts to demonstrate that the plans were necessary and that the districts had examined race-neutral alternatives.[40] A plurality of the Court stridently emphasized that "[t]he way to stop discrimination on the basis of race is to stop discriminating on the basis of race."[41] The Court's decision in *Parents Involved* sent a strong cautionary signal to school districts that employed race-conscious approaches to advance diversity and avoid racial isolation.[42]

In short, the courts in a series of decisions since *Brown v. Board of Education* have significantly limited the tools available to remedy racial segregation in public school systems across the United States. Schools still have available race-neutral alternatives to integrate the schools as well as narrowly tailored race-conscious ones.[43] Up to this point in time, however, minority schoolchildren have been unable to secure through desegregation efforts the educational equality promised by *Brown v. Board of Education*.

Disparate Educational Outcomes

Racial segregation in modern public schools is particularly harmful because it is accompanied by disparities in access to educational opportunities for minority students.[44] Heavily concentrated in segregated and poorly funded school districts, racial minorities not surprisingly experience disparate and substandard educational outcomes.

In 2015, Latina/os graduated from high school at remarkably lower rates (66.7 percent) than did African Americans (87 percent), Asian Americans (89.1 percent), and non-Hispanic whites (93.3 percent).[45] The failure to graduate high school has long-term labor-market and social-mobility consequences, with nongraduates earning significantly less than graduates over the course of their lifetimes. On the positive side of the educational ledger, the Latina/o dropout rate recently hit a new low, while college enrollment is at an all-time high.[46]

Graduation rates are not the only educational outcome in which today's US public schools generate glaring racial disparities. Due to educational disparities, "Latino students are overrepresented in lower educational outcomes; nationally they tend to have lower grades, lower scores on standardized tests, and higher dropout rates than do students from other ethnic groups."[47] Latina/o schoolchildren have lower mean reading and math scores than whites do; Latina/o achievement, with regard to obtaining associate degrees, lags behind that of other racial groups.[48]

"The academic performance of an average African American or Hispanic student is equivalent to the performance of an average white student in the lowest quartile of white achievement. . . . One education policy organization concretely stated the implications of this achievement gap: '17-year-old African American and Latino students have skills in English, math, and science similar to those of 13-year-old Whites.'"[49] In addition, African American and Latina/o students are more likely than white students to lose school days to suspensions.[50] Disparate discipline rates result in fewer classroom hours for minority students and contribute to disparate achievement outcomes.

Latinas in particular lag in college completion, have the lowest percentage of graduate degrees, and are much less likely than other groups to obtain a degree in science, technology, engineering, and mathematics.[51] Gender disparities have prompted efforts to improve Latina access to, and retention in, colleges and universities.

In sum, education serves as a critically important avenue for social mobility in the United States. Consequently, deficient educational opportunities and disparate outcomes for Latina/os and other minorities hamper that mobility and reinforce the persistent racial inequality in income and wealth.[52] Put simply, educational disparities have inhibited the full integration of Latina/os in US society. The relationship between education and social mobility helps to explain why, as historically has been the case for African Americans, equal educational opportunity is considered to be a central Latina/o civil rights concern. However, as discussed in the next section, the major efforts to close the Latina/o opportunity gap have not succeeded. A federal right to education would provide Latina/os with an important weapon in the fight for equal educational opportunity.

Efforts to Remedy Latina/o Educational Disparities

Two specific areas of particular focus in the Latina/o quest for equal educational opportunities warrant attention. Although efforts to guarantee access to bilingual education have been on the wane, the push to guarantee access of Latina/o immigrants to equal educational opportunity has been in the ascendance. Concrete educational benefits have resulted from these efforts. However, neither has been completely successful in securing equal educational opportunity for segments of the Latina/o community.

Bilingual Education

Linguistic diversity among Latina/os contributes to the need for programs that promote educational opportunities for non-English speakers. Many Latina/os live in homes in which Spanish is the primary language. "A record 37 million Hispanics ages five and older" spoke Spanish at home in 2016, "up from 25 million in 2000."[53] In California, for example, more than 40 percent of all public school students speak a language other than English at home; unfortunately, many teachers of English-language learners are not adequately trained to teach English-language learners.[54]

Bilingual education historically has been viewed as an important way to improve the educational outcomes for Spanish speakers, including many Latina/o students and other language minorities.[55] Beginning at the height of the civil rights movement, advocates of equal educational opportunity for Spanish-speaking children championed bilingual education programs.[56] At least for a time, Latina/os enjoyed political and litigation success in securing bilingual education in US public elementary and secondary schools.[57]

In 1974, the Supreme Court in *Lau v. Nichols*[58] held that Title VI of the Civil Rights Act of 1964 bars the denial of equal educational opportunities to non-English speakers. The decision served as an important tool for advocates to pursue bilingual education and other programs for English-language learners. Over time, the courts, however, have limited *Lau* by interpreting Title VI to prohibit only intentional discrimination.[59] In its place, the courts have measured the legality of English-language programs pursuant to the Equal Educational Opportunities Act under the standard adopted in *Castañeda v. Pickard*.[60] This court of appeals decision requires a school district to establish that a sound educational theory or a legitimate experimental approach informs its language program, that the district's practices are reasonably calculated to implement the theory or experimental approach, and that language barriers are actually being overcome. Scholars have criticized the *Castañeda* approach as providing a weak and ineffectual standard for mandatory language programs.[61] Moreover, the Supreme Court's 2009 decision in *Horne v. Flores* opened the door to the reconsideration of consent decrees requiring school districts to fund English-language learner programs.[62]

Political resistance to bilingual education finds fuel in the contentious contemporary politics of the "English only" movement[63] and immigration, both of which disproportionately affect Latina/os. In 1998, California voters passed an initiative, Proposition 227, which prohibited bilingual education for non-English-speaking students in the state's public schools and instead required children learning English to be taught through English immersion.[64] Enacted by a racially polarized vote in which Latina/o voters opposed the law by a wide margin, the initiative disparately impacted the Golden State's Spanish-speaking student population, which had grown dramatically in the years before its passage.[65] With its racially disparate impacts, if not discriminatory intent, Proposition 227 was considered in some quarters to be nothing less than anti-Latina/o.[66] Its passage also marked an end of bilingual education as a battleground for Latina/o struggles to secure equal educational opportunity.

Efforts to eliminate bilingual education gained momentum after the passage of Proposition 227. "[T]he English-Only movement has spawned numerous [Proposition 227–type laws], state legislation aimed at abolishing bilingual education by replacing it with English acquisition classes, imposing a time limit on English acquisition, and removing bicultural education from public schools."[67] In the early 2000s, Massachusetts and Arizona voters approved measures similar to the California law.[68] Adding to the decline of bilingual education, Congress in 2002 passed the No Child Left Behind Act,[69] a piece of educational reform legislation that included provisions that, as implemented, effectively operated to discourage bilingual education programs. The act, for example, specifically made English-language acquisition, as opposed to bilingual education, the priority in federal educational policy.[70]

Fortunately, some states have moved toward supporting bilingual education. California and Massachusetts both repealed their bans. In 2016, after Proposition 227 had been in effect for eighteen years, California repealed it.[71] In 2017, Massachusetts repealed its restriction.[72] In addition, some states now explicitly support the use of bilingual or dual-language education programs.[73] However, Arizona continues to limit the use of bilingual education by requiring all students to be taught in English and for English learners generally to be taught in "sheltered English immersion" for no longer than one year.[74] New Hampshire also requires instruction in English for all students; however, the state board and school districts may approve bilingual education programs.[75]

Most recently, the Every Student Succeeds Act (ESSA)[76] sets forth goals designed to improve instruction for English-language learners.[77] The act continues the No Child Left Behind Act's emphasis on English-language acquisition. ESSA requires states to include long-term goals for English-language proficiency in their accountability plans; all schools must show how they are improving English proficiency. In addition, states, schools, and districts must report student outcome data for English-language learners.[78] These changes signal a greater prioritization of the education of students learning English.[79] Local educational agencies also must provide English-language learners annual English proficiency assessments that are aligned to state standards for English-language learners.[80] ESSA also requires states to develop standardized procedures that establish the entrance and exit criteria for English learners.[81]

A federal right to education could build on state and federal support for enhancing the educational opportunities and outcomes for English-language learners. The next subsection considers law and policy affecting the access of undocumented students to elementary and secondary education.

Immigrant Access to Public Education

Today approximately eleven million undocumented immigrants live and work in communities across the United States.[82] Many are school-age and, like other children living in this country, would be expected to attend public schools.

In 1982, the Supreme Court in the landmark 5–4 decision of *Plyler v. Doe*[83] held that states generally cannot, consistent with the Equal Protection Clause of the Fourteenth Amendment of the US Constitution, bar undocumented students from a public elementary and secondary school education. Although limited in scope to the undocumented immigrant segment of the Latina/o community, *Plyler v. Doe* was a watershed decision affecting the access of many Latina/os to the public schools. Over the more than thirty-five years since the Supreme Court decided the case, school districts across the United States have provided an education to millions of undocumented schoolchildren, with many of them from Mexico and Central America.

Despite the longevity of the *Plyler* decision, it continues to generate considerable resistance. Political and legal challenges at the state and local levels regularly have been brought against its mandate. For instance, California voters in 1994 overwhelmingly passed Proposition 187, an initiative that, if it had been fully implemented, would have denied undocumented students access to the state's public elementary and secondary schools, an outcome that is directly at odds with *Plyler v. Doe*. The law also would have rendered undocumented immigrants ineligible for virtually any and all state and local public benefits.[84] Finding that the core of Proposition 187 was preempted by federal immigration law, a federal court barred its implementation.[85] The initiative would have "den[ied] social services, health care services and public education to individuals based on immigration status."[86] The court held that *Plyler v. Doe* precluded the denial of public education on the basis of immigration status.[87] The case did not make its way to the Supreme Court, which has not yet had the opportunity to revisit *Plyler v. Doe*.

Despite the invalidation of Proposition 187, contemporary political challenges to *Plyler v. Doe* continue. They have frequently been tied to advocacy for the restriction of undocumented immigration, a deeply contested issue in modern US politics. Political activists, who also generally decry undocumented immigration as a serious social problem, persist in the efforts to overrule *Plyler*. For example, in 2012, the Alabama legislature passed House Bill 56,[88] one of a number of recent state laws ostensibly designed to facilitate enforcement of the federal immigration laws. Section 28 of the law would have required, among other things, school districts to collect information about the immigration status of public school students and their parents, as well as data about the number of English-as-a-second-language students attending the schools. The Alabama law's school data-collection provisions were designed to gather the information that could be used to persuade the Supreme Court to reconsider *Plyler v. Doe*.[89] A district court found that "there is evidence that the legislative debate on H.B. 56 was laced with derogatory comments about Hispanics. This evidence reinforces the contention that [the] term illegal immigrants (the purported target of H.B. 56) was just a racially discriminatory code for Hispanics."[90]

After an investigation, the US Justice Department concluded that "H.B. 56 has had significant and measurable impacts on Alabama's school children, impacts that have weighed most heavily on Hispanic and English language learner students."[91] That conclusion was based on a finding that, in the wake of the passage of the law, many Latina/o parents moved out of Alabama or, fearing possible removal from the United States, would not allow their children to attend school. Concluding that the law undermined the right of undocumented schoolchildren to a public education, a court enjoined implementation of the data-collection provisions of Alabama's H.B. 56.[92]

Up to this point in time, efforts such as Alabama's to push the Supreme Court to reconsider *Plyler v. Doe* have failed. However, the future vitality of the Court's ruling remains far from certain.[93] Political and legal challenges to the obligation to educate undocumented students seem likely to continue, in part because of the substantial costs imposed on state and local governments of providing an education to undocumented immigrants in an era of tight state and local budgets.[94] Moreover, the states have taken diametrically opposed positions on allowing undocumented students access to public colleges and universities, with some states barring undocumented students from public postsecondary institutions.

Twenty-five years later, California has garnered national attention—and the opposition of the Trump administration—for its "sanctuary" policies.[95] These policies seek to protect immigrants from removal, rather than facilitate removal as Proposition 187 attempted to do. California is not the only state to adopt such policies, and some localities have also sought to limit their cooperation with federal immigration enforcement.[96] Some school districts have even adopted "sanctuary school resolutions," although they are mostly symbolic.[97]

Despite some federal and state education laws and policies that support the education of English-language learners and undocumented students, federal and state laws have been insufficient to ensure that Latina/os receive an education of sufficient quality to ensure that Latina/o students can successfully learn and compete effectively with their non-Latina/o peers in the employment market, as the disparate funding, opportunities, and outcomes documented earlier in this chapter demonstrate. These enduring disparities reveal a need for Latina/os to find new legal avenues to secure high-quality educational opportunities. Therefore, the next section examines how a federal right to education would benefit Latina/os.

The Benefits to Latina/os of a Federal Right to Education

Up to this point in time in US history, existing legal and political strategies have failed to ensure full access to high-quality educational opportunities for minorities in the United States. "Today, Latinos/as constitute the largest group of non-White public school students in the United States. We cannot ignore the substantial educational challenges and substandard educational experiences which continue to plague so many of those students. We also cannot abandon the pursuit of equitable educational opportunities for all students."[98]

Despite these enduring inequities, some political leaders likely would argue that the states, not the federal government, should be the place to best protect educational rights. Some states, such as California, in recent years have been protective of the rights of Latina/os. However, many states have not extended similar protections. And even in California, the segregation of Latina/o students in poorly funded public schools is widespread—and well above the national average. Federal intervention is needed to create a high-quality educational baseline for all students, including Latina/os, across the entire nation.

It is important to understand that in the political process, the power of Latina/os is diluted by the fact that the Latina/o community in the United States is composed of a large immigrant population. Immigrants who have not naturalized to become US citizens cannot vote. Consequently, the rapid Latina/o population growth has not directly translated into anything approximating a commensurate growth in Latina/o political power.[99] In most states, a white-dominated electorate remains in firm control of state and local governments and educational institutions. Disparate educational outcomes have followed from the unequal state and local education budgets approved by public officials elected with support from the white-dominated electorate. As the Latina/o population has grown, Latina/os have been educationally disadvantaged in ever-increasing numbers. Given the limited protections under state laws, federal intervention is necessary.

A federal right to education, perhaps through a favorable Supreme Court decision or a law establishing national educational requirements as explored in part 2 of this volume, holds substantial promise for improving educational opportunities for Latina/os and other minorities on a nationwide basis. Although the burgeoning political power of Latina/os may in the long run ensure enduring legislative solutions to the problem of educational inequality, advances through the state and local political process would take a long time—in this instance, perhaps even a generation or more. State and local measures also would occur in a piecemeal fashion, with Latina/os in each state and district having to fight similar battles.

A federal right to education would allow for greater federal support for Latina/os and other minorities seeking substantive equality in education. Undoubtedly, a federal right to education would not be a panacea for all of the educational challenges that Latina/os confront. Nevertheless, absent a massive and immediate shift of state and local political power in the United States, which is unlikely, a federal right to education would provide an important tool to Latina/os in all states to directly seek to redress the particular inequalities that Latina/os experience within the modern public education systems in the United States. Such a right should promote high-quality educational opportunities for all to ensure that all students, including Latina/os, are on a level playing field sooner, rather than later. A federal right to education would provide greater benefits to Latina/os seeking access to high-quality educational opportunities than the inconsistent and incomplete protections offered under current state and federal law. A federal right to education also would allow Latina/os and other minorities to more effectively challenge the adverse educational outcomes generated by the public schools.

As we know, *Brown v. Board of Education* has not ended segregation in the public schools. Indeed, Latina/os and African Americans have experienced increasing segregation. And there is no end in sight. A federal right to education would serve as a powerful tool in the arsenal of weapons to promote integration and secure equal educational opportunity for Latina/os, including a remedy for state funding schemes that serve to create unequal and overwhelmingly minority schools. A new legal tool at a minimum could strengthen the likelihood that efforts to reduce segregation and demand equitable funding would prove successful.

In addition, although some states have moved away from policies that harm Latina/o students and have adopted policies to support their education, federal action remains necessary to remedy significant disparities in the educational experiences of non-English-speaking Latina/o students. Specifically, a right to education could provide a legal tool to pursue increased availability of bilingual education to English-as-a-second-language learners. A federal right to education that is consistent across the United States would provide Latina/os with a new and formidable tool to seek bilingual education as an integral part of high-quality educational opportunities or at least to challenge state bans and limitations on bilingual education. Furthermore, the funding sufficient to educate a non-English learner, "about twice that of educating an English-proficient child in a standard classroom," can be unattainable for the high-poverty schools that often have substantial concentrations of students learning English.[100] A federal right to education also would empower Latina/os with a means to seek adequate funding for educational programs in states and districts that fail to effectively serve English-language learners.

Finally, a federal right to education would better allow Latina/os to pursue equal educational opportunity in the courts regardless of the immigration status of the students affected. This is a critically important issue to Latina/os as immigrants compose a significant segment of the Latina/o population. State and local sanctuary policies may provide some peace of mind for undocumented students,[101] but they fail to strengthen the precarious constitutional grounds of *Plyler v. Doe.* For these reasons, a federal right to education would benefit the educational opportunities and outcomes of Latina/os.

NOTES

1. 347 U.S. 483 (1954). *See generally* CHARLES J. OGLETREE JR., ALL DELIBER-
   ATE SPEED: REFLECTIONS ON THE FIRST HALF-CENTURY OF *BROWN V.
   BOARD OF EDUCATION* (2005) (examining the legacy of *Brown v. Board of Educa-
   tion* after fifty years).

2. Kimberly Jenkins Robinson, *The Case for a Collaborative Enforcement Model for
   a Federal Right to Education,* 40 U.C. DAVIS L. REV. 1653, 1655 (2007) (footnote
   omitted).

3. The US Census Bureau explains its classification system as follows: "People who
   identify with the terms 'Hispanic' or 'Latino' are those who classify themselves in
   one of the specific Hispanic or Latino categories listed on the decennial census
   questionnaire and various Census Bureau survey questionnaires—'Mexican, Mexican Am., Chicano' or 'Puerto Rican' or 'Cuban—as well as those who indicate
   that they are 'another Hispanic, Latino, or Spanish origin.'" US Census Bureau,
   About Hispanic Origin (Mar. 7, 2018), https://www.census.gov.

4. *See* Gary Orfield et al., Brown *at 62: School Segregation by Race, Poverty and
   State,* UCLA CIVIL RIGHTS PROJECT 5–6 (2016) (data on school segregation of
   Latina/os); EDUCATION TR., FUNDING GAPS 2018, at 10–11 (2018) (funding
   gap data); NAT'L CTR. FOR EDUC. STATISTICS, STATUS AND TRENDS IN
   THE EDUCATION OF RACIAL AND ETHNIC GROUPS 2017, at 45–56 (2017)
   (achievement gap data); NAT'L CTR. FOR EDUC. STATISTICS, *supra,* at 84–86
   (graduation rates).

5. Antonio Flores, *How the U.S. Hispanic Population is Changing,* PEW RES. CTR.
   (Sept. 18, 2017), www.pewresearch.org.

6. Ulrich Boser & Perpetual Baffour, *Isolated and Segregated: A New Look at the
   Income Divide in Our Nation's Schooling System,* CTR. FOR AM. PROGRESS (May
   31, 2017), https://www.americanprogress.org.

7. Jens Manuel Krogstad & Richard Fry, *Dept. of Ed. Projects Public Schools Will Be "Majority-Minority" This Fall,* PEW RES. CTR. (Aug. 18, 2014), www.pewresearch.org.

8. DEBORAH A. SANTIAGO, THE CONDITION OF LATINOS IN EDUCATION: 2015 FACTBOOK 4 (2015) [hereinafter LATINO FACTBOOK], https://files.eric.ed.gov.

9. Eileen Patten, *The Nation's Latino Population Is Defined by Its Youth,* PEW RES. CTR. (Apr. 20, 2016), www.pewhispanic.org.

10. *See* Kurt Bauman, *School Enrollment of the Hispanic Population: Two Decades of Growth,* U.S. CENSUS BUREAU: CENSUS BLOGS (Aug. 28, 2017), https://www.census.gov; WHITE HOUSE INITIATIVE ON EDUC. EXCELLENCE FOR HISPANICS, US DEP'T OF EDUC., EARLY LEARNING: ACCESS TO A HIGH QUALITY EARLY LEARNING PROGRAM (2014).

11. *See* BEING BROWN IN DIXIE: RACE, ETHNICITY, AND LATINO IMMIGRATION IN THE NEW SOUTH (Cameron D. Lippard & Charles A. Gallagher eds., 2011).

12. Flores, *supra* note 5, at 5.

13. Kevin R. Johnson, *The End of "Civil Rights" as We Know It? Immigration and Civil Rights in the New Millennium,* 49 UCLA L. REV. 1481, 1491–1510 (2002) (analyzing the transformation of the civil rights agenda in the modern United States due to the movement of Mexican immigrants to regions across the country).

14. US COMM'N ON CIVIL RIGHTS, PUBLIC EDUCATION FUNDING INEQUALITY IN AN ERA OF INCREASING CONCENTRATION OF POVERTY AND RESEGREGATION 5 (2018), www.usccr.gov.

15. EDUCATION TR., *supra* note 4, at 10.

16. *See* LINDA DARLING-HAMMOND, THE FLAT WORLD AND EDUCATION: HOW AMERICA'S COMMITMENT TO EQUITY WILL DETERMINE OUR FUTURE 22–23, 43 (2010) (discussing inadequate facilities and less qualified teachers in high-minority schools); NAT'L CTR. FOR EDUC. STATISTICS, *supra* note 4, at 58–65, 68–71 (describing inequities in the retention, suspension, and expulsion rate of minorities and disparities in advanced, college-preparatory course taking across racial/ethnic groups).

17. *See, e.g.,* CAL. CONST. art. IX (providing a right to education); Serrano v. Priest, 487 P.2d 1241 (Cal. 1971) (applying strict scrutiny under the California Constitution in evaluating the constitutionality of a school financing scheme); *School Finance Litigation Cases, in* THE ENDURING LEGACY OF *RODRIGUEZ*: CREATING NEW PATHWAYS TO EQUAL EDUCATIONAL OPPORTUNITY 275, 275–80 (Charles J. Ogletree Jr. & Kimberly Jenkins Robinson eds., 2015); James E. Ryan, *Schools, Race, and Money,* 109 YALE L.J. 249, 251–52 (1999).

18. Rachel R. Ostrander, *School Funding: Inequality in District Funding and the Disparate Impact on Urban and Migrant School Children,* 2015 BYU EDUC. & L.J. 271, 271 (2015).

19. Michael A. Rebell, *Safeguarding the Right to a Sound Basic Education in Times of Fiscal Constraint*, 75 ALB. L. REV. 1855, 1857 (2011).

20. Thomas P. DiNapoli, *Foreword: A New Era of State and Local Fiscal Policy*, 6 ALB. GOV'T L. REV. vii, vii (2013).

21. Justin Steil, Jorge De la Roca & Ingrid Gould Ellen, *Desvinculado y Desigual: Is Segregation Harmful to Latinos?*, 660 ANNALS 57, 58 (2015).

22. Krista Kauble, Comment, *Litigating* Keyes: *The New Opportunity for Litigators to Achieve Desegregation*, 31 CHICANA/O-LATINA/O L. REV. 103, 120 (2012) (footnote omitted).

23. Gary Orfield & Erica Frankenberg, Brown *at 60: Great Progress, a Long Retreat, and an Uncertain Future*, UCLA CIVIL RIGHTS PROJECT 23–24 (2014), https://www.civilrightsproject.ucla.edu.

24. Orfield et al., *supra* note 4.

25. Erica Frankenberg et al., *Southern Schools: More than a Half-Century after the Civil Rights Revolution*, UCLA CIVIL RIGHTS PROJECT (2017), https://escholarship.org.

26. Jamie Gullen, *Colorblind Education Reform: How Race-Neutral Policies Perpetuate Segregation and Why Voluntary Integration Should Be Put Back on the Reform Agenda*, 15 U. PA. J.L. & SOC. CHANGE 251, 253–54 (2012) (emphasis added) (footnotes omitted).

27. Sheryll Cashin, *Place, Not Race: Affirmative Action and the Geography of Educational Opportunity*, 47 U. MICH. J. L. REFORM 935, 938 (2014).

28. Orfield & Frankenberg, *supra* note 23, at 22–23.

29. 161 F.2d 774 (9th Cir. 1947). *See generally* PHILIPPA STRUM, *MENDEZ V. WESTMINSTER*: SCHOOL DESEGREGATION AND MEXICAN-AMERICAN RIGHTS (2010) (analyzing the significance of the *Mendez* decision).

30. *See, e.g.*, Fisher v. Tucson Unified Sch. Dist., 652 F.3d 1131, 1143–44 (9th Cir. 2011) (ordering district court to maintain jurisdiction over school desegregation consent decree that had been in place for thirty years); *see also* David Hinojosa & Karolina Walters, *How Adequacy Litigation Fails to Fulfill the Promise of* Brown *(But How It Can Get Us Closer)*, 2014 MICH. ST. L. REV. 575, 584–587, 592–595 (2014) (discussing the initial success of desegregation challenges and the subsequent obstacles faced by Latina/o reformers). *See generally* Kauble, *supra* note 22.

31. *See, e.g.*, Kimberly Jenkins Robinson, *Resurrecting the Promise of* Brown: *Understanding and Remedying How the Supreme Court Reconstitutionalized Segregated Schools*, 88 N.C. L. REV. 787, 811–33 (2010).; Rebecca Klein, *Latino School Segregation: The Big Education Problem That No One Is Talking About*, HUFFINGTON POST (Oct. 26, 2015), www.huffingtonpost.com.

32. *See* Robinson, *supra* note 31, at 811–33.

33. 418 U.S. 717, 744–45 (1974); Robinson, *supra* note 31, at 814.

34. *See* JAMES E. RYAN, FIVE MILES AWAY, A WORLD APART: ONE CITY, TWO SCHOOLS, AND THE STORY OF EDUCATIONAL OPPORTUNITY IN MODERN AMERICA 105 (2010).

35. 413 U.S. 189 (1973).
36. *See id.* at 195; Rachel F. Moran, *Untoward Consequences: The Ironic Legacy of Keyes v. School District No. 1,* 90 DENV. U. L. REV. 1209, 1219–21 (2013).
37. Parents Involved in Cmty. Schs. v. Seattle Sch. Dist. No. 1, 551 U.S. 701, 712 (2007) [hereinafter *Parents Involved*].
38. *Id.* at 716 (citations omitted).
39. *See* Fisher v. Univ. of Tex., 136 S. Ct. 2198 (2016); Grutter v. Bollinger, 539 U.S. 306 (2003).
40. *Parents Involved,* 551 U.S. at 733–35.
41. *Id.* at 748 (plurality opinion).
42. Kimberly Jenkins Robinson, *The Constitutional Future of Race-Neutral Efforts to Achieve Diversity and Avoid Racial Isolation in Elementary and Secondary Schools,* 50 B.C. L. REV. 277, 293–94 (2009).
43. *See id.* at 280.
44. Orfield et al., *supra* note 4, at 1.
45. CAMILLE L. RYAN & KURT BAUMAN, US CENSUS BUREAU, EDUCATIONAL ATTAINMENT IN THE UNITED STATES: 2015, at 2, Table 1 (2016).
46. John Gramlich, *Hispanic Dropout Rate Hits New Low, College Enrollment at New High,* PEW RES. CTR. (Sept. 29, 2017), www.pewresearch.org.
47. Silvia Alvarez de Devila, *Falling Behind: Understanding Challenges Facing Latino Education in the U.S.,* IMPROVING LIVES: CEHD VISION 2020 BLOG (Apr. 29, 2016), https://cehdvision2020.umn.edu.
48. LATINO FACTBOOK, *supra* note 8, at 4.
49. Jared S. Buszin, *Beyond School Finance: Refocusing Education Reform Litigation to Realize the Deferred Dream of Educational Equality and Adequacy,* 62 EMORY L.J. 1613, 1627–28 (2013) (footnotes omitted) (quote from Press Release, Educ. Trust, States Can Close Achievement Gap by Decade's End (Mar. 2, 2001), www.edtrust. org).
50. Daniel J. Losen & Amir Whitaker, *Lost Instruction: The Disparate Impact of the School Discipline Gap in California,* UCLA CIVIL RIGHTS PROJECT 6–10 (2017), https://www.civilrightsproject.ucla.edu.
51. Patricia Gándara, *Fulfilling America's Future: Latinas in the U.S., 2015,* UCLA CIVIL RIGHTS PROJECT 11 (2015), https://sites.ed.gov.
52. Rakesh Kochhar & Anthony Cilluffo, *How Wealth Inequality Has Changed in the U.S. since the Great Recession, by Race, Ethnicity and Income,* PEW RES. CTR. (Nov. 1, 2017), www.pewresearch.org.
53. Flores, *supra* note 5, at 3.
54. Lucrecia Santibañez & Patricia Gándara, *Teachers of English Language Learners in Secondary Schools: Gaps in Preparation and Support,* UCLA CIVIL RIGHTS PROJECT 2 (2018), https://www.civilrightsproject.ucla.edu.
55. *See* Ilana M. Umansky & Sean F. Reardon, *Reclassification Patterns Among Latino English Learner Students in Bilingual, Dual Immersion, and English Immersion*

Classrooms, 51 AM. EDUC. RES. J. 879 (2014) (identifying educational benefits of bilingual education to English-language acquisition).

56. *See* Rachel F. Moran, *Bilingual Education as a Status Conflict*, 75 CALIF. L. REV. 321 (1987).

57. Kristi L. Bowman, *Pursuing Educational Opportunities for Latino/a Students*, 88 N.C. L. REV. 911, 924–31 (2010).

58. 414 U.S. 563, 568–69 (1974).

59. *See, e.g.*, Castañeda v. Pickard, 648 F.2d 989, 1007 (5th Cir. 1981) (reasoning that, although the Supreme Court had not expressly overruled *Lau*, *U.C. Regents v. Bakke*, 438 U.S. 265 (1978), limited Title VI claims to intentional discrimination); *see also* Rachel Moran, *Undone by Law: The Uncertain Legacy of* Lau v. Nichols, 16 BERKELEY LA RAZA L.J. 1, 4–6 (2005) (explaining how the courts have undone the *Lau* decision).

60. 648 F.2d 989, 1009–10 (5th Cir. 1981).

61. Equal Educational Opportunities Act (EEOA), 20 U.S.C. § 1703(f) ("No State shall deny equal educational opportunity to an individual on account of his or her race, color, sex, or national origin, by . . . (f) the failure by an educational agency to take appropriate action to overcome language barriers that impede equal participation by its students in its instructional programs."); *Castañeda*, 648 F.2d at 1009–10; *see also* Eric Hass, *The Equal Educational Opportunity Act 30 Years Later: Time to Revisit "Appropriate Action" for Assisting English Language Learners*, 34 J.L. & EDUC. 361, 369 (2005) (contending that the courts placed an almost impossible burden on plaintiffs under *Castañeda* to show that the educational theory underlying the language program is not sound); Rachel F. Moran, *The Politics of Discretion: Federal Intervention in Bilingual Education*, 76 CALIF. L. REV. 1249, 1320 (1988) (arguing that the third prong of *Castañeda* can be interpreted to require merely "reasonable steps to follow up on program success").

62. *See* Horne v. Flores, 557 U.S. 433 (2009). For analysis of the negative impacts of the Court's decision on English language learners, *see* Bowman, *supra* note 57, at 958–68.

63. Matthew P. O'Sullivan, Note, *Laboratories for Inequality: State Experimentation and Educational Access for English-Language Learners*, 64 DUKE L.J. 671, 687 (2015).

64. Proposition 227, English Language for Immigrant Children, CAL. EDUC. CODE §§ 300–40.

65. *See* Valeria v. Davis, 307 F.3d 1036 (9th Cir. 2002) (affirming the denial of an injunction that would have barred the implementation of Proposition 227).

66. Kevin R. Johnson & George A. Martínez, *Discrimination by Proxy: The Case of Proposition 227 and the Ban on Bilingual Education*, 33 U.C. DAVIS L. REV. 1227, 1268–75 (2000).

67. Jennifer Bonilla Moreno, *¿Only English? How Bilingual Education Can Mitigate the Damages of English-Only*, 20 DUKE J. GENDER L. & POL'Y 197, 198 (2012) (footnotes omitted).

68. *See* An Act Relative to the Teaching of English in Public Schools, 2002 MASS. ACTS 1161–66 (approved by the people Nov. 5, 2002); ARIZ. REV. STAT. ANN. §§ 15–751 to 755 (2000).

69. No Child Left Behind Act of 2001, Pub. L. No. 107-100, 115 Stat. 1425 (2002).

70. Rosemary C. Salomone, *Educating English Learners: Reconciling Bilingualism and Accountability*, 6 HARV. L. & POL'Y REV. 115, 125–32 (2012).

71. *See* Proposition 58, 2016 CAL. STAT. A-42 (approved by voters Nov. 8, 2016); Ashley Hopkinson, *A New Era for Bilingual Education: Explaining California's Proposition 58*, EDSOURCE, Jan. 6, 2017, https://edsource.org.

72. *See* An Act Relative to Language Opportunity for Our Kids, 2017 Mass. Legis. Serv. Ch. 138 (West) (codified in scattered sections of MASS. GEN. LAWS chs. 69, 70 & 71).

73. Noble Ingram, *In These Bilingual Classrooms, Diversity Is No Longer Lost in Translation*, CHRISTIAN SCI. MONITOR, Oct. 30, 2018, https://www.csmonitor.com; US DEP'T OF EDUC., DUAL LANGUAGE EDUCATION PROGRAMS: CURRENT STATE POLICIES AND PRACTICES xviii–xix (2013), https://ncela.ed.gov.

74. ARIZ. REV. STAT. ANN. §§ 15–751 to 753 (2000) (defining sheltered English immersion as "an English language acquisition process for young children in which nearly all classroom instruction is in English but with the curriculum and presentation designed for children who are learning the language" and permitting only minimal use of a student's native language).

75. N.H. REV. STAT. ANN. § 189:19 (2018).

76. Pub L. No. 114-95, 129 Stat. 1802 (2015).

77. Charles Barone, *What ESSA Says: Continuities and Departures, in* THE EVERY STUDENT SUCCEEDS ACT: WHAT IT MEANS FOR SCHOOLS, SYSTEMS AND STATES 59, 65 (Frederick M. Hess & Max Eden eds., 2017).

78. 20 U.S.C. § 6311(c)(4)(A) (Supp. IV 2016) (regarding long-term goals for English-language proficiency); 20 U.S.C. § 6311(h) (Supp. IV 2016) (reporting requirements for states and districts for English-language learners and regarding English proficiency).

79. Scott Sargrad, *Hope for English-Language Learners*, U.S. NEWS, Jan. 13, 2016, https://www.usnews.com.

80. 20 U.S.C. § 6311(b)(2)(G) (Supp. IV 2016).

81. *Id.* § 6821(b)(2).

82. Jeffrey S. Passel & D'Vera Cohn, *Unauthorized Immigrant Population Stable for Half a Decade*, PEW RES. CTR. (Sept. 21, 2016), www.pewresearch.org (estimating that 11.1 million undocumented immigrants lived in the United States in 2014).

83. 457 U.S. 202 (1982). *See generally* MICHAEL A. OLIVAS, NO UNDOCUMENTED CHILD LEFT BEHIND: *PLYLER V. DOE* AND THE EDUCATION OF UNDOCUMENTED SCHOOLCHILDREN (2012) (analyzing litigation strategy and impacts of *Plyler v. Doe*).

84. Proposition 187, 1994 CAL. STAT. A-317.

85. *See* League of United Latin Am. Citizens v. Wilson, 908 F. Supp. 755 (C.D. Cal. 1995).

86. *Id.* at 765.
87. *See id.* at 774.
88. H.B. 56, 2011 Leg., Reg. Sess. (Ala. 2011).
89. In striking down the Texas law effectively barring undocumented immigrants from the public schools, the Supreme Court in *Plyler v. Doe*, 457 U.S. 202, 227–30 (1982), found that the state had failed to provide a compelling justification for denying those students a public education, such as evidence of the allegedly substantial costs associated with providing an education to undocumented students.
90. Cent. Ala. Fair Hous. Ctr. v. Magee, 835 F. Supp. 2d 1165, 1193 (M.D. Ala. 2011), *vacated and remanded in part*, 2013 U.S. App. LEXIS 11316 (11th Cir. May 17, 2013).
91. Letter from Thomas E. Perez, Assistant Attorney General, US Department of Justice, to Dr. Thomas R. Bice, Alabama State Superintendent of Education (May 1, 2012), http://media.al.com.
92. Hispanic Interest Coal. of Ala. v. Gov. of Ala., 691 F.3d 1236, 1245–50 (11th Cir. 2012), *cert. denied sub. nom.*, Alabama v. United States, 569 U.S. 968 (2013).
93. Constitutional law scholars have questioned the doctrinal basis for *Plyler v. Doe. See, e.g.*, Dennis J. Hutchinson, *More Substantive Equal Protection? A Note on* Plyler v. Doe, 1982 SUP. CT. REV. 167, 184 (1982).
94. National Center for Public Policy Research, *Influx of Illegal Immigrant Children Likely to Strain Public Schools* (Aug. 18, 2014), https://nationalcenter.org (contending that unaccompanied minors from Central America coming to the United States in 2014 may strain public school systems).
95. *See* United States v. California, 314 F. Supp. 3d 1077 (E.D. Cal. 2018) (denying US government's motion to enjoin three of four of California's "sanctuary" laws).
96. Christopher N. Lasch et al., *Understanding "Sanctuary Cities,"* 59 B.C. L. REV. 1703, 1738–52 (2018); Rose Cuison Villazor & Pratheepan Gulasekaram, *The New Sanctuary and Anti-Sanctuary Movements*, 52 U.C. DAVIS L. REV. 549, 553–60 (2018).
97. Thomas Fuller, *"Sanctuary Schools" across America Defy Trump's Immigration Crackdown*, GUARDIAN, Aug. 21, 2017, https://www.theguardian.com.
98. Bowman, *supra* note 57, at 991.
99. *See* Kevin R. Johnson, *A Handicapped, Not "Sleeping," Giant: The Devastating Impact of the Initiative Process on Latina/o and Immigrant Communities*, 96 CALIF. L. REV. 1259 (2008).
100. *See* Bowman, *supra* note 57, at 978.
101. *See* Fuller, *supra* note 97 ("Though they don't always carry much legal weight, sanctuary school resolutions help ease parents' and children's anxiety by ensuring that teachers and principals know how to respond if immigration agents go to a school or request student information.").

PART II

How the United States Could Recognize a Federal Right to Education

5

Implying a Federal Constitutional Right to Education

DEREK W. BLACK

Introduction

The idea that education is a right that the federal Constitution protects has long fascinated scholars and litigants. Since at least the 1950s, litigants have tried to convince the federal judiciary to recognize a right to education.[1] The right possesses some allure for judges as well. Courts have always refused to doctrinally recognize the right asserted by plaintiffs but refused to entirely reject the possibility that some other theory might change their position. The Supreme Court has routinely spoken of education as being of the utmost importance to both individuals and our overall democracy.[2] As such, the Court has, on several occasions, hinted that a minimally adequate education might be cognizable, just not in the particular case before it.[3]

These hints at a right, combined with what many people argue was simply the wrong result in *San Antonio v. Rodriguez*, have kept scholars steadily at work on theories that might thread the Supreme Court's doctrinal needles. With little to no favorable precedent on their side, scholars have developed a multitude of theories for why the federal Constitution should protect education. Those ideas run a large doctrinal gambit. They range from Due Process and Equal Protection to the Privileges and Immunities Clause to the rights of citizenship. If there is a constitutional clause within which the right to education might fit, someone has almost assuredly considered it. And even within those broad doctrinal categories, scholars have developed additional subsets of nuanced arguments. Due process alone, for instance, breaks down into claims premised on history, the importance of education, education's intersection with other rights, stigmatic harms, and the necessity of minimal education.

An implied federal constitutional right to education is, in effect, an idea that just will not die. The question of this chapter is whether there is plausible life in the idea or whether the idea is just fodder for idle chatter. A survey of existing theories reveals that a number of them are logically compelling. Compelling theories, interestingly, are not new. The primary problem may not be in logic or doctrine but in practical plausibility. Judicial biases regarding particular doctrines and methods of interpretation simply make otherwise valid theories unlikely to succeed.

The doggedness of advocates and scholars, however, may be on the verge of finally breaking through judicial reticence. Newer theories have begun to gravitate toward originalism arguments rather than focusing merely on the importance of education to individuals. These theories may well strike a perfect balance between meritorious arguments and the predilections of the judiciary.

General Approaches to a Fundamental Right to Education

Most theories, in one way or another, make the claim that education is, or should be, a fundamental right. This framing, however, is overly general. The Supreme Court's fundamental rights analysis technically divides into two categories: due process and equal protection. Distinguishing between fundamental rights sounding in substantive due process and those sounding in equal protection can be difficult. The simplest explanation is that fundamental rights under substantive due process are those rights that individuals possess without government granting them to individuals. One might think of them as inalienable rights—although they are not limited to inalienable rights—such as the freedom of speech, the right to privacy, and the right to life. Government does not "give" citizens these rights; rather, these are individual rights that, in many instances, predate our government. If these rights do not emanate from government, government should not be able to take them away, save extreme circumstances requiring as much.

In contrast, fundamental rights under equal protection are more closely linked to the function of government. They are not akin to freestanding inalienable rights. Rather, fundamental rights under equal protection arise in regard to benefits or privileges that the government extends to citizens and that are so important that the government should not be permitted to treat citizens unequally. In other words, once government extends certain fundamental benefits to individuals, it must ensure it extends them equally.

For instance, federal law does not require state governments to afford their citizens the right to elect persons for each and every type of public office that government establishes. In fact, citizens do not get to vote for most government officials. Moreover, states are presumably free to withdraw the right to vote for certain offices that are currently subject to a vote, such as local school board members. States could pass laws permitting mayors to appoint school board members. But what states and local governments cannot do is treat individuals differently once they grant individuals the right to vote in a particular election.[4] Thus, the right to vote is treated as fundamental under equal protection[5] but not under substantive due process.

Another important practical distinction remains: violations of substantive due process and equal protection rights occur in different contexts. A substantive due process violation occurs when any single person's fundamental right is infringed. But a fundamental equal protection right is most typically violated when a group of individuals is treated differently.

These distinctions are particularly important in assessing a fundamental right to education. The Supreme Court has only squarely confronted the question of a fundamental right to education once, and it decided the case—*San Antonio Independent School District v. Rodriguez*—on the basis of equal protection. There, the Court rejected the idea that education's importance would control whether the Court found it fundamental.[6] For the Court, the question was whether the Constitution affords any explicit or implicit right to education. Given that the term "education" does not appear in the Constitution, the Court quickly moved to the question of an implied right to education. As to the latter, the Court found no implicit right to education either.[7] The fact that education has close intersections with the exercise of other explicit rights—voting and speech—was insufficient.[8] The Court reasoned that education was not unique in its connection to other explicit rights.

A number of scholars argue that the Court was simply wrong in *Rodriguez*.[9] They reason that education is so important as a general matter and sufficiently connected to the exercise of other fundamental rights that the Constitution must afford it special protections.[10] While those arguments may be correct, expecting the Court to reverse itself without some new additional arguments probably does fall into the category of idle chatter. Thus, this chapter focuses primarily on scholarship that makes arguments that are meaningfully distinct from those raised in *Rodriguez* or, at least, raises significant new facts that might influence the Court to decide that things have changed rather than admit it was flatly wrong in *Rodriguez*.

Equal Protection

Some people argue that developments since the Court's holding in *Rodriguez* have undermined the decision's predicates. In particular, state courts have recognized that their constitutions provide for a right or duty in education.[11] State statutes and regulations have established qualitative measures of education by which a court might compare educational opportunities across schools.[12] And local authority over education has substantially decreased, with state authorities playing a much larger role in education.[13]

The most notable change is in regard to state constitutional rights. At the time of *Rodriguez*, the Court may have been correct that education was not significantly different from other public benefits. California was the only state whose supreme court had given any substantive meaning or protection to education under its state constitution, and that had occurred only a little over a year prior to *Rodriguez* and in ambiguous terms.[14] To be clear, the state constitutional provisions themselves were not new. Most had been in place for over a century, but state courts had never enforced them.[15] Thus, the United States Supreme Court had no basis on which to interpret equal and quality education in state constitutions.

In the decades following *Rodriguez*, the status quo completely changed. Immediately following *Rodriguez*, California reaffirmed its position, and a handful of courts followed its lead. A full-fledged state constitutional movement, however, did not fully take hold until the late 1980s, with a number of state courts refusing to intervene in education rights. But after the late 1980s, plaintiffs succeeded in approximately two-thirds of their cases. Now, over half of the state supreme courts have ruled in favor of plaintiffs in these cases.[16]

Some of these courts declared education to be a fundamental right under state constitutional law, and others characterized education as a constitutional duty that obligated the state to provide an adequate education. Even in states where plaintiffs lost their specific claims, some courts recognized that students may have a technical right to education under their state constitution. These courts simply found that the state was meeting its obligation or that separation-of-powers limitations prevented the court from adjudicating cases in this area.

On the whole, these cases dictate that education encompasses more than just the right to enter a school building; states must also deliver a certain qualitative level of education therein.[17] Thus, contrary to the assumption in *Rodriguez*, education is not just any public benefit. Education is an express state constitutional right and one that a legislature is bound to deliver, often above all else.

Scholars reason that this shift provides a basis for federal courts to apply something more than just minimal scrutiny to inequality and inadequacies in education. I, for instance, have previously argued that these state cases may not directly reverse *Rodriguez* but that federal equal protection attaches to state constitutional rights.[18] States cannot declare something to be a constitutional right and then treat their citizens differently in regard to those rights. Thus, state law sets the floor of educational opportunity, but federal law regulates equality of access to those opportunities.

The key question is the appropriate level of scrutiny—intermediate or strict. Strict scrutiny is the most logical but even intermediate would be a marked improvement over current doctrine. This approach, however, has its limits. Because not all states have recognized an enforceable education right or have only recognized a minimal qualitative right, educational inequality might violate the federal Constitution in one state but not another. In short, this approach offers, at best, a partial fix.

Martha Morgan takes a slightly narrower approach.[19] She argues that federal courts should simply read the precise holdings of state supreme courts. Where a state supreme court has declared education to be a fundamental right under state law, federal courts should apply strict scrutiny. Where they have not made such a declaration, federal courts should respect the state ruling and apply the typical rational basis review. In other words, federal courts should treat state fundamental rights the same as they treat federal fundamental rights. Both Morgan and I emphasize that this approach does not ask much of federal courts or disturb federalism norms.[20] Federal courts would merely be asked to follow the lead of states, not create affirmative substantive education rights themselves.

Scholars have also emphasized the growth of qualitative statutory and regulatory requirements. States, for instance, have established standardized end-of-course subject-matter exams, along with graduation exams. The federal government has, likewise, mandated that all students be proficient in core subjects. Scholars argue that these statutory and regulatory baselines establish the minimal thresholds of educational quality that states must provide.[21] When a state fails to provide the required baseline opportunities to a particular class of students, it should trigger heightened scrutiny in some form.[22] This theory would not depend on the state constitutional precedent in a state but simply on the fact that state laws and regulations now provide qualitative measures against which courts can measure inequality and absolute deprivation of educational opportunity.

Substantive Due Process

Far more thought has been devoted to education as a fundamental right under substantive due process's protection of liberty. While the Due Process Clause explicitly protects liberty, it does not define the meaning of liberty. Thus, its meaning is necessarily a matter of interpretation for the courts. In *Washington v. Glucksberg*,[23] the Supreme Court stated the general test for identifying fundamental rights under substantive due process: "First, we have regularly observed that the Due Process Clause specially protects those fundamental rights and liberties which are, objectively, 'deeply rooted in this Nation's history and tradition,' and 'implicit in the concept of ordered liberty,' such that 'neither liberty nor justice would exist if they were sacrificed.' Second, we have required in substantive-due-process cases a 'careful description' of the asserted fundamental liberty interest. Our Nation's history, legal traditions, and practices thus provide the crucial 'guideposts for responsible decisionmaking' that direct and restrain our exposition of the Due Process Clause."[24]

Several scholars argue that education easily meets this test. Susan Bitensky, for instance, writes that "there is overwhelming evidence of American history and traditions which are specifically protective of children's interest in education. . . . [S]chool-age children in the United States can point to an enduring and pervasive historical tradition of receiving state-provided elementary and secondary education."[25] The interest is so important that states compel students to attend school.

Bitensky does not just rely on generalities. She parses history, focusing separately on state governments' provision of education since the nineteenth century, the federal government's financial support for those early state efforts, and the federal government's more recent efforts to regulate certain state educational activities. She also emphasizes that through this period, the Supreme Court has "extolled the virtues of public education, recognizing 'the public schools as a most vital civic institution for the preservation of a democratic system of government' that is intrinsic to American national identity and culture."[26] This history, Bitensky reasons, suffices to establish education as a right deeply "rooted in [this Nation's] history and tradition," as required by the Court.[27] Bitensky is joined in her assessment by a number of other scholars.[28]

Barry Friedman and Sara Solow, more recently, dug even further into this history. They detail nearly two centuries of state constitutional commitments in education, along with the steady growth of the federal commitment, to establish a tradition of education rights that our federal Constitution would treat as fundamental.[29] They argue that this history is so compelling that a court need not engage in theoretical debates over constitutional interpretation and its appropriate standards. Friedman and Solow simply argue, "When one interprets the Constitution as judges and lawyers interpret, it turns out [that] a federal right to an adequate education . . . has emerged over time. . . . [T]he right is every bit as clear as, say, the right to possess and bear arms in self-defense or the right of a woman to choose abortion—or so many other constitutional rights that at their core are part of American life in the early twenty-first century."[30] Drawing on everything from the state and federal commitment to education in the original colonies and the Northwest Ordinance of 1787 to state constitutions, the Fourteenth Amendment, and vastly expanded federal legislation in recent decades,[31] Friedman and Solow posit that education is easily among the "deepest and most fundamentally constitutive" aspects of our legal and constitutional commitments.[32]

Some scholars would even urge that the time is ripe to press the Court to intervene in education on substantive due process grounds. They have gained inspiration from the Court's willingness to intervene on behalf of the LGBTQ community in a series of recent cases. These cases may have expanded the general possibilities of fundamental rights recognition.[33] As the Court wrote in *Obergefell v. Hodges*,

> The identification and protection of fundamental rights is an enduring part of the judicial duty to interpret the Constitution. That responsibility, however, "has not been reduced to any formula." Rather, it requires courts to exercise reasoned judgment in identifying interests of the person so fundamental that the State must accord them its respect. That process is guided by many of the same considerations relevant to analysis of other constitutional provisions that set forth broad principles rather than specific requirements. History and tradition guide and discipline this inquiry but do not set its outer boundaries. That method respects our history and learns from it without allowing the past alone to rule the present.[34]

Those cases, moreover, arguably establish a new lens through which to filter a fundamental right to education: autonomy and dignity. Both concepts weigh heavily in the Court's recent cases adjudicating the rights of the LGBTQ community. Scholars argue that the autonomy and dignity framing represents a "sea change" and offers a "template for recognizing the positive right of access to public education."[35]

Areto Imoukhuede, for instance, points out that the right to privacy in *Lawrence v. Texas* rests on the notion "that privacy is essential to liberty and human dignity."[36] He argues that education is, likewise, central to liberty and dignity, but education is also central to a democratic component of human dignity that may be missing with privacy. Thus, "the case for a dignity-based due process clause protection of the right to public education is even stronger for education than the case for the right to privacy."[37]

In *Obergefell*, the Court wrote that the "right to marry . . . draws meaning from related rights of childrearing, procreation and education," all of which are a "central part" of "the liberty protected by the Due Process Clause."[38] References such as this allowed the litigants in Connecticut to splice quotes from *Obergefell* and argue that "like marriage, '[c]hoices about [education] shape an individual's destiny.'"[39] Moreover, the connection between education and destiny has been an implicit part of the

Court's jurisprudence since *Brown v. Board of Education*. There, the Court wrote, "it is doubtful that any child may reasonably be expected to succeed in life if he is denied the opportunity of an education."[40]

Minimally Adequate Education

While the foregoing line of reasoning offers a basis for what one might call a full-scale fundamental right to education, scholars have increasingly devoted their attention to a potentially smaller prize: a fundamental right to a minimally adequate education. This line of reasoning owes its genesis to the Court itself, which has made reference to the possibility of such a right on more than one occasion. Friedman and Solow see virtue in this narrower approach. They do not concede a full-scale right to education but emphasize that our historical commitment to education supports, at the very least, the protection of a minimal level of education.[41] Other scholars, however, suggest that a minimal education may rest on a rationale distinct from the ones in support of a full-scale right.

Gershon Ratner was one of the earliest scholars to make this point. He argued that because "compulsory education deprives students of constitutionally protected liberties—freedom from physical confinement, freedom of association, freedom to travel, and the right to privacy"—the state takes on a duty to provide students with at least basic education skills.[42] This duty is further justified because the deprivation of liberty is not temporary. Rather, it extends over several years.

Another scholar further developed this idea in light of subsequent Supreme Court decisions.[43] In a series of cases, the Supreme Court has held that the state assumes a duty when it confines, takes custody over, or establishes a special relationship with an individual.[44] While all of these cases occur outside the educational context, *Youngberg v. Romero*[45] involved a person with an intellectual disability who was involuntarily committed to a mental institution. The Court held that he was entitled to "minimally adequate or reasonable training,"[46] reasoning that while the state has no general affirmative duty to provide training to citizens, the particular restriction on liberty created such a duty.[47]

Education involves an analogous impairment of students' liberty. The more difficult question in education would be the nature of the duty that the impairment imposes. As to that question, the theory returns to *Youngberg*. There, the Court, referring to confinement to a mental institution, wrote,

> [T]he minimally adequate training required by the Constitution is such training as may be reasonable in light of respondent's liberty interests in safety and freedom from unreasonable restraints. In determining what is "reasonable"—in this and in any case presenting a claim for training by a State—we emphasize that courts must show deference to the judgment exercised by a qualified professional. . . . [T]he decision, if made by a professional, is presumptively valid; liability may be imposed only when the decision by the professional is such a substantial departure from accepted professional judgment, practice, or standards as to demonstrate that the person responsible actually did not base the decision on such a judgment.[48]

In short, the state's restriction of an individual's liberty requires reasonable compensatory services. Courts should treat services as reasonable so long as they fall within accepted professional norms.

Applying these principles to education, one commentator has argued that "if a state restricts an individual's liberty for the express purpose of educating that individual and then fails to educate her, then the nature of the restraint bears no reasonable relation to the purpose of the restraint, and due process is violated. Hence, litigants might assert a substantive due process right to a minimal level of education."[49] On the other hand, *Youngberg*'s holding might only stand for the principle that the state's duty is to provide services "that would enable confined individuals to realize their personal autonomy interests. . . . Under this analysis, schools would have a duty to educate students to the extent necessary for the students to enjoy their personal autonomy, which might mean educating a student either to her potential or to a certain minimal level."[50] Under either approach, a court looking for professional judgments and norms regarding minimal education standards could turn to federal legislation such as the Every Student Succeeds Act. States, likewise, have codified basic education programs. A school failing to provide students with an education that is generally consistent with these statutes could be said to have deprived students of their liberty without providing a reasonable level of education.

Other scholars and advocates approach the issue of a substantive due process right to a minimally adequate education differently. They note the fact that the state is confining students but focus more heavily on the claim that the state is affirmatively harming students during the course of that confinement.[51] This theory revolves around what one might call stigmatic harm, which the Court has recognized in other contexts. Whereas the *Youngberg* line of reasoning argues the state has assumed a duty to educate students to a minimal level, stigma theory is premised on a negative right: a right to be free from stigma. If the state is stigmatizing students, the only way to eliminate the stigma is the provision of certain education skills. The net result of stigma and confinement theory are the same—a minimally adequate education—but the duty in stigma theory flows more precisely from the affirmative harm that the state appears to be imposing on students.

The recent lawsuit in Detroit, Michigan, involves a paradigmatic claim of education stigma.[52] The lawsuit argues that all persons are entitled to equal and full citizenship, which requires, as a practical matter, access to some basic level of education. But the complaint more specifically charges that the school system is so deficient that it deprives students of literacy.[53] This illiteracy stigmatizes students and consigns them to an economic, political, and social underclass.[54] While these students may be citizens in a formal and technical sense, the failure of the state to ensure their literacy effectively reduces these students to second-class citizens.[55] The state is responsible for the stigma because it controls the horrendous education and compels students to suffer it.[56] Thus, plaintiffs' gripe is not that other students receive a better education elsewhere but that the education they receive from the state is crippling.[57] The right to be free from this stigmatic harm requires the protection of education, at least, at some minimal level.[58]

Hybrid Theories

More recently, scholars have considered the possibility that a fundamental right to education need not fit neatly within substantive due process or equal protection, suggesting that a right to education might emanate from the combined force of due process and equal protection principles. This line of thinking, like some substantive due process theories, has been buoyed in large part by the Court's recent cases protecting the rights of LGBTQ individuals. These and other scholars aptly recognize that the Court's recent jurisprudence is ambiguous—potentially in a good way.[59]

In particular, the Court has refused to moor same-sex couples' right to sexual intimacy and marriage in standard equal protection or due process jurisprudence. Instead, the Court has indicated that those rights have both substantive due process and equal protection dimensions. The Court's past refusal to recognize a right to education may stem from a flawed attempt to pigeonhole the right. *Plyler v. Doe* may be a perfect example.

The equal protection grounds for ruling in plaintiffs' favor there were arguably very weak. Nothing in past equal protection precedent would have suggested a victory. Likewise, the absence of a substantive due process right eliminated the possibility of victory on that ground. Yet the Court offered rhetorical arguments that easily would have made the case for a new general doctrine supporting heightened scrutiny under equal protection scrutiny or a substantive due process right. The Court, however, stopped short of announcing any new doctrine, leaving the outcome of the case resting in some netherworld between equal protection and due process.

Joshua Weishart's recent scholarship attempts to bring form to these hybrid theories and synthesize them with the Court's recent jurisprudence.[60] He argues that this synthesis offers a potentially stronger grounding for a right to education. He writes,

> [A]djudicating the right to education "stereoscopically—through the lenses of both [due process and equal protection]—can have synergistic effects, producing results that neither clause might reach by itself" or that the right to education can have unassisted.
>
> Inasmuch as the Equal Protection and Substantive Due Process Clauses "further[] our understanding" of the "central precepts" of liberty and equality entailed by the "right to marry," they can do the same for the right to education. It may be fair to characterize the resulting amalgamation as an "equality-based and relationally situated theory of substantive liberty." Or, to put it less eloquently, the right to education would remain a mutant of sorts, an aberration in the constitutional order.[61]

Without explicitly stating as much, new federal education rights lawsuits seem to agree, as they straddle the line between equality and substantive due process arguments at times.

Originalism

Another group of scholars argue on originalism grounds that the Constitution guarantees a right to education. The guarantee of education or duty to provide education is distinct from the fundamental rights and equal protection analysis. These scholars do not argue that any grand theory of substantive due process, equal protection, and evolving necessities render education a fundamental right. They argue that the original intent of the Fourteenth Amendment was to protect education. In this respect, these theories stand outside the nuances of modern doctrines regarding rights recognition. Interestingly, however, originalism theory includes its own diversity, with certain arguments situating the right to education in differing clauses of the Fourteenth Amendment.

Goodwin Liu's work could be called the national citizenship theory. Liu argues, based on the language and legislative history of the Fourteenth Amendment and the prevailing practices that followed it, that Congress intended education to be one of the privileges and immunities of national citizenship.[62] He writes, "Before the Fourteenth Amendment mandates equal protection of the laws, it guarantees national citizenship. This guarantee is affirmatively declared; it is not merely protected against state abridgment. Moreover, the guarantee does more than designate a legal status. Together with Section 5 [of the Fourteenth Amendment], it obligates the national government to secure the full membership, effective participation, and equal dignity of all citizens in the national community."[63] While facially sound, the theory is stacked against unfavorable privileges and immunities precedent.[64] How much this matters is uncertain.

The rationale on which the negative privileges and immunities precedent rests is far more questionable than the rationale of *Rodriguez*. Few people dispute that the privileges and immunities of national citizenship were "neutered by a reactionary Supreme Court that perverted the essential meaning of the Civil War Amendments and helped undermine Reconstruction."[65] Contemporaneous observers of the case "recognized national citizenship as a font of substantive guarantees that Congress had the power and duty to enforce."[66] In dissent, Justice John Marshall Harlan expressly adopted this view, and Congress implicitly did the same through its subsequent actions.[67] Moreover, today, even one of the most conservative justices has indicated a need to rethink the Court's privileges and immunities doctrine,[68] suggesting that flawed privileges and immunities doctrine has forced the Court to overexpand other Fourteenth Amendment doctrines to cure the problem.

Unlike so many other scholars, however, Liu's immediate aim is not for courts to recognize an implied right to education. His aim is on Congress. Liu emphasizes the distinction between the adjudicated Constitution and the full meaning of the Constitution itself. He points out that Congress enacts legislation to enforce the full meaning of the Constitution, whereas courts can only enforce narrower aspects of the Constitution. Thus, Liu calls on Congress to legislate to further support education, which is consistent with the full meaning of the Constitution's guarantee of national citizenship.

Like Liu, I have emphasized the importance of the Fourteenth Amendment's citizenship clause, but I point out that the clause guarantees both state and federal citizenship.[69] I argue that education is more appropriately understood as a right of state citizenship. It was the intent of both Congress and the states to make it such. This distinction, however, does not mean that education is entirely left to the discretion of states. Rather, it means that states are obligated to provide education and that other constitutional principles operate as a limit on how states provide education.

I reach this conclusion on the basis of detailed review of the southern states' readmission to the Union and their final ratification of the Fourteenth Amendment. The Fourteenth Amendment required assent from both southern and northern states, but most southern states had yet to rejoin the Union when the ratification process began.[70] To rejoin the Union, Congress required southern states to meet specific terms outlined in the Reconstruction Act of 1867.[71] One of those terms included ratifying the Fourteenth Amendment.[72] In this respect, southern readmission and the final ratification of the Fourteenth Amendment were directly intertwined. And, as a result, the terms and processes of southern readmission came to define the very meaning of the citizenship that the Fourteenth Amendment secured.

History reveals that Congress expected southern states, as a condition of readmission, to provide for education in their constitutions. Both the Reconstruction Act and Article IV of the federal Constitution required states to adopt republican forms of government.[73] As a practical matter, this required southern states to rewrite their constitutions and present them to Congress for approval.[74] Because Congress believed that education was inherent to a republican form of government,[75] it would reject those constitutions that excluded education. In fact, Congress placed special conditions on those Confederate states that were the slowest to act, readmitting them only on the explicit condition that they continued to provide education equally to all their citizens.[76] These and other events reveal that, at the point the Fourteenth Amendment was ratified, education was a right of state citizenship in the constitution of every readmitted state and, thus, implicit in the state citizenship requirement set forth in the Fourteenth Amendment.

Another variation on my point can be found in Steven Calabresi and Michael Perl's examination of original intent regarding school segregation. In the context of answering that question, Calabresi and Perl simply count state constitutional amendments across time and point out that three-quarters of all state constitutions recognized a right to public education in 1868. They treat this fact itself as conclusive. "Any right that existed widely in 1868, the year the Fourteenth Amendment was passed, could fairly be argued to be a fundamental right that is deeply rooted in American history and tradition and that is therefore a 'Privilege or Immunity' of national or state citizenship."[77] As this quote shows, they wrap these facts in the language of modern fundamental rights tests, but at its core their claim is originalist regardless of doctrine.

The final potential originalism theory, but one not yet fully explored, is that the Constitution's republican form of government clause guarantees education. The clause provides that "[t]he United States shall guarantee to every state in this union a republican form of government."[78] This theory is tricky. First, the clause is part of the original Constitution. At that point, only a few states affirmatively provided for education. Thus, it is difficult to claim that education was part of the original understanding of the clause. At best, a republican form of government is an evolving concept that later came to require education.

Second, the clause is more directly a grant of power to Congress. In admitting new states (and readmitting southern states), Congress assesses whether states have a republican form of government.[79] On the basis of my research, Congress's understanding of a republican form of government had clearly evolved to include education by the end of the Civil War. While I emphasize congressional intent in regard to the Fourteenth Amendment itself, it is equally applicable to the republican form of government clause. The only problem with the latter is case law.

The Court has tended to treat the republican form of government clause as nonjusticiable, leaving the matter to Congress.[80] New litigation, however, has attempted to carve out a middle ground that would protect education to some extent. Again, focusing back on Congress's conditioning the readmission of the last few southern states, plaintiffs in Mississippi argue that the state is obligated to provide the educational opportunities that it promised its citizens in its 1868 constitution.[81] Fearing that Mississippi would backslide, Congress, by specific legislative act, provided that "the constitution of Mississippi shall never be so amended or changed as to deprive any citizen or class of citizens of the United States of the school rights and privileges secured by the constitution of said State."[82] Congress did so under its constitutional power to guarantee a republican form of government in Mississippi. Plaintiffs reason that federal courts need not offer their own meaning of a republican form of government in this case because Congress has already done so and Mississippi is bound to comply. In this respect, plaintiffs' claim is technically a request that Mississippi comply with a congressional act, but the claim resonates in constitutional power and authority.

Evaluating the Theories

Equal protection theories are the simplest of all and technically solid. No doubt, students have far more education rights today than they had when the Court decided *Rodriguez*, and many of the rights rise to the level of a fundamental or constitutional right under a state constitution. It is hard to construct an argument in favor of the idea that states should be free to treat citizens unequally in regard to state constitutional rights, while the federal government is prohibited from doing the same in regard to federal rights such as freedom of speech.

The disadvantage of equal protection theories is not their logic but their practical effect. The facts that would give rise to a federal equal protection claim presumably give rise to a state adequacy or equity claim as well. In this respect, federal equal protection theories do not necessarily create any additional claims or remedies beyond those already available under state law. Thus, in states where education is not a fundamental or constitutional right, federal equal protection does nothing to increase protections for education. Federal equal protection law, in effect, becomes a font of state law—a redundancy that the Court has resisted in due process.

The primary benefit, if any, of a federal equal protection claim would be venue. Litigating education claims in federal court might lead to more effective enforcement because federal judges are not subject to election, nor are they constrained by the separation-of-powers limits that dissuade state courts. More effective enforcement of existing rights would be a welcome improvement in some states, but the agenda of a federal right to education is to expand the scope of potential remedies both geographically and substantively. Equal protection theories are not particularly well suited to this end.

Substantive due process theories, in contrast, would produce significant substantive expansions of education rights. Regardless of underlying state law, substantive due process theories would ensure that students have the same right to education across all jurisdictions—a right to some threshold level of education and to challenge inequities in access to it. Yet the doctrinal grounding for a substantive due process claim asks far more of courts than an equal protection claim. And while states' historical commitment to education provides a strong basis to recognize a substantive due process right, a number of countervailing factors also exist.

The first countervailing point is the saliency of the distinction between affirmative and negative rights. Whatever the merits of this distinction, it is a distinction that resonates with courts. Advocates can respond that other fundamental rights impose obligations on the state as well, but they must concede that a substantive due process right to education would impose affirmative duties well in excess of those imposed by other fundamental rights. In other words, even if the distinction between education and other rights is one of quality rather than kind, the qualitative distinction is immense. And so long as a significant distinction persists in kind or quality, the distinction, regardless of the merits of plaintiffs' claims, will prime courts to resist education as a fundamental right of substantive due process.

The second countervailing point is a judicial reluctance to recognize new fundamental rights, even if negative rights. The open-ended nature of fundamental rights inquiry affords courts enormous discretion. When the Court has exercised that discretion, enormous controversy within and outside the Court has followed. The Court is routinely accused of picking winners and losers in the rights sweepstakes on the basis of the personal values of its members rather than neutral principles.[83] To ward off these critiques, the Court has generally become more restrictive in its recognition of rights.[84] In this respect, the recognition of a right to education was more plausible at the time of *Brown* or *Rodriguez* than it is today.

The Court's holdings in LGBTQ cases may be an exception to the Court's general approach rather than indicators of a new general rule itself. And even if the Court's doctrine has become more flexible, it is not clear that the doctrine of those cases translates as well to education as advocates suggest. Analogies can be made, but so can important differences. The basis and need for intervention in LGBTQ discrimination were hard to deny. Basic justice arguably compelled judicial intervention. The LGBTQ community was clearly the subject of intentional discriminatory treatment akin to other forms of discrimination that the Court strikes down as a matter of course.

As the Court emphasized in *Romer v. Evans*, singling out a group for disadvantage is a quintessential violation of equal protection.[85] Once the Court applied that rationale in *Romer* and rejected the morality claims of antigay advocates, it was hard for the Court to back away from other antigay legislation. Subsequent cases, however, required a different rationale because the LGBTQ community had not necessarily been explicitly targeted for disadvantage. Rather, LGBTQ individuals were requesting that they be included in the larger community for the first time. This required the Court to go further and recognize new substantive rights or, at least, that everyone had an equal right to exercise existing rights. The Court may have gone further not because any particular doctrine or precedent required it but because doing so was consistent with the Court's overall constitutional project to treat LGBTQ individuals equally. If so, the precise doctrine or theory by which the Court reached this end may have been secondary and the amorphous nature of its final holdings intentional, which allowed the Court to avoid binding itself to ancillary effects in other areas.

A fundamental right to education does not seem nearly as inevitable or compelling. First, the Court has long hinted at the idea of a federal right but consistently refrained from recognizing it. The only position to which the Court has consistently adhered is one that rejects education as a fundamental right. No outward signs suggest that the Court is transitioning toward a new position. Some people would argue— although I would disagree—that the practical reasons for the Court to make that transition are in decline. The number of states recognizing constitutional rights and duties in education has steadily grown over the past several decades, as has the federal statutory structure aimed at improving educational outcomes.[86] While both of these developments have serious limits, they arguably reduce the pressure on federal courts to intervene—at least on grounds that are not firmly established in doctrine.

Second, even if the LGBTQ cases represent broader general rights of dignity and autonomy, those rights are not implicated as clearly in education as in marriage and privacy. Here, the positive versus negative rights distinction remains important. Some people might argue that prohibitions on homosexual intimate relations or marital bonds are demeaning, stigmatizing, and authoritarian in a way that educational inequality is not. At the most general level of abstraction, the practical effects of anti-LGBTQ policy and educational inequality may be the same—they shrink the life options of disadvantaged groups—but they are different at more specific levels. The purpose of education policy is to create life options. When education policy fails to achieve that goal, it is often the effect of ineffective policy rather than a purposeful design. In contrast, the purpose of anti-LGBTQ policy has to be to actively constrain autonomy, and in doing so, it is unavoidably demeaning.

The efficacy of pursuing claims in support of a minimally adequate education is a closer call. The payoff for such a right is smaller, but the potential for securing it is relatively higher because it asks less of the Court. A narrower right means narrower judicial intervention, which could allow the Court to recognize a right without fully committing to the federalization of education. And, of course, the fact that the Court has always been careful not to rule out the possibility of a minimally adequate education indicates that the Court believes a right could lie there even if it fails in other areas.

According to some newer litigation and scholars, the Court's prior statements regarding education in general and a minimally adequate education in particular simply add up to a right to a minimally adequate education.[87] These arguments, effectively, attempt to outlawyer the Court with its own dicta. The Court's dicta alone, however, are unlikely to motivate the Court to recognize a minimally adequate education.

The Court is well aware of its precedent and the lack thereof, and the substance of the Court's prior statements on education is thin. These prior statements are primarily conclusory laudatory statements and assumptions, not the reasoned doctrinal building blocks of a fundamental right—even if only a minimally adequate one. Without an affirmative theory or rationale, the Supreme Court is no more likely to suddenly recognize a fundamental right to a minimally adequate education than it is to overturn *Rodriguez's* holding regarding a general fundamental right to education. In short, the Court's past commentary is a double-edged sword—sufficient to make a right to education highly plausible but far from sufficient to make the right a reality. Thus, the task of minimally adequate education theories moving forward should be to more fully flesh out the logical and doctrinal underpinnings of such a right.

A full explanation of that logic is beyond the scope of this chapter, but a few avenues appear immediately possible. The first relates to the fact that states are the gatekeepers and guarantors of educational opportunity. Whether they are obligated to play this role as a matter of federal law is debatable, but every state is and has been in the business of running education systems that either create or limit the lifetime opportunities of students. No other entity or institution has the capacity to fill this role.

Second, when the state system miserably fails for some students or, even worse, adopts policies that have the effect of precluding opportunities for some students, the state comes closer to engaging in exclusionary activity and demeaning students in ways that are more equivalent to concerns raised in the LGBTQ cases. A miserably failing education system or one that deprives students of certain opportunities is just one step short of the explicit exclusion that the Court struck down in *Plyler*. If participation in democracy, the workplace, and higher education are the benchmarks, the difference between the total exclusion in *Plyler* and the denial of minimally adequate education may be relatively small in some instances. In seeking a job or higher education, a student who has attended school but failed to acquire basic literacy and math skills is in roughly the same position as students who have been excluded altogether. Both groups of kids are likely to be consigned to an underclass.

Or, in the alternative, one might argue that while *Plyler* involves absolute exclusion, it is the relative difference in opportunity that makes the exclusion problematic. Earlier in our national history when a smaller percentage of students went to school and an even smaller percentage went to school beyond the elementary years, a law excluding certain students from schools would not necessarily consign them to an underclass. Complete exclusion becomes problematic in the modern era because of the relative gap it creates between individuals. If so, a requirement of a minimally adequate education might be understood as a shorthand qualitative identifier of when an unconscionable gap in educational opportunity occurs. Likewise, one might reason that the denial of a minimally adequate education all but forecloses the exercise of other core rights of citizenship: speech and voting.

Putting the logical and empirical merits of the foregoing arguments aside, they face a steep uphill battle because they rest in substantive due process theory. Substantive due process is much maligned both in and out of the Court. An effort to avoid pure substantive due process likely explains why the Court's evolving LGBTQ jurisprudence has been characterized as resting on a hybrid theory of equal protection and due process. While cases such as *Lawrence* and *Obergefell* seemed like perfect cases by which to extend prior substantive due process theories, the Court carefully refrained from offering full-throated substantive due process holdings in those cases. Interestingly, compelling arguments exist for education to similarly follow a hybrid path.[88] After all, *Plyler* seemingly rests on some unarticulated hybrid theory: the Court indicated that undocumented youth are not a suspect class and education is not a fundamental right, and the intersection of these two factors motivated the Court to engage in a more searching scrutiny of the disadvantage.[89]

The most promising path, if possible, is to avoid the general resistance to substantive due process or the ambiguity and complexity of hybrid theories. As Friedman and Solow emphasize, originalism is inherently alluring and instinctual to judges. It cuts through "endless theoretical debates about how the Constitution should be interpreted," as well as "'conservative' and 'liberal' ideologies."[90] While the foregoing debates rage, judges simply interpret the Constitution.

> [T]he way in which judges interpret constitutional and statutory text has not changed notably over history [and remains] dominant today. It involves—are you ready?—examining the constitutional text, the intentions of those who wrote and ratified the document as well as common understandings at the time, social and legislative practices both before and after ratification, constitutional structure, governing precedents, and paying some attention to consequences and ethics. The process is evolutionary—slowly and conservatively evolutionary, as properly fits interpretation of a foundational document—but evolutionary nonetheless. And this method of interpretation is evident in countless familiar and seminal opinions of judges from the right and left alike. There is much on which they differ. But the mechanics by which they interpret the Constitution often displays a stunning similarity.[91]

The Court's most recent recognition of a new fundamental right confirms this sentiment in the judiciary. In *McDonald v. Chicago*,[92] the issue before the Court was whether the right to bear arms was a fundamental right of liberty and protected under due process. In other words, the Court framed *McDonald* as a substantive due process case. While the Court's holding in favor of the fundamental right was deeply divided, the most striking aspect of the case was that both the majority and dissent took up the mantel of originalism. The majority argued that the original meaning of the phrase "right to bear arms" included an individual right, and the dissent argued it referred to the militia and only certain types of "arms."[93]

Originalism could play a similarly central role in education and, ultimately, tip the scales in favor of a positive result. Three of the most compelling articles of the past decade have all been grounded in some form of originalism. First, Friedman and Solow argue, in short, that the Constitution protects education as a fundamental right because education has been treated with the utmost importance by states and the federal government since the enactment of the Fourteenth Amendment. Second, Liu relies on much of that same history but also adds a more detailed examination of congressional actions immediately following the Fourteenth Amendment. On the basis of that history, he argues that the framers' original intent was for education to be a privilege and immunity of federal citizenship. Most recently, I focus on the precise events leading to the ratification of the Fourteenth Amendment. Those events reveal that the ratification of the Fourteenth Amendment was part of an overall compromise that required states to provide education. As such, education became an original right of state citizenship. To this scholarly trend, one should also add the new litigation in Mississippi that argues that Congress, in the exercise of its constitutional authority, guaranteed a republican form of government in newly admitted states to the Union and imposed education as an explicit requirement in those states in which Congress feared the states would backtrack on education.

As an author of one of these originalist theories, my bias renders me unfit to evaluate the comparative merits of the originalist theories here.[94] And for the purposes of this chapter, that comparative analysis is not important because the most striking aspect of these theories is how mutually reinforcing these three independent articles are. The same is true of the Mississippi lawsuit that followed them. All of the theories put forth a core set of facts that are largely beyond dispute. These facts establish a compelling originalism account of education. In the years leading up to and following the enactment of the Fourteenth Amendment, those who wrote, enacted, ratified, and enforced the Amendment—Congress and the states—placed an unmistakable emphasis on the governmental provision of public education. They sought to protect education, to fund education, and to enshrine it through constitutional protections. And as I point out, this collective effort was never in any serious dispute. Rather, it was one of the few issues on which all could easily agree.

The Court could deploy this history through a number of different constitutional doctrines, but the result of all should be that education does warrant federal constitutional protection. An originalist approach, regardless of the doctrinal vehicle, largely relieves the Court of developing rationales that others could more easily label as activist. By heavily relying on history, the Court need not reinterpret doctrine or rely on modern valuations of education or amorphous inquiries of liberty. It need only focus on the facts as they were in the second half of the nineteenth century.

Conclusion

In late 2015 and early 2016, the possibility that the Court might seriously entertain the recognition of some right to education seemed plausible. This sentiment surely played some role in the filing of three new cases in a short time period, particularly when a long fallow period had preceded it. But with Justice Neil Gorsuch taking his seat on the Court, some people might now assume that those chances of winning have dimmed significantly. The ascension of someone such as Goodwin Liu to the Court would have heavily tilted the issue in the other direction. While the possibilities of a Justice Liu or a Justice Merrick Garland feel like distant memories, the possibility of the recognition of a right to education does not.

Maybe I am too naïve, but I resist viewing the Court in the coarse terms of its composition alone. The Court's composition plays an important role, but so too does constitutional text, history, and zeitgeist. Would anyone have predicted the Court's LGBTQ jurisprudence a few years before *Lawrence v. Texas*? Would anyone have predicted the Court would consistently strike down Congress's and the Bush administration's approach to the imprisonment and detainment of "enemy combatants" during the "War on Terror"?[95] Both lines of cases were monumental—the first as progress and the second as bulwark.

History is on the side of education, and originalism is embedded in the Court's thinking about rights. While a prediction that the Court will recognize a right to education in one of the cases pending in the federal courts assumes too much, conceding that the Court will not find an appropriate vehicle to recognize a right to education in the coming years assumes too little. So I remain cautiously optimistic.

NOTES

1. *See, e.g.*, Brown v. Bd. of Educ., 347 U.S. 483 (1954).
2. *See, e.g.*, Plyler v. Doe, 457 U.S. 202, 223 (1982); Ambach v. Norwick, 441 U.S. 68, 76–78 (1979); Wisconsin v. Yoder, 406 U.S. 205, 221 (1972); *Brown*, 347 U.S. at 493.
3. Kadrmas v. Dickinson Pub. Schs., 487 U.S. 450, 466 n.1 (1988) (Marshall J., dissenting) (reasoning that the Court left open the possibility of a "a minimally adequate education"); Papasan v. Allain, 478 U.S. 265, 285 (1986) (emphasizing that *Rodriguez* left open whether a minimally adequate education is a fundamental right).

4. *See, e.g.,* US CONST. amend. XV (prohibiting race discrimination in voting); US CONST. amend. XIX (prohibiting gender discrimination in voting); US CONST. amend. XXIV (prohibiting poll taxes); US CONST. amend. XXVI (reducing the voting age to eighteen); Kramer v. Union Free Sch. Dist. No. 15, 395 U.S. 621 (1969).

5. Reynolds v. Simms, 377 U.S. 533, 561–62 (1964).

6. San Antonio Indep. Sch. Dist. v. Rodriguez, 411 U.S. 1, 34–37 (1973).

7. *Id.*

8. *Id.* at 35–36.

9. *See, e.g.,* Erwin Chemerinsky, *The Deconstitutionalization of Education*, 36 LOY. U. CHI. L.J. 111, 123 (2004); Gregory F. Corbett, Note, *Special Education, Equal Protection and Education Finance: Does the Individuals with Disabilities Education Act Violate a General Education Student's Fundamental Right to Education?*, 40 B.C. L. REV. 633, 668–71 (1999); Stephen E. Gottlieb, *Communities in the Balance: Comments on Koch*, 37 HOUS. L. REV. 711, 718 (2000); Timothy D. Lynch, Note, *Education as a Fundamental Right: Challenging the Supreme Court's Jurisprudence*, 26 HOFSTRA L. REV. 953, 956 (1998).

10. *See, e.g.,* Lynch, *supra* note 9, at 995; Ian Millhiser, Note, *What Happens to a Dream Deferred? Cleansing the Taint of* San Antonio Independent School District v. Rodriguez, 55 DUKE L.J. 405, 431 (2005).

11. *See* Michael A. Rebell, *Poverty, "Meaningful" Educational Opportunity, and the Necessary Role of the Courts*, 85 N.C. L. REV. 1467, 1500–05 (2006) (discussing the results in state cases and the substantive meaning of the constitutional right to education in those cases); *see, e.g.,* Dupree v. Alma Sch. Dist. No. 30, 651 S.W.2d 90, 93 (Ark. 1983); Horton v. Meskill, 376 A.2d 359, 373 (Conn. 1977); Seattle Sch. Dist. No. 1 v. State, 585 P.2d 71, 71 (Wash. 1978); Washakie Cty. Sch. Dist. No. 1 v. Herschler, 606 P.2d 310, 333 (Wyo. 1980).

12. *See, e.g.,* N.C. GEN. STAT. § 115C-81 (2009); VA. CODE ANN. § 22.1-253.13:1 (2006); *see also* Martha I. Morgan, Adam S. Cohen & Helen Hershkoff, *Establishing Education Program Inadequacy: The Alabama Example*, 28 U. MICH. J.L. REFORM 559, 568–71 (1995) (discussing Alabama's legislative and administrative structure for education).

13. *See* Derek Black, *Unlocking the Power of State Constitutions with Equal Protection: The First Step towards Education as a Federally Protected Right*, 51 WM. & MARY L. REV. 1343, 1402–05 (2010) (discussing state legislatures providing a larger portion of education funds).

14. Serrano v. Priest, 487 P.2d 1241 (1971).

15. *See generally* INST. FOR EDUC. EQUITY & OPPORTUNITY, EDUCATION IN THE 50 STATES: A DESKBOOK OF THE HISTORY OF STATE CONSTITUTIONS AND LAWS ABOUT EDUCATION 36 (2009) ("[T]he country correspondingly expanded the right to education [to freedmen] to assure the ability of these new citizens to participate in a democratic society.").

16. *Overview of Litigation*, SCHOOLFUNDING.INFO, http://schoolfunding.info (last visited Dec. 6, 2017); Rebell, *supra* note 11, at 1500–05 (discussing the results in

state cases and the substantive meaning of the constitutional right to education in those cases); SCHOOLFUNDING.INFO, http://schoolfunding.info (last visited Dec. 6, 2017).

17. Rebell, *supra* note 11, at 1500–05.

18. *See, e.g.,* Black, *supra* note 13, at 1393–95.

19. Martha I. Morgan, *Fundamental State Rights: A New Basis for Strict Scrutiny in Federal Equal Protection Review*, 17 GA. L. REV. 77, 101 (1982).

20. Black, *supra* note 13, at 1393–95; Morgan, *supra* note 19, at 101.

21. *See, e.g.,* Black, *supra* note 13, at 1393–95; Gershon M. Ratner, *A New Legal Duty for Urban Public Schools: Effective Education in Basic Skills*, 63 TEX. L. REV. 777 (1985).

22. Morgan, *supra* note 19, at 77–78 (arguing that when a state recognizes a fundamental right, strict scrutiny should apply to federal constitutional analysis of inequities in regard to that state's rights).

23. Washington v. Glucksberg, 521 U.S. 702 (1997).

24. *Id.* at 720–21.

25. Susan H. Bitensky, *Theoretical Foundations for a Right to Education under the U.S. Constitution: A Beginning to the End of the National Education Crisis*, 86 NW. U. L. REV. 550, 586 (1992).

26. *Id.* at 588–89.

27. *Id.* at 585 (paraphrasing Michael H. v. Gerald D., 491 U.S. 110, 124 (1989)).

28. *See, e.g.,* Barry Friedman & Sara Solow, *The Federal Right to an Adequate Education*, 81 GEO. WASH. L. REV. 92 (2013).

29. Friedman & Solow, *supra* note 28.

30. *Id.* at 96.

31. *Id.* at 112–17, 121–45.

32. *Id.* at 155.

33. Matthew A. Brunell, Note, *What* Lawrence *Brought for "Show and Tell": The Non-Fundamental Liberty Interest in a Minimally Adequate Education*, 25 B.C. THIRD WORLD L.J. 343, 345–46 (2005) ("*Lawrence* represents a sea change in the Court's substantive due process analysis, and as a result, decisions such as . . . *Rodriguez* are no longer on firm footing"); Areto A. Imoukhuede, *Education Rights and the New Due Process*, 47 IND. L. REV. 467, 468 (2014) ("Ironically, *Lawrence*, which is a negative-rights and liberty-based holding, can serve as the template for recognizing the positive right of access to public education"); *see also* Note, *A Right to Learn? Improving Educational Outcomes through Substantive Due Process*, 120 HARV. L. REV. 1323, 1327 (2007) ("although substantive due process rests on a shaky foundation, recent Supreme Court decisions not only have reaffirmed its legitimacy, but also might have expanded its scope" (footnotes omitted)); Joshua E. Weishart, *Reconstituting the Right to Education*, 67 ALA. L. REV. 915, 978 (2016).

34. Obergefell v. Hodges, 135 S. Ct. 2584, 2598 (2015).

35. *See, e.g.,* Imoukhuede, *supra* note 33, at 468; Note, *A Right to Learn?, supra* note 33, at 1339.

36. Imoukhuede, *supra* note 33, at 468.
37. *Id.*
38. *Obergefell*, 135 S. Ct. at 2600.
39. Complaint at 53–54, Martinez v. Malloy, No. 3:16-cv-01439 (D. Conn. Filed Aug. 23, 2016) [hereinafter Martinez Complaint] (quoting *Obergefell*, 135 S. Ct. at 2599), https://www.scribd.com.
40. Brown v. Bd. of Educ., 347 U.S. 483, 493 (1954).
41. Friedman & Solow, *supra* note 28.
42. Ratner, *supra* note 21, at 823.
43. Note, *A Right to Learn?*, *supra* note 33, at 1327.
44. *See, e.g.*, Revere v. Mass. Gen. Hosp., 463 U.S. 239, 244 (1983); Youngberg v. Romero, 457 U.S. 307 (1982); Estelle v. Gamble, 429 U.S. 97 (1976).
45. Youngberg v. Romero, 457 U.S. 307 (1982).
46. *Id.* at 319.
47. *Id.*
48. *Id.* at 322–23.
49. Note, *A Right to Learn?*, *supra* note 33, at 1337.
50. *Id.* at 1338–39.
51. *See, e.g.*, Complaint at 1, Gary B. v. Snyder, No. 16-CV-13292, 2016 WL 4775474 (E.D. Mich. Sept. 13, 2016) [hereinafter Gary B. Complaint]; Ratner, *supra* note 21, at 824; Note, *A Right to Learn?*, *supra* note 33, at 1324–25.
52. Gary B. Complaint, *supra* note 51, at 1.
53. *Id.*
54. *Id.* at 16–17.
55. *Id.* ("[T]hey are not citizens invited to participate on equal terms in the economic, civic, and political life of our nation.").
56. *Id.* at 1, 27–28; Martinez Complaint, *supra* note 39, at 13. They are aided in this argument by the fact that the state is also obligated by its own constitution to deliver an education. CONN. CONST. art. VIII, § 1; MICH. CONST. art. VIII, § 2; *see also* Horton v. Meskill, 376 A.2d 359, 375 (Conn. 1977) (holding that Connecticut's school finance system violated the state's equal protection clause).
57. Gary B. Complaint, *supra* note 51, at 57–60.
58. *Id.* at 1–3.
59. Nancy C. Marcus, *Deeply Rooted Principles of Equal Liberty, Not "Argle Bargle": The Inevitability of Marriage Equality after* Windsor, 23 TUL. J.L. & SEXUALITY 17, 18–19 (2014); Aaron J. Shuler, *From Immutable to Existential: Protecting Who We Are and Who We Want to Be with the "Equalerty" of the Substantive Due Process Clause*, 12 J.L. & SOC. CHALLENGES 220, 316–17 (2010); Weishart, *supra* note 33, at 978. *See also* Obergefell v. Hodges, 135 S. Ct. 2584, 2604 (2015) ("[T]he Equal Protection Clause can help to identify and correct inequalities in the institution of marriage, vindicating precepts of liberty and equality under the Constitution.").
60. Weishart, *supra* note 33, at 972–77.

61. *Id.* at 976–77.

62. Goodwin Liu, *Education, Equality, and National Citizenship*, 116 YALE L.J. 330, 392–99 (2006).

63. *Id.* at 335.

64. *See, e.g.,* The Slaughter-House Cases, 83 U.S. (16 Wall.) 36 (1872).

65. Liu, *supra* note 62, at 335.

66. *Id.*

67. The Civil Rights Cases, 109 U.S. 3, 26 (1883) (Harlan, J., dissenting); Liu, *supra* note 62, at 335.

68. *See* Saenz v. Roe, 526 U.S. 489, 527–28 (1999) (Thomas, J. dissenting) (indicating a willingness to reevaluate the meaning of the Privileges and Immunities Clause); Clarence Thomas, *The Higher Law Background of the Privileges or Immunities Clause of the Fourteenth Amendment*, 12 HARV. J.L. & PUB. POL'Y 63, 68 (1989) (positing the idea of overruling the *Slaughter-House Cases*).

69. Derek W. Black, *The Constitutional Compromise to Guarantee Education*, 70 STAN. L. REV. 735, 741 (2018).

70. ERIC FONER, RECONSTRUCTION: AMERICA'S UNFINISHED REVOLUTION, 1863–1877, at 260–61 (1988).

71. Reconstruction Act of 1867, ch. 153, 14 Stat. 428–430.

72. *Id.*

73. U.S. CONST. art. IV, § 4; Reconstruction Act of 1867, *supra* note 71 (requiring a republican form of government).

74. Reconstruction Act of 1867, *supra* note 71; *see also* Steven G. Calabresi & Michael W. Perl, *Originalism and* Brown v. Board of Education, 2014 MICH. ST. L. REV. 429, 461 (2014) (noting that the new education clauses "undoubtedly reflect[] the pressure brought to bear on those states by the Reconstruction Congress, which imposed stern conditions.").

75. *See, e.g.,* CONG. GLOBE, 40th Cong., 1st Sess. 168 (Mar. 16, 1867) (remarks of Sen. Cole and Sen. Sumner indicating that Congress retained the right to withhold admission to states whose constitutions lacked an education clause).

76. *See, e.g.,* An Act to admit the State of Texas to Representation in the Congress of the United States, ch. 39, 16 Stat. 80, 81 (1870); An Act to admit the State of Mississippi to Representation in the Congress of the United States, ch. 19, 16 Stat. 67, 68 (1870); An Act to admit the State of Virginia to Representation in the Congress of the United States, ch. 10, 16 Stat. 62, 63 (1870). *See also* Eric Biber, *The Price of Admission: Causes, Effects, and Patterns of Conditions Imposed on States Entering the Union*, 46 AM. J. LEGAL HIST. 119, 143–44 (2004). Interestingly, new and existing states also began including affirmative education mandates in their constitutions as well, creating a new national norm. JOHN MATHIASON MATZEN, STATE CONSTITUTIONAL PROVISIONS FOR EDUCATION: FUNDAMENTAL ATTITUDE OF THE AMERICAN PEOPLE REGARDING EDUCATION AS REVEALED BY STATE CONSTITUTIONAL PROVISIONS, 1776–1929, at 140–51 (1931).

77. Calabresi & Perl, *supra* note 74, at 442.
78. U.S. CONST. art. 4, § 4.
79. *See id.*; Black, *supra* note 69, at 781.
80. City of Rome v. United States, 446 U.S. 156, 182 n. 17 (1980) (challenging the preclearance requirements of the Voting Rights Act); Baker v. Carr, 369 U.S. 186, 218–29 (1962) (challenging apportionment of state legislative districts); Pac. States Tel. & Tel. Co. v. Oregon, 223 U.S. 118, 140–51 (1912) (challenging initiative and referendum provisions of state constitution).
81. Emma Brown, *Black Parents Use Civil War–Era Law to Challenge Mississippi's "Inequitable" Schools*, WASH. POST, May 23, 2017, https://www.washingtonpost.com.
82. An Act to Admit the State of Mississippi to Representation in the Congress of the United States, ch. 19, 16 Stat. 67, 68 (1870).
83. Washington v. Glucksberg, 521 U.S. 702, 721–22 (1997) (responding to the problem of subjectivity in fundamental rights analysis).
84. *Id.*
85. Romer v. Evans, 517 U.S. 620, 634–35 (1996).
86. *See generally* Rebell, *supra* note 11.
87. Gary B. Complaint, *supra* note 51, at 1–3; Martinez Complaint, *supra* note 39, at 2–3.
88. Weishart, *supra* note 33, at 972–77.
89. Robert C. Farrell, *Successful Rational Basis Claims in the Supreme Court from the 1971 Term through* Romer v. Evans, 32 IND. L. REV. 357, 382 (1999) (examining the Court's hybrid analysis in *Plyler*).
90. Friedman & Solow, *supra* note 28, at 95.
91. *Id.* at 95–96.
92. 561 U.S. 742 (2010).
93. *Id.* at 770–78.
94. My article, however, does offer its critique of the others. Black, *supra* note 69, at 755–65.
95. *See, e.g.*, Boumediene v. Bush, 553 U.S. 723, 732–33 (2008); Hamdi v. Rumsfeld, 542 U.S. 507, 509 (2004).

6

Education for Sovereign People

PEGGY COOPER DAVIS

Introduction

Although the overwhelming majority of constitutional democracies give the right to education explicit constitutional status, the Supreme Court of the United States has only tiptoed toward declaring the right to education "fundamental"[1] and therefore entitled in United States constitutional terms to scrupulous protection. In 1954, in its historic *Brown v. Board of Education* school desegregation case, the Court said that education had become "perhaps the most important function of state and local governments." It noted then that education is compulsory, is "required in the performance of our most basic public responsibilities," and is "the very foundation of good citizenship."[2] In 1973, the Court repeated and embraced its 1954 language about the importance of education but declined by a vote of five to four to declare the right to education "fundamental."[3] Having determined that the Texas school funding scheme at issue in the 1973 case did not require the rigorous testing that constriction of a fundamental right demands, the Court saw no constitutional violation in substantial interdistrict funding disparities. It approved the scheme despite its admittedly negative effects on educational opportunities in low-income communities. In 1982, the Court again considered education policy in Texas, this time in a case that challenged the complete denial of public education to undocumented children. In that context, a majority of the justices did find a constitutional violation.[4] The denial was absolute rather than relative, and five justices were willing to give careful—although not "strict"—scrutiny to its justifications. Since these decisions, the right to education has remained in the Neverland of important but less-than-fundamental rights.

Some justices hesitate to declare the right to education fundamental out of concern that federal protection of a right to education would wrongfully usurp state authority in the field. Moreover, self-proclaimed "textualists" hesitate to declare the right to education fundamental because it is not explicitly mentioned in the United States Constitution. But the Court has been less hesitant with respect to other internationally recognized human rights. It has declared rights of privacy, bodily integrity, marriage recognition, procreation choice, family integrity, and choice in the socialization of one's children fundamental despite the fact that they are importantly regulated at the state level and unmentioned in the Constitution's text. Moreover, the Court has established tests for determining when an unenumerated right is nonetheless fundamental, declaring that the right must be either implicit in the articulation of enumerated rights or consistent with the nation's history and traditions and essential to a balance between order and liberty that permits people to be self-actualizing sovereigns rather than dominated subjects.[5]

As the Supreme Court has tiptoed toward declaring the right to education fundamental, it has told brief and partial stories of the history of education in the United States. The argument of this chapter is that a more inclusive reading of the history of education in the United States establishes that a right to be educated is a prerequisite for the exercise of rights that are enumerated in our Constitution, deeply embedded in our history and traditions, and necessary to achieve the human sovereignty to which those traditions commit us.

We must first consider the Court's stories of education and why a more inclusive reading is needed. In *Brown v. Board of Education*, the 1954 case addressing the constitutionality of official school segregation, the Court considered the post–Civil War status of education in the United States in order to explain why the views of the Fourteenth Amendment's framers were uninformative with respect to their intentions concerning school segregation. The Court noted that in the South education for white children was largely private. It ignored the dearth of educational opportunity for poor white children. It noted that education for blacks was "almost nonexistent" and "forbidden in some states" and that "practically all of the race were illiterate." It observed that education systems in the North were somewhat more advanced but still undeveloped. In light of all of this, the Court found it unsurprising "that there should be so little in the history of the Fourteenth Amendment relating to its intended effect on public education."[6] Against this partial and somewhat misleading account, the Court held, as a matter of equal protection, that where a state "has undertaken to provide" educational opportunities, those opportunities "must be made available to all on equal terms."[7] It did not address the question whether educational opportunities must be provided. Indeed, some officials in Virginia took the Court at its narrow words and shut down local school systems rather than desegregate them.[8]

In 1973, when the Court looked at the educational disadvantages that low-income minority Texas students suffered, it gave a decidedly sympathetic account of the history of education in Texas, noting that the first Texas state constitution had provided for public education and crediting the state for repeated, albeit only moderately successful, efforts to minimize funding disparities across wealthy and impoverished school districts. The justices made no mention of the state's long history of racially exclusive or racially segregated publicly funded schooling or of Texas's slaveholding traditions that forbade black literacy. In the 1982 Texas case, the history of education was not referenced at all.

In the pages that follow, I offer an alternative history of education in the United States to round out—and to some extent correct—the stories that have thus far framed the Supreme Court's deliberations about the status that education holds in our society. This alternative story serves as a foundation for constitutional recognition of the fundamental character of every child's right to a quantum of education sufficient for self-realization and meaningful political participation, for it shows that such recognition is necessary to the exercise of other enumerated rights, consistent with the nation's history and traditions and essential to ordered liberty, understood as the freedom to be responsibly self-actualizing.

The first section describes the criminalization and private punishment of literacy in order to support slavery and other forms of enforced subservience in the colonial and pre–Civil War eras. The second section recounts a neglected history of slave rebellion against literacy bans and freed peoples' embrace of education as a foundation of newfound citizenship. The third section describes national congressional initiatives and those of southern state and local governments in the golden years of congressional Reconstruction to provide universal public education sufficient to support republican government by and for a free people.[9]

The fourth section explains how this history supports an argument for recognition of a fundamental right to education.

Education and the Construction of a Servant Caste

Group-based restrictions on educational opportunity perpetuate group subordination by assuring that lower-caste children's capacities are nurtured no more than those of their parents. Lower-caste children therefore remain locked in a lower social and economic status. Our nation has a history of caste-enforcing education restrictions that intersects in important ways with its history of racial subordination. When what have become the United States were colonies, unpaid menial labor was commonly obtained through term-limited indentured servitude. Both black and white indentured servants could envision upward mobility, at least in theory. The terms of their service were a matter of contract, and some were entitled to a modicum of education and/or to training in a trade. As tobacco and cotton farming grew into large and profitable enterprises, the demand for unpaid labor grew, and the serviceability of a free and upwardly mobile laboring class waned. Racialized chattel slavery satisfied the expanded demand for unpaid labor.[10] It was justified by a belief system according to which Christian Anglo-Americans were manifestly destined for dominance and others were inherently inferior and divinely designed to serve. Black unpaid laborers lost rights to education as well as the right to freedom after a period of service.

The racialization of servitude and the perpetuation of a supremacist belief system facilitated entrenchment and life-limiting treatment of a servant caste. This was conspicuous in the construction of laws and practices around education: Whereas some education of indentured servants had been a potential obligation of the indenturer,[11] the education of black slaves was brutally restricted.[12] Reading, writing, and instruction were variously criminalized and were unofficially punished by "masters," overseers, and supremacist white citizens.[13] Whether the proscriptions were formal or informal, sanctions were regularly imposed and universally feared.

Reported examples abound. An enslaved man who was blinded as punishment for attempting to learn to read insisted that his story be told to children to inspire them to pursue education.[14] A child named

Douglass Dorsey proudly displayed his ability to read and write when his "mistress" commanded him to do so. For this he was dealt a heavy blow across the face and told that if he was again caught reading or writing his arm would be cut off.[15] Albert Brookings was whipped to death for "spoiling good niggers" by teaching them to read.[16] James Lucas reported that his owner "hung the best slave he had" for teaching others to spell.[17] Enoch Golden said on his dying bed that he "had been the death of many a nigger 'cause he taught so many to read and write."[18] The most common punishment for learning was public amputation of fingers.[19]

Education as Rebellion

Learning and teaching reading and writing were among the most impactful acts of resistance to slavery. Literacy yielded access to congenial thoughts about human rights, knowledge of the physical and political world outside slave quarters, and a means of communication within and beyond an owner's domain. It also provided immediate practical benefits, such as the ability to forge documents to exploit the travel-pass system that slaveholders maintained to keep the enslaved within narrow physical spaces. Appreciating this, enslaved people seized education, secretly by firelight after long hours of work and more boldly in unauthorized schools existing against all odds as early as 1819.[20]

It is difficult to know how many enslaved people in the United States became literate despite legal restrictions and terrorist deterrence. It has been estimated that in the face of painful and disabling punishment, at least 5 percent of people held in slavery before the Civil War had learned to read.[21] Several factors suggest that this estimate is conservative.[22] Self and group preservation required that enslaved people keep secret their ability to read or write and to conceal their transmission of reading and writing materials or of literacy skills to other enslaved people. There were slaveholders who found it useful to have slaves who could read and cipher. Other slaveholders thought, or were encouraged by missionaries to think, that they had a moral duty to enable those whom they enslaved to earn salvation by reading the Christian Bible. But slaveholders who facilitated slave literacy were subject to ostracism and to formal and informal sanctions. As a result, they were also prone to keep their efforts and successes secret.

Despite the difficulty of knowing how many African Americans were literate before or just after the Civil War, we now know with certainty that enslaved people took consistent and dangerous actions in pursuit of literacy and the freedom it brought. The leading qualitative account of enslaved people's dangerous quests for literacy is that of the lawyer and historian Heather Williams. In *Self-Taught*, she reports the findings of her necessarily painstaking research to uncover the stories of how people without schools, writing utensils, or written communication gained literacy.

Williams's work is exceptional for bringing to the study of slave literacy a welcome attention to the determined agency of enslaved people. Her powerful accounts go beyond isolated anecdotes to piece together relatively full accounts of enslaved people's multilayered liberation strategies. Her account of Mattie Jackson's liberation struggles begins when Jackson watches as a child as her father and stepfather escape to freedom, each to avoid being sold away from his family. Lacking the off-plantation access that enslaved men could more easily acquire, Jackson and her mother used eavesdropping and a secretly acquired literacy to learn of the outbreak of civil war and the approach of Union troops. This learning emboldened them to take actions to, in Williams's words, "disturb the power relation between master and slave."[23] Threatened with a flogging, Jackson fashioned the flogging switch into the first letter of her name and walked off the plantation. Together with her mother, she engaged in physical combat with their male master (a man whom mother and daughter together seemed fully able to subdue).[24] This correlation between literacy and the capacity to assert power is beautifully confirmed by the historian Shaun Wallace's more recent quantitative study of literacy and fugitivity.[25]

Thomas Weber's work in education history resonates with Williams's work in that it defines education broadly to encompass enslaved people's development of a culture of resistance against white supremacy. Describing self-education as a part of that process, Weber emphasizes examples of black agency in accounts that are more fragmented than Williams's but also powerful. He tells of W. E. Northcross, who went without food in a mountain hideaway, learning to read from the "Blue Back Speller,"[26] the then-ubiquitous primer that Noah Webster created just after the American Revolution to document and celebrate an Americanized conception of the English language. Weber also tells of Thomas Jones, who refused through a severe beating to reveal the hiding place for a precious book;[27] of Austin Steward, who after being flogged for reading "determined to learn to read and write, at all hazards, if [his] life was only spared";[28] and, of Frederick Douglass's well-known depiction of how his "master's" fierce declaration that knowledge would make him unfit to be a slave showed Douglass the path to freedom.[29]

Mattie Jackson's stolen knowledge of the outbreak of civil war led her to escape twice to Union lines, once to be turned away and once to be taken in but then returned to her "master" when he came to claim her. She was, then, part of what W. E. B. Du Bois rightly called a massive labor strike against slavery, attempting to join a tidal wave of African Americans who left bondage to join the Union cause. These people became known as "contrabands" when Union generals began to claim them as confiscated property of the enemy. They are more appropriately thought of as freedom fighters. More than 179,000 of them were in time officially recognized as soldiers in the Union army. In addition, at least 18,000 black men and eleven black women served in the Union navy,[30] and countless more served unofficially as nurses, scouts, blacksmiths, and laborers of every kind. These men and women were not only crucial to Union victory but also central to the African American literacy campaign.

Heather Williams's work is again instructive, for she documents in unusual detail the immediate efforts of Union volunteer forces to educate one another for free citizenship. She tells of Susie King Taylor, who fled bondage at age seventeen and served as adjunct to the First South Carolina Volunteers, 35th Regiment of the Union army. In addition to working as a laundress and nurse for the soldiers, Taylor, who had learned to read through secret perseverance, held classes for the freedom fighters' children and taught the adults who squeezed literacy training into whatever free time they had.[31] Histories of black Civil War freedom fighters' camps recount not only the destitute conditions in which people survived (and in which many perished from exposure and disease) but also an upsurge of learning. The intensity of Union freedom fighters' determination to learn is perhaps best illustrated by reports that on the wards of hospitals for Union wounded, black patients were teaching one another to read.[32]

The efforts of liberated people to educate themselves for free citizenship extended beyond freedom fighters' camps. A contemporaneous survey of freedpeople in liberated territory reported that there were, for example, in a Union-liberated area of Arkansas: a school of forty or fifty students taught by "Rose Anna, a colored girl"; a school of eighty-nine students taught by "Uncle Jack, a colored man"; a school of thirty-nine taught by "Uncle Tom, a colored man" who was so infirm that he taught from his bed; and, a school of sixty students taught by "Wm. Mc-Cutchen, a colored man."[33]

After the war's end, freedpeople intensified their quest for education as a prerequisite to free civic participation. Events on the Sea Islands of South Carolina exemplify this process. With the arrival of Union troops, lands were abandoned by plantation owners, and Union army personnel made direct promises of land grants. Freedpeople flocked to the abandoned plantations with reason to hope for property ownership and other privileges of civic status. Under the direction of the Union army, freedpeople tilled abandoned fields; under its protection, freedpeople began to construct homes and, as an immediate priority, to organize schools. The Freedmen's Bureau, the army, and black and white volunteers from the North joined forces to create and staff a system of education. Those who taught in the new schools were explicitly mindful of the schools' role in supporting free citizenship, and some were also mindful of a corollary need to promote an antisupremacist or anticaste thought. Charlotte Forten, perhaps the best known of thousands of black volunteer teachers from the North,[34] described leading her students in singing "the 'John Brown' song" and telling them about Toussaint-Louverture, "thinking it well they should know what one of their own color had done for his race."[35]

The idea of schooling for free citizenship and antisupremacist activism lived in the Sea Islands to inspire the Freedom Schools that were foundational to the mid-twentieth-century civil rights movement, often aptly referred to as the Second Reconstruction. The educator-activists Septima Clark and Esau Jenkins built on the post–Civil War Sea Islands legacy in the mid-nineteenth century to create Citizenship Schools that prepared opponents of Jim Crow and voter suppression for voter registration and community activism. These schools became models for labor and desegregation movements in the Second Reconstruction of the 1960s.[36]

We will see in the next section that multiracial Reconstruction governments formed after the Civil War's end attempted immediately to establish universal public schooling. But freedpeople did not await this development. Black American citizens continued without government assistance to build schools throughout the South, taxing themselves to maintain those schools and rebuilding them when, as often happened, they were burned by Confederate diehards.

Education as a Linchpin of the United States' Reconstructed Democracy

As federal legislators explored the needs of a post–Civil War United States, there were those who recognized forthrightly that a national entitlement to education was implicit in the country's expanded definition of citizenship. Statements to this effect are scattered throughout congressional debates in the postwar period. Speaking between the end of hostilities and the passage of the Fifteenth Amendment, Senator Timothy Howe observed, "the struggle to emancipate the nation is just ended. The struggle to enfranchise the nation is almost ended. The struggle to educate the nation is just commencing."[37] The need for federal commitment to education was elaborated by Representative Ignatius Donnelly as he argued for extension of the Freedmen's Bureau's education initiatives. He began by saying that Reconstruction was rightly understood as "the birth of a new nation." In this reconstructed nation, he argued, the Constitution would be "read by the light of the rebellion [and] by the light of the emancipation." Reading the reconstructed Constitution in this way, Donnelly argued that "the freedom of the people must rest on the intelligence of the people": "The one great error of our country has been that education was not from the very first made a matter of the State, and as essential to the citizen as liberty itself. Education means the intelligent exercise of liberty, and surely without this liberty is a calamity, since it means simply the unlimited right to err. . . . Suffrage without education is an edged tool in the hands of a child—dangerous to others and destructive to himself."[38] Senator Charles Sumner put it this way: "We are to have universal suffrage, a natural consequence of universal emancipation, but that I fear will almost be a barren scepter in the hands of the people unless we give them also education."[39]

The neglected achievements of post–Civil War multiracial governments in states reconstituted from the former Confederacy speak even more explicitly to the necessity for universal educational opportunity in a free democracy. Here again, South Carolina serves as an example. Before the Civil War, South Carolina had done little to educate the white poor and nothing to educate blacks. The 1811 Act to Establish Free Schools led to meager efforts that were distorted by corruption and a system that was pronounced a failure in 1855.[40] The years leading to the Civil War brought no progress.

After the war, Congress required, as one of the conditions of former Confederate states' readmission to the Union, that new state constitutions be drafted by conventions whose delegates were chosen in elections open to both black and white voters. In part as a result of a boycott by white Democrats, 95 percent of the voters who elected delegates to South Carolina's 1868 convention were black men. A majority of the convention delegates were black—fifteen recruited from northern states and sixty-five from South Carolina. At a time when most southerners had no formal education, fourteen of the black delegates had common school educations; five were graduates of normal schools, and ten had graduated from college or a professional school. Most were literate.[41] White delegates were also a mix of southerners, most of whom had been Union sympathizers, and northern Republican recruits, most of whom had been antislavery advocates.[42]

This convention was viciously derided by the Confederate press. Two examples suffice. One publication referred to the convention as a whole as the "Carolina Gorillas" and wrote that Robert DeLarge, a black delegate who later served in the House of Representatives, "might have lived and died without having his name in print . . . if it had not been for the great social revolution which like boiling water has thrown scum on the surface."[43] The same publication described a white delegate as a man who "could easily be mistaken at a short distance for a cross between a grizzly and a hyena."[44]

One of the first orders of business for this much-derided South Carolina convention was to continue the long-standing antislavery quest for literacy and free citizenship by mandating the creation of a system of free public education.[45] The South Carolina body's reasoning is instructive: "[T]he general and universal diffusion of education and intelligence among the people is the surest guarantee of the enhancement, increase, purity and preservation of the great principles of republican liberty;

therefore, it shall be the duty of the General Assemblies, in all future periods of this Commonwealth, to establish, provide for, and perpetuate a liberal system of free public schools."[46] A state Department of Education was to be created to establish and maintain a system of elementary schools open to children regardless of race. The state was also required to create a normal school for teachers as well as a university and an agricultural college. State schools, colleges, and universities were to be free, funded by property taxes, an education poll tax, and wealth conferred as a result of federal land grants. School attendance was to be compulsory until the age of sixteen. The white Republican J. K. Jillson, who was to become South Carolina's first superintendent of education, was one of many who spoke to the essential character of the measure, arguing that "where the republican form of government prevails, where the government is of the people, and in, through, and by the people," a nation's interest in educating its people is "second to no other interest."[47]

The requirement of compulsory attendance yielded libertarian opposition on the ground that it unduly infringed the liberty of children and their parents. To this, James Ransier, a distinguished African American delegate who was subsequently elected to the federal Congress, replied in a way that revealed an acute consciousness of the nexus between education and free citizenship and the proper bounds of democratic liberty. Pointing out that "the success of republicanism" depended on the educational progress of the nation's people, he insisted that to be free "is not to enjoy unlimited license." If it were, he added, his protesting colleague "might desire to enslave again his fellow men."[48]

Benjamin Franklin Randolph, another black delegate to the convention, also insisted that compulsory schooling was necessary to, rather than inconsistent with, republican democracy. Randolph stood in the tradition of Susie King Taylor. He had served as one of fourteen black chaplains in the Union army, and during that service he had monitored and encouraged education among the black troops, reporting that among the 26th US Colored Troops, with which he served, two hundred men were learning to read, and seventy were learning to write.[49] Schooling was, he said, "a matter of justice which is due to a people," and to compel it was no more antirepublican than to compel their military service.[50]

Randolph did not live to see his vision of free public education realized. He was assassinated, reportedly by Ku Klux Klan members, just months after the South Carolina Constitutional Convention's end.[51] His murder, which resulted in no prosecutions, was but one early sign of the terrorism that ultimately unseated the Republican Reconstruction government in South Carolina.

Advancements in education that were mandated by multiracial, Republican governments across the South were regularly threatened by Confederate terror of the kind that overthrew those governments and killed Benjamin Franklin Randolph. Derek Black's recent scholarship, described in chapter 5 of this volume, calls attention to the important fact that Congress actively resisted the former Confederacy's return to race- and class-based educational deprivation. As Black has explained, federal statutes governing the readmission of three states of the former confederacy (Mississippi, Texas, and Virginia) conditioned those states' readmission on the constitutionalization of education guarantees of the kind put in place by the democratically elected, multiracial constitutional conventions of the early post–Civil War period.

The history of caste-based educational deprivation, followed by education in rebellion against slavery, and the subsequent history of a national commitment to guaranteeing the educational opportunity that democratic republicanism requires should inform any contemporary examination of whether education is a fundamental right under the reconstructed United States Constitution or simply an opportunity that states may or may not choose to provide.

Education as a Fundamental Right

I have noted two principal sources of the Court's hesitation to recognize education as a fundamental right. One is anxiety that assertions of federal power to enforce a right to education might compromise states' control of their education systems in ways that are inconsistent with the terms of United States federalism. The other is the right's unenumerated character. The United States Constitution, unlike more recent constitutions of democratic states, does not explicitly grant a right to education, and the justices have repeatedly expressed anxiety that their authority is dangerously unmoored when they look beyond the text of governing documents. I address the federalist anxiety and the need for judicial moorings in turn.

The federalist anxiety was born of American colonists' distrust of distant power. It is a remnant of times when cross-country communication and travel were difficult in ways that are hard to imagine in a world of electronic communication and supersonic jet travel. It reflects an intuition that small and local government is more responsive to people's needs, but its appeal has been disproportionately broad, for it has been stoked by Confederate resentment of the larger government's interference with slaveholding and Jim Crow.[52] At one level, the federalist anxiety is easily addressed, for the original Constitution's requirements of deference to state authority were transformed by Union victory in the Civil War and by subsequent constitutional amendments giving the federal government the authority—and the responsibility—to define and enforce civil rights.[53] As I have argued elsewhere at length,[54] and as historians have repeatedly documented in the face of the Supreme Court's negligent readings of history,[55] the drafters and ratifiers of the Reconstruction Amendments deliberately transferred to the federal government power to ensure the sovereignty and civil rights of all classes of people. As Justice Wiley Rutledge pointed out in another context, "If that is a great power, it is one generated by the Constitution and the [Reconstruction] Amendments, to which the states have assented and their officials owe prime allegiance."[56] The Supreme Court's reluctance to recognize this power has been encouraged by those who feared its egalitarian implications.[57]

There are, of course, legitimate reasons to be solicitous of states' desires to retain voice and authority with respect to their education systems, but there are equally sound reasons to honor Reconstruction's promise of federal guarantees of civic freedom. As Kimberly Jenkins Robinson argues in this volume and elsewhere, the responsibility to educate post-Reconstruction is shared between states and the federal governments such that a coordinated system of education best satisfies the needs of the nation, and the federal government is obligated both to assure that states do their part to educate their citizens and to contribute substantially to that effort.[58] Time has taught the wisdom of her argument. Immediately after the Civil War, when some people opposed federal education initiatives in the name of broad, Confederate-backed states'-rights principles, Congressman Richard Yates gave an apt response: "we are a nation, not States merely, but a nation, with the powers and attributes of sovereignty as a nation." The Confederate doctrine of states' rights had, he said, "resulted in woes immeasurable" and "in the loss of hundreds of thousands of lives and millions of treasure." "Sir," he concluded, "we need a center for our educational system."[59] This need is greater today than it was in the congressman's less complex times and less competitive marketplaces.

With respect to the need for judicial moorings in the articulation of unenumerated rights, there are principles other than strict adherence to text that appropriately cabin judicial discretion. Justices have rightly held that unenumerated rights warrant special protection when they are necessary to the exercise of an important enumerated right (and therefore implicitly conferred by the Constitution's guarantee of that right) or when they follow the nation's history and traditions to strike an appropriate and workable balance between liberty and order. The right to education easily meets both of these criteria. The proof of this lays out simply: I identify five explicit constitutional guarantees and briefly explain why each implicitly includes a right to education. I then explain why the implicit right to education is also necessary to the US conception of ordered liberty, understood as the freedom to be a responsibly self-defining and self-actualizing member of a free polity. Full elaboration of these arguments could span an entire book, but a concise presentation of each conveys the weight of their totality.

Due Process Liberty

The Fourteenth Amendment's Due Process Clause, which forbids states to "deprive any person of life, liberty or property without due process of law," is the constitutional language most frequently relied on to ground a fundamental right. The (quite reasonable) rationale is that some deprivations are so momentous that they require weighty justification as well as procedural protection. Moreover, an entitlement to due process of law is fairly understood as a protection against arbitrary or unreasonable laws. The Due Process Clause is therefore deemed to have substantive content as a set of liberty interests.

The history of indenture, slavery, and emancipation in the United States described in this chapter exposes the link between education and personal, political, and economic liberty. It shows that education was denied—and even prohibited—for the express purpose of inhibiting liberty, of binding men and women to forced and uncompensated labor and preventing them from exercising agency to improve their conditions and determine the course of their lives. Contemporary deprivations of quality education have similar, if less extreme, effects, for they lock the undereducated within low-wage labor markets and limit their potential for civic agency.

Equal Protection

When the Civil War ended and citizenship status and political equality were acknowledged as birthrights, Congress and the ratifying states rejected the caste principle that had justified slavery[60] and adopted a principle of equality. As the history described earlier shows, the nation had seen how neglect of a group's basic rights corresponded with its subordination. To take the example most pertinent to this constitutional argument, slaveholding states denied conscripted workers the freedom to acquire and disseminate knowledge, and that denial was for the express purpose of keeping those workers and their descendants locked in a subordinate status and without civic agency. The lesson is that limitations on the acquisition and dissemination of knowledge are constitutionally suspect not only because they inhibit the self-determination, self-fulfillment, and civic participation protected by other clauses but also because they perpetuate an unequal status. As Justice Anthony Kennedy has noted, constitutional clauses "may converge in the identification and definition of [a] right," and the "interrelation of . . . two principles furthers our understanding of what freedom is and must become." As Justice Kennedy also noted, the liberty protected by the Fourteenth Amendment's Due Process Clause converges in this way with its Equal Protection Clause.[61]

Privileges and Immunities of Citizenship

Enforcing the Fourteenth Amendment's guarantee of citizenship and the privileges and immunities associated therewith has been made difficult by the Supreme Court's adherence to unreasonably narrow interpretations of the Citizenship Clause: the Supreme Court held in the 1873 *Slaughter-House Cases* that the privileges and immunities guaranteed by the Citizenship Clause were limited to privileges and immunities that flow uniquely from national citizenship.[62] That holding was wrong, and it should be overruled.[63]

But even if one holds to the belief that the privileges of citizenship protected by the Fourteenth Amendment are no more than the privileges of national citizenship, it must be said that education is fundamental to national civic participation just as it is fundamental to participation in the civic life of a state. Education is as essential to officeholding, policy advocacy, or intelligent exercise of the franchise at the federal level as it is to the exercise of those functions at the state level. This realization strengthens Kimberly Jenkins Robinson's arguments, in this volume and elsewhere,[64] that education must be a coordinated responsibility of state and federal governments. It also suggests that the obligation to assure education is both joint and several: on the default of one obligor, the other becomes fully responsible.

Thirteenth Amendment Freedom

The Supreme Court has at times recognized that the Thirteenth Amendment's prohibition of slavery and other forms of involuntary servitude extends to protect against what the Court has called the "badges and incidents" of slavery, and it has acknowledged that these include all things required to maintain human freedom.[65] The history related earlier establishes that illiteracy was a badge or mark of slavery and that withholding education was deliberately incidental to keeping people in bondage. It is reasonable to posit, therefore, that access to education is an aspect of the freedom assured by the Thirteenth Amendment.

A Republican Form of Government

The Supreme Court has shied away from enforcing the federal government's obligation under the original Constitution to guarantee in each state a republican form of government. The requirements of republicanism are contested, and the Court's hesitation to enforce its guarantee has resulted from disinclination to interfere in states' political choices. Prior litigation under the requirement has involved situations in which reasonable people could disagree as to whether a state's structural or political choices had undermined the state's republican character. None of this should, however, deter the Court from considering whether an educated citizenry is essential to a republican form of government. Reconstruction debates establish that, without challenge, those who debated the terms of Reconstruction governments at both the state and the federal levels saw an educated citizenry as foundational. It was uncontroversial then, as now, that a republican form of government is one in which the people through their elected representatives are sovereign, and as Reconstruction legislators insisted, popular sovereignty without the capacity for informed and reasoned judgment is chaos.

History, Tradition, and Ordered Liberty

Recognition that the right to education is implicit in five broader constitutional guarantees should be sufficient to establish its fundamental character. It is important to add, however, that the right to education meets each of the Supreme Court's commonly articulated tests for establishing a constitutional right as fundamental. Justice John Marshall Harlan II's 1961 statement that the test of a fundamental right has not been reduced to a formula[66] remains apt despite the certain-sounding language of justices who aspire to impose the discipline of rules on the identification of fundamental rights (or to embed or expand particular notions about what rights are fundamental). Nonetheless, as the Court has recognized in other contexts, the discipline of adherence to history and tradition and the requirement that a right be declared fundamental only if its protection is necessary to a fair balance between freedom and order are sufficiently constraining interpretive guides. The fundamental character of the right to education is therefore evident. With respect to history and tradition, we can look to the history of educational prohibitions for a servant caste, an uprising in which members of the servant caste demanded freedom with education as one of its necessary incidents, constitutional revision to prohibit caste-based servitude, and corollary efforts to establish public schools for all children nationwide. This history supports the conclusion that although the nation has at times taken an elitist view of educational entitlement, it has consistently regarded the right to education as fundamental to civic, political, and economic participation and human fulfillment. With respect to a concept of ordered liberty, we can say with Randolph and Ransier and Jillson and Yates and

Donnelly that an uneducated people cannot be sovereign or free. As Congressman Donnelly put it in 1866, without an educated populace, "a Republican form of government, resting on the intelligent judgment of the people, [is] an impossibility."[67] Finally, with respect to Justice Kennedy's concept of a constitutional right to liberty sufficient for responsible and autonomous self-realization, the history recited earlier is proof that education is prerequisite. To be enslaved is to be controlled and used rather than free to realize one's own life projects. The lives of people such as Mattie Jackson embody the message that education is the gateway to autonomy and self-realization in a modern democracy.

The United States began with a declaration that all men—by which we assume today that they must be taken to have meant all people—are created equal. The Civil War was the culmination of a struggle to resolve the nation's founding compromise with chattel slavery. Reconstruction presented a profound challenge to the re-United States. They could keep the Declaration's promise and create a government in which the people are sovereign and equal in political status, or they could find ways to abolish the then-untenable institution of slavery and yet maintain racial, gender, and caste subordination. The country's history since its Civil War can be seen as a struggle between those two choices. It has been, in other words, a struggle to define a new polity. The definition will always depend on an underlying and often subconscious[68] conception of who the people of the United States are. We must hope that one day there will be a Supreme Court majority that conceives the people to include the descendants of Mattie Jackson, Douglass Dorsey, Albert Brookings, James Lucas, Enoch Golden, W. E. Northcross, Thomas Jones, Austin Steward, Susie King Taylor, William McCutchen, Charlotte Forten, "colored girl" Rose Anna, and "colored men" Jack and Tom. And we must hope that one day there will be a Supreme Court majority that conceives the people as including the descendants of politicians such as Randolph, Ransier, Jillson, Yates and Donnelly. A Court with such a majority would understand the rights implicit in the reconstructed Constitution to include a right to education that is entitled to scrupulous protection.

NOTES

1. *See* Barry Friedman & Sara Solow, *The Federal Right to an Adequate Education*, 81 GEO. WASH. L. REV. 92, 117–20 (2013) (analyzing the Supreme Court's mixed

signals on a right to education); Courtney Jung, Ran Hirschl & Evan Rosevear, *Economic and Social Rights in National Constitutions*, 62 AM. J. COMP. L. 1043, 1053–54 (2014) (reporting that 80 percent of the world's constitutions provide a right to education). In United States constitutional discourse, certain rights are designated as fundamental to indicate that, although they are never absolute, people in the United States are specially protected against their official—and sometimes unofficial—limitation. Restriction or denial of a right that is "fundamental" in United States constitutional parlance warrants very strong justification and very narrow scope, whereas restriction or denial of other rights is permitted with weaker justification and broader sweep. The review given to a fundamental right is sometimes called "strict scrutiny."

2. Brown v. Bd. of Educ., 347 U.S. 483, 493 (1954).

3. San Antonio Indep. Sch. Dist. v. Rodriguez, 411 U.S. 1, 37 (1973).

4. Plyler v. Doe, 457 U.S. 202 (1982).

5. It was Justice Benjamin Cardozo (addressing the issue of double jeopardy in a criminal case) who first announced the requirement that a fundamental right be "implicit in the concept of ordered liberty," such that "neither liberty nor justice would exist if [it] were sacrificed." Palko v. Connecticut, 302 U.S. 319, 325–27 (1937). Justice Anthony Kennedy's opinion for the Court in the 2015 same-sex marriage cases gathered a number of precedents to instruct that a newly recognized right may be deemed fundamental when it "extend[s] to . . . personal choices central to individual dignity and autonomy." Obergefell v. Hodges, 135 S. Ct. 2584, 2597 (2015).

6. *Brown*, 347 U.S. at 493.

7. *Id.*

8. *See generally* Carl Tobias, *Public School Desegregation in Virginia during the Post-Brown Decade*, 37 WM. & MARY L. REV. 1261 (1996).

9. The term "golden years" can now be applied confidently to the period between congressional rejection of President Andrew Johnson's policies of Confederate appeasement and the Confederate "Redemption" brought about by southern terrorism and northern political compromise.

10. *Re Negro John Punch*, decided in 1640, has been cited as the first judicial recognition of the distinction between white and black bound servants. Two white men and one black man were convicted of running away. The white men were sentenced to "thirty stripes" and an additional four years of servitude, whereas the black man was sentenced to serve the remainder of his life. JUDICIAL CASES CONCERNING AMERICAN SLAVERY AND THE NEGRO, 5 vols. (Helen Tunnicliff Catterall ed., 1926; reprint, New York: Octagon Books, 1968).

11. *See* Mark R. Snyder, *The Education of Indentured Servants in Colonial America*, 33 J. TECH. STUD. 65 (2007).

12. For an account of changing attitudes toward and increasing opposition to education among the enslaved, *see generally* CARTER WOODSON, THE EDUCATION OF THE NEGRO PRIOR TO 1861: A HISTORY OF THE EDUCATION OF THE

COLORED PEOPLE OF THE UNITED STATES FROM THE BEGINNING OF SLAVERY TO THE CIVIL WAR (1915).

13. *See generally* JANET D. CORNELIUS, WHEN I CAN READ MY TITLE CLEAR (1992); HEATHER A. WILLIAMS, SELF-TAUGHT: AFRICAN AMERICAN EDUCATION IN SLAVERY AND FREEDOM (2005).

14. QUALITY EDUCATION AS A CONSTITUTIONAL RIGHT: CREATING A GRASSROOTS MOVEMENT TO TRANSFORM PUBLIC SCHOOLS ix (Theresa Perry et al. eds., 2010).

15. THOMAS WEBBER, DEEP LIKE THE RIVERS: EDUCATION IN THE SLAVE QUARTER COMMUNITY 1831–1865, at 134–35 (1978).

16. CORNELIUS, *supra* note 13, at 66.

17. *Id.*

18. WEBBER, *supra* note 15, at 135.

19. CORNELIUS, *supra* note 13, at 65–66.

20. W. E. B. DU BOIS, BLACK RECONSTRUCTION IN AMERICA 528 (1935).

21. *Id.* at 523.

22. *See* EUGENE GENOVESE, ROLL, JORDAN, ROLL 563 (1976).

23. WILLIAMS, *supra* note 13, at 7.

24. *Id.* at 11.

25. Shaun Wallace, *Fugitive Slave Advertisements and the Rebelliousness of Enslaved People in Georgia and Maryland 1790–1810*, at 171–204 (2017) (unpublished Ph.D. dissertation, University of Stirling), https://dspace.stir.ac.uk.

26. WEBBER, *supra* note 15, at 133.

27. *Id.* at 135.

28. *Id.*

29. *Id.* at 135–36.

30. Joseph Reidy, *Black Men in Navy Blue during the Civil War*, 33 PROLOGUE (2001), www.archives.gov.

31. WILLIAMS, *supra* note 13, at 49.

32. *Id.* at 51 ("[T]hough usually only one or two men in a ward could read, they would gather about one of these, who would read aloud.").

33. *Id.* at 36–37.

34. *See* RONALD E. BUTCHART, SCHOOLING THE FREED PEOPLE 18–20 (2010) (concluding that "black teachers were by any measure the most important of those who entered the black classrooms" in the period after the Civil War).

35. *See* Charlotte Forten, *My Life on the Sea Islands*, ATLANTIC (May 1868), www.theatlantic.com.

36. Elizabeth Cooper Davis, *Making Movement Sounds* 65–70 (2017) (unpublished Ph.D. dissertation, Harvard University).

37. CONG. GLOBE, 39th Cong., 2nd Sess. 1843 (1867).

38. CONG. GLOBE, 39th Cong., 1st Sess. 586 (1866).

39. CONG. GLOBE, *supra* note 37.

40. DU BOIS, *supra* note 20, at 524.

41. BENJAMIN GINSBERG, MOSES OF SOUTH CAROLINA 70–71 (2010).

42. *Id.*

43. *Id.* at 72–73. The author collects quotes from a variety of Confederate publications to document the negative perceptions of the convention among embittered Confederate whites. He includes this "ditty" hummed by white Carolinians in reference to the convention:
    Some are black.
    Some are blacker.
    And some are the color of a chaw of tobaccer.

44. *Id.* at 73.

45. As Derek Black explains in chapter 5 in this volume, some constitutional conventions in the former Confederacy can be understood to have embraced public education under federal mandate. This was a probable motivation for conventions called after Confederate "Redemption," but the integrated state bodies formed under congressional Reconstruction were motivated by a commitment to public education.

46. Proceedings of the Constitutional Convention of South Carolina of 1868, at 264 (hereinafter Proceedings).

47. *Id.* at 696.

48. *Id.* at 688.

49. WILLIAMS, *supra* note 13, at 55.

50. Proceedings, *supra* note 46, at 698.

51. William C. Hine, *Randolph, Benjamin Franklin*, SOUTH CAROLINA ENCYCLOPEDIA, www.scencyclopedia.org (last visited Apr. 26, 2019).

52. Peggy Cooper Davis et al., *The Persistence of the Confederate Narrative*, 84 TENN. L. REV. 301–05 (2017). As historians have made clear, narrow interpretations of Reconstruction's enhancement of federal power were driven to a great extent by bigoted and politically driven misinterpretations of Reconstruction's history. *See* Eric Foner, *The Supreme Court and the History of Reconstruction—and Vice Versa*, 112 COLUM. L. REV. 1585 (2012).

53. Davis et al., *supra* note 52, at 310–12.

54. *See, e.g.*, Peggy Cooper Davis, *Contested Images of Family Values: The Role of the State*, 107 HARV. L. REV. 1348 (1994).

55. *See* Foner, *supra* note 52.

56. Screws v. United States, 325 U.S. 91, 133–34 (1945).

57. *See* Davis et al., *supra* note 52.

58. *See generally* Kimberly Jenkins Robinson, *Disrupting Education Federalism*, 92 WASH. U. L. REV. 959 (2015).

59. CONG. GLOBE, 39th Cong., 2nd Sess. 843–44 (1867).

60. *See* Plessy v. Ferguson, 163 U.S. 537, 559 (1896) (Harlan, J., dissenting) ("There is no caste here.").

61. Obergefell v. Hodges, 135 S. Ct. 2584, 2603 (2015).

62. 83 U.S. (16 Wall) 36, 74–80 (1872).

63. *See* Kermit Roosevelt III, *What If* Slaughter-House *Had Been Decided Differently?*, 45 IND. L. REV. 61, 62–63 (2011) (noting an "academic consensus [that] *Slaughter-House* was wrong—blatantly, maliciously, egregiously. (Pick your adverb.)").

64. *See generally* Robinson, *supra* note 58.

65. *See* Jones v. Alfred H. Mayer, Co., 392 U.S. 409, 439–40 (1968).

66. Poe v. Ullman, 367 U.S. 497, 542 (1961) (Harlan, J., dissenting).

67. CONG. GLOBE, 39th Cong., 1st Sess. 586 (1866).

68. For an understanding of the persistence and the unconscious character of supremacist conceptions of "we, the people," *see* Peggy Cooper Davis, *Performing Interpretation: A Legacy of Civil Rights Lawyering in* Brown v. Board of Education, *in* RACE, LAW, AND CULTURE: REFLECTIONS ON *BROWN V. BOARD OF EDUCATION*, 23, 23–24 (Austin Sarat ed., 1997).

7

A Congressional Right to Education

Promises, Pitfalls, and Politics

KIMBERLY JENKINS ROBINSON

Introduction

Congress has enacted a wide variety of legislation to expand educational opportunity for well over half a century. In the Civil Rights Act of 1964, Congress authorized the attorney general to bring desegregation suits, thereby relieving nonprofit and private groups from solely bearing the costs of desegregation lawsuits.[1] The Elementary and Secondary Education Act of 1965 (ESEA) subsequently provided over $1.3 billion in federal aid for education, including $1.06 billion to support supplemental services for economically disadvantaged students through Title I of the law.[2] President Lyndon Johnson ushered ESEA through Congress to empower education to serve as a vehicle to lift children out of poverty and to empower education to fulfill its purpose as the engine of the American dream. The widespread distribution of federal funds under ESEA combined with the Civil Rights Act's prohibition of recipients of federal financial assistance discriminating on the basis of race, color, or national origin also expanded the ability of the federal government to use federal aid as a hook to accomplish desegregation.[3]

Congressional expansion of the federal role in ESEA paved the way for subsequent legislation to address the needs of handicapped children, girls and women, and English-language learners. More recently, Congress has widened its attention to include ensuring states adopt high standards and closing achievement gaps through such legislation as the Improving America's Schools Act, the No Child Left Behind Act, and the Every Student Succeeds Act. The Every Student Succeeds Act represents a significant return of education authority to the states, even as Congress maintained its broad aims of incentivizing states to ensure that children learn the content of state standards and reducing achievement gaps.[4]

Throughout Congress's involvement in education, it has stopped short of guaranteeing all children a federal right to education. Such a law has been proposed several times in both the Senate and the House. For instance, Senator Christopher Dodd (D-CT), along with cosponsors Ted Kennedy (D-MA) and Richard Durbin (D-IL), introduced the Student Bill of Rights Act in 2007. The bill would have required all states that receive federal financial assistance to provide all children with an education that "enables the students to acquire the knowledge and skills necessary for responsible citizenship in a diverse democracy, including the ability to participate fully in the political process through informed electoral choice, to meet challenging student academic achievement standards, and to be able to compete and succeed in a global economy." The bill included a private right of action.[5] Senator Dodd introduced similar bills four times in the Senate before he left office in 2011, and the 2007 bill was his final attempt.[6] Congressman Chaka Fattah introduced similar bills in the House of Representatives eight times, and the 2003 bill gained the support of 188 cosponsors.[7] However, these bills have not moved past the introduction stage.[8] More recently, in 2015, Congressman Mike Honda (D-CA) gathered thirty-five cosponsors to support the Equity and Excellence in American Education Act of 2015, which aimed to establish an excellent and equitable education system in the United States and would have offered grants to states with substantial concentrations of English-language learners, minority, Native American, or migratory students, or students in poverty, but this bill also failed to outlive the introduction phase.[9]

Yet rights hold a privileged status in US society. They convey a sense of national values and priorities and serve as the bedrocks of our democracy. They also can serve as bulwarks against the tyranny of the majority.[10] The absence of a federal right to education undoubtedly allows states great autonomy over education. Although this autonomy has sometimes been used for innovation, experimentation, and excellence, it also has been used to create and maintain educational opportunity gaps that disadvantage many schoolchildren, particularly poor and minority schoolchildren.[11]

This chapter explores how Congress should recognize a right to education. I contend the process through which Congress recognizes such a right is critical for both its political viability and its sustainability. Therefore, Congress should engage in incremental shifts to education federalism that partner with the laboratory of the states to test potential approaches to a federal right to education before adopting enduring legislation to recognize such a right. Once Congress decides to enact a long-standing federal right to education, Congress should include a collaborative enforcement model for the right and create a private right of action as a last resort when collaboration fails. This chapter then considers the advantages that Congress enjoys for creating a federal right to education over the judiciary. The chapter concludes by analyzing the promises, pitfalls, and politics of a congressional right to education in light of my recommendations. This chapter builds on the array of scholarship arguing that Congress should enact a federal right to education or play a critical role in the enforcement of such a right that is created by the judiciary.[12]

How Should Congress Enact a Federal Right to Education?

In analyzing how Congress should enact a federal right to education, I make two recommendations. Most who contend that Congress should enact a right to education envision a firm directive to the states. However, I contend that Congress should take an incremental path to a federal right to education by experimenting with the contours of an education right through incentives and conditional spending legislation before enacting a directive to the states. In addition, I recommend that Congress adopt a collaborative enforcement model for a right to education that insists on collaboration between the federal government and states to expand educational opportunity. An aggrieved student would only have a claim in court when the collaborative process fails. These incremental and collaborative approaches are presented in the following subsections.

An Incremental Approach to a Congressional Right to Education

Congress should enact a federal right to education through an incremental process that engages Congress and the laboratory of the states in a dialogue that improves the potential for lasting and effective reform. This incremental approach avoids the dramatic shifts to education federalism in the No Child Left Behind Act and the Every Student Succeeds Act.[13] An incremental shift of the federal role in education should include publicizing the need for reform, inviting incentives, and compelling conditions for federal funding before Congress enacts a mandate for a federal right to education. Here, I explain how each phase would work.

First, the United States should expand its emphasis on the need for every child to receive a high-quality education that prepares her or him for college or a career. Federal law and policy makers, including the president, must highlight the need for additional reforms that seek to reduce the long-standing links between educational opportunity on the one hand and zip code, class, race, national origin, and disability on the other. The federal government should explain the national interest in achieving this goal so that the nation can promote a robust economy, maintain its national security, and ensure a just and effective democracy. This campaign should publish the costs of the current opportunity and achievement gaps along with highlighting reforms that have demonstrated an ability to close these gaps.[14]

Once the need for additional reforms is well established, the federal government should create incentives that invite states to adopt reforms that establish the foundation for a federal right to education. Considering the potential guarantees of a federal right to education that are analyzed in part 3 of this book, incentives could be created for states to undertake such reforms as implementing or strengthening progressive funding that recognizes the additional costs of educating children in poverty, adopting programs that increase the supply of high-quality teachers in high-need areas, and restructuring educational opportunities to ensure an adequate and equitable education system.

Incentives would take several forms. The United States Department of Education would draw on its superior research capacity to provide research that would increase the understanding of states and localities about reforms that effectively close opportunity and achievement gaps and the conditions needed for the reforms to be successful. This research would increase the capacity of state departments of education, local school districts, and schools to address the impediments to equitable and excellent educational opportunities and outcomes. The United States Department of Education also would offer technical assistance to states, districts, and schools to help them replicate reforms that have proven successful. This research and technical assistance should encourage collaboration between states and localities facing similar challenges. It also would embrace economies of scale that prevent the unnecessary duplication of state and local experiments.

Finally, federal financial aid could be used to support the work of experts to provide a fresh perspective on impediments to and opportunities for reform at the state and local levels. These experts could study the positive and negative impacts of existing approaches to education as well as the costs and benefits of an array of reforms. Federal aid also can reward innovation and expand the breadth, depth, and reach of reforms.

This additional federal aid should be given out over several years and require states and localities to meet specific conditions to receive further aid. This approach avoids the historical pitfall of federal aid, which sometimes resulted in distributing aid without requiring consistent implementation of federal objectives. Instead, this approach requires continuous improvement. These incentives ultimately should encourage state and local leaders to embrace reform by both increasing the likelihood that reforms will be successful and providing financial rewards for reforms. The financial incentives also should spark state and local pressure for reform as states observe neighboring states benefiting from a new infusion of federal education aid.[15]

A critical advantage of federal incentives is that the Department of Education can create conditions for discretionary funds as long as the conditions are consistent with the terms of the funds. This means that Congress does not have to determine the conditions. This allows the testing of incentives to enact a federal right to education to occur without the support needed to secure passage of new legislation each time new or modified conditions are needed.

Once the federal incentives have sparked additional innovation and reform that begins to test approaches to a federal right to education, Congress should include conditions within the Elementary and Secondary Education Act that test potential approaches to a federal right to education. Such conditions could be created as a separate program, a condition for Title I funding, or as a condition for any ESEA funding. Congressional conditions on funding adopted pursuant to Congress's authority under the Spending Clause cannot cross the line from coercion to compulsion. The United States Supreme Court struck down new federal conditions to a large amount of old Medicaid funds in *National Federation of Independent Businesses v. Sebelius* because the conditions, which threatened loss of all Medicaid funding and constituted more than 10 percent of a state's total budget, amounted to "economic dragooning that leaves the States with no real option but to acquiesce in the Medicaid expansion."[16] However, as I have explained in other scholarship, this case continues to allow Congress to attach new conditions to new education funds in ways that would permit a substantial and even dramatic expansion of the federal role in education as long as the states retain a genuine choice to reject the funds and thus are not essentially compelled to accept the conditional funds.[17]

ESEA provides an effective vehicle for new federal conditions because all states and the District of Columbia accept ESEA funds. However, given the novel terrain that a federal right to education ultimately would entail, conditions based on the eventual components of a federal right to education, such as those outlined in part 3 of this book, should begin as a separate program. A separate program invites the laboratory of the states to test out the various approaches and assess their benefits and drawbacks. This approach would allow other states to learn from implementing states and localities before Congress includes specific requirements as conditions in Title I.[18] Also, including such conditions as a separate program could reduce the likelihood that this single program alone would forestall a successful ESEA reauthorization. When the conditions are a separate program, states can choose to opt out of the program while still receiving other ESEA funds.

Once greater certainty on the optimal terms for a federal right to education have been determined by the laboratory of the states, these conditions should be included within a future reauthorization of Title I. Conditions within Title I will exert a greater coercive effect because of its long-standing history and widespread buy-in from states and localities. Therefore, the separate program conditions should demonstrate some successes before Congress considers incorporating the conditions into Title I. Including these conditions within Title I would benefit from the need to reauthorize the ESEA on a regular basis. However, the almost-eight-year delay to reauthorize ESEA after the No Child Left Behind Act demonstrates that a political stalemate can forestall reauthorization even when the nation badly needs it. As discussed later in this chapter, the political will that establishes the need for a federal right to education will be essential to including such language within Title I.

Including conditions for all education funding that require states to provide the components of a federal right to education offers the most enduring approach for federal conditions. However, this approach also will be the most contested. This approach builds on such statutes as Title IX of the Education Act of 1972, which prohibits discrimination on the basis of sex in federally funded education programs.[19] An enduring condition for all education funding benefits from only one enactment, compared to the potential for more than one reauthorization for various ESEA conditions. A single enactment signals the importance of and commitment to the components of a federal right to education in a way that ESEA conditions do not. To implement the conditions, administrative agencies would enact regulations to interpret the conditions and would build expertise over time regarding enforcement.[20] Yet the stand-alone and enduring nature of permanent conditions for all education funds means that it would require even greater support than ESEA conditions. Therefore, ESEA conditions that have tested the costs and benefits of enduring conditions would be beneficial for building sufficient political will to garner enactment.[21]

Ultimately, a congressional right to education should be enacted as a directive that must be followed by all states. A clear and unequivocal directive would overcome the shortcomings of past federal policies that have been too attenuated and indirect.[22] Such a directive also would benefit from the need to be enacted only once, in contrast to the reauthorizations required for ESEA. Both the political Right and the Left have supported such directives for education, with congressional Democrats sponsoring Title IX and congressional Republicans sponsoring the Equal Access Act, which ensures that school facilities are available to school clubs in an evenhanded fashion.[23] This history confirms that both parties will support an educational directive when Congress is persuaded of its benefits. States and school districts routinely follow federal directives that require or prohibit specific actions even when those directives have not provided additional funds.[24]

A robust and clear directive on a right to education signals an unambiguous and unequivocal commitment to equitable access to an excellent education. Over the history of federal involvement in education, it should come as no surprise that more forceful federal policies have had the greatest effect.[25] Numerous examples support this commonsense understanding of federal policy in education. For instance, the initial tepid approach to school desegregation in *Brown v. Board of Education II* invited defiance on the part of school boards and delay and evasion by federal judges. As a result, only 2 percent of African American students attended desegregated schools in the South a decade after the decision.[26] It took the Court's clear pronouncements in *Green v. County School Board of New Kent County* and *Swann v. Charlotte-Mecklenburg Board of Education* that school districts must end segregation and remedy all vestiges of segregation by creating integrated schools, combined with unequivocal guidance from the Department of Health, Education, and Welfare that insisted on effective desegregation plans, for school districts to take meaningful steps to desegregate.[27] Similarly, it took the explicit right to an individualized education plan for disabled students, as well as thorough procedural mechanisms in the Individuals with Disabilities Education Act, to transform the education of disabled students from the margins of education to a mainstream and beneficial approach.[28] This history suggests that even if a less forceful policy should be used to assess the most efficacious approach to a federal right to education, ultimately a robust and clear congressional right to education will make the greatest impact on the educational opportunities of schoolchildren.

Although most who support a federal right to education imagine it being enacted once as a directive, such a right is more likely to become an enduring part of the US landscape if it is preceded by thorough testing through federal education incentives and conditions. By testing a federal right to education before it becomes a directive, Congress could take the lessons learned from this process to craft an enduring right that gains bipartisan support because it has been crafted to benefit most, if not all, schoolchildren.

A Collaborative Enforcement Model for a Right to Education

A federal right to education also should include a collaborative enforcement model. This model includes four components, as I have developed in prior scholarship.[29] First, once Congress defines the requirements of a right to education in a statute, states must report to the federal government on their provision of this right on a periodic basis. The federal government would establish a panel or commission of experts to review state reports and provide feedback. The panel or commission would create reporting guidelines that state reports must follow. The panel or commission would publish its findings widely, and this information should be used within states to spark community and government involvement in reforms that improve the provision of the right to education. The panel or commission would include recommendations while encouraging states to develop their own solutions to the impediments to protecting the federal right to education. In addition, the periodic reporting requirement recognizes that the right will take years to fully implement while encouraging continual progress toward the right.[30]

The second and third components incorporate tools of the incremental approach. The federal government through the United States Department of Education would conduct research and provide technical assistance to empower states to address obstacles to providing the federal right to education. The federal government also would increase its financial assistance to states to support their provision of a federal right to education. This assistance aims to expand states' capacities to implement a federal right to education, in light of research indicating that states lacked or currently lack the capacity to implement recent reauthorizations of ESEA. Federal funds also would incentivize states to comply with the requirements of the right.[31]

Finally, a collaborative enforcement mechanism for the right to education would provide individuals and groups a federal judicial remedy when states refuse to provide the right to education. A private right of action would become available once the collaborative approach has been exhausted. This organization of remedies encourages collaboration but does not leave schoolchildren and their families helpless if a state refuses to implement the right to education. The collaborative enforcement approach must have definite timelines for responses and reforms so that a child could proceed to court in time for the ruling to benefit her or him.[32]

A collaborative enforcement model for a federal right to education enjoys numerous benefits over a right that first turns to the judiciary for enforcement. The collaborative enforcement approach encourages the federal and state governments to work together as partners with a joint interest in closing opportunity and achievement gaps, in contrast to litigation that presents the federal and state governments as combatants with competing interests. Federal and state governments possess aligned interests in improving educational opportunities that promote a strong economy, engaged and knowledgeable citizens, and a just society. Therefore, the federal and state governments should be working as partners toward common goals for education rather than as adversaries.[33]

Collaborative enforcement of a federal right to education also focuses enforcement authority within the democratically elected branches of the federal government. Federal action must serve as a counterweight to the state and local interests that are invested in preserving the status quo for education because it benefits their children or their constituents.[34] Collaborative enforcement also can avoid some of the backlash that great expansions of federal authority over education can engender because the approach builds on a mutually beneficial alliance to achieve shared goals rather than an edict from on high to unwilling participants. Cooperation is more likely when collaborative enforcement is preceded by a widespread effort to educate the nation about the urgent need for implementing a federal right to education.[35]

Collaborative enforcement also maintains more state and local control over education than a litigation-centered approach. Each state would decide how to provide a federal right to education, while the federal government would ensure that each state's approach is consistent with the right and that particular groups of students are not disadvantaged by the state's approach. This process preserves the ability of states to experiment and innovate in education within federally defined parameters.[36]

In addition, collaborative enforcement harnesses the expertise that a federal panel or commission would bring to education, and this expertise would surpass the knowledge and expertise of federal judges. A federal panel or commission also could accomplish some consistency in defining a right to education that federal courts might lack until the United States Supreme Court weighs in. A federal panel or commission avoids the Supreme Court becoming the overseer of the education provided in all fifty states, a role that it has indicated it wants to avoid.[37]

Ultimately, if the political will to recognize a federal right to education is lacking, a judicial private right of action may be required for such a right to be recognized. The next section considers the advantages that Congress enjoys over courts in creating and enforcing a federal right to education.

The Advantages of Congress Creating a Federal Right to Education Rather than the Judiciary

A congressional right to education enjoys distinct advantages that a judicial right does not. When Congress expands its role in education, it claims the imprimatur of a majoritarian branch. This majoritarian imprimatur is essential for many of the changes that a successful federal right to education would require. For instance, a substantial shift to education federalism that increases the federal role in education will occur if Congress enacts a federal right to education. However, when rejecting remedies that would have advanced equal educational opportunity, the Supreme Court has repeatedly noted that it does not want to upset the balance of education federalism or diminish local control.[38] Specifically, the more conservative members of the Court may believe that a substantial shift to education federalism should only come from a majoritarian branch. When Congress decides to recalibrate education federalism, it avoids the countermajoritarian difficulties that the Supreme Court would face, and Congress signals the need for a new approach to education federalism.

A majoritarian approach also should garner more support for implementation by the states and localities that participated in the political process of enacting the right. In contrast, court decisions often encounter political resistance that can undermine long-standing reform. In addition to the well-known example of sharp resistance to school desegregation, successful school finance litigation has brought important beneficial increases in funding[39] but also largely has failed to initiate fundamental changes to most education systems, such as equal resources or ending the heavy reliance on property taxes.[40] Resistance most often has been substantial because comprehensive education reform requires implementation by legislatures that typically lack the political will to invest more in education or to redistribute education funding. This resistance results in long battles between the state legislature and the court following successful litigation and suggests that courts may be encountering limits to their institutional capacity to accomplish reform.[41] Congress provides a superior avenue for recognizing a federal right to education because such legislation would express the will of the people.

In addition, courts in school finance cases oftentimes have resisted defining educational objectives and how to advance them and instead simply declare the existing system unconstitutional. Courts then defer resolution of these issues to the legislature.[42] This approach respects the primacy of the legislature in setting education law and policy. A congressionally centered process enables Congress to simultaneously establish both clear objectives and the means to achieve them and thereby mitigate the long battles between courts and legislatures that a judicially defined right could engender.

Although the process of enacting legislation also can be quite slow, this process is not hindered by the constraints of litigation, which also can be a protracted process, as the decades of school finance litigation have demonstrated. The courts must await litigation to establish a right, while Congress is not tied to the wish lists of litigators. Congress also can design a right focused on national interests, while a court remedy must be responsive to the evidence and parties before it.[43] Congress also has proven that it can act quickly on education legislation. For example, President George W. Bush introduced the No Child Left Behind Act on his second day in office, January 21, 2001, and the legislation was signed into law on January 8, 2002.[44] Congress can act swiftly when it decides to do so.

Vesting authority to define and revise a federal right to education within Congress also allows citizens through their lawmakers to revisit and redefine the right to education to reflect new research and insights about how best to define and enforce the right. Although this makes the right vulnerable to political shifts, it also can encourage greater buy-in from states and localities that gain a voice in the scope and enforcement of the right through their federal representatives.[45] In contrast, courts must wait for parties to bring a lawsuit to adjust the contours of a right and even then must only respond to the issues brought before the court.

When enacting a right to education, Congress also can simultaneously allocate the federal expertise and resources that will be needed to empower states to close opportunity and achievement gaps.[46] The nation's experience with the No Child Left Behind Act revealed, among other things, that many states lacked the capacity to engage in the substantial reform required by the law.[47] States similarly have indicated that under the Every

Student Succeeds Act they lack the capacity to offer support to large numbers of schools, and thus these states set modest performance benchmarks for identifying low-performing schools.[48] An impactful federal right to education will require expanding the capacity of states to undertake comprehensive reform. Only Congress can insist on the resource allocation needed to accomplish this. Courts would be limited to ordering a state to remedy only the inequities and inadequacies within the state's control. This would leave behind the states that lack the capacity to remedy opportunity and achievement gaps.[49]

When considering the challenges of garnering the political will to support a congressional right to education when compared to seeking judicial recognition of a federal right to education, it is important to recognize that far too often the courts have failed to serve as effective change agents within education. University of Virginia president Jim Ryan has commented that "it seems with courts generally in the context of education: they are more willing and able to make marginal rather than fundamental changes." He supports this assertion by noting that successful school finance suits can increase funding, but schools remain isolated by poverty and race; and winning does not address the disparate property values that lie at the heart of the inequality.[50] Similarly, some people criticize court involvement in desegregation as undermining desegregation.[51] Building the political will for Congress to pass a federal right to education may be essential to effective implementation of the right.

Most importantly, Congress is the only branch that could adopt both the incremental and collaborative approaches that I think will help to address some of the political obstacles to a federal right to education and increase the likelihood of the right's beneficial impact. The next section turns to some of the potential political obstacles and pitfalls that a congressional right must overcome to be enacted and impactful.

Navigating the Politics and Pitfalls to Achieve the Promises of a Congressional Right to Education

The incremental and collaborative approaches address some, but not all, of the political concerns surrounding congressional enactment of a federal right to education. Changing the politics of education remains essential for securing education reform that advances equal educational opportunity because, as Jim Ryan succinctly put it, "politics matter as much as policy."[52]

An incremental approach can help to secure passage of a federal right to education. Designing a federal education law that benefited most districts was essential for securing the expansion of the federal role in education in the 1965 Elementary and Secondary Education Act.[53] Similarly, demonstrating the widespread benefits of a congressional right to education will be essential for securing passage of such a right. The incremental approach to enacting a federal right to education envisions a gradual and substantial infusion of additional federal funds into education. In addition, maintaining ongoing support for a right to education will require comprehensive support, because such support has proved critical for sustaining other federal education programs, such as Title IX and the IDEA, in the face of skepticism and criticism.[54]

Transforming the US education system from one that privileges some students at the expense of others to one that provides all children an excellent and equitable education undoubtedly will be expensive. The Kentucky Supreme Court acknowledged in its pathbreaking recognition of a right to an adequate education for the children of Kentucky, "The taxpayers of this state must pay for the system, no matter how large, even to the point of being 'unexpectedly large or even onerous.'"[55] The same is true for the taxpayers of the United States. US taxpayers must be willing to invest in the education not just of their own children but of other people's children to support the robust economy, engaged democracy, and just society that most Americans want.

A congressional right to education must learn from past programs that appropriated millions of dollars that, when widely distributed, became small amounts with very little impact.[56] The federal government has the ability to substantially raise its contribution to education through its ability to cut waste and institute taxes. A substantial increase in federal funding for education would increase the stability of support for education, just as Congress chose to do for several years through the American Recovery and Reinvestment Act.[57] The amount of funding should be determined based on the lessons from past successful federal incentives and conditions.[58]

An incremental approach to a congressional right to education also would accomplish gradual shifts to education federalism. As noted earlier, a transformation of education federalism is essential for securing passage of a right to education. At its core, this transformation must eschew the approach to education that puts the federal government on the sidelines trying to coax behavior while states and districts remain in the driver's seat, oftentimes with the federal government pursuing different policies than states and localities.[59] Instead, the federal, state, and local governments must embrace a joint partnership that respects federal leadership, expertise, and resources as well as state and district innovation, experimentation, and authority.[60] This transformation of education federalism is essential because one of the critical reasons that past federal programs such as Title I and the standards and accountability movement have failed is because the key factors for driving education reform, such as influencing teachers and classrooms, were considered untouchable.[61]

An incremental approach also increases the political support for reform by creating a federal right based on lessons from federal incentives and conditions. This gradual approach will appeal to those who embrace ongoing education reform over a quick transformation. In this way, the incremental approach is consistent with the very nature of education, which thrives on innovation and experimentation with more modest reforms.[62]

Unfortunately, it will take far longer to enact a congressional right to education through an incremental approach than it will to enact a single statute. However, the benefits of experimentation, even if only done through federal incentives, could help to prevent Congress from creating a right that is quickly repealed because it is not informed by actual experimentation within states and localities. Increasing the likelihood that the right would stand the test of time outweighs the need to act quickly.

A collaborative approach also can increase political will for a federal right to education. The approach does not immediately create a cause of action against all fifty states, as the Court was concerned about in *San Antonio Independent School District v. Rodriguez*.[63] Instead, collaboration between the federal and state governments would remain the focus of the federal right, thereby reducing concerns about immediate litigation. States also are more likely to view the federal assistance provided through a collaborative approach as support for a common goal rather than an unfunded mandate, which is a common complaint about federal education legislation.[64]

Ultimately, greater equity, adequacy, and excellence in education may require a social movement to incentivize Congress to seriously consider and ultimately enact a federal right to education. A substantial body of research indicates that social movements are often necessary to accomplish wide-scale legal and social reform.[65] Such a social movement may be essential for providing the impetus to change the nation's long-standing approach to education that leaves behind too many children.

There are signs in the United States that such a social movement is brewing. For instance, the waves of school funding and teacher litigation suggest an ongoing willingness for parents and communities to demand more equitable and adequate educational opportunities.[66] Organizations across the nation are engaging in education reform and demands for greater equity.[67] If these efforts and organizations joined together with others demanding greater economic justice, a social movement may ignite that includes among its demands a federal right to education.[68]

Conclusion

History confirms that the interests of those who are harmed by the status quo oftentimes require federal intervention to address and remedy the injustices of the current approach.[69] The reforms and investments that would be necessary to accompany a transformative federal right to education would require politicians to be willing to upset the status quo and follow uncharted territory.[70] Such substantial reforms are essential because tinkering at the margins of public education has failed to remedy the inequitable and inadequate distribution of educational opportunities. Although the politics of today undoubtedly would prevent the enactment of such a right, no one believed that Congress would authorize widespread support for the education of poor children long before the Elementary and Secondary Education Act of 1965 was enacted. Nor did many predict that a Republican president would usher through the No Child Left Behind Act and accomplish the largest expansion of the federal role in education in the nation's history.

We must not shy away from considering the potential promises and pitfalls of a federal right to education because the politics of today might prevent us from enacting it in the near future. Our nation is already failing far too many schoolchildren, so we collectively already wear the mantle of failure. Therefore, we should thoughtfully analyze why and how Congress should enact a federal right to education to prepare for when such a right is demanded by those who are unwilling to tolerate the unjust education system that has endured for generations.

NOTES

1. Title IV of the Civil Rights Act of 1964, 42 U.S.C. § 2000c-6 (2012).
2. Title VI of the Civil Rights Act of 1964, 42 U.S.C. § 2000d-7 (2012); Elementary and Secondary Education Act of 1965, Pub. L. No. 89-10, 79 Stat. 27; PATRICK J. MCGUINN, NO CHILD LEFT BEHIND AND THE TRANSFORMATION OF FEDERAL EDUCATION POLICY, 1965–2005, at 31 (2006).
3. *See* MCGUINN, *supra* note 2, at 29–31; MICHAEL J. KLARMAN, *BROWN V. BOARD OF EDUCATION* AND THE CIVIL RIGHTS MOVEMENT 124, 212 (2007).
4. Education for All Handicapped Children Act of 1975, Pub. L. No. 94-142, 89 Stat. 773 (codified as amended at 20 U.S.C. §§ 1400–82 (2012 & Supp. IV 2016)); Individuals with Disabilities Education Act Amendments of 1997, Pub. L. No. 105-17, 11 Stat. 37 (codified as amended at 20 U.S.C. §§ 1400–82 (2012 & Supp. IV 2016)); Title IX of the Education Amendments of 1972, Pub. L. No. 92-318, 86 Stat. 304 (codified as amended at 20 U.S.C. §§ 1681–88 (2012 & Supp. IV 2016)); the Equal Educational Opportunities Act of 1974, Pub. L. 93-380, tit. II, 88 Stat. 514 (codified as amended at 20 U.S.C. §§ 1701–58 (2012 & Supp. IV 2016)); Improving America's Schools Act of 1994, Pub. L. No. 103-382, 108 Stat. 3518 (codified as amended in scattered sections of 20 U.S.C.); No Child Left Behind Act of 2001, Pub. L. No. 107-110, tit. V, §501, 115 Stat. 1425 1806-10 (codified as amended at 20 U.S.C. §§ 7231–31j (2012 & Supp. IV 2016)); Every Student Succeeds Act, Pub. L. No. 114-95, 129 Stat. 1802 (2015) (codified as amended in scattered sections of 20 U.S.C.); Kimberly Jenkins Robinson, *Restructuring the Elementary and Secondary Education Act's Approach to Equity*, 103 U. MINN. L. REV. 915 (2018) (analyzing how the Every Student Succeeds Act aspires to, but falls short, of advancing equity).
5. Student Bill of Rights Act, S. 2189, 110th Cong. §§ 101, 401 (2007) (two cosponsors).
6. *See* Student Bill of Rights, S. 2828, 109th Cong. (2006) (ten cosponsors); Student Bill of Rights, S. 2428, 108th Cong. (2004) (thirteen cosponsors), Student Bill of Rights, S. 2912, 107th Cong. (2002).
7. Student Bill of Rights, H.R. 1070, 114th Cong. (2015) (zero cosponsors); Student Bill of Rights, H.R. 378, 113th Cong. (2013) (zero cosponsors); Student Bill of Rights, H.R. 1295, 112th Cong. (2011) (eight cosponsors); Student Bill of Rights, H.R. 2451, 111th Cong. (2009) (zero cosponsors); Student Bill of Rights, H.R. 2373, 110th Cong. (2007) (sixty-seven cosponsors); Student Bill of Rights, H.R. 2178, 109th Cong. (2005) (128 cosponsors); Student Bill of Rights, H.R. 236, 108th Cong.

(2003) (188 cosponsors); Student Bill of Rights, H.R. 5346, 107th Cong. (2002) (125 cosponsors).

8. *See* Actions Overview H.R.1070—114th Congress (2015-2016), Congress. gov; Actions Overview H.R.378—113th Congress (2013-2014), Congress. gov; Actions Overview H.R.1295—112th Congress (2011-2012), Congress. gov; Actions Overview H.R.2451—111th Congress (2009-2010), Congress.gov; Actions Overview S.2189—110th Congress (2007-2008), Congress.gov; Actions Overview H.R.2373—110th Congress (2007-2008), Congress.gov; Actions Overview S.2828—109th Congress (2005-2006), Congress.gov; Actions Overview H.R.2178—109th Congress (2005-2006), Congress.gov; Actions Overview S.2428—108th Congress (2003-2004), Congress.gov; Actions Overview H.R.236—108th Congress (2003-2004), Congress.gov; Actions Overview H.R.5346—107th Congress (2001-2002), Congress.gov; Actions Overview S.2912—107th Congress (2001-2002), Congress.gov (last visited Sept. 27, 2018).

9. *See* Actions Overview H.R.4013—114th Congress (2015-2016), Congress.gov (last visited Sept. 27, 2018).

10. *See* ANNE NEWMAN, REALIZING EDUCATIONAL RIGHTS: ADVANCING SCHOOL REFORM THROUGH COURTS AND COMMUNITIES 24, 95 (2013); RONALD DWORKIN, TAKING RIGHTS SERIOUSLY xi (1977); Michael A. Rebell, *The Right to Comprehensive Educational Opportunity*, 47 HARV. C.R.-C.L. L. REV. 47, 52 (2012).

11. Kimberly Jenkins Robinson, *Disrupting Education Federalism*, 92 WASH. U. L. REV. 959, 968-83 (2015) (critiquing the benefits of education federalism as well as the substantial costs that it imposes); Kimberly Jenkins Robinson, *The High Cost of Education Federalism*, 48 WAKE FOREST L. REV. 287, 293-330 (2013).

12. Several scholars rely on Congress's authority under the Spending Clause to attach conditions to education funds as a potential source of authority for a federal right to education. *See, e.g.*, JACK JENNINGS, PRESIDENTS, CONGRESS, AND THE PUBLIC SCHOOLS: THE POLITICS OF EDUCATION REFORM 216-17 (2015) (recommending that a congressional right to education could serve as an effective alternative to closing opportunity gaps if the Supreme Court refuses to recognize a right to education and a constitutional amendment guaranteeing such a right is not enacted); Kristi Bowman, *The Failure of Education Federalism*, 51 U. MICH. J.L. REFORM 1, 43-44 (2017) (acknowledging the ability of Congress to set a "minimum quality level" for education through reauthorizations of the ESEA and highlighting the benefits of this approach); Christopher Edley, *Keynote Address*, 4 STAN. J. C.R. & C.L. 151, 157 (2008) (contending that NCLB and its reauthorizations provided and will continue to provide an opportunity to incrementally develop and define a federal right to education); Rebell, *supra* note 10, at 66 (arguing that Congress created "an implicit right to comprehensive educational opportunity" for economically disadvantaged students through the No Child Left Behind Act); *but cf.* Daniel S. Greenspahn, *A Constitutional Right to Learn: The Uncertain Allure of Making a Federal Case out of Education*, 59 S.C. L. REV. 755,

775–82 (2008) (arguing against a judicially recognized federal right to education because of the federal judiciary's withdrawal from education, reluctance of the current conservative Court to recognize new substantive rights, the emphasis of courts on federalism and deference in education, the success of state finance litigation, and the benefits of local control of education); Michael Heise, *The Political Economy of Education Federalism*, 56 EMORY L.J. 125, 154 (2006) (emphasizing the value of local accountability for reform that would be lost if the focus of reform shifted to the federal level). In prior scholarship, I proposed that Congress should enact a federal right to education that aims to develop each child's mental and physical abilities, talents, and personality to his or her fullest potential and to reduce interstate inequalities. Kimberly Jenkins Robinson, *The Case for a Collaborative Enforcement Model for a Federal Right to Education*, 40 U.C. DAVIS L. REV. 1653, 1712 (2007). In addition, at least two scholars argue that the Fourteenth Amendment recognizes substantial substantive protection for education and that Congress must play a critical role in promoting equal educational opportunity. *See* Derek W. Black, *The Constitutional Compromise to Guarantee Education*, 70 STAN. L. REV. 735, 746–47, 835 (2018) (recommending that Congress exercise its authority under the Fourteenth Amendment to protect education as a right of state citizenship and embracing congressional oversight to prevent and address particular education abuses, thereby engaging in "'process-based' oversight" of education, but not calling for a federal right to education); Goodwin Liu, *Education, Equality, and National Citizenship*, 116 YALE L.J. 330, 334 (2006) (arguing that the Citizenship Clause of the Fourteenth Amendment grants the authority and creates an obligation for Congress to guarantee "a meaningful floor of educational opportunity throughout the nation"). Derek Black's chapter 5 in this volume examines scholarship that argues for judicial creation or recognition of a federal right to education.

13. For a full exploration of this idea, *see* Kimberly Jenkins Robinson, *No Quick Fix for Equity and Excellence: The Virtues of Incremental Shifts in Education Federalism*, 27 STAN. L. & POL'Y REV. 201, 220–49 (2016).

14. *See id.* at 221–22.

15. *See id.* at 222–25; JENNINGS, *supra* note 12, at 196.

16. 567 U.S. 519, 580–82 (2012) (plurality opinion); *id.* at 680–81, 689 (Scalia, Kennedy, Thomas & Alito, J.J., dissenting).

17. *See* Robinson, *Disrupting Education Federalism*, *supra* note 11, at 1010–12.

18. *See* Robinson, *supra* note 13, at 227.

19. Title IX of the Education Amendments of 1972, Pub. L. No. 92-318 (codified as amended at 20 U.S.C. §§ 1681–88 (2012 & Supp IV 2016)).

20. *See* Robinson, *supra* note 13, at 231.

21. *See id.* at 231–32.

22. JENNINGS, *supra* note 12, at 186.

23. *Id.* at 146.

24. *Id.*

25. *Id.* at 144.

26. Kimberly Jenkins Robinson, *Resurrecting the Promise of* Brown: *Understanding and Remedying How the Supreme Court Reconstitutionalized Segregated Schools*, 88 N.C. L. REV. 787, 797–801 (2010) (analyzing the impact of Brown v. Bd. of Educ., 349 U.S. 294 (1955)).

27. *Id.* at 787, 805–11, 840 (citing Green v. Cty. Sch. Bd. of New Kent Cty., 391 U.S. 430, 442 (1968)).

28. Individuals with Disabilities in Education Act, 20 U.S.C. §§ 1414, 1415 (1202 & Supp. V 2017) *et seq.*; JENNINGS, *supra* note 12, at 145, 147.

29. *See* Robinson, *supra* note 12, at 1715–22.

30. *See id.* at 1716–19.

31. *See* PAUL MANNA, COLLISION COURSE: FEDERAL EDUCATION POLICY MEETS STATE AND LOCAL REALITIES 49, 83–85 (2011); Robinson, *supra* note 12, at 1719–21; NATASHA USHOMIRSKY ET AL., EDUC. TR., TRENDS IN STATE ESSA PLANS: EQUITY ADVOCATES STILL HAVE WORK TO DO 9 (2017).

32. *See* Robinson, *supra* note 12, at 1721–22.

33. *See id.* at 1733–34.

34. *See id.* at 1728–30.

35. *See* Robinson, *supra* note 13, at 242–47.

36. *See* Robinson, *supra* note 12, at 1730–31.

37. *See id.* at 1731–32, 1734–35.

38. *See, e.g.,* Missouri v. Jenkins, 515 U.S. 70, 98–99, 102 (1995); Freeman v. Pitts, 503 U.S. 467, 489–90 (1992); Bd. of Educ. of Okla. City Pub. Schs. v. Dowell, 498 U.S. 237, 248 (1991); Milliken v. Bradley, 418 U.S. 717, 741–44 (1974); San Antonio Indep. Sch. Dist. v. Rodriguez, 411 U.S. 1, 44 (1973). For a full account of how the Supreme Court has relied on education federalism to deny efforts to advance equal educational opportunity, *see* Robinson, *The High Cost of Education Federalism*, *supra* note 11, at 294–314.

39. C. Kirabo Jackson et al., *The Effects of School Spending on Educational and Economic Outcomes: Evidence from School Finance Reforms*, 131 Q.J. ECON. 157, 160 (2016) ("Although we find small effects for children from affluent families, for low-income children, a 10% increase in per pupil spending each year for all 12 years of public school is associated with 0.46 additional years of completed education, 9.6% higher earnings, and a 6.1 percentage point reduction in the annual incidence of adult poverty. The results imply that a 25% increase in per pupil spending throughout one's school years could eliminate the average attainment gaps between children from low-income . . . and nonpoor families.").

40. *See* KLARMAN, *supra* note 3, at 155–74; JAMES E. RYAN, FIVE MILES AWAY, A WORLD APART: ONE CITY, TWO SCHOOLS, AND THE STORY OF EDUCATIONAL OPPORTUNITY IN MODERN AMERICA 153 (2010).

41. *See* RYAN, *supra* note 40, at 153 ("Most legislatures are slow to act; some ignore the decision altogether"); William S. Koski, *Beyond Dollars? The Promises and Pitfalls*

of the Next Generation of Educational Rights Litigation, 117 COLUM. L. REV. 1897, 1909–15 (2017) ("[C]ourts may also be deterred by the prospect of having reached their institutional limitations in the face of legislative recalcitrance.").

42. RYAN, *supra* note 40, at 151.

43. DONALD L. HOROWITZ, THE COURTS AND SOCIAL POLICY 257 (1977).

44. *See* MCGUINN, *supra* note 2, at 1, 166; Alyson Klein, *How ESSA Passed: The Inside Scoop, in* THE EVERY STUDENT SUCCEEDS ACT: WHAT IT MEANS FOR SCHOOLS, SYSTEMS AND STATES 43, 57 (Frederick M. Hess & Max Eden eds., 2017).

45. *See* Robinson, *supra* note 13, at 242–47.

46. Robinson, *Disrupting Education Federalism, supra* note 11, at 994–1000; JEN-NINGS, *supra* note 12, at 208; Rebell, *supra* note 10, at 52–53.

47. MANNA, *supra* note 31, at 49, 83–85.

48. USHOMIRSKY ET AL., *supra* note 31, at 9.

49. *See* BRUCE D. BAKER, MARK WEBER, AJAY SRIKANTH, ROBERT KIM, AND MICHAEL ATZBI, THE REAL SHAME OF THE NATION: THE CAUSES AND CONSEQUENCES OF INTERSTATE INEQUITY IN PUBLIC SCHOOL INVEST-MENTS 38–39 (2018).

50. RYAN, *supra* note 40, at 303.

51. GERALD N. ROSENBERG, THE HOLLOW HOPE: CAN COURTS BRING ABOUT SOCIAL CHANGE? 155–56 (1991); Michael J. Klarman, Brown *and* Lawrence *(and* Goodridge*)*, 104 MICH. L. REV. 431, 473–82 (2005).

52. *See* RYAN, *supra* note 40, at 14.

53. MCGUINN, *supra* note 2, at 31.

54. JENNINGS, *supra* note 12, at 214.

55. Rose v. Council for Better Educ., 790 S.W.2d 186, 208 (Ky. 1989) (quoting Carroll v. Bd. of Educ. of Jefferson Cty., 410 F. Supp. 234 (W.D.Ky.1976), *aff'd,* 561 F.2d 1 (6th Cir. 1977)).

56. JENNINGS, *supra* note 12, at 148.

57. *Id.* at 201.

58. Jack Jennings has proposed a federal statute to support teaching and learning that would double the amount of federal funding from 10 to 20 percent as well as create a separate federal guarantee of a good education if *Rodriguez* cannot be overturned and a constitutional amendment cannot be secured. *Id.* at 201, 216–17.

59. *Id.* at 188.

60. Robinson, *Disrupting Education Federalism, supra* note 11, at 1002–05, 1014–16; JENNINGS, *supra* note 12, at 187.

61. DAVID K. COHEN & SUSAN L. MOFFITT, THE ORDEAL OF EQUALITY: DID FEDERAL REGULATION FIX THE SCHOOLS? 188 (2009).

62. *See generally* DAVID TYACK & LARRY CUBAN, TINKERING TOWARD UTO-PIA: A CENTURY OF PUBLIC SCHOOL REFORM 7 (1995) ("[H]istory provides a generous time frame for appraising reforms. It is not driven by the short-term needs of election cycles, budgets, foundation grants, media attention, or the

reputations of professional reformers. Certain reforms may look successful when judged soon after adoption, but in fact they may turn out to be fireflies, flickering brightly but soon fading.").

63. San Antonio Indep. Sch. Dist. v. Rodriguez, 411 U.S. 1, 44 (1973).

64. For instance, state leaders and some members of Congress criticized No Child Left Behind for inadequate funding. *See* MANNA, *supra* note 31, at 61–64, 157.

65. *See* DONATELLA DELLA PORTA & MARIO DIANI, SOCIAL MOVEMENTS: AN INTRODUCTION 248 (2nd ed., 2006); ERIC FONER, THE STORY OF AMERICAN FREEDOM (1998); SOCIAL MOVEMENTS AND AMERICAN POLITICAL INSTITUTIONS 1 (Anne Costain & Andrew S. McFarland eds., 1998).

66. *See generally* Charles J. Ogletree, Jr. & Kimberly Jenkins Robinson, *The Enduring Legacy of* San Antonio Independent School District v. Rodriguez, *in* THE ENDURING LEGACY OF *RODRIGUEZ*: CREATING NEW PATHWAYS TO EQUAL EDUCATIONAL OPPORTUNITY 1 (Charles J. Ogletree, Jr. & Kimberly Jenkins Robinson eds., 2015); William S. Koski, *Notes from California on the Potential and Pitfalls of Teacher Quality Litigation, in* THE ENDURING LEGACY OF *RODRIGUEZ, supra,* at 119.

67. *See* Jean Anyon, *Progressive Social Movements and Educational Equity*, 23 EDUC. POL'Y 194, 206, 213 (2009) (noting that "[t]he past 15 years have witnessed the appearance and rapid growth across the nation of community organizing specifically for school reform, or education organizing" and that such efforts would need to connect to other alliances to build a social movement); NEWMAN, *supra* note 10, at 88 ("Organizing groups engaged in education reform are proliferating across the United States, as is scholarship that examines their principles, strategies, and outcomes."). *But see* David Shepard, *Will a Social Movement Save Education?*, KENNEDY SCHOOL REV., Apr. 10, 2011, http://ksr.hkspublications.org (arguing that a social movement will not save education while also acknowledging that "[r]egardless of what we call it, the energy that has swept the education reform community in the past five years exceeds the energy we have generated in the previous five decades").

68. *See* Anyon, *supra* note 67, at 200–01.

69. JENNINGS, *supra* note 12, at 216.

70. *Id.* at 203.

8

No Time to Lose

Why the United States Needs an Education Amendment to the US Constitution

SOUTHERN EDUCATION FOUNDATION

Introduction

This chapter outlines the case for an Education Amendment to the US Constitution to reduce radical disparities in the allocation of resources and funds for the education of the nation's public school students. The chapter argues that an Education Amendment is the best way to fundamentally reform the structural arrangements that are limiting the talent and productive capacities of millions of Americans. Such an amendment would provide a permanent framework for the exercise of federal power in the area of public education and provide sorely needed clarification of the federal role. Enactment of an Education Amendment requiring the federal government to augment state resources and finances to ensure that all Americans have fair and equal access to quality public education is an idea, a possibility, whose time has come.

The Southern Education Foundation (SEF) is the South's only and longest standing public, nonprofit organization devoted to advancing equity and excellence in education, from preschool through higher education. In this interconnected world, providing more and better education to all Americans should be a national priority of the utmost magnitude and importance. For over 150 years, SEF has not shied away from putting inconvenient truths about public educational opportunities or their structures before the public and policy makers while continually pressing for change. This chapter is written in the spirit of carrying forward in that tradition.

Since the nation's founding, the United States has experimented with highly decentralized systems of public education, primarily financed and controlled by state and local government. The results have been decidedly mixed. The status quo in public education—disturbingly low rates of educational access, achievement, and attainment—constitutes a crisis that, though unheralded, is every bit as important to present and future national well-being as the economic emergency that earlier this century turned all eyes toward Wall Street.

This chapter begins with an examination of the federal, state, and local roles in education—both historically and today—as critical background for understanding how an Education Amendment to the US Constitution might impact these roles. It also examines why there is no mention of education made in the US Constitution, as well as the ways in which federal, state, and local government roles are intertwined in education policy and practice. It considers the effects of shared governmental responsibility for public education, now spread across many entities, on the accountability and transparency needed to effect fundamental change and improvements. It questions whether it is any longer feasible to diffuse responsibility for education finance, resources, content, and quality control in light of changed circumstances and emergent challenges. It concludes with an examination of different models of an amendment to the US Constitution and how each model could improve public education.

The United States is in the midst of a global sea change, in which no existing education arrangement should be accepted without critical analysis and in which informed suggestions for structural change—a vision of what might be—are a fit subject for exploration. As the saying goes, "You can't get to where you want to go with the same old thinking that got you where you are." It is time for bold ideas and action. There is no time to lose.

In this time of extraordinary complexity and of daunting challenges to the environment, governance structures, human rights, and national defense, the United States must enhance and expand its increasingly diverse human capital at a scale equal to the challenges ahead. The single most powerful investment that any nation can make in its future is in the education of its people.

The United States was once a global leader in education. It can regain its place and a renewed position of strength by drawing on the talent, capacity, ingenuity, and innovation of a well-educated people. It must.

> We must . . . give our children the fairness of a start which will equip
> them with such an array of facts and such an attitude toward truth that
> they can have a real chance to judge what the world is and what its greater
> minds have thought it might be.
>
> —W. E. B. Du Bois[1]

Understanding the Constitution's Silence on Education

Since the nation's founding, the federal government has taken a piece-meal approach to setting education policy, practice, funding, and standards among the states. The federal government's engagement in these areas has been critically important but inadequate. The gross disparities in resources and funding illuminated in this and other chapters will not and cannot be solved by state and local governments alone. The country needs a new national strategy and commitment to address these issues. SEF believes that such efforts should begin with serious consideration of an Education Amendment to the US Constitution.

The US Constitution is the embodiment of the nation's collective aspirations of its people and the values they cherish. Its virtue is its permanence. The US Constitution provides the essential structure for apportionment of power between the government and the governed; among local, state, and national governments; and, within the national government itself. As the country's supreme law, the Constitution mediates the interests and aspirations of Americans, both as individuals and as groups. It embodies the collective identity of the people through its articulation of timeless values, rights, protections, and safeguards under whose influence all Americans live.

Often called a "living document," the US Constitution provides a framework through which issues and challenges, including those not envisioned or foreseeable by its authors, may be addressed. The US Constitution was not meant to reflect in detail all aspects of life in the nation but rather to serve as a distillation of fundamental, guiding principles for use over time.

Given the present and growing importance of public education to national well-being, it is anomalous for the US Constitution to remain silent on education. The Supreme Court of the United States, the ultimate interpreter of the Constitution, has declined to hold that education is a fundamental right guaranteed to the people, due to the absence of an explicit reference to education in the Constitution and the primacy of state government in this area under the nation's extant "federalist" system.

The US Constitution's silence on education has historical roots. First, the Constitution was written at a time when most Americans made their living through manual labor. Education, far from universal, was largely the prerogative of upper-class white males and those who were training for church ministry. Public education was originally intended only for white, male property owners.

Second, the authors of the US Constitution were primarily concerned with establishing structures and securing political rights. Social and economic rights, as understood today in international human rights instruments, were not among the prevailing political challenges of the day. The framers created a document largely focused on restraint rather than use of federal power.

As John Vile, dean and professor of political science at Middle Tennessee State University, has noted, "Although the delegates who assembled in Philadelphia at the Constitutional Convention of 1787 faced many crises and perceived crises, education was not among them. The problems that brought delegates to Philadelphia were more immediate—the inability of the national government to raise adequate revenues and provide adequate protections to the states, weak executive authority, difficulty in enforcing treaties and negotiating with foreign powers, lack of federal control over interstate commerce, the difficulty of adopting constitutional amendments, and perceived injustices at the state level."[2]

In colonial times, education was conducted mostly in the family or the church. The Massachusetts Bay colony enacted a law requiring elementary schooling in towns where more than fifty families resided, with the intent of combating "that old deluder, Satan."[3] Very few schools existed in the South, which was predominantly rural. As time wore on, education was increasingly viewed as the means of creating citizens capable of participation in democratic processes, a matter that grew in importance as colonial governments became democratic state governments.[4]

Perhaps the most compelling reason why the US Constitution did not originally address public education issues is that the newly created United States of America—unlike its modern-day counterpart—did not have the financial means to develop or support a national system of education.

National Engagement in Public Education

Despite the failure of the US Constitution to mention the word "education," the federal government has a long history of engagement in public education. In 1789, shortly after adoption of the US Constitution, Congress promulgated the Northwest Ordinances, which required the setting aside of lands for schools. Congress enacted the Morrill Act in 1862, initiating the creation of land-grant colleges. In 1867, the US Department of Education was established in clear recognition of the national interest in education.

After the abolition of slavery, the federal Freedmen's Bureau established a network of schools for blacks in the South, often with the help of religious bodies and groups such as the Peabody Fund, the Slater Fund, and the Jeanes Fund, that later came together as the Southern Education Foundation. The rationale for this extension of education by the federal government was that former slaves, now citizens, needed to be able to knowledgeably participate in democracy.

By the late 1860s, there was clear evidence that southern states were denying full rights of citizenship, including equal public education, to formerly enslaved African Americans, notwithstanding the intent of the Fourteenth Amendment. In response, Congress conditioned readmission of selected southern states to the Union by requiring them to provide free public schools and abide by race-blind voting requirements. In 1870, Representative George Hoar of Massachusetts introduced a bill for "a system of national education" for children ages six to eighteen, calling on the federal government to monitor and inspect schools operated by the states in order to determine which states might be delinquent in their obligation. The bill would have authorized the federal government to build national schools and prescribe textbooks where states failed in their duties to educate, and the national schools would have been supported by a federal tax.[5] The proposal was defeated, as was a later bill introduced by Senator Charles Sumner calling for integration of all of the nation's schools.

In 1875, President Ulysses S. Grant proposed amending the Constitution to enlarge the federal role in the nation's public schools, arguing that public schools should be free, nonsectarian, and accessible to all children. Four years later, Senator Ambrose Burnside moved to sell parcels of federal lands to raise funds for public schools, as well as for the new land-grant colleges. Neither President Grant nor Senator Burnside prevailed in his proposal, in large measure because an enhanced exercise of federal power in education was conflated with racially mixed schools and because of distrust for a centralized authority in education policy and practice.

In one of the final attempts in the nineteenth century to establish a federal role in K–12 education, Senator Henry Blair of New Hampshire repeatedly introduced a bill during the 1880s to grant federal appropriations to the states according to their illiteracy rates for residents aged ten and older. The bill included a provision for equal per-pupil amounts to both African American and white public schools. Senator Joseph Brown of Georgia argued on behalf of Blair's unsuccessful act that "if Congress has power to protect the voter in the free exercise of the use of the ballot, it must have power to aid in preparing him for its intelligent use."[6] The bill, if enacted, would have provided massive federal funds to many southern states, including those that were segregated. Southern resistance to federal intervention, coupled with a desire to maintain segregation, doomed the Blair bill. In a discussion of nineteenth-century attempts to expand the role of the federal government in public education, Goodwin Liu, now an Associate Justice of the Supreme Court of California, argues, "The Constitutional underpinnings of those early proposals are as compelling today as they were then: Congress is duty-bound to secure equal national citizenship by serving as the ultimate guarantor of educational opportunity."[7] Despite such a persuasive constitutional need for a larger federal role, competing interests and politics have continued to push back.

In the twentieth century, the US Congress enacted a series of federal statutes for education, thereby augmenting the federal government's role in addressing the need for a well-educated citizenry. The Servicemen's Readjustment Act of 1944, inspired by President Franklin D. Roosevelt, was a "GI Bill of Rights" that helped millions of military veterans attain education beyond high school after World War II. The National Science Foundation was created in 1950 to encourage and support research at colleges and universities and, eventually, curriculum development and training of teachers in elementary and secondary schools. The National Defense Education Act (1958), a response to Cold War fears, supported and advanced education in math, science, and foreign languages and proved to be a harbinger of large-scale federal aid for college students.

In 1965, the federal government launched a new era in K–12 education with the passage of the Elementary and Secondary Education Act (ESEA). Over the course of more than five decades, Title I, the centerpiece of this legislation, has generated tens of billions of dollars in aid to states for the education of economically disadvantaged students. In recent years, however, a flawed formula for distributing funds through Title I has begun "to reinforce, not reduce, the wide disparities in educational resources that exist across states."[8] As Liu observes, "our current policies treat the nation's schoolchildren not as 'citizens of the United States' but foremost as 'citizens of the state wherein they reside.'"[9]

A straight line connects ESEA to the much-debated No Child Left Behind Act (NCLB). Enacted in 2001, NCLB sought to raise the achievement of all elementary and secondary school students, with special emphasis on students enrolled in low-performing schools. The act required the disaggregation of test results for discrete subgroups in order to spotlight those schools that, despite overall achievement levels, failed to make adequate yearly progress in advancing all subgroups. The legislation had measures to promote competition among schools and required, as a last resort, that the states assume responsibility for underperforming schools that failed to meet prescribed standards over time. It also required that all public K–12 teachers of core academic subjects be certified as "highly qualified." The act, though prescriptive, did not provide full funding to ensure implementation and achievement of its goals.

The federal government also deepened its involvement in elementary and secondary schools with the creation and expansion of the National Assessment of Educational Progress (NAEP) in 1969, which conducts nationally representative assessments of students' knowledge and performance in various subject areas. NAEP results became the nation's measuring stick for gauging scores on the many different tests that individual states used to calculate NCLB's requirements for yearly progress. NAEP's tests, developed in recognition of the United States' need to compete in the global economy, have established the nation's own benchmarks for academic achievement at the elementary and secondary school levels as all students complete the same test. No federal standards exist, however, for establishing a baseline for the necessary funding and resources to provide a high-quality public education.

In retrospect, NCLB had a number of unintended consequences that were criticized by parents and teachers (and test-fatigued students). Its high-stakes barrage of state testing and the unrealistic expectations it set led to school closures; virtually all the underperforming schools were those with predominantly students of color and low-income students. The increased accountability led to the spread of the idea that the United States' schools were failing, which shifted the idea of charter schools as labs of innovation to being solutions in themselves. Further, the testing criteria's laser focus on English and math led to an unhealthy de-emphasis of other subjects such as the arts, science, and history; even physical education became endangered. Art, music, and other curricula that cultivate and nourish other areas of student growth and creativity were devalued as the standardized tests became conflated with teachers' jobs and the prestige and economic viability of the schools themselves. The consensus from many students was that school had become a place where they were drilled in rote facts, detached from any wider perspective or critical thinking, in order to know whether to select A, B, or C on a test. Some students found themselves hindered rather than helped when they entered college and discovered they had to think beyond multiple choice.

One positive contribution of NCLB is that it became a new source for an important piece of information: disaggregated student data. Schools were no longer able to hide or ignore subgroups of students in their overall school averages. This important component may be lost moving forward. While each state developed its own standards by the 2000s, there was no interstate consistency in proficiency standards. Therefore, in 2009, state leaders launched the Common Core State Standards (CCSS). According to the CCSS website, "State school chiefs and governors recognized the value of consistent, real-world learning goals and launched this effort to ensure all students, regardless of where they live, are graduating high school prepared for college, career, and life."[10] By

2015, forty-two states, Washington, DC, and several territories had adopted the CCSS for literacy and math.

Ultimately, a new approach was adopted to address the inherent weaknesses of NCLB and implement some of the lessons learned. NCLB effectively ended when President Barack Obama signed the Every Student Succeeds Act (ESSA) into law in 2015. According to Alyson Klein, when ESSA debuted, it was "in many ways a U-turn from the . . . much-maligned version of the ESEA law, the No Child Left Behind Act."[11] While ESSA still calls for benchmark testing in grades 3 through 8 and once in high school, "beyond that, states get wide discretion in setting goals, figuring out just what to hold schools and districts accountable for, and deciding how to intervene in low-performing schools. And while tests still have to be a part of state accountability systems, states must incorporate other factors that get at students' opportunity to learn, like school-climate and teacher engagement, or access to and success in advanced coursework."[12] Depending on the state plan, some level of disaggregated data is still provided.[13] This varies, however, as states define subgroups differently. This lack of specificity by ESSA is resulting in various approaches to tracking achievement of all students.

Despite stipulated requirements and objectives, current federal statutes allow states to devise educational goals of widely varying rigor. Some states have high expectations of student achievement, while others have far less ambitious targets. Some state constitutions have been interpreted to set high bars of proficiency; others have set the bar remarkably low. In the current arrangement, the federal government is not obliged to provide monies or resources to enable states to meet their own or voluntary federal NAEP standards of proficiency. As a result, today's taxpaying public is confused by differing reports issued by various education bodies pointing to deficiencies in relation to one set of standards, while other standards are used to demonstrate progress or achievement. It is a condition that at best has produced a stalemate instead of national reform.

The Federal Government Should Protect Vulnerable Groups: A Fair Opportunity to Learn Should Be National in Scope

One of the most significant turning points in US education was reached after years of test-case litigation when the United States Supreme Court outlawed de jure racial segregation in public elementary and secondary education in *Brown v. Board of Education*. The High Court said with prescience,

> Today, education is perhaps the most important function of state and local governments. Compulsory school attendance laws and the great expenditures for education both demonstrate our recognition of the importance of education to our democratic society. It is required in the performance of our most basic public responsibilities, even service in the armed forces. It is the very foundation of good citizenship. Today it is a principal instrument in awakening the child to cultural values, in preparing him for later professional training, and in helping him to adjust normally to his environment. In these days, it is doubtful that any child may reasonably be expected to succeed in life if he is denied the opportunity of an education. Such an opportunity, where the state has undertaken to provide it, is a right which must be made available to all on equal terms.[14]

The plaintiffs in *Brown* were fundamentally seeking redress from the unequal and inferior education provided to black students. They believed that through integration, blacks would have a fair chance of receiving an education as good as their white counterparts, because blacks and whites would attend the same public schools and be afforded the same opportunities.

Since 1954, many cases have sought to enforce the mandate of *Brown* and undo the system of unequal access to quality education that has unjustly marginalized African Americans. Despite progress in desegregation, gains were in many instances transitory, due to changing judicial mandates or racially identifiable housing patterns over ensuing years, declining socioeconomics, and the phenomenon known as "white flight." Ultimately, the United States Supreme Court set a very high bar for plaintiffs seeking redress for racial segregation and discrimination in public education. The Court also sanctioned mechanisms for jurisdictions long under federal desegregation orders to be released from further compliance obligations. The back door to ensuring that African American students have access to a quality education commensurate to that provided to whites through use of desegregation was effectively shut by the High Court's 2007 decision in *Parents Involved in Commu-*

nity Schools v. Seattle. In this case, the High Court invalidated voluntary integration efforts undertaken by the school districts that relied on race as the basis for making school assignments.

De jure segregation in public education is now clearly unlawful. But de facto segregation, which may be attributed to class or to school district boundaries and assignment policies, is pervasive and difficult to challenge.

Education Finance, Equity, and Adequacy Litigation: Important but Only "Half Measures"

As the desegregation door began to close on integration as a means by which to challenge unequal education opportunity afforded to blacks, a new line of cases came to the forefront. Although it came nearly half a century ago, the 1973 Texas case *San Antonio Independent School District v. Rodriguez,* described in chapter 1 of this volume, epitomizes cases that have sought to establish that the US Constitution provides a cognizable right to equal education opportunity. Plaintiffs in such cases sought to upend state public education finance schemes that, due to reliance on local property taxes by a school district, resulted in gross disparities in amounts of funds and resources available for the public education of low-income students compared to affluent students. The plaintiffs in these cases relied largely on the US Constitution and the Equal Protection Clause to argue their claims of deprivation of rights.

The High Court held that education is not a fundamental right whose unequal provision requires "strict scrutiny." It declined to hold that there is either an implied or explicit right to education within the US Constitution or to hold "wealth" as a "suspect classification" requiring the highest level of judicial examination. Rebuffed by the High Court, lawyers for low-income students and school districts turned to state courts to litigate a series of cases, relying on state constitutional provisions with mixed results. "Equity" cases, for example, sought to secure equal per-pupil expenditures as a means by which to reduce large-scale funding and resource disparities by school districts.[15]

Though some of the equity cases were successful and yielded important improvements in public education finance equalization, this line of litigation has now been largely supplanted by "education adequacy cases." Adequacy cases rely heavily on education clauses in state constitutions to challenge the adequacy of school finance systems in districts where the quality of education fails to meet constitutionally mandated standards, as demonstrated by an examination of educational inputs, outputs, or both. These cases spotlight issues such as the achievement gap and its causes, inequitable funding between low-income and affluent school districts, disparities in coursework, teacher assignments, retention, access to technology, physical plants of schools, and other such concerns. They raise critical questions about the standards by which to measure adequacy and "what it costs" to educate a child to a level deemed appropriate in the state at issue. These cases seem to be more attractive to courts than cases reliant primarily on challenges to education finance per se, because they allow the courts to receive specific evidence documenting the denial of students' state-provided constitutional rights to receive an adequate education.

Such cases often invoke standardized test results to demonstrate noncompliance with state standards. But the use of these test results can also lead, ironically, to unfair consequences for students and teachers in underfinanced and underresourced schools. As Jack Boger, professor of law at the University of North Carolina School of Law and former dean of that school, writes, "[I]f high stakes testing programs are implemented in circumstances where educational resources are inadequate . . . there is potential for serious harm. Policy makers and the public may be misled . . . ; students may be placed at increased risk of educational failure and dropping out; [and] teachers may be blamed or punished for inequitable resources over which they have no control."[16]

Limited funds and resources such as those mentioned in chapter 1 are invariably major factors in the failure to meet given standards as articulated in state constitutions or statutes. Although many state constitutional provisions and statutes set a relatively low standard of "adequacy," such cases have had a generally positive impact on public education financing and resourcing.

At least forty-five states have been party to lawsuits initiated by low-income groups, often composed largely of members of minority groups, who argue that public education in the states in which they reside is inadequate to meet specified achievement norms set forth in state constitutions.[17] Depending on the language of the state constitutional provision at issue, the courts have variously articulated the standard of achievement to be used for purposes of assessing education adequacy. "The common approaches have been to define adequacy as (1) the spending levels of districts of schools with high levels of performance; (2) the spending necessary for specific resources (qualified teachers, certain pupil-teacher ratios, sufficient textbooks, etc.) that professionals judge to be adequate; or, (3) a level of spending sufficient to bring all students to some adequate level of outcomes, which itself needs to be explained."[18]

The results of the litigation have been variable, as have the theories used by experts to evaluate ways to achieve adequacy and methods for determining projected costs. As documented in voluminous literature, some adequacy lawsuits have resulted in increases in funding and other mandated policy and practice changes for prevailing parties. Others have achieved only partial success and have been unable to realize the full desired impact. Still others have prompted public demands for education improvements even when formal litigation has failed. In most cases, courts have shied away from requiring recalcitrant state executives or legislatures to provide the necessary resources for generous implementation of remedies, frustrating the potential transformative impact of such litigation. Many such lawsuits are still pending.

In states with large numbers of low-income people and limited tax bases, state defendants have sometimes asserted simple lack of money to provide resources for the achievement of required remedial action. In these cases, geography and the inability of states or local subdivisions to comply with state constitutional provisions have become a reality that state courts are loath to address. The absence of a federal obligation or duty to provide a baseline of resources or monies necessary to ensure compliance speaks to the need for a new arrangement, a new relationship between the states and the federal government in relation to public education finance.

Education adequacy cases, moreover, are unable to address a pernicious aspect of disparate financing and resourcing of public education: radical inequality in the capacities of discrete states to raise requisite funds and resources or the disinclination to do so for reasons unrelated to what students need for a quality opportunity to learn. The interstate issues, reflective of demographics, in addition to tax bases of varying dimensions and productivity levels and diverse political inclinations regarding the role of government and education, can only be addressed through federal leadership. Unless students are to be forever consigned to "geography as destiny," the federal government must be called upon to address these concerns.

An Education Amendment Is the Best Way to Reduce Radical Intra- and Interstate Disparities in the Opportunity to Learn

The Introduction and Chapter 1 of this book highlight data establishing that the United States' many systems of public education constitute a patchwork of radical inequality in resources and finance, which yields learning opportunities of widely variable quality depending on place, class, and race. Within states, the amount of money and resources allocated for public education also varies greatly. Some students are provided a second-class opportunity to learn, while others are privileged to enjoy a good-quality public education. Radical disparities in funding and resources are even greater between states, and regional disparities exist as well.

Clearly locales and states have dramatically different capacities and inclinations to fund public education improvements. Liu sums up the present moment:

> Although interstate inequalities have decreased since Reconstruction, it is unlikely that lingering disparities will become much narrower without a more robust federal role. The overall level of interstate inequality in per-pupil spending has changed little in recent decades despite school finance litigation and policy reforms touting high standards for all children. Unfavorable interstate comparisons have spurred improvement in some states but not others, and substantial disparities in fiscal capacity constrain the extent of interstate equalization that states can achieve on their own.... [T]he constitutionally motivated project of affording all children an adequate education for equal citizenship remains a work in progress.[19]

The only way to address the gross disparities in education resources and finance within and among states is for the federal government to assume the duty of safeguarding against such disparities. An amendment might impose such a duty on the federal government to ensure that states provide all students with the opportunity for public education of a quality determined and articulated through legislation, irrespective of place, class, or race. Ultimately, however, for such an amendment to have optimal impact, it would have to oblige the federal government itself to provide resources and guidance to ensure that gross inequality in the opportunity to learn is addressed. The import of either approach is clear. The federal government would be the guarantor of fairness in the opportunity to learn, irrespective of venue.

This is an area of complexity, to be sure, for which diverse formulas would need to be developed—and implemented through legislation enacted by Congress—to assess what state, local, and federal governments must do to ensure a baseline of equitable finance and resource allocation in public education. A first step in this direction might be to convene a high-level, independent, national commission to assess these complexities and recommend options for the way forward.

By inserting education into the highest law in the land, a permanent framework for recognition of the federal role in education would be created, a framework that would not be subject to rapid or quixotic change for political reasons. An Education Amendment would codify a commitment to development of the nation's human capital to its utmost potential. It would also position the United States within the global community of nations that acknowledge education as a fundamental and universal human right.

There ought to be nothing sacrosanct about the current vesting of primary responsibility for public education in the states or about the apportionment of governmental obligations for the provision of public education. Rather, it is anomalous to have a federal Constitution that has no safeguards or requirements regarding the national interest in education, while all fifty state constitutions explicitly recognize the importance of education. If the United States is one nation, there ought to exist an overarching framework for the vetting and making of decisions related to quality public education opportunity.

Only by vesting in the federal government a leadership role in public education can all fifty states work together to improve education in the national interest and gain access to resources necessary to make real change. In the interest of US business, national security, and a basic commitment to equal rights, the federal government should no longer tolerate radical disparities in the quality of education provided by state and local governments or at best urge piecemeal reform while providing limited incentives for change. What is needed is leadership, combined with resources and money, to forge new partnerships between levels of government so that all US students, especially those who need help the most and are receiving the least, are treated fairly and receive the requisite skills for productive participation in democratic society.[20]

An Education Amendment could help set the standard of achievement necessary to serve the national interest and to provide both the means and methods by which to meet that standard. It would help to ensure that patterns of education opportunity stratification do not become permanently calcified at a time when the nation is becoming more diverse and when maintenance of healthy intergroup relations and unity are vitally important to the country's future.

An Education Amendment Would Ratify Existing Public Support for National Leadership in Education

According to a poll of American adults conducted by the Pew Research Center in January 2018, "improving education" is the number-two priority of Americans—just below "fighting terrorism" and just above the economy.[21] While the ultimate outcome of an Education Amendment effort would be the best predictor of public sentiment and will, there is little to suggest that such an effort would not be well received by many, if not most, Americans.

An effort to frame an Education Amendment and secure its enactment would codify what some people have called the "popular Constitution," that is, the general understanding among Americans of their rights and entitlements. An amendment effort would catalyze development of new approaches to public education cost sharing and the establishment of a common benchmark, actual and/or aspirational, against which to measure national progress and achievement. Ultimately, if a new framework for delivery, financing, and resourcing of public education were to be developed, it is likely that cost savings attributable to reduction in duplicative processes and jurisdictional overlapping would be realized.

An Education Amendment and concomitant legislation to implement its provisions would establish accountability at the highest level of government. It would call for national leadership to address thorny issues of policy in relation to the national interest. Presidential candidates of both parties often speak of what they would do to improve US education, conveying the impression to voters that the real power to fund public education, to problem-solve and lead, reposes in federal hands. There is a need to align federal responsibility and authority with public expectations and create a focal point for education improvements that are tangible and in the national interest.

At present, efforts to ensure accountability notwithstanding, there are approximately fourteen thousand school districts in fifty states, with tiered responsibility for public education funding and content decision-making. When everyone is responsible for something, effectively no one is accountable.

State-based efforts that rely on state standards to set appropriate benchmarks for education achievement and attainment are both variable and an uneven means by which to ensure high levels of education for the entire nation. Were the federal government clearly responsible for the elimination and/or reduction of radical disparities in public education finance, it would promote effective change and transparency in decision-making.

An Education Amendment Process Would Foster National Consensus and Build Public Will for Change

SEF believes that the American people at every level need to become involved in a searching inquiry about the intrinsic value of quality public education. The best way to ensure this type of national, democratic consensus building is through the laborious constitutional amendment process, state by state. Such a process would ensure that the outcome reflects the collective, informed will of the voting public and has the force of public will and consensus behind it.

The process by which the US Constitution may be amended permits changes only after a full, deliberative, and broad-based process of engagement of the American people. The US Constitution sets a high but not insuperable bar for passage of amendments. Article V provides,

The Congress, whenever two thirds of both houses shall deem it necessary, shall propose amendments to this Constitution, or, on the application of the legislatures of two thirds of the several States, shall call a
convention for proposing amendments, which, in either case, shall be
valid to all intents and Purposes, as part of this Constitution, when ratified by the legislatures of three fourths of the several States, or by conventions in three fourths thereof, as the one or the other mode of ratification
may be proposed by the Congress. Provided that no amendment which
may be made prior to the Year one thousand eight hundred and eight
shall in any manner affect the first and fourth clauses in the ninth Section
of the first article; and that no State, without its consent, shall be deprived
of its equal Suffrage in the Senate.[22]

James Madison, one of the framers of the US Constitution, commented
on the language finally approved, "The mode preferred by the convention seems to be stamped with every mark of propriety. It guards equally
against that extreme facility, which would render the Constitution too
mutable; and that extreme difficulty, which might perpetuate its discovered faults. It, moreover, equally enables the general and the State
governments to originate the amendment of errors, as they may be
pointed out by the experience on one side, or on the other."[23]

An earnest national debate about the causes and consequences of
education inequality in light of changing national demographics is long
overdue. A full, democratic, participatory effort is required to effect
changes and enhancements in public education finance of the scale necessary to meet national needs.

In fact, the nation has already begun this consensus-building process, as most recently demonstrated by the enactment of Common Core
Standards. There is growing awareness among Americans of the need
for binding national standards to provide both an achievement destina-
tion for public education in key subject matters and measures by which
to assess progress made or the lack thereof. This is an important first
step toward providing a shared set of standards for all students that the
country could build on to develop common assessments to measure academic progress.

However, there is not and has not been an equivalent effort to establish national resource and funding benchmarks in order to reduce radi-

cal disparities that in many venues result in denial of the opportunity to learn among low-income students. Such national resource and funding benchmarks are also necessary.

An Effort to Pass an Education Amendment Would Have Positive Effects Even If the Effort Were Unsuccessful

Even if ultimately unsuccessful, an effort to amend the US Constitution in relation to education would achieve the following:

- Underscore the importance of public schools to the preservation of democratic values and national security
- Draw attention to the question of whether the current system of resource allocation for public schools is sufficient to meet the needs of the twenty-first century
- Remind Americans that the quality of education now depends extensively on venue—where a child lives—and that inequity is built into the current system
- Lead to consideration of whether the federal government should be obliged to assist schools that serve students in low-resource states or districts to gain access to more funding and resources
- Create "space" for intermediate measures to reduce inequality by legislation or the reform of existing practices

One of the lessons of the unsuccessful effort to enact the Equal Rights Amendment (ERA) is that it mobilized public awareness of the reality of gender-based discrimination, encouraged creative and voluntary responses to it, created a focal point for the development of public policy related to diverse manifestations of gender-based discrimination, and mobilized key constituencies to use political processes to secure redress of grievances. There is general consensus today that, though the ERA was unsuccessful, many of the aims to which the amendment was devoted have been achieved, at least to a degree.

Over time, several amendments to the US Constitution related to education have been proposed. None have been successful. These proposals have included amendments to create a national university, to restrict aid to parochial schools, to authorize prayer in public schools, to limit affirmative action in education, to define circumstances under which busing to achieve integration cannot be undertaken, and to designate English the "official" language of the nation and its public schools.[24] More general education amendments have likewise failed to win sufficient support.

Time for Change

SEF believes that the United States is just beginning to come to terms with the new, interconnected, "flat" world of which it is a part. It has gone through a period of appropriate precursors to an amendment effort and, at the very least, has come to understand the limitations of piecemeal efforts in response to problems as large and complex as those presented by nearly fourteen thousand school districts in fifty states. As skilled jobs are exported and well-educated people are imported to fill jobs that Americans have been deprived of the requisite education to handle, a consensus supportive of the need for change is building momentum.

It is beyond the scope of this chapter to propose or promote particular language for an Education Amendment to the US Constitution. A measure of such importance should be the product of in-depth deliberation by the American people and their representatives and leaders at all levels. The specific language of such an amendment is best left to those who can invest significant time to frame it with precision.

It is appropriate to note, however, that a federal Education Amendment could be modeled in several different ways, depending on its primary aim, and that each approach would have varying potential impacts. Examples that demonstrate the range of choices follow (without regard to order of priority):

Adequacy Model: This type of amendment could vest within the federal government the obligation to ensure that Americans have access to education of a specified type and quality. The constitutions of states offer many examples of language that could provide a point of departure for this approach.

Equitable Finance Model: If written primarily to require the federal government to provide money and resources necessary to ensure access to quality public education, this type of amendment could help ameliorate disparities within and between states.

Intrastate Finance Equalization Model: An amendment could require finance and resource equalization within states. Such an approach would help to address intrastate disparities but would leave interstate disparities largely intact.

Interstate Finance Equalization Model: If written to ensure that all states have equivalent resources for the public education of students within a range to be delimited by legislation, this approach could address problems experienced by low-wealth states and/or school districts.

International Human Rights Model: This type of amendment could declare that all Americans have an equal right to education of a particular type or quality without regard to location, class, or economic status. Were a formulation of this type to be adopted, it would be the first amendment to focus primarily on economic rather than political rights.

Civil Rights Model: This type of amendment might prohibit the states from relying on particular forms of education finance and resource allocation or require provision of a right to education of equally high quality.

Whatever the form of the amendment, SEF believes that its aim must be to ensure that the fundamental resource and finance disparities documented in this book are addressed and resolved. Without equalized funding and resources across districts, states, and the nation, Americans will continue to be deprived of equal rights in education.

The language of an education amendment should be simple and general but clear enough in intent so that it can be neither subverted nor ignored. Details of specific strategies to achieve the ends articulated in the amendment would be left to implementing legislation enacted by Congress. Accountability measures would have to be addressed, and decisions about enforceability and standing would have to be resolved.

No Time to Lose

The time is nigh for a sustained and substantive examination by the American people of the likely consequences of an Education Amendment to the US Constitution. While some people will earnestly or reflexively oppose an Education Amendment on grounds that it would give rise to a new body of litigation or undue federal encroachment into state prerogatives, what is the alternative? To continue to allow state and local education policies to hobble national economic growth and competitiveness? To ignore the very real risk of eroding our country's standing in the world community of nations?

Although the nuances of education reform are many, the United States' educators know the building blocks of a quality education. A proliferation of studies shows that the following elements, all of which require resources and money, are fundamental:

- Early childhood services, including quality prekindergarten
- Full-day kindergarten
- Classes and schools small enough for students to receive individual attention
- Quality standards for content and for performance
- Appropriate, restorative discipline practices that aim to keep students in school
- Community-centered strategies
- High expectations for all students
- Qualified teachers who are culturally competent
- Principals who are instructional leaders
- Flexible approaches to help meet needs of English-language learners
- Student-centered, project-based learning
- Parental engagement and outreach to encourage and facilitate learning

If Americans were designing public education *de novo*, it is unlikely that anyone would create the current unequal, decentralized patchwork of educational decision-making, finance, and resource distribution. Such a system would be widely recognized as inefficient, inadequate, and unjust.

In relation to education, the point of no return for the United States may be imminent. The country will simply have too many uneducated, undereducated, or miseducated people to generate resources at a level required to effect fundamental change. An Education Amendment offers the possibility of change before it is too late.

This chapter has sought to show what is at stake and why it is important to consider how the US Constitution can be instrumental in helping the nation solve one of its most pressing challenges. An Education Amendment to the US Constitution would not constitute an end point of efforts to improve public education. However, it would and could be the most powerful point of departure for a national effort to do so.

At the heart of the United States' commitment to notions of fairness and equality lies a contradiction. Simply stated, it is that equal opportunity in the United States means little if one cannot develop, through access to a quality education, the capacity to take advantage of equal opportunity. Without a fair, high-quality public education system, the United States' promise of democracy is a hollow formalism.

SEF believes that the strategy for addressing structural infirmities in US public school education should begin with consideration of the nation's founding document, the US Constitution. The Constitution is the primary and most effective source of redress for issues of magnitude affecting the American people. Daniel Webster said it best: "We may be tossed upon an ocean where we can see no land—nor, perhaps, the sun and stars. But there is a chart and a compass for us to study, to consult, and to obey. The chart is the Constitution."[25]

The United States has no time to lose.

NOTES

The Southern Education Foundation thanks Lynn Huntley, who was president of the Southern Education Foundation when she wrote "No Time to Lose: Why America Needs an Education Amendment to the Constitution." This work was revised to become the chapter "Why the United States Needs an Education Amendment to the US Constitution." Kelley Ditzel provided excellent editorial assistance to revise the original publication.

1. W. E. B. DUBOIS SPEAKS: SPEECHES AND ADDRESSES 1920–1963 255 (Philip S. Foner ed., 1970).

2. John Vile, The Constitutional Amending Process and Federal Educational Reform 4–5 (2006) (unpublished SEF-commissioned report).

3. ELLWOOD P. CUBBERLEY, PUBLIC EDUCATION IN THE UNITED STATES 18 (1919).

4. INST. FOR EDUC. EQUITY AND OPPORTUNITY, EDUCATION IN THE 50 STATES: A DESKBOOK OF THE HISTORY OF STATE CONSTITUTIONS AND LAWS ABOUT EDUCATION 10 (2008).

5. Goodwin Liu, Education, Equality and National Citizenship, 116 YALE L.J. 330, 375–76 (2006).

6. Id. at 386–87, 390.

7. Goodwin Liu, *Interstate Inequality in Educational Opportunity*, 81 N.Y.U. L. REV. 2044, 2049 (2006). Support for this view may also be found in *Education in the 50 States: A Deskbook of the History of State Constitutions and Laws about Education*, *supra* note 4, at 3, which makes the case that one reason education was not mentioned in the US Constitution is because it was assumed to be an attribute of "citizenship." The report says that having "the intellectual skills necessary for meaningful participation in the community's political and economic life" was "a well recognized part of the landscape," and hence the framers found it unnecessary to articulate what was understood to be an implicit right to education.

8. Liu, *supra* note 5, at 402–03.

9. *Id.* at 403.

10. Common Core State Standards Initiative, *Development Process*, www.corestandards.org. (last visited June 12, 2018).

11. Alyson Klein, *Accountability and the ESEA Reauthorization Deal: Your Cheat Sheet*, EDUC. WK.: POLITICS K–12 (Nov. 23, 2015, 7:31 AM), http://blogs.edweek.org.

12. *Id.*

13. *Id.*

14. Brown v. Bd. of Educ., 347 U.S. 483, 493 (1954).

15. Michael A. Rebell, *Adequacy Litigations: A New Path to Equity*, *in* BRINGING EQUITY BACK: RESEARCH FOR A NEW ERA IN AMERICAN EDUCATIONAL POLICY 293, 295–97 (Janice Petrovich & Amy Stuart Wells eds., 2005) (discussing the "shift from 'equity' to 'adequacy' claims").

16. American Educational Research Association, *Position Statement on High-Stakes Testing* (July 2000), www.aera.net.

17. Liu, *supra* note 7, at 2046.

18. Norton W. Grubb, What Should Be Equalized? Litigation, Equity and the "Improved" School Finance (paper presented at the Rethinking Rodriguez: Education as a Fundamental Right Symposium, Berkeley, California, April 27–28, 2006).

19. Liu, *supra* note 5, at 399.

20. There are some who argue that public education is fatally flawed and broken and ought to be privatized. Certainly in contemporary times, the United States has witnessed considerable experimentation with public-private arrangements and charter schools. SEF does not oppose this experimentation but believes that education is too important to place into private hands, away from the bright light of public accountability. Nor is there any absorptive capacity now or in the foreseeable future for private entities to provide a quality education for millions of low-income students. Moreover, many private schools and charter schools have admissions requirements that low-income students would be unable to meet. Vouchers provide, in most cases, only partial reimbursement for private school education. The solution to the problems described in this chapter does not repose in these options.

21. Valerie Strauss, *New Poll of Americans' Top Priorities for 2018 Has Education at No. 2—Ahead of the Economy*, WASH. POST, Jan. 25, 2018, https://www.washington-post.com.

22. U.S. CONST. art. V.

23. THE FEDERALIST NO. 43, at 225 (James Madison) (Ian Shapiro ed., 2009).

24. Vile, *supra* note 2.

25. Daniel Webster, *The Mexican War, in* THE WRITINGS AND SPEECHES OF DANIEL WEBSTER IN EIGHTEEN VOLUMES, Vol. 13, at 365 (1903). The speech was delivered in Springfield, Massachusetts, on September 20, 1847.

PART III

What a Federal Right to Education Should Guarantee

9

Assuring Essential Educational Resources through a Federal Right to Education

LINDA DARLING-HAMMOND

I think by far the most important bill in our whole code is that for the diffusion of knowledge among the people. No other sure foundation can be devised for the preservation of freedom and happiness. . . . [The Education Act is] to avail the commonwealth of those talents and virtues which nature has sown as liberally among the poor as rich, and which are lost to their country by the want of means for their cultivation.
—Thomas Jefferson

Of all the civil rights for which the world has struggled and fought for 5000 years, the right to learn is undoubtedly the most fundamental. . . . The freedom to learn . . . has been bought by bitter sacrifice. And whatever we may think of the curtailment of other civil rights, we should fight to the last ditch to keep open the right to learn.
—W. E. B. Du Bois

That an adequate public education is essential to a functioning democracy, to liberty, and to equality has been a cornerstone of American thought since the founding fathers devised the fundamental principles of our nation. Even while education was denied to many citizens, the legal arguments for universal public education of a particular quality were being fashioned. The organization of education fell to the states, and every state constitution has a clause requiring something like "free appropriate," "sound basic," or "thorough and efficient" education. The federal Fourteenth Amendment brings an equity dimension to the evaluation of that education as it is provided within states—and, arguably, across states as well.

The meaning of these clauses with respect to the guaranteed provision of education quality has been litigated for well over a century, in part because of de jure and de facto segregation and in part because the historical expectation that local towns would fund schools—typically with property taxes—resulted in a highly inequitable distribution of burden and dollars. More than forty states have engaged or are currently engaged in school finance equity lawsuits, often in an iterative, recurring cycle of litigation. As Schott Foundation president John Jackson has quipped, "Each state has its state flag, its state bird, and its state school finance lawsuit." Defining what each state constitution requires is an ongoing arm wrestle between plaintiffs from low-wealth, low-spending districts, state governments, and the courts.[1]

In this chapter, I describe recent federal requirements for education that may establish an emerging federal standard on which a right to education may stand. I then outline the potential elements of that right, with regard to access to an appropriate curriculum, supported by necessary materials for learning and well-qualified educators. I conclude with recommendations for what the federal government could do to support equal access to those key elements for learning.

An Emerging Federal Standard for Education

Over the past twenty years, a new standard has emerged to judge what an adequate education is. Beginning in the 1990s, the federal Elementary and Secondary Education Act (ESEA)—then called the Improving America's Schools Act—required that states develop and set standards for student learning that could be used to guide assessments, educator training, and funding.[2] The authors of the notion of "standards-based reform" felt that "Opportunity to Learn" standards should also be required: when the national standards movement was first launched with the Goals 2000 Act in the Clinton administration, concerns about resources were squarely on the table. The report of the National Council on Education Standards and Testing (NCEST) argued both for national performance standards for students and for "school delivery standards" that would ensure the investments needed to meet the standards. The NCEST's Standards Task Force noted,

[I]f not accompanied by measures to ensure equal opportunity to learn, national content and performance standards could help widen the achievement gap between the advantaged and the disadvantaged in our society. If national content and performance standards and assessment are not accompanied by clear school delivery standards and policy measures designed to afford all students an equal opportunity to learn, the concerns about diminished equity could easily be realized. Standards and assessments must be accompanied by policies that provide access for all students to high quality resources, including appropriate instructional materials and well-prepared teachers. High content and performance standards can be used to challenge all students with the same expectations, but high expectations will only result in common high performance if all schools provide high quality instruction designed to meet the expectations.[3]

However, school delivery standards—or "Opportunity to Learn" standards, as they were also called—were a no-win proposition in the Congress, when representatives realized that outlining the resources expected for students would pave the way for more successful school funding lawsuits. So standards for what students should learn moved ahead without standards for what schools, districts, or states should provide.

Nearly three decades later, there is plentiful evidence that—while standards and assessments have been useful in clarifying goals and focusing attention on achievement—tests alone have not improved schools or created educational opportunities without investments in curriculum, teaching, and school supports.[4] In fact, in some states offering the harshest sanctions for students' failures to pass tests, inequality in access to resources has grown, fewer well-qualified teachers are available and willing to teach in the schools that are labeled failures, and more students are held back and pushed out of school. The school-to-prison pipeline has been the greatest beneficiary of this approach, especially in states that serve large numbers of students of color and new immigrants in systems that are highly unequal.[5]

The next iteration of the law—No Child Left Behind—took this notion further and required that schools achieve continuous improvement on test scores mapped to these standards for all students and for each of several subsets of students—defined by race, family income, special education status, and language background—and suffer consequences if specific test-score targets were not met each year. Furthermore, the federal Department of Education created strong monetary and regulatory incentives for states to adopt a set of standards, known as the Common Core State Standards, in English-language arts and mathematics. Although the standards were not federally created, the department's incentives created a strong federal role in defining outcome adequacy through conditions for federal funds.[6]

Although the current version of the ESEA, known as the Every Student Succeeds Act, has eliminated incentives for adopting the Common Core, it still requires states to set "challenging academic standards" for all public school students in English-language arts, mathematics, and science. These standards must be aligned with both the entrance requirements for credit-bearing coursework in the state's public higher-education system and the state's career and technical education standards. States must measure progress toward the standards with annual tests for which the state sets goals and targets for improvement overall and for each subset of students. The reporting of these scores also has to meet federal standards.

The Every Student Succeeds Act also requires states to track and set progress targets on additional measures, such as federally defined graduation rates and tested progress toward English proficiency of English learners, along with other state-determined measures. The law obligates states to intervene in and support low-performing schools or those that have large performance gaps among subgroups. States also must guarantee comparability in the quality of teachers available to students in low- and high-poverty schools (as measured by experience, subject-matter knowledge, and "effectiveness"), and states must make expenditure data for every school publicly available.[7]

Thus, the definition of an adequate education as meeting college- and career-ready standards is not only substantially more specific than it has been before; it is substantially more influenced by the federal government than it was when *San Antonio Independent School District v. Rodriguez* was decided in 1973. Congress has decided that there are specific elements associated with the education that states must provide if they want to receive federal funding.

Elements of a Right to Learn

A new spate of equity litigation has been stimulated by state efforts to set standards for all students without fully ensuring opportunities to learn. These lawsuits—which may be said to constitute the next generation of efforts begun by *Brown v. Board of Education*—argue that if states (as now required by the federal government as a condition for federal education funds) require all students to meet the same educational standards, they must assume a responsibility to provide resources adequate to allow students a reasonable opportunity to achieve those standards, including a curriculum that fully reflects the standards; teachers who are well qualified to teach the curriculum; and, the materials, texts, supplies, and equipment needed to support this teaching.

The logic is straightforward. Yet the path to educational opportunity through the state courts is tortuous, both because of differing interpretations regarding what courts should take on and in part because opponents of school finance reform have argued that centralized funding of schools would violate traditions of local control of schools. This argument continues to be made in finance lawsuits, despite the fact that local ability to meet standards for education quality is even more dependent on equitable funding than when the California Supreme Court unseated the myth of local control in its 1971 *Serrano* decision requiring reform:

> We need not decide whether such decentralized financial decision-making is a compelling state interest, since under the present financing system, such fiscal freewill is a cruel illusion for the poor school districts. . . . [S]o long as the assessed valuation within a district's boundaries is a major determinant of how much it can spend for its schools, only a district with a large tax base will be truly able to decide how much it really cares about education. The poor district cannot freely choose to tax itself into an excellence which its tax rolls cannot provide. Far from being necessary to promote local fiscal choice, the present financing system actually deprives the less wealthy districts of that option.[8]

Although parent and community involvement in public schools remains an important way to focus resources and decisions on local needs and to maintain accountability to parents and students, such participation does not depend on the local production of dollars for education. In many other countries that fund schools centrally and equally, local schools have extensive flexibility to design programs and interventions and decide how funds are used. Finland, Switzerland, Canada, Australia, and even highly centralized Singapore are all places where local communities and school-based educators are actively involved in deciding what goes on in their centrally funded schools. Indeed, one could argue that a level playing field of resources might be a precondition for genuine local control of educational decisions that matter.

A number of studies in recent years have shown that equalized investments in education that allocate more funds to the students with greater needs have strong positive effects on student outcomes,[9] which in turn create benefits for the population as a whole in the form of reduced costs for welfare, health care, crime, and incarceration, coupled with greater wage rates and tax payments.[10] For example, one recent analysis of the long-term effects of state school finance reforms found that a 10 percent increase in per-pupil spending for children from low-income families throughout all twelve school-age years led to a 9.8-percentage-point increase in graduation rates and, on average, an additional half year of educational attainment for these children, plus significantly higher family income and lower poverty rates for these children when they reached adulthood.[11] These improved outcomes were associated with increases in the numbers of teachers and their salaries, suggesting the likelihood of higher-quality staff and smaller class sizes and/or more instructional specialists available to support children's learning. State-level studies of school finance reforms have reached similar conclusions in Massachusetts, Vermont, Michigan, and California, among others.[12]

Other studies have documented how specific resources—including better-qualified teachers, smaller class sizes, and strong curriculum systems—contribute to student achievement gains.[13] On the strength of this research, for example, the North Carolina Supreme Court declared in its *Leandro* decision that a "sound, basic education" must aim to prepare students with the full curriculum needed to gain formal education or gainful employment in a "complex and rapidly changing society" as well as to discharge the duties of citizenship and that this requires the following:

1. That every child has the right to attend a public school with access to at least the following educational resources:
   a. In every classroom, a competent, certified, well-trained teacher who is teaching the standard course of study by implementing effective educational methods that provide differentiated, individualized instruction, assessment and remediation to the students in that classroom.
   b. In every school, a well-trained competent principal with the leadership skills and the ability to hire and retain competent, certified and well-trained teachers who can implement an effective and cost-effective instructional program that meets the needs of at-risk children so that they can have the opportunity to obtain a sound basic education by achieving grade level or above academic performance.
   c. In every school, the resources necessary to support the effective instructional program within that school so that the educational needs of all children, including at-risk children, can be met.[14]

In the remainder of this chapter, I consider research regarding the resources that students need to receive an excellent and equitable educational opportunity, including high-quality teachers and principals, access to a rigorous curriculum geared to the demands of the twenty-first-century society and economy, and the course materials and technology needed for such an education. I argue that a federal right to education—which may be considered a corollary of the now-strong federal prescriptions for educational standards, coupled with Fourteenth Amendment requirements—should guarantee these resources for all children as the nation strives to eliminate achievement gaps.

The Quality of Teachers

In the United States, teachers are the most inequitably distributed school resource. By every measure of qualifications—certification, subject-matter background, pedagogical training, selectivity of college attended, test scores, or experience—less qualified teachers are found in schools serving greater numbers of low-income and minority students.[15] As Kati Haycock, the founder and former CEO of the Education Trust, has noted, these statistics on differentials in credentials and experience, as shocking as they are, actually understate the degree of the problem in the most impacted schools: "For one thing, these effects are additive. The fact that only 25% of the teachers in a school are uncertified doesn't mean that the other 75% are fine. More often, they are either brand new, assigned to teach out of field, or low-performers on the licensure exam. . . . There are, in other words, significant numbers of schools that are essentially dumping grounds for unqualified teachers—just as they are dumping grounds for the children they serve."[16]

How Unequally Distributed Are Teachers?

Whenever teacher shortages occur—which is frequently, given the low wages that teachers earn in many states relative to other college-educated workers—states are likely to hire individuals without preparation to teach, and these individuals are most likely to be hired in the low-wealth, high-poverty schools serving the highest-need students.

In 2016–17, as standards were lowered to fill vacancies, nearly 50 percent of California's new teachers entered without having completed—or often having begun—training, and the vast majority of them were assigned to teach in high-need schools. In some districts more than 50 percent of newly hired teachers were uncertified.[17] Across the state, students in high-minority schools are nearly three times more likely to have unqualified teachers than are students in low-minority schools.[18] Similar inequalities have been documented in lawsuits challenging school funding in Massachusetts, New Jersey, New York, North Carolina, South Carolina, and Texas, among other states,[19] and in recent data from the US Department of Education's Office for Civil Rights.[20]

Does Teacher Quality Matter for Student Learning?

But do these aspects of teacher quality matter for student learning? A large body of research indicates that they do: studies at the state, district, school, and individual level have found that teachers' academic background, preparation for teaching, and certification status, as well as their experience, significantly affect their students' achievement.[21]

In combination, teachers' qualifications can have very large effects. For example, a study of high school students in North Carolina found that students' achievement was significantly higher if they were taught by a teacher who was certified in his or her teaching field, was fully prepared upon entry, had higher scores on the teacher licensing test, graduated from a competitive college, had taught for more than two years, or was National Board Certified.[22] While each of these traits made teachers more effective, the combined influence of having a teacher with most of these qualifications as compared to one having few of them was larger than the effects of race and parents' education combined. That is, the difference between the effect of having a very well-qualified teacher rather than one who was poorly qualified was larger than the average difference in achievement between a typical white student with college-educated parents and a typical black student with high-school-educated parents. The achievement gap would be much reduced if low-income minority students were routinely assigned such highly qualified teachers rather than the poorly qualified teachers they more often encounter.

A similar study of teachers in New York City also found that teachers' certification status, pathway into teaching, teaching experience, graduation from a competitive college, and math SAT scores were significant predictors of teacher effectiveness in mathematics in elementary and middle grades.[23] A student's achievement was most enhanced by having a fully certified teacher who had graduated from a university preservice program, who had a strong academic background, and who had more than two years of experience. Students' achievement was hurt most by having an inexperienced teacher on a temporary license—again, a teaching profile most common in high-minority, low-income schools. In combination, improvements in these qualifications reduced the gap in achievement between the schools serving the poorest and most affluent student bodies by 25 percent.

Because of public attention to these disparities and to the importance of teacher quality, Congress included a provision in the No Child Left Behind Act of 2001 that states should ensure that all students have access to "highly qualified teachers," defined as teachers with full certification and demonstrated competence in the subject-matter field(s) they teach.[24] This provision was historic, especially since the students targeted by federal legislation—students who are low income, low achieving, new English-language learners, or identified with special education needs—have been in many communities those least likely to be served by experienced and well-prepared teachers.

At the same time, reflecting a key Bush administration agenda, the law encouraged states to expand alternative certification programs, and regulations developed by the Department of Education allowed candidates who had just begun, but not yet completed, such a program to be counted as "highly qualified" classroom teachers—a ruling that caused California parents of low-income, minority students taught by such teachers to sue the US Department of Education. The parents claimed that the department's rule sanctioned inadequate teaching for their children and masked the fact that they were being underserved, thus reducing pressure on policy makers to create the incentives that would have given their children access to fully prepared teachers.[25] Unfortunately, Congress ultimately supported the Department of Education's definition with an amendment to NCLB that enabled teachers to be considered "highly qualified" if they had begun an alternative certification program.[26]

While there are some high-quality alternative programs, most of them—generally targeted for high-turnover urban schools—offer only a few weeks of training before teachers step into the classroom on their own, with variable access to mentoring or support. These efforts to address shortages in high-need schools by reducing training rather than increasing the incentives to teach have, in many cases, actually exacerbated staffing problems—since unprepared teachers leave at two to three times the rates of fully prepared teachers.[27] They also undermine efforts to raise student achievement, as teachers in training are less effective than those who have completed their training,[28] and high rates of teacher turnover also reduce achievement.[29]

One study of alternatively certified teachers, which noted that teachers from these alternative programs were almost exclusively found in high-minority, high-poverty schools, found that the least prepared group—teachers in "low coursework" programs (who receive little or no student teaching or training in areas such as child development and learning; how to teach reading, mathematics, or other subjects; how to manage a classroom productively; or, how to teach special education students or English learners) actually depressed the reading and math achievement of students over the course of the academic year.[30]

These findings are similar to those in other studies. In the North Carolina study cited earlier, the largest negative effects on student achievement were found for inexperienced teachers and for teachers who had entered teaching on the state's "lateral entry" program, an alternate route that allows entry for midcareer recruits who have subject-matter background but no initial training for teaching. In addition, three large, well-controlled studies, using longitudinal individual-level student data from New York City and Houston, Texas, found that teachers who entered teaching without full preparation—as emergency hires or alternative-route candidates—were significantly less effective when they started than were fully prepared beginning teachers working with similar students, especially in teaching reading.[31] This is not surprising, given the sophisticated knowledge and skills needed to teach beginning reading, especially to students who have few literacy experiences outside of school and those who are new English-language learners.

Even if those who stay in teaching catch up to their peers later, however, students who have had such teachers when they were novices suffer and may never catch up, especially if the students have a revolving door of such beginners year after year. In reading, for example, the negative differential for upper elementary students taught by underprepared novices in two of these studies was estimated to be the loss of about one-third of a grade level.[32] When children in hard-to-staff schools experience several such teachers in a row, it is easy for the students to fall further and further behind. And when teachers who quit are replaced by other new, underprepared teachers, the achievement level within a school or district remains depressed. Those who enter without having completed preparation also leave at more than twice the rate of those who are well prepared.[33] This turnover itself has negative effects, with lower achievement for students who attend schools with greater churn.[34]

The totality of this research indicates that well-prepared and fully qualified teachers must be an essential component of a federal right to education if such a right aims to help close opportunity and achievement gaps.

The Quality of Principals

Principals have been found to be the second most important school-level factor associated with gains in student achievement and attainment—right behind teachers.[35] Principals influence both the quality and stability of teachers who enter and remain in a given school. Turnover of teachers is also associated with the quality of school leadership. In fact, the quality of administrative support is often the top reason teachers identify for leaving or staying in the profession.[36] High-quality leaders influence student achievement both indirectly—through their ability to recruit, support, and retain teachers—and directly through their own actions. What principals do in establishing a vision for the school, developing teachers and school staff, redesigning the school to support all students' learning, and leading instruction has been found to be associated with their effectiveness in supporting achievement gains.[37] As one study observed, "There are virtually no documented instances of troubled schools being turned around without intervention by a powerful leader."[38]

In addition, committed principals who remain in their schools are associated with improved school-wide student achievement. As a corollary, principal turnover is associated with lower gains in student achievement.[39] Principal turnover has a more significant, negative effect in high-poverty, low-achieving schools—the schools where students most rely on education for their future success.[40] And principal turnover is related to principal preparation: those who are better prepared are more likely to be exhilarated rather than stressed by their jobs and to stay longer in their positions.[41]

Like teachers, experienced, qualified, and stable principals are unequally distributed, with more affluent communities having more well-prepared and experienced principals who are also more likely to stay. As with teachers, gaining access to well-prepared principals is a matter of both ensuring access to high-quality preparation and distributing principals more equitably, by equalizing salary levels and working conditions. A well-prepared and effective principal is necessary for a federal right to education to significantly improve educational opportunities and outcomes for those who are disadvantaged by the current education system.

Access to Quality Curriculum

To learn effectively to the level of college and career-ready standards, as required in the federal Every Student Succeeds Act, young people must have a stable and well-qualified teacher and leader workforce teaching a curriculum that is responsive to the standards, addressing the demands of entering college and the expectations for entering careers. This, too, is a source of inequality that can deny students the right to learn in ways that will make them well-prepared citizens able to contribute to the society and economy they are entering. In addition to students of color and low-income students being taught by less expert teachers than their white and middle class counterparts are, these students often face stark differences in courses, curriculum programs, materials, and equipment, as well as in the human environment in which they attend school. High-quality curriculum and instruction—which is shaped by all of these factors—has been found to matter more for school outcomes than students' backgrounds do.

Allocating Knowledge

Unequal access to knowledge is structured in a variety of ways. In US schools, far more than those in high-achieving nations around the world, this occurs through the allocation of different course-taking opportunities to different students very early in their school experience. Sorting often begins as early as kindergarten or first grade, with decisions about which students will be placed in remedial or "gifted" programs and with differentials among affluent and poor schools in what is offered. For example, wealthy districts often offer foreign languages early in elementary school, whereas poor districts offer few such courses even at the high school level. Richer districts typically provide extensive music and art programs, project-based science with well-outfitted labs, and elaborate technology supports, while poor districts often have none of these and offer stripped-down drill-and-practice approaches to reading and math learning, rather than teaching for higher-order applications.[42]

Research has found that schools serving African American, Latino, and Native American students are "bottom heavy"—that is, they offer fewer academic and college-preparatory courses and more remedial and vocational courses, which tend to train specifically for low-status occupations.[43] For example, in 2017, the National Center for Education Statistics reported that students in schools serving predominantly African American and Latino students consistently earn less credit in advanced, college-preparatory courses than their white peers do.[44] According to the same report, three times as many white students completed high school calculus as African American students (18 percent versus 6 percent), and whites completed calculus at almost twice the rate of Latinos (18 percent versus 10 percent). A lower percentage of African American students (23 percent) and Hispanic students (34 percent) earned credit in AP/IB classes than did white (40 percent) and Asian students (72 percent).[45] Furthermore, recent scholarship suggests that schools serving lower-income communities, that is, those with the largest shares of workers without college degrees, routinely "devote a larger share of their course offerings to subbaccalaureate career-related coursework and a smaller share to AP/IB courses."[46]

Tracking is another well-established mechanism used in the US system to differentiate access to knowledge. Sometimes schools call these pathways "streams" or "lanes" that, essentially, flow in distinctive directions, as they are intended to prepare students for different futures. In elementary schools, these may be called "gifted and talented" or "advanced" programs, or sometimes magnet schools or programs focused on particular curriculum areas, versus "regular" ones. By middle and high school, the various tracks are known by terms such as "honors," "advanced," "college preparatory," "basic," "remedial," or "vocational."

In racially mixed schools, the tracks are generally color coded. Honors or advanced courses are reserved primarily for white students, while the lower tracks are disproportionately filled with students of color.[47] A recent lawsuit in New Jersey brought by black parents whose daughter was denied access to a higher-level mathematics class, despite having the grades and test scores required, reflects complaints to the US Department of Education's Office for Civil Rights from across the country and has triggered new standards of review from the department.[48] Unequal access to high-level courses and challenging curriculum explains much of the difference in achievement between minority students and white students, as course taking is strongly related to achievement, and there are large race-based differences among students in course taking, especially in such areas as mathematics, science, and foreign language.

By contrast, there is very little curriculum differentiation in the education offerings for students in contemporary high-achieving European and Asian nations, such as Finland, Sweden, Korea, Singapore, and Hong Kong, which have sought, as part of their reforms, to equalize access to a common, intellectually ambitious curriculum.[49] These nations typically do not track or sort most students until the end of high school, when, in the last two years, there is often differentiation of courses by interest and academic achievement. An international study found that the spread of achievement between high and low achievers is much greater in countries that track students into curriculum streams from an early age than in those that do not.[50]

Indeed, access to high-quality curriculum for what many people call "twenty-first-century learning" is by many accounts relatively rare in the United States. Tony Wagner, for example, describes a global achievement gap: "the gap between what even our best suburban, urban, and rural public schools are teaching and testing versus what all students will need to succeed as learners, workers, and citizens in today's global knowledge economy." Wagner describes the skills that students need in terms very similar to those that others have outlined in reform reports around the world: critical thinking and problem solving; collaboration; agility and adaptability; initiative and entrepreneurialism; effective oral and written communication; accessing and analyzing information; curiosity and imagination.[51] The kind of curriculum that supports these qualities has typically been rationed to the most advantaged students in the United States—a strategy that is increasingly problematic as demand for these skills becomes universal.

Does Curriculum Access Influence Learning?

The curriculum-rationing system that we have inherited was justified on the grounds that it was best for students, so that they could be educated in the most appropriate ways, at their own "levels," and find their way into society. However, a substantial body of research over the past forty years has found that the combination of teacher quality and curriculum quality explains most of the school's contribution to achievement and that access to curriculum opportunities is a more powerful determinant of achievement than initial achievement levels are. That is, when students of similar backgrounds and initial achievement levels are exposed to more and less challenging curriculum material, those given the richer curriculum opportunities ultimately outperform those placed in less challenging classes.[52] For example, a rigorously designed experimental study that randomly assigned seventh-grade "at-risk" students to remedial, average, and honors mathematics classes found that at the end of the year, the at-risk students who took the honors class offering a prealgebra curriculum outperformed all other students of similar backgrounds.[53]

Similarly, a study by Jeannie Oakes in a California city found that, among students scoring at about the median on the district's standardized test, those placed in low-track classes lost an average of 2.0 normal curve equivalents (NCEs) after one year and sustained these losses for three years, while those who were placed into an accelerated course gained 6.5 NCEs after one year and 9.6 NCEs after three years.[54] These patterns held true for students who were initially much lower in the achievement distribution (for example, near the twentieth percentile) and for those much higher in the achievement distribution (for example, near the eightieth percentile)—a finding reinforced by other studies.[55] In these ways, tracking exacerbates differential access to knowledge.

Tracking is associated with curriculum differences that can dramatically restrict students' encounters with knowledge and their opportunities to learn. Decades of research have shown that teachers who produce high levels of learning for initially lower- and higher-achieving students alike provide active learning opportunities involving student collaboration and many uses of oral and written language, connect to students' prior knowledge and experiences, provide hands-on learning opportunities, and engage students' higher-order thought processes, including their capacities to approach tasks strategically, to hypothesize, to predict, and to evaluate, integrate, and synthesize ideas.[56]

However, many studies have found that students placed in the lowest tracks or in remedial programs tend to experience instruction geared only to rote skills, working at a low cognitive level on fill-in-the-blank worksheets and test-oriented tasks that are profoundly disconnected from the skills they need to learn. Teacher interaction with students in lower-track classes is less motivating and less supportive, more likely to focus on behavioral criticisms, especially for minority students, and less focused on higher-order reasoning and responses. In these classes, students are rarely given the opportunity to talk about what they know, to read real books, to research and write, or to construct and solve problems in mathematics, science, or other subjects.[57] Thus, they are denied access to the development of higher-order thinking skills that sustain academic achievement.

Curriculum Materials and Equipment

In order to teach to a learning standard, schools also need adequate curriculum materials and equipment that support teaching to the standards. These, too, are inequitably distributed. Multiple school finance lawsuits have demonstrated that students in many underresourced schools lack access to any or up-to-date textbooks, library resources, science labs, and other supports for learning.[58] The inequalities extend to the availability of computers—including adequate bandwidth for connectivity, so central to research and representation of knowledge in the twenty-first century.[59] All of these inequalities must be remedied if students are to have access to the college- and career-ready standards required by federal law. This research demonstrates that equal access to a rigorous curriculum and high-quality educational resources also should be guaranteed through a federal right to education so that all students gain access to the knowledge and skills necessary for college or career success.

What Should the Federal Government Do?

While the main responsibility for education funding resides in the states, a strategic federal role is necessary to create an infrastructure for strong teaching and school leadership across the country, tied to curriculum and materials that can allow educators to teach diverse students effectively to the high standards now required. Individual innovative programs at the local level will not alone solve the inequalities that now exist.

The United States Commission on Civil Rights' recent report *Public Education Funding Inequity in an Era of Increasing Concentration of Poverty and Resegregation* argued that Congress should declare education a federal right. The Commission suggested that Congress should incentivize states to adopt equitable school finance systems and should increase federal funding to supplement state funding; promote collection, monitoring, and evaluation of school spending data; and, develop mechanisms to monitor and evaluate the effectiveness of federal spending.[60]

A federal right to education could be pursued by tying federal education funding to each state's movement toward equitable access to key education resources, just as federal funding is tied to enforcement of civil rights laws. There are a number of components under the new Every Student Succeeds Act (ESSA)—the nation's largest federal education law—that would support this approach, but they need to be enforced and, in some cases, expanded. Here I identify three strategies that could inform federal, as well as state, actions that provide a right to adequate education.

- Enforce comparability provisions for ensuring equally qualified teachers and resources to schools serving different populations of students. ESSA requires that states develop policies to balance the qualifications of teachers—as well as the financial resources—across schools serving more and less advantaged students; but this aspect of the law has been weakly enforced, and wide disparities continue.
- Require states to report on opportunity indicators to accompany their reports of academic progress for each school, reflecting the dollars spent; availability of well-qualified teachers; strong curriculum opportunities; books, materials, and equipment (such as science labs and computers); and, adequate facilities. Evaluate progress on opportunity measures in state plans and evaluations under the law and require states to meet a set of opportunity-to-learn standards for schools identified as failing.
- Launch federal initiatives to ensure an adequate supply of qualified teachers and leaders across all communities, as the federal government currently does in medicine.

Comparability

A traditional federal role in education policy has been to require comparability in the conditions in schools receiving federal funds on behalf of low-income children in comparison to schools that do not serve concentrations of such children. For many years, federal law has required that districts receiving Title I funds demonstrate "comparability" in access to qualified teachers,[61] because schools serving concentrations of low-income students and students of color have historically been more likely than schools serving more advantaged students to employ inexperienced and uncredentialed teachers.[62] Furthermore, in hard-to-staff schools, with high numbers of students living in poverty and/or English learners, disproportionate numbers of underprepared, substitute, and out-of-field teachers are assigned to classrooms with the highest-needs students.[63] All of these factors have been found to undermine student achievement. However, federal requirements on this issue have not been effectively enforced, and thus these inequitable disparities have remained entrenched.

Under ESSA, state plans must address disproportionate rates of ineffective, out-of-field, or inexperienced teachers in schools that serve low-income students and students of color. This is an opportunity for states and districts to examine root causes of inequities across and within both districts and schools and to develop plans for addressing these issues. Where inequities do exist, state plans will need to outline how they will evaluate access to effective teachers, address inequities, and publicly report progress. Another requirement is that states must publish spending data for all schools, including "actual personnel expenditures and actual non-personnel expenditures of federal, state, and local funds, disaggregated by source of funds, for each local educational agency and each school in the state" and then establish the comparability of funding across Title I and non–Title I schools.[64] If education was treated as a civil right, these requirements for comparability would be strongly enforced.

Indicators of Opportunities to Learn

As noted earlier in this chapter, federal leverage could be used to ensure that information about opportunities to learn is routinely collected and made available at the state level, something that ESSA begins to do with its encouragement for states to add additional indicators of school quality and student success to multiple indicators of outcomes. A number of states have responded by adding indicators of college and career readiness, extended-year graduation rates, suspension rates, and school climate, as well as chronic absenteeism.[65] These and other measures can be used to both gauge and increase students' opportunity to learn, by revealing students' abilities to access a full and rigorous curriculum. Furthermore, these indicators can encourage schools and other stakeholders to pay close attention to the resources and conditions that influence student learning outcomes and to address inequalities that exist. Especially in the context of schools identified for intervention and support, states should be required to provide a minimum adequate level of curriculum opportunities coupled with teaching quality.

- *Curriculum Access:* Increasing student access to a high-quality "thinking curriculum," traditionally available to only a privileged few, is an important step toward more equitable schooling. Reporting this kind of information by group should leverage greater access, while also offering a more holistic picture of students' learning.[66] Indicators of access to a full, rich curriculum and rigorous coursework could include
  - student participation in college-preparatory courses or completion of a full college-preparatory curriculum;
  - completion of a high-quality career technical course sequence, including work-based learning opportunities or internships;
  - access to a well-rounded curriculum that includes science, history, writing, a world language, music, physical education, and arts, in addition to reading and math; and,
  - student participation in and completion of Advanced Placement courses, International Baccalaureate courses, or dual-credit college courses.
- *Access to Well-Qualified Teachers:* As the "comparability provisions" of ESSA acknowledge, the distribution of in-field, experienced, and effective teachers is often highly uneven across districts and schools. Indicators of equal access to teacher qualifications shown to be associated with teacher effectiveness could include, at minimum, the proportions of educators who are (1) fully certified for the courses they teach, (2) have more than three years of experience, or (3) have demonstrated higher levels of accomplishment through National Board Certification.
- *Access to Resources:* Looking closely at the distribution of resources across schools and districts offers important information about how they might address existing inequities in opportunities and outcomes. For schools to be held accountable for providing a rich curriculum, they need resources, such as
  - sufficient funding;
  - up-to-date curriculum materials, including access to computers and other technology; and,
  - adequate and timely professional development opportunities for educators.

In each instance, because these indicators are disaggregated by subgroup, schools would be encouraged to provide a stronger curriculum for all students to ensure that children from all backgrounds not only have greater access to these opportunities but are also provided the support to succeed.

Supply of Qualified Educators

Federal strategies for enhancing the supply of teachers and school leaders have precedents in the field of medicine. Since 1944, the federal government has subsidized medical training to meet the needs of underserved populations, to fill shortages in particular fields, and to build teaching hospitals and training programs in high-need areas. This consistent commitment has contributed significantly to the United States' world-renowned system of medical training and care.

Intelligent, targeted subsidies for teacher and leader preparation, coupled with stronger supports at entry and incentives for staying in high-need schools, could help ensure that all students have access to teachers who are indeed highly qualified. Effective strategies include the following:

1. Service scholarships or forgivable loans for entering teachers who will teach for four to five years in high-need fields and locations can expand the pipeline of teachers and direct them to where they are needed, improving the capacity of schools in high-need communities.
2. Mentoring programs for beginning teachers, launched through matching grants to states, can ensure expert support in the first two years on the job, improving both teacher retention and expertise.
3. Recruitment incentives, including increased compensation, can bring expert, experienced teachers and leaders to teach, mentor, and lead in high-need schools, as can opportunities to take on new leadership roles and to participate in school redesign initiatives.
4. Improved preparation for teaching high-need students and for programs in high-need areas, including teacher residency programs, can address shortages by underwriting training for recruits in high-need fields such as mathematics, science, and special education while providing them with a yearlong apprenticeship alongside

an expert mentor teacher. Recruited by districts and partnering universities as midcareer entrants or recent college graduates, residents simultaneously complete credential coursework that is tightly integrated with their clinical placement as they are coteaching. In exchange for tuition remission and a stipend, as well as two years of mentoring, they commit to teach for three to five years in the districts' schools and usually stay much longer, with retention rates typically more than 80 percent over five years, as well as evidence of strong effectiveness.[67]

5. Leadership residency programs for increasing the pipeline of well-prepared principals for high-need school districts have also proven successful and can be funded federally.[68] ESSA permits states to set aside 3 percent of their Title II formula funds to strengthen the quality of school leaders, including by investing in the recruitment, preparation, induction, and development of school leaders.[69] Federal funds can encourage initiatives that reflect the evidence base for what makes an effective program, including purposeful and targeted recruitment, curricular coherence, problem-based learning methods, field-based internships and coaching by an expert, cohort groups, on-the-job coaching and continued professional learning, and close collaboration between programs and school districts.[70]

Conclusion

Acknowledging the federal right to education that is implicit in recent federal education laws, as well as the constitutional equality standard, is a first step toward securing the quality and kind of education resources needed to provide every student with the ability to engage productively in the twenty-first-century economy and society in which we live. Ensuring access to the curriculum and materials geared to college- and career-ready standards required by federal law, as well as the qualified teachers and leaders needed to teach and support learning, should be guaranteed by a federal right to education.

NOTES

Epigraphs: Thomas Jefferson, *Elementary School Act, 1817, in* 17–18 THE WRITINGS OF THOMAS JEFFERSON 440 (Albert E. Bergh ed., 1907); Letter from Thomas

Jefferson to George Wythe (Aug. 13, 1786), ME 5:396; W. E. B. Du Bois, *The Freedom to Learn* (1949), *in* W. E. B. DU BOIS SPEAKS 230–31 (P. S. Foner ed., 1970).

1. For a review of cases, *see* LINDA DARLING-HAMMOND, THE FLAT WORLD AND EDUCATION: HOW AMERICA'S COMMITMENT TO EQUITY WILL DETERMINE OUR FUTURE (2010); Charles J. Ogletree, Jr. & Kimberly Jenkins Robinson, *The Enduring Legacy of* San Antonio Independent School District v. Rodriguez 1, 12, *in* THE ENDURING LEGACY OF *RODRIGUEZ*: CREATING NEW PATHWAYS TO EQUAL EDUCATIONAL OPPORTUNITY (Charles Ogletree, Jr. & Kimberly Jenkins Robinson eds., 2015). For current information on school finance litigation, *see* SchoolFunding.Info: A Project of the Center for Educational Equity at Teachers College, http://schoolfunding.info (last visited June 21, 2018).

2. Improving America's School Act of 1994, Pub. L. No. 103-382, 108 Stat. 3518.

3. NAT'L COUNCIL ON EDUC. STANDARDS & TESTING (NCEST), RAISING STANDARDS FOR AMERICAN EDUCATION 79–80 (1992).

4. *See* DARLING-HAMMOND, *supra* note 1, at 74.

5. *See generally* JOHANNA WALD & DANIEL J. LOSEN, DECONSTRUCTING THE SCHOOL-TO-PRISON PIPELINE (2003).

6. No Child Left Behind Act of 2001, Pub. L. No. 107-110, 115 Stat. 1425 (codified as amended in scattered sections of 20 U.S.C.); Patrick McGuinn, *Stimulating Reform: Race to the Top, Competitive Grants and the Obama Education Agenda*, 26 EDUC. POL'Y 136, 143–45 (2012).

7. 20 U.S.C. § 6311(h)(1)(C)(x) (Supp. IV 2016).

8. Serrano v. Priest, 487 P.2d 1241, 1260 (Cal. 1971).

9. For a summary, *see generally* BRUCE D. BAKER, LEARNING POLICY INST., HOW MONEY MATTERS FOR SCHOOLS (2017).

10. *See generally* CLIVE R. BELFIELD & HENRY M. LEVIN, THE PRICE WE PAY: ECONOMIC AND SOCIAL CONSEQUENCES OF INADEQUATE EDUCATION (2007).

11. *See* C. Kirabo Jackson, Rucker C. Johnson & Claudia Persico, *The Effects of School Spending on Educational and Economic Outcomes: Evidence from School Finance Reforms*, 131 Q.J. OF ECON. 157, 160 (2016).

12. *See generally* BAKER, *supra* note 9; *see also* RUCKER C. JOHNSON & SEAN TANNER, LEARNING POL'Y INST., MONEY AND FREEDOM: THE IMPACT OF CALIFORNIA'S SCHOOL FINANCE REFORM (2018).

13. *See, e.g.*, BAKER, *supra* note 9; DARLING-HAMMOND, *supra* note 1; Alan B. Krueger, *Economic Considerations and Class Size*, 113 ECON. J. F34 (2003).

14. Hoke County Bd. of Educ. v. State, 599 S.E. 2d 365, 389 (N.C. 2004).

15. *See generally* Hamilton Lankford, Susanna Loeb & James Wyckoff, *Teacher Sorting and the Plight of Urban Schools: A Descriptive Analysis*, 24 EDUC. EVALUATION & POL'Y ANALYSIS 37 (2002); OFFICE FOR CIVIL RIGHTS, U.S. DEP'T OF EDUC., CIVIL RIGHTS DATA COLLECTION: DATA SNAPSHOT (TEACHER EQUITY) (2014), www.ed.gov.

16. Kati Haycock, *No More Settling for Less*, *in* 4 THINKING K–16, at 3, 11 (2000).

17. *See generally* LEIB SUTCHER, DESIREE CARVER-THOMAS & LINDA DARLING-HAMMOND, LEARNING POLICY INST., UNDERSTAFFED AND UNDERPREPARED: CALIFORNIA DISTRICTS REPORT ONGOING TEACHER SHORTAGES (2018).

18. DESIREE CARVER-THOMAS & LINDA DARLING-HAMMOND, LEARNING POLICY INST., ADDRESSING CALIFORNIA'S GROWING TEACHER SHORT-AGE: 2017 UPDATE 12 (2017).

19. *See* DARLING-HAMMOND, *supra* note 1.

20. *See generally* LEIB SUTCHER, LINDA DARLING-HAMMOND & DESIREE CARVER-THOMAS, LEARNING POLICY INST., A COMING CRISIS IN TEACHING? TEACHER SUPPLY, DEMAND, AND SHORTAGES IN THE U.S. (2016).

21. For a review, *see generally* DARLING-HAMMOND, *supra* note 1.

22. Charles T. Clotfelter, Helen F. Ladd & Jacob L. Vigdor, *How and Why Do Teacher Credentials Matter for Student Achievement?* 24–29 (Nat'l Bureau of Econ. Research, Working Paper No. 12828, 2007).

23. *See* Donald Boyd et al., *The Narrowing Gap in New York City Teacher Qualifications and Its Implications for Student Achievement in High-Poverty Schools*, 27 J. POL'Y ANALYSIS & MGMT. 793 (2008).

24. 20 U.S.C. § 6319, *repealed by* Every Student Succeeds Act, Pub. L. No. 114-95, § 1000(1), 129 Stat. 1802, 1814.

25. *See* Renee v. Duncan, 686 F.3d 1002 (9th Cir. 2012); Frank Adamson & Linda Darling-Hammond, *Funding Disparities and the Inequitable Distribution of Teachers: Evaluating Sources and Solutions*, 20 EDUC. POL'Y ANALYSIS ARCHIVES 1, 8 (2012).

26. Continuing Appropriations and Surface Transportation Extensions Act, Pub. L. No. 111-322, 124 Stat. 3518 (2010).

27. DESIREE CARVER-THOMAS & LINDA DARLING-HAMMOND, LEARNING POLICY INST., TEACHER TURNOVER: WHY IT MATTERS AND WHAT WE CAN DO ABOUT IT 14 (2017).

28. *See* JILL CONSTANTINE ET AL., NAT'L CTR. FOR EDUC. EVALUATION & REG'L ASSISTANCE, INST. EDUC. SCI., US DEP'T OF EDUC., AN EVALUA-TION OF TEACHERS TRAINED THROUGH DIFFERENT ROUTES TO CERTI-FICATION (2009).

29. *See generally* Matthew Ronfeldt, Susanna Loeb & James Wyckoff, *How Teacher Turnover Harms Student Achievement*, 50 AM. EDUC. RES. J. 4 (2013).

30. LINDA DARLING-HAMMOND, STANFORD CTR. FOR OPPORTUNITY POLICY EDUC., EDUCATIONAL OPPORTUNITY AND ALTERNATIVE CERTIFICA-TION: NEW EVIDENCE AND NEW QUESTIONS 2 (2009).

31. *See* Donald Boyd et al., *How Changes in Entry Requirements Alter the Teacher Workforce and Affect Student Achievement*, 1 EDUC. FIN. & POL'Y 176 (2006); Linda Darling-Hammond et al., *Does Teacher Preparation Matter? Evidence about Teacher Certification, Teach for America, and Teacher Effectiveness*, 13 EDUC. POL'Y ANALYSIS ARCHIVES, no. 42, 2005, at 1; Thomas J. Kane, Jonah E. Rock-

off & Douglas O. Staiger, *What Does Certification Tell Us about Teacher Effectiveness? Evidence from New York City*, 26 ECON. EDUC. REV. 615 (2008). *See also* Clotfelter, Ladd & Vigdor, *supra* note 22 (presenting the North Carolina findings regarding inexperienced teachers and lateral entry teachers).

32. *See* Darling-Hammond, *supra* note 30; Ildiko Laczko-Kerr & David C. Berliner, *The Effectiveness of 'Teach for America' and Other Under-Certified Teachers on Student Academic Achievement: A Case of Harmful Public Policy*, 10 EDUC. POL'Y ANALYSIS ARCHIVES 2 (2002).

33. *See* CARVER-THOMAS & DARLING-HAMMOND, *supra* note 27, at 14.

34. Ronfeldt, Loeb & Wyckoff, *supra* note 29, at 5, 18.

35. For summaries, see KENNETH LEITHWOOD ET AL., WALLACE FOUND., HOW LEADERSHIP INFLUENCES STUDENT LEARNING (2004); Kenneth Leithwood et al., *How Successful Leadership Influences Student Learning: The Second Installment of a Longer Story*, in 23 SPRINGER INTERNATIONAL HANDBOOKS OF EDUCATION 611 (2010).

36. *See* THOMAS G. CARROLL, NAT'L COMM'N ON TEACHING & AMERICA'S FUTURE, POLICY BRIEF: THE HIGH COST OF TEACHER TURNOVER 3 (2007); NAT'L CTR. FOR EDUC. STATISTICS, SCHOOLS & STAFFING SURVEYS: TEACHER FOLLOW-UP SURVEY (2013); VERMONT WORKING CONDITIONS SURVEY (2013), www.tellvermont.org.

37. *See generally* Leithwood, *How Leadership Influences Student Learning, supra* note 35.

38. *Id.* at 5.

39. *See generally* Ashley Miller, *Principal Turnover and Student Achievement*, 36 ECON. EDUC. REV. 60 (2013).

40. Tara Béteille, Demetra Kalogrides & Susanna Loeb, *Stepping Stones: Principal Career Paths and School Outcomes*, 41 SOC. SCI. RES. 904, 906–07 (2012).

41. *See generally* LINDA DARLING-HAMMOND ET AL., PREPARING PRINCIPALS FOR A CHANGING WORLD: LESSONS FROM EXEMPLARY LEADERSHIP DEVELOPMENT PROGRAMS (2009).

42. DARLING-HAMMOND, *supra* note 1, at 52.

43. *See generally* JEANNIE OAKES, KEEPING TRACK: HOW SCHOOLS STRUCTURE INEQUALITY (2d ed. 2005).

44. *See* NAT'L CTR. FOR EDUC. STATISTICS, US DEP'T OF EDUC., STATUS AND TRENDS IN THE EDUCATION OF RACIAL AND ETHNIC GROUPS 2017, at 58–65 (2017).

45. *Id.* at 64–65.

46. April Sutton, *Preparing for Local Labor: Curricular Stratification across Local Economies in the United States*, 90 SOC. EDUC. 172, 183 (2017).

47. OAKES, *supra* note 43, at 66–67.

48. Sonali Kohli & Quartz, *Modern-Day Segregation in Public Schools*, ATLANTIC, Nov. 18, 2014, https://www.theatlantic.com; Press Release, US Dep't of Educ., U.S. Department of Education Announces Resolution of South Orange-Maplewood, N.J., School District Civil Rights Investigation (Oct. 28, 2014).

49. DARLING-HAMMOND, *supra* note 1, at 52.

50. *See* Eric A. Hanushek & Ludger Woessmann, *Does Educational Tracking Affect Performance and Inequality? Differences-in-Differences Evidence across Countries,* 116 ECON. J. C63, C75 (2006).

51. TONY WAGNER, THE GLOBAL ACHIEVEMENT GAP 8 (2008); *see also* TONY WAGNER, THE GLOBAL ACHIEVEMENT GAP 14–42 (2d ed. 2014).

52. For a review, *see* OAKES, *supra* note 43, at 226.

53. John M. Peterson, *Remediation Is No Remedy,* 46 EDUC. LEADERSHIP 24, 24–25 (1989).

54. OAKES, *supra* note 43, at 236–38.

55. *Id.* at 231–38.

56. *See generally* NAT'L RESEARCH COUNCIL, HOW PEOPLE LEARN: BRAIN, MIND, EXPERIENCE, AND SCHOOL (John D. Bransford, Ann L. Brown & Rodney R. Cocking eds., 1999).

57. OAKES, *supra* note 43, at 227.

58. *See* DARLING-HAMMOND, *supra* note 1.

59. LINDA DARLING-HAMMOND, MOLLY ZIELINSKI & SHELLY GOLDMAN, STANFORD CTR. FOR OPPORTUNITY POLICY EDUC., USING TECHNOLOGY TO SUPPORT AT-RISK STUDENT'S LEARNING 14–15 (2014).

60. US COMM'N ON CIVIL RIGHTS, PUBLIC EDUCATION FUNDING INEQUITY IN AN ERA OF INCREASING CONCENTRATION OF POVERTY AND RESEGREGATION (2018).

61. 20 U.S.C. § 6321(c) (2012).

62. *See generally* Adamson & Darling-Hammond, *supra* note 25; CAL. DEP'T OF EDUC., CALIFORNIA STATE PLAN TO ENSURE EQUITABLE ACCESS TO EXCELLENT EDUCATORS (2015); OFFICE FOR CIVIL RIGHTS, *supra* note 15, at 10.

63. *See generally* Adamson & Darling-Hammond, *supra* note 25.

64. 20 U.S.C. §§ 6311(g)(1)(B), 6311(h)(1)(C)(x) (Supp. V 2017), 6321(c)(1)(A) (2012).

65. *See* STEPHEN KOSTYO, JESSICA CARDICHON & LINDA DARLING-HAMMOND, LEARNING POLICY INST., MAKING ESSA'S EQUITY PROMISE REAL: STATE STRATEGIES TO CLOSE THE OPPORTUNITY GAP (2018).

66. *See generally* SOUNG BAE & LINDA DARLING-HAMMOND, STANFORD CTR. FOR OPPORTUNITY POLICY EDUC., RECOGNIZING COLLEGE AND CAREER READINESS IN THE CALIFORNIA SCHOOL ACCOUNTABILITY SYSTEM (2014).

67. *See* RONEETA GUHA, MARIA E. HYLER & LINDA DARLING-HAMMOND, LEARNING POLICY INST., THE TEACHER RESIDENCY: AN INNOVATIVE MODEL FOR PREPARING TEACHERS (2016).

68. *See* LEIB SUTCHER, ANNE PODOLSKY & DANNY ESPINOZA, LEARNING POL'Y INST., SUPPORTING PRINCIPALS' LEARNING: KEY FEATURES OF EFFECTIVE PROGRAMS 5–8 (2017).

69. 20 U.S.C. § 6611(c)(3) (Supp. IV 2016).

70. *See* SUTCHER, PODOLSKY & ESPINOZA, *supra* note 68.

10

The Constitution of Opportunity

Democratic Equality, Economic Inequality,
and the Right to Compete

RACHEL F. MORAN

Introduction

Inequality in US schools has profound consequences for students. Consider, for example, Alondra Jones, who attended a public high school in San Francisco with a student body that was overwhelmingly non-white and poor. The school was strapped for resources and reported test scores near the bottom of California's Academic Performance Index, even when compared to other high-poverty schools.[1] Alondra and her classmates described a lack of textbooks, constant teacher turnover, and decrepit facilities—conditions that were described as "shock[ing] the conscience."[2] As bad as the situation was, Alondra did not feel deeply wronged until she visited far-better-supported public schools in affluent areas of the city and an exclusive private academy in Marin County. The differences were so striking that Alondra felt demeaned by the state's lack of investment in her future.[3] Deprived of any meaningful opportunity to compete with privileged peers, Alondra ultimately sued the state to demand at least an adequate, if not equal, education.[4]

In navigating through the "political thicket[]"[5] of establishing a right to education, experiences such as Alondra's should remain uppermost in our minds. Her sense of injury reflects not just the abject conditions in her own school but also the notably superior conditions at other schools. Initially, school finance lawsuits focused on resource gaps and demanded equity through the equalization of per-pupil funding.[6] In 1973, in *San Antonio Independent School District v. Rodriguez*,[7] the

United States Supreme Court halted the federal campaign to make equity a federal constitutional mandate, and suits seeking resource equalization have since had a mixed reception in the states.[8] These setbacks prompted reformers to turn to a new strategy that calls for an adequate education for all public schoolchildren. This approach prevents the denial of access to education but permits significant funding disparities to persist. Adequacy suits often rely on standards-based testing to define the core components of an elementary and secondary education.[9]

The movement from equity to adequacy reflects larger social trends. The campaign for equity sprang from the civil rights movement's pursuit of democratic equality but foundered on political backlash and resistance. The adequacy movement, by contrast, is built on the business community's growing anxiety that an underprepared US workforce will not be competitive in a global economy. With the shift from equity to adequacy, growing judicial tolerance for pronounced resource disparities has tested the long-standing belief that public schools are pathways to political voice and personal mobility.[10] The schools have been simultaneously asked to serve as sites of equal opportunity and to sort students for increasingly unequal jobs in the workplace.[11] These dual roles—propelling students forward and putting them in their place— has been a source of significant tension in school finance reform efforts.

For schools to continue to serve as pathways to mobility, students must be prepared to compete "in today's market as well as in the marketplace of ideas."[12] A number of state courts have acknowledged the importance of a fair opportunity to compete, but none has fully operationalized the concept to redress gaps in school resources. At a minimum, the opportunity to compete requires that low-income students in schools with limited resources have a meaningful chance to approximate the achievements of affluent students in better-supported institutions. Otherwise, students such as Alondra will find that they continue to inhabit separate and unequal educational worlds.

The Evolution of Democratic Values and Economic Imperatives in Public Education

Tensions between equity and adequacy stem from historical changes in the relative significance of education for citizenship and preparation for work. When our nation was founded, public schools played a critical role in advancing democratic ideals by forging a common identity and fostering civic engagement.[13] Training for the labor force was not such an urgent concern because most skills could be learned from parents on the family farm or from neighbors in the artisan shop.[14] Despite recognition of schools as bulwarks of republicanism, the founders did not include a right to education in the Constitution. Responding to widespread fears of coercive centralized power, they instead treated schooling as primarily a state and local matter.[15]

A decentralized approach did not prevent the federal government from promoting nation-building through strategic educational incentives and inducements. With rapid expansion westward in the late 1700s and early 1800s, Congress approved land grants to create schools and spur settlement. In addition, territories had to develop public school systems as a condition of statehood.[16] State governments independently recognized the importance of cultivating strong communities and responsible citizens through education. During the 1840s and 1850s, the common school movement successfully pressed for state constitutional clauses declaring a right to education.[17] Whether incentivized at the federal level or constitutionalized at the state level, public school systems educated students to shoulder the responsibilities of civic life.[18]

Strategies based on democratic concerns proved remarkably effective in advancing educational attainment. By the mid-nineteenth century, per-capita primary school enrollments and literacy rates among the free population in the United States exceeded those in Europe.[19] Unfortunately, those who were not considered full members of the body politic, most notably slaves and free blacks, were excluded from this progress.[20]

Despite impressive advances, the educational system in the United States remained rudimentary at the dawn of the twentieth century.[21] In the late 1800s and early 1900s, as industrialization and urbanization transformed the US economy, progressive elites stressed the need to prepare students for an increasingly demanding job market by professionalizing school systems.[22] The imperative of efficiency dominated in "the one best system."[23] In an earlier era, a common approach to schooling had evoked democratic preoccupations with equal citizenship. Now, progressives decried uniform programs of instruction for all students as ineffective, unscientific, and ill suited for the modern economy.[24] Vocational education to train students for different careers became a salient feature of public schooling,[25] and compulsory education laws were designed to ensure that all children received workforce training.[26]

Progressive elites clearly prioritized economic needs over democratic concerns. The notable exception was a struggle over how best to socialize immigrant children. As the foreign born arrived in unprecedented numbers to satisfy a seemingly insatiable demand for labor, populists feared that newcomer children would not become good Americans.[27] The assimilationist—and at times, nativist—fervor to inculcate loyalty and patriotism grew so intense, particularly during World War I, that some states required students to attend public schools with a curriculum that would reliably reflect American values. Eventually, the United States Supreme Court upheld the right of parents to enroll children in private schools that reflected the families' educational and cultural preferences.[28] Even so, the balance of power had shifted. The one best system allowed dissenting parents to opt out of public schools but not necessarily to change them from within.

With the success of the civil rights movement after World War II, concerns about full inclusion and democratic flourishing once again came to the fore. In *Brown v. Board of Education*,[29] the United States Supreme Court struck down state-mandated racial segregation of the public schools as a violation of equal protection. In doing so, the justices offered an eloquent tribute to education's central place in shaping a child's future:

> Today, education is perhaps the most important function of state and local governments. Compulsory school attendance laws and the great expenditures for education both demonstrate our recognition of the importance of education to our democratic society. It is required in the performance of our most basic public responsibilities, even service in the armed forces. It is the very foundation of good citizenship. Today it is a principal instrument in awakening the child to cultural values, in preparing him for later professional training, and in helping him to adjust normally to his environment. In these days, it is doubtful that any child may reasonably be expected to succeed in life if he is denied the opportunity of an education. Such an opportunity, where the state has undertaken to provide it, is a right which must be made available to all on equal terms.[30]

Despite earlier tensions between democratic equality and economic efficiency, the justices saw education for citizenship and preparation for the workforce going hand in hand to ensure a child's success. The soaring rhetoric led reformers to hope that the Court would recognize not just a right to be free of racial discrimination but also a right to be educated.[31] Ultimately, however, intense resistance to school integration revealed the limits of the federal judiciary's power to recalibrate the United States' commitment to equality.[32]

Equity and Adequacy in the Courts: Ongoing Tensions between Democratic Values and Economic Imperatives

In the 1970s, federal courts grew increasingly reluctant to enforce school integration orders, and many schools reverted to the segregated conditions that *Brown* had sought to eradicate.[33] As a result, advocates began to search for alternative strategies to preserve the promise of equal opportunity. An obvious choice was recognition of a right to education, which seemed implicit in the Court's paean to the importance of public schooling.[34] School finance litigation began auspiciously enough in *Serrano v. Priest*.[35] There, the California Supreme Court held that substantial disparities in school districts' per-pupil funding were unconstitutional because reliance on a local property-tax system resulted in wealth discrimination and denied children a right to equal education.[36] With a strong nod to *Brown's* legacy, the state high court characterized education as "universally relevant," a "sustained, intensive" experience, "unmatched" in the formation of identity, and "so important that the state has made it compulsory."[37] Indeed, schooling was essential to prepare students for "economic and social success in our competitive society" as well as for "participation in political and community life."[38]

Rather than mandate a program of resource equalization, the California Supreme Court asked the state legislature to craft a solution.[39] Lawmakers responded by requiring comparable levels of per-pupil funding for school districts.[40] The high court accepted this approach and insisted on strict equivalency. In 1976, five years after the initial *Serrano* decision, the justices ordered the California legislature to ensure that differences in per-pupil expenditures would not exceed $100.[41] For those who believed that parents are "consumer-voters"[42] who should be able to secure a high-quality education for their children in property-rich districts, the decision was an affront to the privileges that families earn in a free-market system. In 1978, a "taxpayer revolt" led to substantial changes in the property tax under Proposition 13, a change attributed—at least by some observers—to a popular backlash against *Serrano*.[43] Whether or not this causal account is accurate, *Serrano* became a cautionary tale about the potentially perverse consequences of equity mandates, and the California Supreme Court eventually retreated from a strict equality standard as unduly rigid.[44] Yet the damage already had been done. Property-tax limits reduced the resources available to public schools, and equalization came to mean leveling down rather than up.[45]

Immediately following the victory in *Serrano* (and before its aftermath became clear), Mexican American plaintiffs brought a class action in *San Antonio Independent School District v. Rodriguez*[46] to challenge large disparities in per-pupil funding under the local property-tax system in Texas. A *Serrano*-style strategy succeeded before a three-judge federal district court,[47] but on appeal, the United States Supreme Court firmly rebuffed the plaintiffs' arguments. With respect to wealth discrimination, the majority concluded that there was no proof that students in districts with low property values were themselves poor, nor that they had been completely deprived of education as a result of their poverty.[48] As for the right to education, the Court acknowledged the centrality of public schooling[49] but observed that "the importance of a service performed by the States does not determine whether it must be regarded as fundamental."[50] The Court found no express right to education in the Constitution and declined to imply one based on schooling's role in promoting admittedly fundamental interests in freedom of expression and exercise of the franchise.[51] The justices did leave open the possibility that students might have a cognizable claim if they suffered "an absolute denial of educational opportunities,"[52] though nothing so dramatic had been alleged in *Rodriguez*.[53]

Serrano and *Rodriguez* each struck a very different balance between democratic values and economic imperatives. The California high court treated equity as an expression of the public schools' pivotal role in promoting democratic ideals of inclusion and participation. The United States Supreme Court, on the other hand, was willing to tolerate substantial disparities in school funding; at most, there might be a democratic obligation to provide a minimally adequate education. With *Serrano* and *Rodriguez* coexisting as state and federal precedent, the dialectic between equity and adequacy began in earnest. During the wave of state school finance litigation following *Rodriguez*, equity advocates initially seemed to prevail. In the 1970s, state high courts invoked *Serrano* to strike down local property-tax systems that produced significant school funding disparities.[54] These decisions sometimes backfired in the face of strong legislative resistance.[55] As a consequence, state courts became increasingly reluctant to take up the mantle of equity. School finance reform lost momentum after "an initial flurry of proplaintiff decisions in the mid-1970s," so that "a decade later, the pendulum had decisively swung the other way. Plaintiffs won only two decisions in the early 1980s, and, as of 1988, fifteen years after *Rodriguez*, fifteen of the state supreme courts had denied any relief to the plaintiffs, compared with the seven states in which plaintiffs had prevailed."[56]

If more state courts were to recognize education as a constitutional right, another strategy would be needed.[57] The federal government laid the groundwork for a new approach in the 1980s. National leaders faced growing pressure from the business community to do something about US schools. International test results indicated that students in the United States were lagging so far behind their peers in other countries that the nation's economic dominance was threatened. As the National Commission on Excellence in Education warned, "If an unfriendly foreign power had attempted to impose on America the mediocre educational performance that exists today, we might well have viewed it as an act of war. As it stands, we have allowed this to happen to ourselves. . . . We have, in effect, been committing an act of unthinking, unilateral educational disarmament."[58] With dire pronouncements such as these, the federal government started to push for greater accountability in elementary and secondary education.[59] In 1989, President George H. W. Bush hosted a national summit of governors that endorsed systematic assessment of student performance.[60] In 1994, Bill Clinton built on these efforts with the Goals 2000: Educate America Act,[61] which encouraged states to adopt high standards and implement accountability testing with the support of federal grants.[62]

But Congress really flexed its federalist muscle in 2002 when it passed the No Child Left Behind Act.[63] To obtain federal funding, states had to adopt rigorous standards, monitor all students' progress in meeting those standards, and close achievement gaps based on race, ethnicity, language, poverty, and disability. Though the act was primarily driven by economic concerns, President George W. Bush invoked the rhetoric of equality when he argued that testing would enable traditionally disadvantaged students to overcome "the soft bigotry of low expectations."[64] Civil rights advocates had their doubts, given the lack of federal resources to support the act's lofty goals, the stigma that could accompany unsatisfactory test scores, and the punitive consequences that would ensue for low-performing schools.[65] States in turn complained about federal overreaching, especially when more and more jurisdictions were unable to meet goals for 100 percent proficiency. The ensuing controversy grew so intense that Congress was unable to extend the No Child Left Behind Act when it expired in 2007.[66] In 2015, Congress passed the Every Student Succeeds Act (ESSA).[67] This legislation restores substantial autonomy to states in setting standards and greatly reduces federal oversight of student performance.[68]

Though primarily designed to promote competitiveness in the global economy, the accountability framework that emerged in the 1980s provided a new tool to pursue educational opportunity. Advocates argued that all students have the right to an adequate education, one that meets the minimum standards that states impose on themselves.[69] This insight gave rise to a new round of school finance litigation, which so far has garnered a number of victories. Since 1989, plaintiffs have prevailed in twenty-one of the twenty-eight state high courts, a success rate of 75 percent.[70] In at least seven of the twenty lawsuits, the state supreme court has endorsed an adequacy rationale after rejecting demands for equity only a few years before.[71] The success of adequacy claims in part reflects the widespread sentiment that simple fairness requires minimum access to education for every child.[72]

Despite these victories, there are growing concerns that adequacy suits have strayed far from school finance reform's initial vision of equity. Critics question the propriety of using state standards that can be "dumbed down" to avoid labeling large numbers of schools underperforming and thus vitiate adequacy claims.[73] ESSA has only heightened these worries because, according to reformers, it imposes "a bunch of vague responsibilities for states" that jeopardize educational opportunities for the neediest children.[74] Fearing that courts will become increasingly amenable to overlooking serious resource disparities, some advocates have demanded a return to equity principles.[75] Others have argued that adequacy claims should expand to address disadvantaged students' needs for special instructional programs as well as their unique harms due to isolation by race, ethnicity, and poverty.[76] All of these proposals greatly complicate adequacy litigation, so perhaps unsurprisingly, the changes have yet to materialize.[77]

Revisiting *Rodriguez*: The Right to Education and an Opportunity to Compete

Given the uncertain prospects in state courts, some reformers have concluded that the time is ripe for federal action, whether the Court revisits its 1973 decision in *Rodriguez* or the Constitution is amended to include an express right to education.[78] One major obstacle to either federal or state innovation in school finance reform is the unresolved tension between equity and adequacy claims. Any right to education must be defined in a way that prevents a race to the bottom among public schools and limits gross disparities in per-pupil expenditures. Yet the Supreme Court's focus on an absolute deprivation of education is the sort of bare-bones approach that could dilute any sort of commitment to educational parity. Although state courts have increasingly shifted from equity to adequacy rationales, there are some decisions that define access in expansive terms. The opinions recognize that public schools are pathways to participation in civic and economic life and therefore must offer students a fair opportunity to compete. Though not requiring perfect equality, these precedents are mindful that students such as Alondra Jones suffer injury not just because their own schools are poorly supported but also because other schools are far superior.

In truth, equity and adequacy claims have much in common. Equalization of resources is not an authentic remedy if it fails to ensure meaningful access, and access is illusory if gross disparities in resources persist. Guaranteeing students an opportunity to compete can avoid a false dichotomy between these two concepts by insisting that minimum access be assessed in light of relative disadvantage. So, for example, whether students such as Alondra are receiving a sound basic education must be determined not only by looking at whether they meet threshold requirements on competency tests but also by considering how their performance compares to that of privileged peers. These students do not have a meaningful opportunity to compete if they inhabit a separate academic world—one in which their scholastic achievements bear little or no resemblance to those of students in better-supported, more affluent schools.

Because the opportunity to compete resonates with popular notions of fairness, it can avert the dangers of backlash that accompany strict equality claims. In *Serrano*, the California Supreme Court explicitly recognized education's role in preparing students for life in a competitive society.[79] When Proposition 13 led to a race to the bottom in public schools, Alondra and students like her were forced to pursue adequacy claims to challenge "schools that shock the conscience" and "lack the bare essentials" needed to "meet basic minimal educational norms."[80] Although the complaint referred to "dreams of college and productive careers" that would be dashed as a result of not receiving "an opportunity to learn,"[81] the plaintiffs demanded only "the minimal educational essentials."[82] This approach did not explicitly link those essentials to an opportunity to compete, a concept that seemingly disappeared in the aftermath of *Serrano*.

The downward spiral in California school funding may have crimped advocates' sense of what is possible under an adequacy claim. Elsewhere, state courts have acknowledged students' need to vie for civic voice and economic security and have bolstered the meaning of a sound basic education accordingly. In *Campaign for Fiscal Equity v. State of New York*,[83] for example, the trial court found that the state constitution mandates "a sound basic education," though not one that is "state of the art."[84] In defining adequacy, the court noted that productive citizenship means "more than just being qualified to vote or serve as a juror, but to do so capably and knowledgeably."[85] Moreover, students must have an opportunity to compete in the workforce so that they can "move beyond" the ranks of "low-level service jobs" that will not pay "a living wage."[86]

An intermediate appellate court disagreed, concluding that adequacy requires only an eighth- or ninth-grade education. In reaching this conclusion, the court emphasized the level of training needed to reach the bottom rung of the labor market: "[T]he ability to 'function productively' should be interpreted as the ability to get a job, and support oneself, and thereby not be a charge on the public fisc. Society needs workers in all levels of jobs, the majority of which may very well be low level."[87] Under this view, an opportunity to compete was irrelevant in defining adequacy, and the constitutional standard fell accordingly. The New York high court ultimately adopted the trial court's more robust approach to defining minimum access based on the imperative of preparing students to pursue "meaningful civic participation in a contemporary society."[88]

Just as acknowledging an opportunity to compete can support a rigorous threshold for minimum access, the concept can further invigorate adequacy by limiting resource disparities above that threshold.[89] Gross differences cannot be tolerated because "what it takes to be an equal citizen—that is, where to set the adequacy threshold—invariably turns on what educational resources others have."[90] In a competitive world, a sound basic education cannot put students "at such a relative disadvantage as to offend their dignity or self-respect, relegate them to second-class citizenship, cut them off from any realistic prospect of upward social mobility, or deprive them of the ability to form social relationships with others on a footing of equality."[91] The opportunity to compete makes clear that underfunded schools can shock the conscience if they relegate students to an educational caste system without any meaningful chance to vie with privileged peers in the labor force and society at large.[92]

A number of state courts have endorsed the comparative and competitive aspects of adequacy by recognizing the importance of an opportunity to compete. For example, in *Rose v. Council for Better Education, Inc.*,[93] the Kentucky Supreme Court mandated not only that students be minimally prepared for citizenship and work but also that they be ready "to compete favorably with their counterparts in surrounding states, in academics or in the job market."[94] The North Carolina Supreme Court similarly found that the state's education clause mandated "sufficient academic and vocational skills to enable the student to compete on an equal basis with others in further formal education or gainful employment in contemporary society."[95] South Dakota's high court held that an adequate education must prepare students "for their future roles as citizens, participants in the political system, and competitors both economically and intellectually."[96] The Washington Supreme Court offered an especially strong endorsement of the opportunity to compete, recognizing that adequacy goes beyond teaching basic skills to include "broad educational opportunities needed in the contemporary setting to equip our children for their role as citizens and as potential competitors in today's market as well as in the market place of ideas."[97] The judges added that the principle of adequacy "would be hollow indeed if the possessor of the right could not compete adequately in our open political system, in the labor market, or in the market place of ideas."[98]

In a number of adequacy cases, then, state courts have concerned themselves with disparities substantial enough to undermine the opportunity to compete. These concerns are even more pressing today because of the dramatic growth in inequality in the United States over the past several decades. Consider, for example, the education scholar Sean Reardon's startling findings on the widening gap in academic attainment between rich and poor. In a 2011 study, he found that the differences were "roughly 30 to 40 percent larger among children born in 2001 than among those born twenty-five years earlier."[99] A 2010 study went beyond average attainment to document a significant and widening "excellence gap" between high-ability low-income and minority students on the one hand and high-ability affluent and white students on the other.[100] Since then, researchers have consistently found that high achievers from disadvantaged groups are less likely than privileged peers to maintain an advanced level of proficiency and to grow academically. Moreover, efforts to improve minimum performance levels among poor and minority students have done little to narrow the gap for these high-performing learners.[101] Recognizing an opportunity to compete could serve as an important tool in addressing this troubling divide, which threatens the public schools' traditional role as an avenue of upward mobility.

To operationalize the concept more fully, courts should examine patterns of attainment at low-resource schools serving disadvantaged students and high-resource schools serving privileged students. Rather than focus exclusively on average levels of achievement at each school, judges should consider the distribution of achievement levels across the top, middle, and bottom range of the student bodies. This process should be facilitated by a new provision in ESSA that requires schools to provide not only statistics on average performance but also measures of student growth and indicia that allow for meaningful differentiation in school performance.[102] To get a rough sense of how this approach might work, consider recent findings on college completion rates. Relying on the 2000 follow-up data from the National Education Longitudinal Study of 1988, the political scientist Robert D. Putnam reported that children with low test scores from wealthy families are now ten times more likely to graduate from college than children with similar scores from poor families. The gap is over six to one for students with midrange scores and over two and a half to one for students with high scores.[103] Putnam finds it "even more shocking" that poor students with high test scores are now slightly less likely to obtain a college degree than wealthy students with low test scores.[104] He concludes that this kind of disparity is "hard to square with the idea at the heart of the American Dream: equality of opportunity."[105]

Putnam's findings call into question whether less advantaged students in the United States have a meaningful opportunity to compete. In litigation, advocates could use the same technique to compare schools in a particular state or district. Courts would assess not just rates of college completion but other measures of educational attainment, such as grade point averages, standardized test scores, college-preparatory courses completed (including Advanced Placement classes), types of college attended (whether two-year or four-year), and selectivity of college attended. Judges concerned with preparation for civic and political life could also look at completion of courses related to civics and US history, performance on tests of civic knowledge, and involvement in extracurricular activities that develop leadership skills or inculcate an ethic of service. The metrics would vary depending on grade level and available data. The content of the curriculum and test scores would probably be key indicators in the early grades, while high school completion, postsecondary success, and extracurricular activities would play a larger role in later grades. Though this approach would not require perfect equality, the opportunity to compete would at the very least reject a dual system in which the most successful, low-income students at poorly supported schools cannot approximate the accomplishments of the least successful, affluent students at highly supported institutions.[106]

It is worth noting that comparing the distribution of educational resources to determine whether students have a fair opportunity to compete is not unprecedented. One instructive example is a 1999 class action challenging admissions policies at the University of California at Berkeley under Title VI and the Equal Protection Clause.[107] Berkeley's admissions process assigned extra weight to Advanced Placement classes in calculating applicants' academic scores.[108] The plaintiffs, who were black, Latino, and Filipino, argued that although they had outstanding high school records, they lacked a fair opportunity to compete because they went to schools that offered few, if any, such courses. Meanwhile, students who attended affluent white high schools had substantially greater access to Advanced Placement classes.[109] One student, Jesus Rios, described his dismay when he was denied admission to Berkeley despite a perfect academic record at his rural California high school: "I thought if you do the right things, you get what you want."[110] Eventually, the lawsuit was settled, and Berkeley agreed, among other things, to use holistic review that attached less weight to Advanced Placement courses.[111] Although this litigation was based on federal antidiscrimination law rather than a right to education, it suggests that decision-makers can make comparative judgments to determine whether educational disparities deny students a meaningful opportunity to compete.

Conclusion

Recognition of a right to education, for all its symbolic force, will not serve the nation's democratic values well if it produces a race to the bottom or permits gross disparities in educational resources to persist. Public schools are platforms for political voice and personal mobility, and a basic education can be sound only if all students have meaningful ways to prepare for civic and economic life. The opportunity to compete expresses a collective regard for students such as Alondra Jones by making clear that they will have an authentic chance to vie for political voice and productive employment. The constitution of opportunity in the public schools may not guarantee perfect equality, but neither can it tolerate inequalities so profound that they estrange the nation's most vulnerable students from the American dream.

NOTES

I am grateful for valuable comments on this chapter from Jonathan Glater, Stephen D. Sugarman, and Mark G. Yudof as well as helpful research assistance provided by Elizabeth Arias. In addition, I appreciate the careful editorial oversight of Kimberly Robinson.

1. PETER SCHRAG, THE FINAL TEST: THE BATTLE FOR ADEQUACY IN AMERICA'S SCHOOLS 15–16 (2003).
2. First Amended Complaint for Injunctive and Declaratory Relief at 6, Williams v. California, (Cal. Super. Ct. Aug. 14, 2000) (No. 312236); SCHRAG, *supra* note 1, at 104–07.
3. SCHRAG, *supra* note 1, at 21.

4. *Id.* at 15. Nor is Alondra's experience unique. A recent broadcast of *This American Life* told the story of Melanie, a gifted high school senior in the Bronx, who gave up on her dreams of college in part because she was discouraged by the vast disparities between her public high school and an elite private school just a few miles away. *This American Life: Three Miles,* CHICAGO PUBLIC RADIO (Mar. 13, 2015), www.thisamericanlife.org.

5. MICHAEL A. REBELL, COURTS AND KIDS: PURSUING EDUCATIONAL EQUITY THROUGH THE STATE COURTS 105 (2009). The education scholar Mark Yudof went even further, likening school finance to a Russian novel because "[i]t's long, tedious, and everybody dies at the end." JAMES E. RYAN, FIVE MILES AWAY, A WORLD APART: ONE CITY, TWO SCHOOLS, AND THE STORY OF EDUCATIONAL OPPORTUNITY IN MODERN AMERICA 145 (2010).

6. Equalization strategies were not identical. For example, some advocates wanted "one pupil, one dollar." ARTHUR E. WISE, RICH SCHOOLS POOR SCHOOLS: THE PROMISE OF EQUAL EDUCATION OPPORTUNITY 156 (1968). Others promoted fiscal neutrality through power district equalizing. This meant that the state adjusted the funding generated by local property taxes so that each school district received equivalent allocations based on the tax rate levied, regardless of property values in the district. *See* JOHN E. COONS, WILLIAM H. CLUNE III & STEPHEN D. SUGARMAN, PRIVATE WEALTH AND PUBLIC EDUCATION 202 (1970). Still others sought to recognize individual differences among students with special needs through weighted student formulas for funding allocation. John G. Augenblick, John L. Myers & Amy Berk Anderson, *Equity and Adequacy in School Funding,* 7 FUTURE CHILDREN 63, 66 (1997). *See generally* Stephen D. Sugarman, *Two School-Finance Roles for the Federal Government: Promoting Equity and Choice,* 17 ST. LOUIS U. PUB. L. REV. 79, 89–91 (1997) (summarizing three different approaches to equity litigation).

7. 411 U.S. 1 (1973).

8. Michael A. Rebell, Rodriguez *Past, Present, and Future, in* THE ENDURING LEGACY OF *RODRIGUEZ*: CREATING NEW PATHWAYS TO EQUAL EDUCATIONAL OPPORTUNITY 65, 68 (Charles J. Ogletree, Jr. & Kimberly Jenkins Robinson eds., 2015).

9. Michael A. Rebell, *Adequacy Litigations: A New Path to Equity?, in* BRINGING EQUITY BACK: RESEARCH FOR A NEW ERA IN AMERICAN EDUCATIONAL POLICY 291, 303 (Janice Petrovich & Amy Stuart Wells eds., 2005).

10. ROBERT D. PUTNAM, OUR KIDS: THE AMERICAN DREAM IN CRISIS 41–44 (2015).

11. Emily Beller & Michael Hout, *Intergenerational Social Mobility: The United States in Comparative Perspective,* 16 FUTURE CHILDREN 19, 29–31 (2006); Eric Grodsky et al., *Testing and Social Stratification in American Education,* 34 ANN. REV. SOC. 385, 394–97 (2008).

12. Seattle Sch. Dist. No. 1 v. State, 585 P.2d 71, 94 (1978).

13. DAVID TYACK, THOMAS JAMES & AARON BENAVOT, LAW AND THE SHAPING OF PUBLIC EDUCATION, 1788–1954, at 21, 23–24 (1987).

14. DAVID B. TYACK, THE ONE BEST SYSTEM: A HISTORY OF AMERICAN URBAN EDUCATION 15 (paperback ed. 1974).

15. *See* TYACK, JAMES & BENAVOT, *supra* note 13, at 24 (describing the republican challenge of preserving individual rights and liberties while building a common identity and national loyalty).

16. *Id.* at 21–22.

17. *Id.* at 55–60.

18. *Id.* at 55.

19. Claudia Goldin, *A Brief History of Education in the United States* 1, 8–9 (Nat'l Bureau of Econ. Research, Working Paper on Historical Factors in Long Run Growth, Historical Paper No. 119, 1999), www.nber.org.

20. *Id.* at 2.

21. TYACK, *supra* note 14, at 13, 79–80; TYACK, JAMES & BENAVOT, *supra* note 13, at 109–10.

22. TYACK, *supra* note 14, at 43–56.

23. This is a term coined by David Tyack to describe the progressives' agenda for school reform. The term is rooted in observations such as those of the educator John D. Philbrick that there was "one best way" of educating children because "[t]he best is the best everywhere." *Id.* at 39–40.

24. *Id.* at 188.

25. *Id.* at 188–90.

26. *Id.* at 183–84.

27. *Id.* at 180–81, 229–55.

28. Farrington v. Tokushige, 273 U.S. 284 (1927); Pierce v. Soc'y of the Sisters, 268 U.S. 510 (1925); Meyer v. Nebraska, 262 U.S. 390 (1923). *See generally* David B. Tyack, *The Perils of Pluralism: The Background of the* Pierce *Case*, 74 AM. HIST. REV. 74, 75 (1968) (describing how World War I and its aftermath led to passage of restrictions on private schooling). Although the doctrine of substantive due process eroded over the years, the Court reaffirmed its commitment to constitutionally protected parental autonomy in *Wisconsin v. Yoder*, 406 U.S. 205 (1972). More recently, the home-schooling movement has asserted the rights of parents to opt out by educating children at home rather than in a private school. *Keep It in the Family: Home Schooling Is Growing Ever Faster*, ECONOMIST, Dec. 22, 2012, at 40, col. 2.

29. 347 U.S. 483 (1954).

30. *Id.* at 493.

31. Ken Gormley, *Education as a Fundamental Right: Building a New Paradigm*, 2 F. ON PUB. POL'Y 207, 209–11 (2006) (describing how Thurgood Marshall and other black civil rights activists hoped that *Brown* would lead to high-quality education for students of all races and how those hopes were dashed by the Court's rejection of a right to equal education). Not only did the Court decline to declare such a right, but it also refused to remedy the effects of de facto segregation due to neighborhood housing patterns. Instead, the justices limited intervention to

cases of de jure segregation, intentionally inflicted by government officials. Keyes v. Sch. Dist. No. 1, 413 U.S. 198 (1973). *See also* Milliken v. Bradley, 418 U.S. 717 (1974) (rejecting interdistrict remedy without proof of an interdistrict violation or interdistrict effect).

32. *See* MARTHA MINOW, IN *BROWN'S* WAKE: LEGACIES OF AMERICA'S EDU- CATIONAL LANDMARK 22–32 (2010).

33. *See generally* Dana N. Thompson Dorsey, *Segregation 2.0: The New Generation of School Segregation in the 21st Century,* 45 EDUC. & URB. SOC'Y 533 (2013); Sean F. Reardon, et al., Brown *Fades: The End of Court-Ordered Desegregation and the Resegregation of American Public Schools,* 31 J. POL'Y ANALYSIS & MGMT. 876 (2012); GARY ORFIELD, JOHN KUCSERA & GENEVIEVE SIEGEL-HAWLEY, E PLURIBUS . . . SEPARATION: DEEPENING DOUBLE SEGREGATION FOR MORE STUDENTS (2012).

34. Robert A. Garda Jr., *Coming Full Circle: The Journey from Separate but Equal to Separate and Unequal Schools,* 2 DUKE J. CONST. L. & PUB. POL'Y 1, 15–22 (2007); William S. Koski & Rob Reich, *When "Adequate" Isn't: The Retreat from Equity in Educational Law and Policy and Why It Matters,* 56 EMORY L. J. 545, 555 (2006); REBELL, *supra* note 5, at 15.

35. Serrano v. Priest (*Serrano I*), 487 P.2d 1241 (1971). The litigation strategy in the *Serrano* case was based on work done by three leading education law scholars. *See* COONS, CLUNE & SUGARMAN, *supra* note 6.

36. *Serrano I,* 487 P.2d at 1244–46, 1255–59, 1262–63.

37. *Id.* at 1259.

38. *Id.* at 1256.

39. *Id.* at 1265–66.

40. Jon Sonstelie, *Is There a Better Response to* Serrano?, *in* SCHOOL FINANCE AND CALIFORNIA'S MASTER PLAN FOR EDUCATION 155, 161–62 (Jon Sonstelie & Peter Richardson eds., 2001); Kirk Stark & Jonathan Zasloff, *Tiebout and Tax Revolts: Did* Serrano *Really Cause Proposition 13?,* 50 UCLA L. REV. 801, 835–36 (2003).

41. Serrano v. Priest (*Serrano II*), 557 P.2d 929, 940 n.21 (1976); William A. Fischel, *Did* Serrano *Cause Proposition 13?,* 42 NAT'L TAX J. 465, 465 (1989). *But cf.* Sonstelie, *supra* note 40, at 165 (contending that a closer reading might have led to the conclusion that the $100 limit referred to disparities in per-pupil funding generated only when districts' tax rates were equal).

42. Charles M. Tiebout, *A Pure Theory of Local Expenditures,* 64 J. POL. ECON. 416, 418–20 (1956). As Richard Briffault has observed, this analysis treats differences in municipal services as largely a product of consumer-voters' tastes and ignores the role of disparities in wealth. Richard Briffault, *The Role of Local Control in School Finance Reform,* 24 CONN. L. REV. 773 (1992).

43. Fischel, *supra* note 41, at 467–71; William A. Fischel, *Did John Serrano Vote for Proposition 13? A Reply to Stark and Zasloff's "Tiebout and Tax Revolts: Did* Serrano *Really Cause Proposition 13?,"* 51 UCLA L. REV. 887, 895–920 (2004). *But*

cf. Isaac Martin, *Does School Finance Litigation Cause Taxpayer Revolt?* Serrano *and Proposition 13*, 40 LAW & SOC'Y REV. 525, 535–48 (2006) (rejecting Fischel's claim that *Serrano* prompted the passage of Proposition 13 and the decline in education spending in California); Paul A. Minorini & Stephen D. Sugarman, *School Finance Litigation in the Name of Educational Equity: Its Evolution, Impact, and Future, in* EQUITY AND ADEQUACY IN EDUCATION FINANCE 34, 49–50 (Helen F. Ladd, Rosemary Chalk & Janet S. Hansen eds., 1999) (same); Stark & Zasloff, *supra* note 40, at 813–41 (same).

44. Serrano v. Priest (*Serrano III*), 226 Cal. Rptr. 584, 600–04 (1986).

45. MATTHEW H. BOSWORTH, COURTS AS CATALYSTS: STATE SUPREME COURTS AND PUBLIC SCHOOL FINANCE EQUITY 46–47 (2001) (noting that the results in California were described as "equalized mediocrity"). *But cf.* Minorini & Sugarman, *supra* note 43, at 49 (describing claims that *Serrano* led to leveling down in California as "oversimplistic and overstated"). Although California has improved its relative position with respect to per-pupil spending in recent years, it remains in the bottom half among states. EDUC. FIN. BRANCH, US CENSUS BUREAU, PUBLIC SCHOOL FINANCES: 2013, at xv, 28 (2015). In addition, it has the largest student-teacher ratio in the country, suggesting that its investment in instructional staffing remains extremely depressed. NAT'L EDUC. ASS'N, RANKINGS & ESTIMATES: RANKINGS OF THE STATES 2013 AND ESTIMATES OF SCHOOL STATISTICS 2014, at 18 (2014).

46. 411 U.S. 1 (1973).

47. 337 F. Supp. 280 (W.D. Tex. 1971), *rev'd*, 411 U.S. 1 (1973).

48. *Rodriguez*, 411 U.S. at 18–29.

49. *Id.* at 30–31.

50. *Id.* at 30.

51. *Id.* at 35–36.

52. *Id.* at 37.

53. *Id.* at 36–37.

54. Horton v. Meskill, 376 A.2d 359 (Conn. 1977); Robinson v. Cahill, 303 A.2d 273 (N.J. 1973); Pauley v. Kelly, 255 S.E.2d 859 (W. Va. 1979).

55. REBELL, *supra* note 5, at 16–17.

56. *Id.* at 17.

57. *See* Rebell, *supra* note 8, at 68 ("Accordingly, at the end of the 1980s, civil rights lawyers changed their focus from equal protection claims based on disparities in the level of educational funding among school districts to claims based on opportunities for a basic level of education.").

58. NAT'L COMM'N ON EXCELLENCE IN EDUC., A NATION AT RISK: THE IMPERATIVE FOR EDUCATIONAL REFORM 5 (1983), http://files.eric.ed.gov. Concerns such as these persist to this day. *See, e.g.*, Greg Toppo, *U.S. Education System No Longer Top Dog*, USA TODAY, Nov. 25, 2015, at 4A, col. 2.

59. Rosemary C. Salomone, *The Common School before and after* Brown: *Democracy, Equality, and the Productivity Agenda*, 120 YALE L.J. 1454, 1483–88 (2011).

60. Alyson Klein, *1989 Education Summit Casts Long Shadow*, EDUC. WK., Sept. 24, 2014, at 1. The participants produced a report that described ambitious educational goals for the nation. THE NATIONAL EDUCATION GOALS: A REPORT TO THE NATION'S GOVERNORS (1990).

61. Pub. L. No. 103-227, 108 Stat. 125, 103d Cong., 2d Sess. (1994).

62. Michael Heise, *Goals 2000: Educate America Act: The Federalization and Legalization of Educational Policy*, 63 FORDHAM L. REV. 345, 356–60 (1994) (summarizing key incentives in the act).

63. Pub. L. No. 107-110, 115 Stat. 1425, 107th Cong., 1st Sess. (2002).

64. George W. Bush, Acceptance Speech at the Republican National Convention (Sept. 2, 2004).

65. LINDA DARLING-HAMMOND, THE FLAT WORLD AND EDUCATION: HOW AMERICA'S COMMITMENT TO EQUITY WILL DETERMINE OUR FUTURE 73–80 (2010).

66. Press Release, US Dep't of Educ., States Granted Waivers from No Child Left Behind Allowed to Reapply for Renewal for 2014 and 2015 School Years (2013), www.ed.gov (describing Congress's failure to renew the act in 2007 and the need to extend waivers granted to thirty-four states and the District of Columbia in 2012–13).

67. Pub. L. No. 114-95, 129 Stat. 1802, 114th Cong., 1st Sess. (2015).

68. *See* Julie Hirschfeld Davis, *Revamping of No Child School Act Is Signed*, N.Y. TIMES, Dec. 11, 2015, at A22.

69. Garda, *supra* note 34, at 25–26; REBELL, *supra* note 5, at 19–20; Michael A. Rebell, *Educational Adequacy, Democracy, and the Courts, in* NAT'L RESEARCH COUNCIL, ACHIEVING HIGH EDUCATIONAL STANDARDS FOR ALL: CONFERENCE SUMMARY 218, 229–31, 236 (Timothy Ready, Christopher Edley Jr. & Catherine E. Snow eds., 2002), www.schoolfunding.info.

70. MICHAEL A. REBELL, "JUDICIAL ACTIVISM" REVISITED: A COMPARATIVE INSTITUTIONAL ANALYSIS OF THE STATE COURTS' ROLE IN ENSURING EQUAL EDUCATIONAL OPPORTUNITY 1 (2006).

71. REBELL, *supra* note 5, at 17. *But see* William S. Koski, *Of Fuzzy Standards and Institutional Constraints: A Re-examination of the Jurisprudential History of Educational Finance Reform Litigation*, 43 SANTA CLARA L. REV. 1185, 1276–83 (2003) (questioning whether the shifts in judicial outcomes can be attributed to relying on adequacy rather than equity or whether the changes reflect other factors, such as changes in the composition of the court or in the judges' attitudes toward education).

72. Koski & Reich, *supra* note 34, at 561.

73. James E. Ryan, *Standards, Testing, and School Finance Litigation*, 86 TEX. L. REV. 1223, 1247–50 (2008); Salomone, *supra* note 59, at 1480–81 (describing the impulse to "dumb down" accountability tests to avoid sanctions for failure).

74. Alia Wong, *The Bloated Rhetoric of No Child Left Behind's Demise*, THE ATLANTIC, Dec. 9, 2015; *see also The Every Student Succeeds Act: Explained*, EDUC. WK., Dec. 8, 2015, at 17. The Every Student Succeeds Act accords significant discretion

to the states to establish and implement standards in mathematics, language arts, and science. Pub. L. No. 114-95, § 1111 (G)(ii), 129 Stat. 1825 (2015) ("The Secretary [of Education] shall not have the authority to mandate, direct, control, coerce, or exercise any direction or supervision over any of the challenging State academic standards adopted or implemented by a State.").

75. Avidan Y. Cover, *Is Adequacy a More Political Question than Equality? The Effect of Standards-Based Education on Judicial Standards for Education Finance*, 11 CORNELL J. LAW & PUB. POL'Y 403, 426 (2002); Koski & Reich, *supra* note 34, at 589–91, 604–05; Koski, *supra* note 71, at 1283–93; Kevin Randall McMillan, *The Turning Tide: The Emerging Fourth Wave of School Finance Reform Litigation and the Courts' Lingering Institutional Concerns*, 58 OHIO ST. L.J. 1867, 1881–88 (1998).

76. McMillan, *supra* note 75, at 1896–1902 (citing Sheff v. O'Neil, 678 A.2d 1267 (Conn. 1996), as an example of this approach); Michael A. Rebell, *The Right to Comprehensive Educational Opportunity*, 47 HARV. C.R.-C.L. L. REV. 47, 53 (2012). The philosopher Elizabeth Anderson goes even further, arguing that integration is essential for privileged students to understand the breadth of human experience, an understanding that is essential for them to assume positions of future leadership. Elizabeth Anderson, *Race, Culture, and Educational Opportunity*, 10 THEORY & RES. EDUC. 105, 124–25 (2012); Elizabeth Anderson, *Fair Opportunity in Education: A Democratic Equality Perspective*, 117 ETHICS 595, 601–02 (July 2007). She therefore argues that the state should impose some requirements that public schools in wealthy areas integrate low-income and minority students. Anderson, *Race, Culture, and Educational Opportunity*, *supra*, at 124–25; Anderson, *Fair Opportunity in Education*, *supra*, at 619.

77. McMillan, *supra* note 75, at 1900–02 (questioning the viability of a new wave of litigation focused on concerns about both resources and integration).

78. *See, e.g.*, Susan H. Bitensky, *Theoretical Foundations for a Right to Education under the U.S. Constitution: A Beginning to the End of the National Education Crisis*, 86 NW. U. L. REV. 550 (1991–92); Erwin Chemerinsky, *The Deconstitutionalization of Education*, 36 LOY. U. CHI. L.J. 111, 119–24, 131–34 (2004); Barry Friedman & Sara Solow, *The Federal Right to an Adequate Education*, 81 GEO. WASH. L. REV. 92 (2013); Goodwin Liu, *Education, Equality, and National Citizenship*, 116 YALE L.J. 330 (2006); Stephen Lurie, *Why Doesn't the Constitution Guarantee the Right to Education?*, THE ATLANTIC, Oct. 16, 2013; Note, *A Right to Learn? Improving Educational Outcomes through Substantive Due Process*, 120 HARV. L. REV. 1323 (2007); Jeannie Oakes et al., *Grassroots Organizing, Social Movements, and the Right to High-Quality Education*, 4 STAN. J. C.R. & C.L. 339 (2008); Kimberly Jenkins Robinson, *The Case for a Collaborative Enforcement Model for a Federal Right to Education*, 40 U.C. DAVIS L. REV. 1653 (2007).

79. Serrano v. Priest (*Serrano I*), 487 P.2d 1241, 1255–56 (1971).

80. First Amended Complaint for Injunctive and Declaratory Relief, *supra* note 2, at 6.

81. *Id.* at 7.

82. *Id.* at 8.

83. Campaign for Fiscal Equity v. State, 719 N.Y.S.2d 475 (N.Y. Sup. Ct. 2001), rev'd, 744 N.Y.S.2d 130 (N.Y. App. Div. 2002), rev'd, 801 N.E.2d 326 (N.Y. 2003). For a general description of the litigation, see SCHRAG, supra note 1, at 175–204.

84. Campaign for Fiscal Equity, 719 N.Y.S.2d at 483–84.

85. Id. at 485.

86. Id. at 486.

87. Campaign for Fiscal Equity, 744 N.Y.S.2d at 138.

88. Campaign for Fiscal Equity, 801 N.E.2d at 330. In 2006, the New York Court of Appeals approved the state's school funding plan as meeting the constitutional requirements for providing a sound basic education. The high court reached this conclusion, although the amount that the New York legislature appropriated fell well below what the trial court deemed necessary to provide a sound basic education. Campaign for Fiscal Equity v. State, 861 N.E.2d 50, 55–58 (N.Y. 2006). Justice Judith Kaye in a partial dissent noted that "the majority does not resolve the inadequate funding of the New York City public schools and reaches a result that is well below what the governmental actors themselves had concluded was required." Campaign for Fiscal Equity, 861 N.E.2d at 62.

89. For a description of these concerns, see Koski & Reich, supra note 34, at 604; but cf. Rob Reich, Equity, Adequacy, and K–12 Education, in EDUCATION, JUSTICE & DEMOCRACY 43, 48–49 (Danielle Allen & Rob Reich eds., 2013) (later acknowledging that adequacy embodies some comparative assessments though it tolerates large degrees of relative deprivation).

90. Lesley A. Jacobs, Equality, Adequacy, and Stakes Fairness: Retrieving the Equal Opportunities in Education Approach, 8 THEORY & RES. EDUCATION 249, 251 (2010); Joshua E. Weishart, Transcending Equality versus Adequacy, 66 STAN. L. REV. 477, 527 (2014). See also Debra Satz, Equality, Adequacy, and Education for Citizenship, 117 ETHICS 623, 636 (2007).

91. Satz, supra note 90, at 638.

92. Id. See also Debra Satz, Unequal Chances: Race, Class and Schooling, 10 THEORY & RES. EDUCATION 155, 156–57 (2012) (noting the dangers that schools that replicate racial and socioeconomic inequality will "carry the aroma of caste privilege"); Debra Satz, Equality, Adequacy, and Educational Policy, 3 EDUC. FIN. & POL'Y 424, 434 (2008) (citing the need for fair opportunities to compete as measured by leadership in the political sphere and personal mobility in the workplace).

93. 790 S.W.2d 186 (Ky. 1989).

94. Id. at 212.

95. Leandro v. State, 488 S.E.2d 249, 255 (N.C. 1997).

96. Davis v. State, 804 N.W.2d 618, 641 (S.D. 2011). The plaintiffs did not succeed in their challenge to the state's school finance system, however. Id.

97. Seattle Sch. Dist. No. 1 v. State, 585 P.2d 71, 94 (Wash. 1978).

98. Id. at 94–95.

99. Sean Reardon, The Widening Achievement Gap between the Rich and the Poor: New Evidence and Possible Explanations, in WHITHER OPPORTUNITY? RISING

INEQUALITY, SCHOOLS, AND CHILDREN'S LIFE CHANCES 91, 93 (Greg J. Duncan & Richard J. Murnane eds., 2011).

100. JONATHAN A. PLUCKER, NATHAN BURROUGHS & RUITING SONG, CTR. FOR EDUC. EVALUATION & POLICY ANALYSIS, MIND THE (OTHER) GAP: THE GROWING EXCELLENCE GAP IN K–12 EDUCATION 28 (2010).

101. JONATHAN PLUCKER, JACOB HARDESTY & NATHAN BURROUGHS, CTR. FOR EDUC. EVALUATION & POLICY ANALYSIS, TALENT ON THE SIDE-LINES: EXCELLENCE GAPS AND AMERICA'S PERSISTENT TALENT UNDER-CLASS 2, 4 (2013).

102. 20 U.S.C. § 6311(c)(4)(B)(ii)(Supp. IV. 2016) (requiring measures of student growth and indicia that allow for meaningful differentiation); *id.* § 6311(c)(4)(B)(v) (defining indicia of meaningful differentiation); *id.* § 6311(h)(1)(C)(iii) and (h)(2)(C) (requiring that information on growth and meaningful differentiation be included in state and local reports).

103. PUTNAM, *supra* note 10, at 189–90.

104. *Id.* at 190.

105. *Id.*

106. *See* Alan Bersin, Michael W. Kirst & Goodwin Liu, Getting Beyond the Facts: Reforming California School Finance 7 (Chief Justice Earl Warren Institute on Race, Ethnicity, and Diversity Issue Brief, Apr. 2008), https://www.law.berkeley.edu ("In California, the highest API [Academic Performance Index] scores of high-poverty schools tend to be lower than the lowest API scores of low-poverty schools. In other words, there is virtually no overlap between the performance distributions of high versus low-poverty schools."). It is worth noting that even in the absence of litigation, some policy makers are already moving to redress the excellence gap by diversifying gifted and talented programs, providing more advanced classrooms at schools marked by poverty and segregation, and changing standards for admission to selective public high schools. Dana Goldstein, *Educators Turn to Programs for Top Students to Narrow the "Excellence Gap,"* N.Y. TIMES, June 25, 2018.

107. Complaint for Declaratory and Injunctive Relief, Rios v. Regents of the Univ. of Cal. (N.D. Cal. Feb. 2, 1999) (No. 99-0525) (later renamed *Casteneda v. Regents*).

108. *Id.* at 12–13.

109. *See* Angela Stephens, *California Students Strike Back: A Class-Action Suit Has Been Filed against the University of California Charging the New Admissions Policy Discriminates against Students of Color*, 15 BLACK ISSUES HIGHER EDUC. 28 (1999) (plaintiffs' counsel alleged that whites had over a 30 percent greater opportunity to take Advanced Placement courses than nonwhite students).

110. Evelyn Nieves, *Civil Rights Groups Suing Berkeley over Admissions Policy*, N.Y. TIMES, Feb. 3, 1999, at A9.

111. [Proposed] Consent Decree at 4–5, Castaneda v. Regents of the Univ. of Cal. (N.D. Cal. June 19, 2003) (No. C 99-0525); *see also* CHARTING THE FUTURE OF COLLEGE AFFIRMATIVE ACTION: LEGAL VICTORIES, CONTINUING ATTACKS, AND NEW RESEARCH 166 (Gary Orfield et al. eds., 2007).

11

Lessons from State School Finance Inform a New Federal Right to Equal Access to a High-Quality Education

CARMEL MARTIN, ULRICH BOSER, MEG BENNER, AND
PERPETUAL BAFFOUR

Introduction

It has been close to fifty years since the US Supreme Court ruled that the federal Constitution does not provide a fundamental right to education in *San Antonio Independent School District v. Rodriguez*. A sheet-metal worker named Demetrio Rodriguez brought the case in 1968. He decided to file a lawsuit against the Edgewood Independent School District, a high-poverty district located just outside of San Antonio, Texas. Rodriguez was frustrated that the schools were dramatically underfunded and marred by dilapidated facilities and weak instruction.

Since Rodriguez lost his case, not much has changed. Indeed, Demetrio Rodriguez's daughter now teaches in Edgewood Independent School District, and the district still gets less than its fair share of dollars.[1] According to one recent analysis, Edgewood receives about $5,000 less per pupil in education funding than does Alamo Heights, a neighboring, wealthier school district.[2] The district continues to lag behind on academic measures, and many students in the district score below grade level.[3]

Funding disparities and inequitable access to a quality education are a national problem. Since the 1970s, school finance advocates have filed dozens of lawsuits across the country. That litigation spurred conversation and important progress, but many problems remain. In nearly half of all states, affluent districts still receive more money for their students than do poorer districts. In some states, the funding gap is egregious; for instance, high-poverty districts in Illinois receive 22 percent less in per-pupil funds in state and local dollars than do the wealthiest school districts.[4] Most recently, in November 2018, public school students filed suit in the federal court of Rhode Island to establish a federal right to education that, among other things, prepares them to be effective citizens who are capable of voting and serving on a jury and that would begin to address the inequities and inadequacies that state school funding litigation has left behind.[5]

Funding must be at the start of every conversation around equity. Funding is a central component to providing a high-quality education and often leads to improved outcomes. A 2016 study found that states that reformed school finance policies to allocate more funding to high-poverty school districts narrowed the achievement gap by an average of one-fifth between 1990 and 2011.[6]

But allocating equal funding does not guarantee that all students will have a rigorous educational experience.[7] Low-income students demand more because they often enter school behind their more affluent peers.[8] In addition, reformers and advocates must focus on the quality of the school, from the excellence of the instruction to the rigor of the classes, in order to support all students. They also must build the political support and will necessary for lasting change.

These ideas are at the heart of this chapter. We argue that the debate over school finance reform needs to move beyond funding, and reforms must focus on both funding levels and equal access to resources shown to be fundamental to a high-quality education. We argue that a federal right to equal educational opportunities must include two central reforms: first, there need to be additional resources—not the same resources—in order to meet the needs of at-risk students. Second, there should be accountability frameworks to ensure that the key ingredients to student success—access to early childhood programs, effective teachers, and rigorous curricula—are available to students irrespective of their race, zip code, or economic status. We came to this conclusion after examining the remedies implemented at the state level—in response to a court order or as a result of political pressure created by state litigation. Therefore, in this chapter we review the history of school funding litigation and some of the outcomes and lessons that should be gained from these cases that can inform a federal right to a high-quality education.

Our chapter contributes to existing research by building on arguments that political will is central to successful school finance reform.[9] We show that specific state constitutional language does not dictate the way a state or even federal court will apply a right to education and thus is a red herring for advocates and reformers. Instead, advocates and reformers should focus on the policy efforts and public will to create clear change that supports more equitable school finance systems that improve outcomes for all students.

As part of our research, we analyzed state constitutions as well as state litigation. In the first round of state cases, the plaintiffs argued that the educational funding inequities violated state constitutional requirements. The next round of state cases focused on adequacy—usually defined as a minimum amount of school funding. In these cases, the court was more likely to consider the quality of education than in previous cases.[10]

On the basis of our analysis of these efforts, we put forth a framework for approaching the issue of school finance that is rooted in political realities. This third-generation approach incorporates the lessons from state fiscal reforms, including focusing school finance on education delivery, providing additional money to low-income students, and taking a comprehensive approach to fiscal reform, including checks on access and outcomes. We argue that there is a growing consensus that education is a right and that its protection requires crucial political support. Our high-quality federal school funding approach builds out of these principles.

What Can We Learn from School Finance Fights in the Courts? Equity versus Adequacy?

Two of the earliest and most well-known instances of state equity cases occurred during the mid-1970s. Both resulted in victories: one in California (*Serrano v. Priest*) and the other in New Jersey (*Robinson v. Cahill*). In both cases, the respective courts used state constitutional provisions requiring equal protection to strike down local property-tax-based systems and to order states to build new funding systems that did not heavily rely on a district's property wealth.[11]

Following the success of these cases, equity cases were brought in many states. Many states have modified, although not completely eradicated, their property-tax-based systems by increasing the state's share in total education spending. As a result, resource differences among districts in some states have declined.[12]

Advocates in various states have taken different approaches to advance equity—some with success and some with unintended outcomes. In many cases, the goal has been to literally "equalize" per-pupil funding without analyzing the necessary level of funding, while other states have attempted to define what level of funding would be "adequate" to provide equal opportunities. In the following subsections, we outline some examples of each approach and highlight some of the unintended outcomes as well as the most positive aspects of the remedies in order to inform a new framework for a potential federal right to a high-quality education.

The Debate over Equity: The First Generation of State School Finance Reform

Both California and Texas have struggled through decades of debate around their school finance systems. In both states, the frame for the debates was equalizing funding levels rather than determining whether funding was sufficient or whether all students had access to fundamental services. The focus on equalized funding also pitted high-wealth and low-wealth districts against each other and led to a drive toward the lowest common denominator rather than lifting up the system as a whole.

In 1976, the California Supreme Court's ruling in *Serrano* declared that California's school finance system violated the state's equal protection clause and was unconstitutional. Following *Serrano*, California prioritized a property-tax-based solution that would close spending gaps between poorer and wealthier districts so that differences in per-pupil spending levels would be no more than $100 by 1980.[13] In 1978, Proposition 13, a resolution that placed a cap on property-tax rates and restricted annual increases on a property's value limited the opportunity to use tax bases as a means to equalize school funding.[14] Instead, local districts could only rely on state revenue for funding parity, making it nearly impossible for districts to pay for new initiatives. Some researchers challenge the extent to which the court's decision led to Proposition 13, but the progression of events is indisputable.[15]

Since California's primary concern was equity of per-pupil funding, the state did not consider the adequacy of funding levels. By 1986, more than 90 percent of California students resided in school districts with a per-pupil funding disparity of less than $100 between them.[16] But the victory was shortsighted. Both the state and districts lowered their overall expenditures, and California no longer led the nation in education expenditures.[17]

In fact, in 1965, pre-*Serrano*, California ranked fifth in the nation in per-pupil spending, but by 1995, the state fell to forty-second.[18] In 2017, California ranked forty-fourth based on National Assessment for Educational Progress (NAEP) scores, graduation rate, college readiness, and access to preschool.[19] In 2013, California finally tackled the issue of school funding and created a new formula called the Local Control Funding Formula.[20] The formula is not based on property taxes and provides additional resources for students needing additional supports, including students from low-income families, English learners, and students with disabilities. We highlight some of the preliminary outcomes from the new California formula later in the chapter.

Similarly, the *Edgewood* case in Texas, which was filed after the *Rodriguez* decision, turned the issue of school finance into a zero-sum game. In 1989, the Texas Supreme Court ruled the state finance system unconstitutional on grounds of equity.[21] In response, the Texas legislature attempted to reduce differences in local tax revenue by recapturing a wealthy district's excess revenues and redistributing them to poorer districts, which some people label a Robin Hood approach.[22]

Texas reduced funding disparities between wealthier and poorer districts from 700:1—as it was during the first Edgewood decision—to 28:1 by the early 2000s.[23] However, the Robin Hood approach in Texas proved problematic, and advocates on the left and the right railed against the provision. The "recapture" approach, in particular, created a disincentive for taxpayers in wealthier districts to increase support through local property taxes.[24] Moreover, a later court case prohibited Texas from capping district property taxes.[25]

Texas then attempted to equalize funding across districts by supplementing district budgets with state funds, but the state struggled to allocate sufficient funds.[26] The average per-pupil spending declined, except for the years 2009, 2010, and 2011, when Texas received additional federal funding from the American Recovery and Reinvestment Act.[27] Today, little is likely to change in Texas. In 2016, the Texas Supreme Court ruled that Texas met its minimal constitutional duty and that the court should not "usurp legislative authority" in deciding how the state should allocate funds to education.[28]

In the end, equity cases spurred policy change to minimize funding inequities, but in some states the focus on equal dollars rather than the quality of services provided to students led to a leveling out of public investment in education.[29] In later cases, litigants and courts moved beyond the concept of equal funding levels, instead adopting "adequacy" as the framework, as discussed in the next subsection.

Issues of Adequacy: The Second Generation School Funding Fight

Over the past few decades, an increasing number of state fiscal cases have focused on issues of adequacy, or a minimum amount of per-pupil funds. These cases rely on states to articulate educational goals for all students, to identify programs or resources to meet those expectations, and to allocate funds to support necessary inputs.[30] In some cases, this framework created a context for weak policy, and the court interpreted "adequate" to mean a bare minimum defined by the state.[31] In several cases, however, this legal framework has driven efforts to articulate what level of funding and what types of resources are necessary to ensure equal educational opportunity. The cases in New Jersey and Massachusetts provide examples of the latter.

In *Abbott v. Burke*, the road to adequacy was a long one. In the original case and subsequent suits, the New Jersey Supreme Court required the legislature to take specific action to increase funding and access to core services for low-income districts. The plaintiff districts—the poorest urban districts in the state—argued that the state was failing to provide them the funds necessary for a "thorough" and "efficient" education, which was required by the state constitution.[32] The court orders called for reforms that both "equalized" funding across districts and also provided additional funds for specific programs for the plaintiff districts.[33]

In the later rulings, the court began mandating funding for specific programs that could improve student outcomes and close achievement gaps.[34] In the 1998 *Abbott V* decision, the court mandated full-day kindergarten, "whole-school reform" for elementary schools, and "on-site social services" in the *Abbott* districts.[35] Subsequent decisions further clarified these requirements and focused on the provision of state funding for school renovation and construction.[36]

The *Abbott* decisions have been critical to improving both fiscal equity and school quality in New Jersey. The state's approach was aggressive and expansive, and the court was involved in enforcing parity and increasing resources for underresourced districts. New Jersey consistently ranks high in education performance and quality, as well as in progress toward narrowing the achievement gap.[37] Many observers believe that the fiscal remedies have helped to improve student outcomes in the state.[38]

In Massachusetts, *McDuffy v. Secretary of the Executive Office of Education* propelled similar education funding reform.[39] In 1993, the Massachusetts Supreme Judicial Court sided with the plaintiffs' argument that the state failed to meet its constitutional duty to provide all students with an adequate education of sufficiently high quality. After the ruling, the state legislature passed one of the most comprehensive reform bills of its time, the Massachusetts Education Reform Act (MERA), which restructured the school finance system and required changes to other areas of education, including new standards, an accountability system, and an authorization of charter schools.[40]

One hallmark of the bill was its introduction of a foundation formula, which aimed to bring all school districts to an adequate level of per-pupil funding by 2000, or over a seven-year phase-in period.[41] By 2000, all districts were at or above their targeted foundation level.[42] By 2002, the total education funding doubled to nearly $3 billion.[43] In 2005, the court ruled in *Hancock v. Commissioner of Education* that the state had established a system that sufficiently addressed inequities and met the state constitutional standard.[44]

Student outcomes remain strong. Massachusetts has some of the highest growth rates of any state on NAEP.[45] Observers have argued that the state's fiscal reforms are partially responsible for the gains.[46] Other research also supports this view, showing that an adequacy frame is more effective at improving outcomes for students.[47] A National Bureau of Economic Research (NBER) study from 2016 showed that, of the various approaches to school spending reform, fiscal initiatives that guarantee a baseline amount of per-pupil funds—otherwise known as foundation plans—were the most effective in increasing overall per-pupil spending and in reducing funding disparities between poor and affluent districts.[48] Foundation plans are similar to the adequacy framework. Compared to equalization plans, foundation plans tend to result in increases in spending across all districts over time.[49]

To be sure, adequacy has its limitations. When defined narrowly, adequacy can serve as a barrier to progress. For instance, the US Supreme

Court discussed adequacy in *Rodriguez* but upheld the Texas funding scheme as rational given that "the State's contribution . . . was designed to provide an adequate minimum educational offering in every school in the State" as well as local control for determining the amount and use of funds.[50] Similarly, the Connecticut Supreme Court in *Connecticut Coalition for Justice in Education Funding v. Rell* ruled that the state allocated sufficient funding for minimally adequate facilities, materials, curricula, and teachers and determined that decisions about the types of services a district provides were "quintessentially legislative in nature."[51] In the following section, we discuss how political will and public support are often the most important predictors of success for adequacy reforms.

A New Approach to Ensuring Equal Access to Educational Opportunities

Recognition of a federal right to education creates an opportunity to address the educational inequities within and across state lines. Scholars and advocates debate the approaches that will best ensure that students receive equitable funding and the essential resources discussed in this chapter and in chapter 9, by the leading education scholar Linda Darling-Hammond. For example, the prominent education economist Eric Hanushek and his sometime coauthor litigator Al Lindseth argue for greater accountability and performance-based school finance reform that aims for transparency and the autonomy that allows districts to tailor incentives to meet accountability goals.[52] Hanushek and Lindseth also argue for greater school choice when a school is underperforming, as an incentive for improving performance.[53] In contrast, Michael Rebell, a highly regarded legal scholar and advocate for school finance reform, critiques Hanushek and Lindseth's work, including noting the mixed results for the array of performance-based and choice reforms that they propose and disputing the contention that struggling schools lack effective incentives rather than inadequate funds. He acknowledges the importance of accountability for school reform while emphasizing the importance of addressing the significant impacts of poverty on student outcomes and child well-being through effective inputs, such as out-of-school services.[54] Despite the scholars' divergent viewpoints on how to remedy deficiencies in funding, Rebell, Hanushek, and Lindseth agree that courts should provide state and district accountability for improved performance, that school funding must acknowledge the disparate needs and challenges of students, and that schools must be equipped to succeed.[55]

Drawing from our analysis and the work of scholars such as Hanushek and Rebell, we recommend that federal school finance reform emphasize a high-quality education program for all students.[56] To reach this aim, students with greater needs must receive additional funding, and that funding needs to be targeted at the services and supports that research demonstrates matter most.[57] Finally, accountability systems and academic standards are necessary to measure quality and shine a light on inequities in ways that will encourage public support for reform.[58]

Putting Forth a High-Quality Finance System: The Third Wave of School Finance

The issue of quality has long been a part of the school funding debate. Justice Thurgood Marshall mentioned the delivery of a high-caliber education in his dissenting opinion in the *Rodriguez* case.[59] As Marshall condemned the majority ruling, "The Court today decides, in effect, that a State may constitutionally vary the quality of education which it offers its children in accordance with the amount of taxable wealth located in the school districts within which they reside."[60] But the issue of quality needs to move front and center and drive school funding debates moving forward. In short, low-income students need more than equity or adequacy; they need sufficient funding to ensure success—which means more funding, not equal funding—and equal access to core services, with accountability for outcomes.

We believe the following principles should guide any school finance reform that is required by a federal right to education.

School funding should provide additional resources for low-income students and end across-state inequities. In order to overcome issues of poverty, low-income students need additional funds. Some research shows that students in poverty require twice the funding relative to students from affluent backgrounds.[61] These dollars should attract effective teachers, improve curricula, and fund programs such as early childhood education.

States with successful remediation efforts have provided more funds to their low-income students, and in some areas, low-income students receive almost double the amount of funding that their affluent peers receive.[62] In New Jersey, for instance, students in the poorest districts receive $3,000 more in per-pupil revenue than do students in the wealthiest districts. Similarly, California now spends about a third more on low-income students in its new funding system.[63] An innovative and robust funding system should follow these models and heed the research that money matters, especially for low-income students.

Weighted student funding can help navigate the balance between higher-quality educational opportunities and better services. Under this program, districts give low-income students, students with disabilities, and other at-risk populations extra "weights," so that additional funding is provided above the base, per-pupil level. Funding is allocated to schools on the basis of the number and demographics of students they serve.[64] Weighted student funding models provide principals with discretion over the use of the schools' budgets. Principals can build their school budget, staff, and program options to best serve their students.

Several states, including California and Rhode Island, have rolled out comprehensive school funding reforms that include weighted student funding. The impact of these programs is yet to be determined, but early results show at least some promise. California's new policy, it seems, has had a positive impact on high school graduation rates. Specifically, the graduation rate of high-need students who received an additional $1,000 in per-pupil spending from the state increased by an average of 5 percent.[65]

Weighted student formulas should be tied to accountability frameworks that look at outcomes, as well as at equal access to core services, including early childhood education, effective teachers, and rigorous college- and career-ready curricula, as discussed in the next subsection. School equity debates must go beyond funding, and states must support equal access to robust services. The New Jersey court described this issue well. The focus should shift from "financing [to the issue of] education itself."[66] The New Jersey court minimized educational disparities by requiring the legislature to implement high-quality policies and programs that are linked to improved student outcomes.

Using this approach as a model, school finance advocates should identify the core components of a high-quality education and ensure equal access to those services as a check on a weighted student funding formula. There are many factors that contribute to a school and a student's success, but the research is compelling that, at a minimum, a next-generation system should have procedures to ensure access to a strong teaching workforce,[67] high-quality early childhood programs,[68] and a robust curriculum and instructional tools.[69]

Specifically, policy makers should fund critical programs to increase the quality of all teachers. Policy makers and school funding advocates should protect and increase funding for teacher compensation and professional development, targeting low-income schools. Programs designed to reduce the cost of teacher preparation, such as the federal TEACH loan-forgiveness program, should be enhanced for those who are willing to teach in high-poverty schools.[70]

The federal government and state policy makers must play a role in ensuring an equitable distribution of skilled and experienced teachers. Under the recently passed Every Student Succeeds Act (ESSA), states are required to describe how they will ensure that low-income students and students of color are not disproportionately taught by teachers that are out of field, less effective, or less experienced.[71] Some states took this requirement seriously and used it as an opportunity to develop clear goals and timelines for reducing these inequities, developed specific strategies for reaching these goals, and included in their plans reporting requirements that ensure transparency should the state fail to reach its goals.[72] However, many states did not make nearly this effort and have significant room to improve, both on the equitable distribution of teachers and on their response to the problem.[73]

Access to rigorous standards, curricula, and courses is also a key ingredient to a high-quality education. At a minimum, states should ensure that all students have access to algebra in eighth grade, as well as access to Advanced Placement or similar rigorous courses in high schools. Indiana provides an example. Starting in 2007, Indiana Core made a rigorous high school curriculum aligned with entry coursework in Indiana's public universities the default curriculum for all students.[74] Indiana wanted to incentivize and support its low-income students to complete rigorous coursework, so "students who complete a Core 40 diploma and meet other financial aid and grade requirements can receive up to 90% of approved tuition and fees at eligible colleges."[75] In 2017, 87 percent of Indiana's public school students earned at least a Core 40 diploma, including 78 percent of African American students, 83 percent of Hispanic students, 90 percent of white students, and 83 percent of low-income students.[76] A student and his or her family must meet with a high school counselor and agree that lower academic standards are better suited for the student's needs before the student can enroll in less rigorous coursework.[77]

Finally, policy makers and school funding advocates must ensure equitable access to early childhood programs and other programs that offer child care. This could be accomplished at the federal or state level through a refundable tax credit or expanded grant programs.[78] Moreover, public investment should incentivize programs to adopt rigorous standards and offer teachers in early childhood programs a living wage to improve the quality of all early childhood programs.

Outcomes-Based Accountability Should Serve as a Check on School Funding Systems

Fiscal reform must include efforts to increase the rigor of academic standards and strengthen accountability provisions. Such reforms make more data available to evaluate the quality of every public school and also ensure that students are held to the same high levels of performance—irrespective of their race, income, or zip code.

Indeed, research has shown that states that adopt rigorous academic standards are more successful in improving outcomes of low-income students. A 2016 analysis found that states that fully embrace standards-based reform are more successful at improving the academic outcomes of low-income students, and states that are more resistant to adopting rigorous assessments post poorer results.[79]

In other words, we agree with other prominent school finance scholars who argue that school funding reform is not a replacement for accountability systems.[80] ESSA requires all states to adopt rigorous standards and hold all schools accountable for student performance. ESSA maintains a requirement that every school must disaggregate student performance by student population—such as low-income students, English-language learners, homeless students, foster youth, and more.[81]

Relatedly, weighted student funding also works best in conjunction with other reforms that foreground quality and outcomes. Many districts have implemented weighted student funding in the past decade, including Houston, Baltimore, and New York City. The districts that have also included thoughtful indicators on student performance and maximized principals' budget autonomy appear to be most successful in narrowing achievement gaps.[82]

Given the level of flexibility afforded to local actors in most weighted student formula frameworks, accountability for outcomes is essential to ensuring that the additional resources reach the students most in need. In addition, there must be a check to ensure that weighted formulas increase access to fundamental core services such as early childhood education.

Accountability systems should also require districts to report transparent school-level outcome data. School "report cards" should specify student outcomes, as is required by ESSA.[83] School report cards also should include the availability and quality of core services that research shows are essential to provide a high-quality education. Such reporting must also be married with efforts to turn around low-performing schools and ensure support for schools that need the most help.

Political Realities

Establishing education as a federal right is a long-term effort. But even if Congress or the Supreme Court establishes this right, it is not a fix-all. Legal precedents cannot take effect without strong political will. As an example, consider the 1963 *Gideon v. Wainwright* decision.[84] While the ruling asserted a defendant's right to appointed counsel during a trial, defendants still often appear in court—and plead guilty—without an attorney present. Part of the issue is that state and local governments do not prioritize spending on public defenders, and so many public defenders are underpaid and overworked.[85]

Similarly, despite legal mandates, many states have not made significant progress to reduce school funding inequities due to a lack of political will, as we found after a careful scan across the states. For example, in Ohio, the media and some legislators strongly objected to the series of decisions related to *DeRolph v. State*. There was little consensus or motivation to substantially rework the school funding system.[86] Eventually, the Ohio Supreme Court relinquished jurisdiction not because inequities significantly decreased but because the court had "no reason to doubt [the] defendants' good faith."[87] As Michael Rebell argues, successful school finance reform is often the result of careful collaboration among all three branches of government.[88] Popular support and political will are essential for guiding the branches in adopting impactful changes.

To be sure, the courts can be a powerful lever for change. But Congress and state legislatures can pass legislation to address inequities absent a court mandate. Moreover, even if a federal right to education is not recognized, Congress can begin to tackle funding inequities by increasing federal funding sources for school districts serving low-income populations under Title I, Part A, of the Elementary and Secondary Education Act. Congress could also improve Title I funding by reforming the formula, which currently does not adequately weight funding toward the districts with low-income students. Congress could also expand other federal funding streams for special needs populations, such as the Individuals with Disabilities Education Act.

Political Will Has a Greater Impact on Outcomes than the Language of the Right to Education

Most state constitutions indicate that it is the state's responsibility to provide for the state's education system. State constitutions tend to use similar or identical language to describe the mandate for public education. Other states also incorporate the principle of nondiscrimination into the education clause.

Surprisingly, though, the language in state education clauses alone is not a strong predictor of legal or fiscal outcomes. States with similar education clauses can have significantly different litigation outcomes. For instance, the state constitutions in Idaho and New Jersey both call for a "thorough" system of public schools, but these states have seen different results.[89]

In 2005, the Idaho state supreme court ruled that the "thorough schools" provision requires the state to provide adequate funding for school facilities construction, but legislative action in Idaho has been fairly limited.[90] The court did not issue any remedial orders or explicitly compel legislative reform. Idaho currently has one of the lowest levels of per-pupil spending in the country.[91]

On the other hand, the *Abbott v. Burke* rulings in New Jersey were successful not only in improving the state school finance system but also in boosting student outcomes. The courts ruled on adequacy grounds on the basis of the "thorough and efficient system of public schools" provision, and the judiciary played an active role in directing targeted interventions.[92] Consequently, New Jersey has seen a narrowing of funding disparities and achievement gaps.[93]

It is important to note that judicial action does not always trigger change, but strong political will almost always makes a difference. When the courts mandate a school finance remedy, the courts typically allow the state legislature to develop the details of the remedy. In some places, such as New Jersey and Massachusetts, the legislature took strong action. In other states, such as South Carolina and Ohio, the legislatures resisted the court mandate and were slow to act.[94] In South Carolina and Ohio, the plaintiffs filed a subsequent suit because they believed the legislature did not take sufficient action. Both states' courts dismissed these suits because each state had worked in "good faith" to minimize inequities.[95] Moreover, there are states, such as Rhode Island, that have rolled out more equitable school finance systems without court-ordered remedies.[96]

In short, the language of an education clause does not necessarily dictate the way a court will interpret and apply a constitutional right. The key to successful reform is the policy framework and political will to make change. As a result, advocates and policy makers must seek to build political will that supports policies that address the components outlined here: sufficient resources to meet the needs of low-income students, equal access to core services, and accountability for outcomes.

Conclusion

Much can be learned from the states, and it is clear that neither equity nor adequacy alone is enough. Looking forward, a federal right to education could begin to address some of the long-standing funding disparities that state funding litigation has failed to remedy. The most important first step is to build political support and a demand for change that remedies these disparities. Building on this support, greater federal involvement in education—through a federal right or legislation—should include additional federal funding for low-income students and must focus on high-quality educational opportunities and the desired outcomes.

Justice Thurgood Marshall once argued that "sometimes history takes things into its own hands," and he was right.[97] But at the same time, the nation must also take school finance into its own hands—and do right by students. A federal right to equal access to a high-quality education provides one way to accomplish this essential national goal.

NOTES

Carmel Martin and Ulrich Boser would like to thank Jessica Yin, special assistant at the Center for American Progress, for her help confirming citations.

1. *See Revenue per Student*, NAT'L CTR. FOR EDUC. STATISTICS (2016), https://nces.ed.gov.

2. *Id.*

3. TEX. EDUC. AGENCY, TEXAS ACADEMIC PERFORMANCE REPORT 2016–2017 DISTRICT PERFORMANCE 1–10, https://rptsvr1.tea.texas.gov (last visited June 12, 2018).

4. IVY MORGAN & ARY AMERIKANER, EDUC. TR., FUNDING GAPS 2018: AN ANALYSIS OF SCHOOL FUNDING EQUITY ACROSS THE U.S. AND WITHIN EACH STATE 6 (2018), https://edtrust.org.

5. Complaint at 2–4, A.C. ex rel. Waithe v. Raimondo, No. 18-cv-00645 (D.R.I. Nov. 28, 2018).

6. JULIEN LAFORTUNE, JESSE ROTHSTEIN & DIANE WHITMORE SCHANZENBACH, WASH. CTR. FOR EQUITABLE GROWTH, CAN SCHOOL FINANCE REFORMS IMPROVE STUDENT ACHIEVEMENT? 2, 4 (2016).

7. *Id.* at 2.

8. *See generally* VALERIE E. LEE & DAVID T. BURKAM, INEQUALITY AT THE STARTING GATE: SOCIAL BACKGROUND DIFFERENCES IN ACHIEVEMENT AS CHILDREN BEGIN SCHOOL (2002).

9. *See generally* MICHAEL REBELL, COURTS AND KIDS: PURSUING EDUCATIONAL EQUITY THROUGH THE STATE COURTS (2009).

10. *See* Abbott v. Burke, 710 A.2d 450 (N.J. 1998); Campaign for Fiscal Equity, Inc. v. State, 655 N.E.2d 661 (N.Y. 1995); McDuffy v. Sec'y of the Exec. Office of Educ., 615 N.E.2d 516 (Mass. 1993).

11. Robinson v. Cahill, 355 A.2d 129 (N.J. 1976); Serrano v. Priest, 487 P.2d 1241 (Cal. 1971).

12. *See* MATTHEW CHINGOS & KRISTIN BLAGG, URBAN INST., HOW HAS EDUCATION FUNDING CHANGED OVER TIME? (2017), http://apps.urban.org.

13. Serrano v. Priest, 557 P.2d 929 (Cal. 1976).

14. Kirk Stark & Jonathan Zasloff, *Tiebout and Tax Revolts: Did* Serrano *Really Cause Proposition 13?*, 50 UCLA L. REV. 801, 807–08 (2003).

15. *See generally id.*

16. *See* Serrano v. Priest, 226 Cal. Rptr. 584 (Cal. Ct. App. 1986).

17. Michael A. Rebell, *Educational Adequacy, Democracy and the Courts, in* ACHIEV-ING HIGH EDUCATIONAL STANDARDS FOR ALL: CONFERENCE SUMMARY 218, 227 (Timothy Ready et al. eds., 2002).

18. *Id.*

19. *Pre-K–12 Rankings: Measuring How Well States Are Preparing Students for College,* U.S. NEWS, https://www.usnews.com (last visited June 13, 2018).

20. *Local Control Funding Formula Overview,* CAL. DEP'T OF EDUC., www.cde.ca.gov (last visited June 13, 2018).

21. Edgewood Indep. Sch. Dist. v. Kirby, 777 S.W.2d 391, 392 (Tex. 1989).

22. *"Robin Hood" School Funding Formula OK'd by Texas Supreme Court,* ABC13 NEWS (May 13, 2016), http://abc13.com.

23. Angela Marie Shimek, *The Road Not Taken: The Next Step for Texas Education Finance,* 9 SCHOLAR 531, 542–43 (2007).

24. *"Robin Hood," supra* note 22.

25. Neeley v. W. Orange-Cove Consol. Indep. Sch. Dist., 176 S.W.3d 746, 798–800 (Tex. 2005).

26. H.B. 1, 79th Leg., 3d Sess. (Tex. 2006).

27. CHANDRA VILLANUEVA, CTR. FOR PUB. POLICY PRIORITIES, THE TEXAS SCHOOL FINANCE CHALLENGE AND WHAT TO DO ABOUT IT 4 (2016).

28. Morath v. Tex. Taxpayer & Student Fairness Coal., 490 S.W.3d 826, 886 (Tex. 2016).

29. Matthew G. Springer, Keke Liu & James W. Guthrie, *The Impact of School Finance Litigation on Resource Distribution: A Comparison of Court-Mandated Equity and Adequacy Reforms,* 17 EDUC. ECON. 421, 439–40 (2009).

30. Rebell, *supra* note 17, at 219.

31. Conn. Coal. for Justice in Educ. Funding, Inc. v. Rell, 176 A.3d 28, 34 (Conn. 2018); Morath v. Tex. Taxpayer and Student Fairness Coal., 490 S.W.3d. 826, 855 (Tex. 2016) ("[T]he constitutional standard demands not the best education, but only an educational system that is adequate to provide a general diffusion of knowledge.").

32. Abbott v. Burke, 710 A.2d 450, 454 (N.J. 1998).

33. *Id.*

34. *Id.* at 456.

35. *Id.* at 473.

36. Geoffrey D. Borman & Gina M. Hewes, *The Long-Term Effects and Cost-Effectiveness of Success for All,* 24 EDUC. EVALUATION & POL'Y ANALYSIS 243, 246 (2002); *The History of* Abbott v. Burke, EDUC. L. CTR., http://edlawcenter.org (last visited June 13, 2018).

37. *Education Reform New Jersey Students Need,* EDUC. L. CTR., www.edlawcenter.org (last visited June 13, 2018).

38. BRUCE BAKER ET AL., IS SCHOOL FUNDING FAIR? A NATIONAL REPORT CARD 4 (6th ed. 2017).

39. 615 N.E.2d 516 (1993).

40. MITCHELL CHESTER, MASS. DEP'T OF ELEMENTARY & SECONDARY EDUC., BUILDING ON 20 YEARS OF MASSACHUSETTS EDUCATION RE-FORM 2 (2014).

41. *Id.* at 5.

42. *Id.*

43. Noah Berger & Jeff McLynch, *Public School Funding in Massachusetts*, MASSA-CHUSETTS BUDGET AND POLICY CENTER (2006), www.massbudget.org.

44. Hancock v. Comm'r of Educ., 822 N.E.2d 1134 (Mass. 2005).

45. *State Performance Compared to the Nation*, THE NATION'S REPORT CARD, https://www.nationsreportcard.gov (last visited June 13, 2018).

46. Phuong Nguyen-Hoang & John Yinger, *Education Finance Reform, Local Behavior, and Student Performance in Massachusetts*, 39 J. EDUC. FIN. 297 (2014).

47. *See* C. Kirabo Jackson, Rucker C. Johnson & Claudia Persico, *The Effects of School Spending on Educational and Economic Outcomes: Evidence from School Finance Reforms*, 131 Q.J. ECON. 157 (2016).

48. *Id.* at 212–14.

49. *Id.*

50. San Antonio Indep. Sch. Dist. v. Rodriguez, 411 U.S. 1, 45–55 (1973).

51. Conn. Coal. for Justice in Educ. Funding, Inc. v. Rell, 176 A.3d 28, 34 (Conn. 2018).

52. *See* ERIC A. HANUSHEK & ALFRED A. LINDSETH, SCHOOLHOUSES, COURTHOUSES, AND STATE HOUSES: SOLVING THE FUNDING-ACHIEVEMENT PUZZLE IN AMERICA'S PUBLIC SCHOOLS 235, 250–51, 264 (2009); Michael Rebell, Alfred Lindseth & Eric A. Hanushek, *Many Schools Are Still Inadequate, Now What?*, EDUC. NEXT 39, 40–41 (Fall 2009), https://www.educationnext.org. *See also* Eric A. Hanushek, *Education and the Nation's Future*, *in* BLUEPRINT FOR AMERICA 89, 98 (George P. Shultz ed., 2016).

53. *See* HANUSHEK & LINDSETH, *supra* note 52, at 223.

54. *See* Michael A. Rebell, *Poverty, "Meaningful" Educational Opportunity, and the Necessary Role of the Courts*, 85 N.C. L. REV. 1467, 1487, 1512–13, 1518, 1544 (2007); Rebell, Lindseth & Hanushek, *supra* note 52, at 42–43.

55. Rebell, Lindseth & Hanushek, *supra* note 52, at 46.

56. *See generally* HANUSHEK & LINDSETH, *supra* note 52; REBELL, *supra* note 9; Rebell, *supra* note 17; Rebell, *supra* note 54.

57. *See* REBELL, *supra* note 9, at 30–41; Rebell, Lindseth & Hanushek, *supra* note 52, at 42–43.

58. *See* HANUSHEK & LINDSETH, *supra* note 52, at 217–19.

59. San Antonio Indep. Sch. Dist. v. Rodriguez, 411 U.S. 1, 70–71 (1973).

60. *Id.* at 70.

61. William D. Dumcombe & John Yinger, *How Much More Does a Disadvantaged Student Cost?* 18 (Syracuse Univ. Ctr. for Policy Research, Working Paper No. 60, 2004).

62. Educ. Fin. Statistics Ctr., *Table A-1: Current Expenditures Minus Federal Revenue Other Than Impact Aid per Pupil in Membership, by Poverty Quartile and State*, NAT'L CTR. FOR EDUC. STAT., https://nces.ed.gov (last visited June 13, 2018).

63. *Funding Formula, supra* note 20; *Table 3: Percentage Distribution of Public School Teachers Based on Years of Teaching Experience, by Selected School Characteristics (2015–16),* NAT'L CTR. FOR EDUC. STAT., https://nces.ed.gov (last visited June 13, 2018).

64. MIKE PETKO, NAT'L EDUC. ASS'N, WEIGHTED STUDENT FORMULA 6–10 (2005).

65. RUCKER JOHNSON & SEAN TANNER, LEARNING POLICY INST., MONEY AND FREEDOM: THE IMPACT OF CALIFORNIA'S SCHOOL FINANCE REFORM 9 (2018), https://learningpolicyinstitute.org.

66. Abbott v. Burke, 710 A.2d 450, 469 (N.J. 1998).

67. Linda Darling-Hammond, *Teacher Quality and Student Achievement: A Review of State Policy Evidence,* 8 EDUC. POLICY ANALYSIS ARCHIVES 1, 32–33 (2000).

68. Ellen Frede & W. Steven Barnett, *Why Pre-K Is Critical to Closing the Achievement Gap,* PRINCIPAL, May–June 2011, at 8, 10.

69. AMY M. HIGHTOWER ET AL., EDITORIAL PROJECTS IN EDUC., IMPROVING STUDENT LEARNING BY SUPPORTING QUALITY TEACHING: KEY ISSUES, EFFECTIVE STRATEGIES 35 (2011).

70. *TEACH Grants,* FED. STUDENT AID, https://studentaid.ed.gov (last visited June 13, 2018).

71. 20 U.S.C. § 6311(g)(1)(B) (Supp. IV 2016).

72. *Fall 2017 ESSA Educator Equity Best Practices Guide,* NAT'L COUNCIL ON TCHR. QUALITY, https://www.nctq.org (last visited June 13, 2018).

73. Madeline Will, *States' ESSA Plans Fall Short on Educator Equity, NCTQ Analysis Finds,* EDUC. WK.: TEACHER BEAT (Nov. 14, 2017), http://blogs.edweek.org.

74. Ind. Dept' of Educ., Opt-Out Process for Indiana's New Graduation Requirements, https://www.doe.in.gov.

75. Ind. Dept' of Educ., Core 40, General Information, https://www.doe.in.gov.

76. Ind. Dept' of Educ., 2017 Graduation Rate Data., https://www.doe.in.gov.

77. Ind. Dept. of Educ., *supra* note 74. Interestingly, the most recent lawsuit advocating for the federal right to education, *A.C. v. Raimondo,* focuses on access to coursework among other opportunities. Specifically, the plaintiffs argue that because the state does not require students to complete any civics or history courses, it does not provide all students with an adequate preparation for citizenship. The complaint also argues that the state prevents all students from exercising their constitutional rights to vote and form a legal assembly. Complaint at 19-38, A.C. ex rel. Waithe v. Raimondo, No. 18-cv-00645 (D.R.I. Nov. 28, 2018).

78. Child Care for Working Families Act, H.R. 3773, 115th Cong. (2017); Katie Hamm & Carmel Martin, *A New Vision for Child Care in the United States,* CTR. FOR AM. PROGRESS (Sept. 2, 2015), https://www.americanprogress.org.

79. Ulrich Boser & Catherine Brown, *Lessons from State Performance on NAEP,* CTR. FOR AM. PROGRESS (Jan. 14, 2016), https://www.americanprogress.org.

80. HANUSHEK & LINDSETH, *supra* note 52, at 217–58; REBELL, *supra* note 9, at 34–41; Rebell, Lindseth & Hanushek, *supra* note 52, at 41–42, 45.

81. 20 U.S.C. § 6311(b)(2)(B)(xi) (Supp. IV 2016) (requiring disaggregation of test data); *Id.* § 6311(c)(4)(D) (requiring intervention in schools in the bottom 5 percent of state performance and in public high schools in which more than one-third of students fail to graduate); *Id.* § 6311(b)(1)(A), (D) (requiring all states to adopt challenging standards); *Id.* § 6311(d)(2)(A), (B) (requiring intervention when a subgroup consistently underperforms); *Id.* § 6311(d)(2)(C) (requiring intervention when a subgroup of students consistently tests in the bottom 5 percent of students).

82. *See* Lisa Snell & Katie Furtick, *Weighted Student Formula Yearbook 2013*, REASON FOUND. (Dec. 5, 2013), https://reason.org.

83. 20 U.S.C. § 6311(h)(1)(A), (B) (Supp. IV 2017).

84. 372 U.S. 335 (1963).

85. Lincoln Caplan, *The Right to Counsel: Badly Battered at 50*, N.Y. TIMES, Mar. 9, 2013, www.nytimes.com.

86. *See* Larry J. Obhof, DeRolph v. State *and Ohio's Long Road to an Adequate Education*, 2005 BYU EDUC. & L.J. 83, 85 (2005).

87. DeRolph v. State, 754 N.E.2d 1184, 1201 (Ohio 2001).

88. REBELL, *supra* note 9, at 42–55; Rebell, Lindseth & Hanushek, *supra* note 52, at 45.

89. IDAHO CONST. art. IX, § 1; N.J. CONST. art. VIII, § 4, cl. 1.

90. Idaho Sch. for Equal Educ. Opportunity v. State, 129 P.3d 1199, 1202–03 (Idaho 2005).

91. Educ. Wk. Research Ctr., *Corrections to Quality Counts 2016, Idaho—State Highlights 2016*, CALLED TO ACCOUNT: NEW DIRECTIONS IN SCHOOL ACCOUNTABILITY (2016).

92. *History of* Abbott, *supra* note 36.

93. *See generally* LINDA DARLING-HAMMOND, THE FLAT WORLD AND EDUCATION: HOW AMERICA'S COMMITMENT TO EQUITY WILL DETERMINE OUR FUTURE (2010).

94. *See, e.g.*, Abbeville Cty. Sch. Dist. v. State, 767 S.E.2d 157 (S.C. 2014); Obhof, *supra* note 86, at 85.

95. *Abbeville*, 767 S.E.2d at 179–80; DeRolph v. State, 754 N.E.2d 1184, 1201 (Ohio 2001).

96. KENNETH K. WONG, CTR. FOR AM. PROGRESS, THE DESIGN OF THE RHODE ISLAND SCHOOL FUNDING FORMULA 1 (2011).

97. David Kurtz, *A Long Road Ahead*, TALKING POINTS MEMO (Mar. 26, 2013), http://talkingpointsmemo.com.

12

Protecting a Federal Right to Educational Equality and Adequacy

JOSHUA E. WEISHART

Introduction

More than half a century of legal challenges to racially segregated and chronically underfunded public schools teaches us that the right to education is meant to protect children's equality and liberty interests. Courts have interpreted those equality interests narrowly, as a protection against state-sanctioned racial discrimination, and broadly, to protect children from disparities in educational opportunity. Courts have also construed the liberty interests both narrowly, as a privilege against state interference in parents' education decisions, and broadly, as a claim on the state to educate children to function as responsible, productive, and autonomous citizens. The wide range of these judicially recognized interests lends to the impression that they are misaligned or, worse, that they reflect profound discord between equality and liberty.

Emblematic of this discord, some scholars say, is the debate about whether children are entitled to an "equal" or an "adequate" education.[1] Lawsuits challenging the constitutionality of state school finance systems sparked this equality versus adequacy debate. Equality proponents insisted on eliminating funding disparities by equalizing per-pupil spending across school districts or targeting funds to the neediest children. Adequacy proponents, more tolerant of funding disparities in deference to the choices (i.e., liberties) of parents and school districts, demanded instead a level of spending sufficient to ensure that all children can meet an absolute, rather than relative, educational quality threshold. Even as scholars contrasted these paradigms, however, courts adjudicating the state constitutional right to education gradually embraced the need for equality and adequacy.[2] In short, practice outpaced theory.

In contemplating a more robust federal right to education, we should absorb two critical lessons from decades of jurisprudence regarding the state right to education. First, state courts have been better served by being pragmatic about equality and adequacy, moderating these demands to account for political and practical feasibility concerns. In the process, they have unwittingly cast aside stale versions of equality (treating all children identically) and liberty (respecting negative freedoms from state interference with education). Instead, some courts have begun to recognize the value of treating differently situated children as equals according to their needs, so as to cultivate, through state action, children's positive freedoms to become equal citizens. Advocates for an effective and sustainable federal right to education should seize on such reconceptualization of children's equality and liberty interests and align them under a claim for equal liberty. In short, theory must keep pace with practice.

Second, federal courts must at the same time not repeat the experience of state courts that have struggled with fashioning an enforceable remedy under the right to education. The difficulty can be explained in part by the lack of standards for mutually enforcing equality and adequacy. It is also partly explained by courts not perceiving the right to education for what it is, a constitutional aberration that spans the positive and negative rights spectrum to both compel and block state action. A federal right to education could unify both forms because it implicates the federal constitutional guarantees of substantive due process and equal protection. In that union lies potential standards to enforce the right's core function to protect children from the harm of educational disparities and deprivations.

This chapter discusses both lessons, beginning with the legal developments that helped shape contemporary conceptions of equality of educational opportunity and educational adequacy. It then unfolds their points of convergence, suggests that their extremes should be abandoned, and unites them behind the conviction that all children are owed an equally adequate, adequately equal education. The latter part of the chapter posits that a federal right to education guaranteeing equal liberty can avoid the challenges that have plagued the state right to education by developing the interrelation of equal protection and substantive due process.

Equality of Educational Opportunity

Brown v. Board of Education preludes most discussions of the right to education and for good reason. A unanimous Supreme Court declared that "the opportunity of an education . . . is a right which must be made available to all on equal terms" under the US Constitution.[3] To the extent this right to an equal educational opportunity guaranteed children access to a racially integrated education, however, that promise has never been fulfilled. In fact, public schools are as racially segregated today as they were in the 1960s.[4] The Court bears part of the blame. Its subsequent decisions eroded *Brown's* holding to forbid only intentional, state-imposed, racial segregation and limited the remedial measures that courts could mandate to achieve integration.[5] Adding insult to injury, the Court also severely curbed voluntary integration plans, viewing such plans that considered race as probably discriminatory.[6] As a result, the right to equal educational opportunity in the desegregation context merely prohibits rare or exceedingly difficult to prove instances of intentional, state-sponsored racial discrimination, which oddly enough can include the state's voluntary consideration of race designed to achieve racial integration.

Any latent promise of an otherwise all-encompassing right to equal educational opportunity implicit in the US Constitution was revoked when the Court turned its attention to wealth discrimination. In *San Antonio Independent School District v. Rodriguez,* a divided Court held that education was not a fundamental right under the Equal Protection Clause and that neither poor people nor families concentrated in high-poverty school districts were worthy of heightened judicial scrutiny.[7] Thus, funding disparities caused by the state's overreliance on local property taxes to finance public schools need only be rationally related to a legitimate state interest. The five-justice majority thought that test was satisfied, having deemed the preservation of "local control" of school districts a "vital" interest worth "some inequality."[8] In sum, the Supreme Court went from signaling in *Brown* that inequality was inexcusable to holding in *Rodriguez* that it was rational. With that about-face, *Rodriguez* virtually halted equality-based school funding challenges in federal courts.

Advocates then took their cases to state courts, petitioning them to effectuate state constitution education clauses and equal protection guarantees and thereby define educational equality in their own right. Early state court decisions negated *Rodriguez* by embracing formal equality (nondiscrimination) as the aim of equal educational opportunity—the idea being that children should not be discriminated against based on the wealth of the school district in which they happened to reside.[9] The remedy for such discrimination seemed deceptively simple at first: eliminate the formal barriers that caused unequal spending through "either horizontal equity among school districts, such that per-pupil revenues were roughly equalized by the state, or at least fiscal neutrality, such that the revenues available to a school district would not depend solely on the property wealth of the school district."[10] Those remedies thus served to effectuate the principle that all children should be treated the same ("one scholar, one dollar").[11]

To achieve absolute fiscal equalization, however, would require (1) leveling down educational spending overall by capping expenditures in wealthy districts while recapturing and redistributing tax revenues to poorer districts and/or (2) leveling up through continual state tax increases to support guaranteed tax bases and supplemental aid to poorer districts to match the spending in wealthy districts. Neither form of leveling is sustainable politically, and leveling down is undesirable from almost every perspective. Most relevant here, leveling down constrains liberty by preventing parents from deciding collectively to spend more on their children's education and by arresting the development of talents and abilities to "the lowest common denominator," thereby denying all children their full potential.[12]

Courts thus began to realize that, by interpreting the right to education as a blanket prohibition against unequal treatment, judges would be compelled to enforce politically infeasible and undesirable remedies that might conflict with individual liberties. Moreover, the formal equality remedies endorsed in the early cases were inherently flawed for two reasons: (1) Equalizing per-pupil funding does not in itself improve the quality of education, which again can be leveled down to achieve formal equality. (2) Equalization does not address the needs of disadvantaged children, who require not equal but more spending to approximate the educational opportunities and attainment of their peers.

Modest legislative endeavors, meanwhile, had sought to provide such compensatory resources and services to disadvantaged children, for example, Title I of the Elementary and Secondary Education Act and the Individuals with Disabilities Education Act. Several state courts also gradually began to articulate a substantive brand of equal educational opportunity—one directed against inequitable (as opposed to unequal) spending.[13] The Supreme Court of New Jersey, for example, determined that its state constitution's education clause obligated the legislature not only "to assure that poorer urban districts' educational funding is substantially equal to that of property-rich districts" but also to provide additional funding "for the special educational needs of these poorer urban districts and address their extreme disadvantages."[14] In essence, legislative and judicial decisions have slowly come to recognize the principle that differently situated students should be treated according to their needs.

Vertical equity, as this principle is frequently termed in the literature, is achieved through remedial efforts to mitigate natural and social disadvantages by allocating greater resources to the neediest students. Such remedial measures are most often implemented minimally through weighted student funding formulas, which apportion additional weights to certain student demographic categories that have more expensive educational needs. Through these more equitable inputs, vertical equity measures attempt to achieve more equitable outputs. The ideal of equality of educational opportunity emerging from legislative and judicial incorporations of vertical equity principles is that "all students should have an equal chance to succeed, with actual observed success dependent on certain personal characteristics, such as motivation, desire, effort, and to some extent ability . . . [, and not] on circumstances outside the control of the child, such as the financial position of the family, geographic location, ethnic or racial identity, gender, and disability."[15]

Despite the focus on resource equity in school finance litigation, for many scholars the notion of equal educational opportunity still signifies equality in one important sense: the social equality manifest in racial and socioeconomic integration. Armed with extensive social science evidence, scholars have urged school finance litigants to incorporate "an argument that racial and socioeconomic integration are necessary components of a student's constitutional right to an equal or adequate education."[16] Very few litigants have pressed that argument, which to date has prevailed in only one state court decision.[17] This is most unfortunate because vertical equity and integration are indeed complementary. "Although the relative importance of redistributing students versus redistributing resources will be a question for the ages, it would be surprising if genuine equality of educational opportunity did not ultimately require both."[18]

Educational Adequacy

The liberty interests protected by a right to education evolved as the equality interests did: curtailed by federal courts, amplified by state courts. The Supreme Court has recognized that the US Constitution confers on parents and guardians the privilege to decide whether their children will receive a public or private education and the privilege to control their children's education and upbringing generally, including their religious education.[19] As such, the federal right to education held by parents and guardians secures liberty in its traditional negative sense—freedom from state interference.[20] When children are deemed the right holder, however, the federal right to education arguably protects liberty in a positive sense—freedom to be and do. Although the 5–4 majority in *Rodriguez* declined to recognize a fundamental right to equal educational opportunity, the Court reserved the possibility that there exists a right to "some identifiable quantum of education" implicit in the US Constitution.[21] Part of the reason that the Court kept this door open was because it acknowledged that a basic education is essential to protect children's "enjoyment of the rights of speech and of full participation in the political process."[22] That is, the Court understood that education instills in children the capabilities, the freedom, to be citizens who can exercise their rights.

This link between education and positive liberty is even more pronounced in state constitutions that express the right to education as a safeguard of democracy. The text of several state constitutions declares explicitly that education is "essential to the preservation of the rights and liberties of the people"[23] and to a "free,"[24] "good,"[25] or "republican form"[26] of government "by the people."[27] Several courts have so interpreted the right even absent such explicit language in the state constitution.[28] The New Jersey Supreme Court perhaps put it best when it acknowledged that education "bestows the capacity to function as a citizen—as a contributing and participating member of society and one's community."[29]

Beyond education for citizenship, a few state constitutions explicitly emphasize the economic importance of education to "commerce, trades, manufactures" as well as "vocational," "mining," "agricultural," "scientific," and "industrial" improvements.[30] Where state constitutions do not declare such purposes explicitly, courts have explained that education equips children with the capabilities "to attain productive employment and otherwise contribute to the state's economy,"[31] "to compete favorably" on the job market,[32] and to "lead economically productive lives to the benefit of us all."[33] Once again, the rationale here is that the state has some obligation to endow children with capabilities to be productive members of the economy.

Being the state's civilizing engine of democracy and catalyst for economic prosperity, education has instrumental value as a public or collective good. But courts adjudicating the right to education have also recognized education's intrinsic value as a private, individual good that should be enhanced by nurturing children's capabilities to be autonomous generally—through "the development of mind, body, and social morality (ethics),"[34] cultivating the "maturity and understanding,"[35] "self-knowledge,"[36] and capacity to "flourish in the twenty-first century."[37]

The nexus between education and positive liberty has been unmistakable and most influential in court decisions interpreting state constitutions to require educational adequacy. In the most influential of those decisions, the Kentucky Supreme Court determined that an adequate education is one that instills "seven capacities" enabling children to "function" in society, "make informed choices," and "understand the issues" as responsible citizens and to "compete favorably" in their education and the job market.[38] The Kentucky decision has been "adopted or relied on in nearly every other successful state court case [for] two decades nationwide, regardless of differences in the substantive language of the education clauses among the states."[39]

To be sure, no court has even so much as mentioned the term "positive liberty" or "freedom" in relation to adequacy. Rather than emphasize liberty, adequacy has been couched in terms of educational quality.[40] Yet when tasked to justify adequacy as the qualitative standard that the state has to meet to discharge its duty, courts repeatedly returned to the notion that education fortifies children's positive liberties—that a liberty interest actually underwrites the adequacy standards.[41] Courts did not have to venture into unchartered judicial terrain with talk of positive liberties because every state constitution has an education clause that can provide a textual basis for an adequacy mandate.[42] Legislators and governors, who lacked the political will to equalize funding, also found adequacy politically expedient.[43] Adequacy was initially billed as "the more achievable, but more modest" alternative to equity.[44] It did not demand equalization of tax capacity or expenditures across school districts; it only required that each district have enough funding so that all of its students could achieve a minimum qualitative threshold. Because adequacy posed no threat of leveling down educational spending, the wealthy and politically powerful school districts would remain free to spend more to provide a greater-than-adequate education to their students.

Adequacy's tolerance for such inequality is explained by the view that relational or "democratic equality" is more worthy of pursuit than equality of resources.[45] On this view, it is not important "that everyone should have the same but that each should have enough."[46] Hence, adequacy theorists assert that all children should have access to a quality education up to a certain threshold—enough to acquire the capabilities (substantial freedoms) to function as equal citizens and avoid political, economic, and social subjugation. Yet they presumptively deny the moral significance of inequalities above that threshold. Indeed, adequacy theorists contend that permitting wealthy school districts to spend more above the threshold is not simply tolerable but valuable because it preserves parental liberty, enhances the intrinsic value of education for the beneficiaries of the additional spending, and, by maximizing the development of their human capital, creates a social surplus that will "redound to everyone's absolute advantage."[47]

Whether one finds this provocative philosophical view convincing, there is no denying that, in the law, adequacy owes its moral force to the inextricable link between education and liberty: the idea that education functions to protect children by instilling basic capabilities—positive liberties—that enable responsible citizenship, economic productivity, personal development, and self-respect.

Equal Liberty: Educational Equality and Adequacy

Despite the theoretical differences between equality and adequacy, state courts interpreting the right to education frequently fuse the concepts.[48] In practice, they have been reconciled along two significant points of convergence. First, adequacy, like equality, can be "a relative concept."[49] For what it takes for a child to function as an equal, responsible, and productive citizen—that is, where to set the adequacy threshold—invariably turns on what educational resources other children have.[50] Courts deciding adequacy cases have therefore made comparative judgments (as they would in equality cases) about the educational resources needed to prepare students in the competition for higher education and high-quality jobs.[51] Assessing the adequacy of New York City schools, for example, the state's highest court compared them with schools in the rest of the state, explaining, "City schools have the most student need in the state and the highest local costs yet receive some of the lowest per-student funding and have some of the worst results."[52]

Second, the vertical equity measures that have been employed in equality cases are also necessary in adequacy cases because more educational resources are required to lift disadvantaged students "above the specified threshold."[53] Several adequacy court decisions have thus approved vertical equity funding "to compensate for differences in regional costs and student needs that translate into higher costs to supply the same quality of education throughout the state."[54] Courts and legislatures have also imported vertical equity principles in utilizing the methods for "costing-out an adequate education, that is, attaching a price tag to the resources necessary for all children to reach specified educational outcomes."[55] Such cost studies, which have been commissioned in at least forty states, can highlight vertical inequities and price the additional resources needed by disadvantaged children to reach the adequacy thresholds.[56] The Kansas Supreme Court recently relied on an albeit-dated cost study in highlighting the disproportionately poor academic performance of certain minority and low-income students in light of funding inadequacies.[57]

Equality and adequacy therefore converge in addressing the educational opportunities of children below a certain threshold—both require assessments of the comparative needs and distributions to compensate for particular needs. Where they continue to diverge, at least in theory, is on the question of how to shape educational opportunities after vertical equity measures have been taken and there remains a considerable gap between those drifting at the threshold and those sailing above it. Predictably, equality would require us to do more, and adequacy would require us to do nothing—each misses the mark.

Equality would require more because education is a positional good; that is, in the competition for selective-college admissions and high-quality jobs, the value of one's education depends on the quantity and quality of education had by others. Thus, "getting 'enough' will not give one a fair chance in competitions to which education is relevant, if others are getting more than enough."[58] The problem, however, comes not with wanting to do more to level the playing field but with setting the end goal at equal chances for educational achievement.

Although this principle of equal chances enjoys broad appeal, it should be tempered by the reality that it cannot be fully realized. In the extreme, it would require the state to neutralize all of the differential effects of social circumstances (e.g., race, class, and gender) and natural endowments (innate talents and (dis)abilities) on every child's chances for educational achievement. The state simply cannot marshal enough resources to accomplish such a feat. Indeed, for some children, the resources that they would need would be virtually insatiable.[59] Even if scarcity were not an issue, chances for educational success would still be unequal so long as family life remains a prevalent influence on a child's prospects—that is, so long as parents retain the liberty to raise children in diverse ways.

Lauding equal chances for educational achievement as a guiding moral principle when it is, in fact, infeasible violates the maxim "ought implies can."[60] If we have a moral obligation to ensure equal chances for educational achievement, then we should be able to bring that about. Otherwise, the danger with equal chances is that it resonates not as an ideal but as reality. Equality defenders take adequacy to task for sending the wrong message to children receiving the threshold level of education, that they are in a sense disfavored because they are not expected to succeed at the same rate as children receiving an above-threshold education.[61] But that message is no more harmful than the one conveyed by perpetuating the fiction that equal chances for educational achievement are attainable. That fiction distorts expectations about the evenness of the playing field and enables the "winners" on the field to cast judgments on the "losers." Those "who fail are further stigmatized because they presumably manifest—to winners more than to losers, to be sure—weakness of will or lack of talent."[62]

None of this should be mistaken for an endorsement of the "do nothing" argument. To those who contend that disadvantaged students "simply cannot make it, the constitutional answer is, give them a chance."[63] Indeed, we owe them an effective, meaningful chance of educational success—one that approximates equal chances by diminishing the positional returns that the advantaged hold over the disadvantaged in the competition for higher education and high-quality jobs. To do so, we can equitably distribute and financially incentivize quality teachers, integrate schools, and target resources to improve academic growth, close achievement gaps, raise graduation rates, reduce class size, enhance the curriculum, and improve school facilities and access to technology. All of that is within our reach.

On the other hand, adequacy in its extreme would require nothing more to level the playing field because there is no perceived injustice in permitting inequalities above the threshold, provided all children have access to enough educational opportunities to function as equal citizens. Again, the end goal is not equality of resources but relational or democratic equality such that the better off are not able to subjugate the worst off politically, economically, or socially and all are able to participate. For democratic equality to endure, "those who occupy positions of responsibility and leadership in society," namely, the elite, must be socially integrated and responsive to "all sectors of society, not just themselves."[64] Such integration requires disadvantaged students to have effective access to the elite ranks, meaning "access within the realistic reach of students exercising substantial but not extraordinary effort and within the financial reach of their families."[65]

Yet large-scale inequalities in educational opportunities above the threshold make it unrealistic to expect disadvantaged children to be able to join the elite. Indeed, at a certain point, those inequalities begin to undermine the very purpose of adequacy—the ability of students to function as equal citizens and compete for admission to higher education and high-quality jobs on comparable terms—democratic equality, however broadly or narrowly defined. Hence, courts "generally do not seek to enforce some absolute notion of adequacy, where disparities in resources are ignored."[66] Rather, courts tend to view adequacy as a "dynamic standard," recognizing that there will come a point where above-threshold spending "will create intolerable disparities in opportunities."[67]

Advocates for a more effectual federal right to education should abandon the extremes of adequacy and equality in favor of distributive rules that capitalize on the reconceptualization of children's equality and liberty interests. Embracing the vertical equity principle that differently situated children should be treated according to their needs, the federal right should call for adequately equal educational opportunities. This demands equitable (not equal) distributions of educational resources designed (1) to mitigate social and natural disadvantages so that all children can meet adequacy thresholds and (2) to diminish positional returns above those thresholds so that the competition for higher education and high-quality jobs is fairer.

This form of equality is conducive to the positive and negative demands of liberty: It does not impinge on the negative liberties of parents to spend above adequacy thresholds, provided that the state meets the needs of all children. It facilitates positive liberty by affording disadvantaged children with compensatory resources and services needed to achieve those thresholds.

Accepting the centrality of positive liberty, the federal right should also entail an equally adequate education. This demands that all children have access to a quality education expressed by high adequacy thresholds that are dynamic and sensitive to children's capabilities to function as equal citizens and to compete for admission to higher education and for high-quality jobs.[68] If met, high adequacy thresholds can also diminish positional returns. For instance, we could expect a considerable reduction of inequalities if the threshold were a K–12 education that would enable students to complete a four-year residential college curriculum designed to prepare them for success in a postgraduate or professional education. "Defining the equal standing of citizens in a robust manner, such that opportunities to participate in civic life are roughly equal, will bring the adequacy orientation much closer to the equality orientation in practice."[69]

This form of positive liberty is then equality enhancing, fostering a relational, democratic equality through equal citizenship. It is also conducive to egalitarian demands for race- and class-based integration in K–12 and higher education—adequacy theorists view such integration as a moral imperative and essential to fulfilling the aims of democratic equality.[70]

Advocates can encapsulate the conviction that children are owed "an equally adequate and adequately equal education" by framing the federal right to education as guaranteeing equal liberty. This phrase invokes an ancient tradition, reflected in the most influential and foundational democratic documents,[71] and it enjoys plenty of constitutional cachet.[72] More importantly, it captures what we mean to equalize—what we can actually equalize—through public education, and that is access to a baseline set of capabilities, positive liberties, that, when exercised, promotes full and equal citizenship. Properly construed, in other words, "a large measure of equality, so far from being inimical to liberty, is essential to it."[73]

Constituting a Federal Right to Education

Safeguarding the viability of a federal right to education will require that advocates address lingering doubts about the right's justiciability. Separation-of-powers concerns have long troubled state courts in school finance litigation.[74] In fact, courts in six states declined even to consider the merits of those cases, reasoning that their state constitution education clauses vest complete discretion in the legislature—thus rendering the right to education in those states nonjusticiable.[75] The vast majority of state courts, nevertheless, have entertained the merits, and more than twenty have declared their school finance scheme unconstitutional.[76] Yet even these courts have struggled with the remedy, faced with the prospect of enforcing the right in ways that might continuously encroach on legislative prerogatives, including ordering the legislature to apportion resources differently or increase educational spending.[77]

Some courts have thus declined to specify a remedy or give guidance about necessary remedial action, in deference to the legislature.[78] This strategy has backfired. The Ohio Supreme Court engaged in a thirteen-year battle with an outright resistant legislature, declaring the school finance system unconstitutional in four separate decisions.[79] The court's remedial deference allowed the legislature to hedge and stall. Eventually, the court surrendered "its jurisdiction over the matter, effectively waiving the white flag and washing its hands of the dispute."[80] Other courts have specified a remedy or given more remedial guidance only to confront stiff legislative resistance.[81] In an unprecedented move, the Washington Supreme Court was forced to impose contempt sanctions ($100,000 per day) on the legislature for its repeated failure to devise a constitutional school finance plan.[82]

Such "under-enforcement of education rights and duties is a product of their past under-theorization by courts."[83] That deficit contributes to the lack of standards for the mutual enforcement of equality and adequacy. The Kansas Supreme Court, for instance, has recognized that "equity and adequacy" are "two components" of the state constitutional right to education, yet the court treats them as separate "challenges," subject to separate constitutional "tests."[84] Essentially, courts have not come to terms with the dual nature of the right to education as both a positive claim to an adequate education (compelling state action) and negative immunity against inequitable distributions of educational opportunity (blocking state action). Consequently, courts have not synchronized both dimensions of the right in a way that directs the state to effectuate the right's core function: to protect children from being disadvantaged in life by educational disparities and deprivations.

A federal right to education could achieve that synchronization by drawing on the demands and guarantees of equal protection and substantive due process. Subjecting the right to either substantive due process or equal protection separately would impede its enforcement because each is doctrinally flawed. Marrying the egalitarian principles of equal protection with the substantive demands of due process à la *Obergefell v. Hodges* could yet overcome these flaws and facilitate judicial enforcement of a federal right to education.[85]

"The Inadequacy of Equal Protection"[86]

Federal equal protection analysis is frequently criticized for its "rigid tiers of scrutiny" and the discriminatory purpose required to prove a violation, regardless of a law's discriminatory effects.[87] Most state courts in lockstep with federal courts have had to contend with these limitations in equality-based school funding challenges. Apart from the strictures of the federal doctrine, the inadequacy of equal protection is apparent in "the struggle of courts to resolve how the concept of equality should be defined and measured"—and particularly whether equal protection entails "formal and substantive equality."[88] This struggle has persisted for decades in the school finance context, perplexing scholars, courts, and legislatures alike.[89] As previously discussed, the state right to education has been trending toward substantive equality; a federal right to education should follow suit. Otherwise, if equal protection demands only formal equality, then it affords no protection "against inadequate funding, provided that inadequacy is equally shared."[90] Nor does it require (as opposed to permit) that educational spending be adjusted to the needs of differently situated children, and thus it fails to protect those who need it most.

Substantive equal protection requiring vertical equity is the answer. Addressing the needs of students could nevertheless pose implementation problems without a qualitative constitutional standard by which to assess the significance of absolute and relative disparities.[91] "For once a court agrees to impose a remedy based upon vertical equity, upon what basis should it rely to authorize or limit how much more money a low-income school or student should receive than an affluent one?"[92] Answering that question seems to turn on "determining what set of knowledge and skills schools should teach to each student" and "what types of supplemental assistance students with special needs require, and how much that assistance will cost."[93] There must be, in other words, "specific targets that can be used to determine whether vertical equity has been reached."[94]

State constitution education standards already exist, so applying equal protection would not necessarily require "independent qualitative judgments by a federal court."[95] Courts would be leery of making such judgments because, as *Rodriguez* emphasized, "[i]t is not the province of [courts] to create substantive constitutional rights in the name of guaranteeing equal protection of the laws."[96] Equal protection, then, may not be the appropriate doctrinal vehicle for adopting any new standards.[97] Enforcing only preexisting state standards through equal protection, however, would leave intact low standards in some states as well as *inter*state inequities that can be much larger than *intra*state inequities.[98] Presumably, those interstate inequities would be a major impetus for seeking a more effectual federal right to education in the first place. Yet, without universal, qualitative, constitutional standards for assessing both absolute and relative disparities, equal protection compelling vertical equity may render a federal right to education an unmanageable and thus inadequate protection.

The Inequity of Substantive Due Process

The notion that substantive due process underpins an affirmative, liberty-based right to education has been suggested for decades.[99] Substantive due process is triggered by state compulsory education laws that not only restrict children's negative liberties but profoundly shape their positive liberties as well.[100] Educational deprivation causes "social economic, intellectual, and psychological" harms that may be fairly attributed to the state's denial of an adequate education.[101] Under federal substantive due process precedent, the threat of these state-created dangers imposes an affirmative duty on states to protect children from such harms.[102] Along those lines, some commentators have suggested a substantive due process path toward the recognition of a federal right to education based on the "human dignity-based holding of *Lawrence v. Texas*."[103] That assertion has been reinforced by *Obergefell* given the Court's reliance on substantive due process in recognizing the fundamental right of same-sex couples to marry.[104]

The problem with substantive due process is not that the Court's precedents fail to support its application to education. The problem is that "substantive due process decisions typically rest essentially or entirely on claims of *non*comparative right" judged on an individual basis without reference to interpersonal relations or effects.[105] A liberty-based right to education grounded in substantive due process could thus tolerate wide disparities in educational opportunities among students, provided that each individual student has what the state deems to be an adequate share.[106] Again, this is one of the main criticisms leveled against adequacy—that in its noncomparative extreme, it confers unfair advantages in the competition for higher education and jobs to students who receive more than the adequate level of educational opportunities. Adequacy encased solely in substantive due process would therefore license and exacerbate inequity.

Equal Protection and Substantive Due Process

There has been an erratic yet enduring relationship between equality and liberty in the constitutional jurisprudence of equal protection and substantive due process. Joined together, these doctrines could offset their respective limitations and ameliorate the right to education's enforcement standards. Substantive due process exerts leverage in the demand for a qualitative, constitutional adequacy threshold to protect children's negative liberties (freedom from educational deprivation) and positive liberties (freedom to be responsible, productive, autonomous citizens). The resulting substantive standards could alleviate some of the implementation concerns by providing a "baseline of adequacy"[107] from which the vertical equity required by equal protection can be measured and adjusted.[108]

Equal protection, in turn, pivots the analysis squarely on the educational disparities. First, equal protection that embraces substantive equality demands vertical equity in the distribution of educational opportunities. As a result, equal protection will necessitate funding to compensate for differences in regional costs and student needs and thus tend to require that disadvantaged students receive additional resources to afford them a meaningful opportunity to meet the adequacy threshold. Second, equal protection intercedes when the disparities between children at the threshold and children above it become objectionable—that is, when such disparities imperil equal liberty by undermining children's capabilities to function as equal citizens and compete for admission to higher education and high-quality jobs on comparable terms. This would implicate both substantive due process, requiring adequacy thresholds to be set higher to diminish positional returns held by those above the threshold, and equal protection, requiring adjustments in the distribution of educational opportunities to ensure vertical equity necessary to meet the higher thresholds. In other words, equal protection translates the adequacy required by substantive due process into a relational or comparative demand.

At bottom, constituting a federal right to education with both equal protection and substantive due process "can have synergistic effects, producing results that neither clause might reach by itself" or that the right can have unassisted.[109] Those effects could manifest themselves in the outgrowth of legal standards for protecting educational equality and adequacy.

Conclusion

The only consensus to have emerged from the age-old project to reconcile equality and liberty is the recognition that these principles can be mutually exclusive or reinforcing, depending on their conceptions.[110]

Although we cannot reconcile every potential conflict between these principles in one interpretive sweep, we can and should align children's educational equality and liberty interests together. Envisioning a more robust federal right to education need not begin on a blank slate, with more than four decades of state court precedent as our guide. That precedent instructs us to moderate the demands of educational equality and adequacy toward a guarantee of equal liberty that is practically feasible, morally acceptable, and legally sustainable. To that end, we can quell doubts about justiciability by developing the interrelation of equal protection and substantive due process to facilitate the enforcement of a federal right to education guaranteeing equal liberty.

NOTES

The author is grateful for the generous support of the Hodges Research Fund at the West Virginia University College of Law.

1. *See* William S. Koski & Rob Reich, *When "Adequate" Isn't: The Retreat from Equity in Educational Law and Policy and Why It Matters*, 56 EMORY L.J. 545, 593–94 (2006) (citing Peter Enrich, *Leaving Equality Behind: New Directions in School Finance Reform*, 48 VAND. L. REV. 101, 160–61 (1995)).

2. *See, e.g.*, Lake View Sch. Dist. No. 25 v. Huckabee, 91 S.W.3d 472, 500 (Ark. 2002) (recognizing that the state must "determine whether equal educational opportunity for an adequate education is being substantially afforded"); Gannon v. State (*Gannon I*), 319 P.3d 1196, 1219 (Kan. 2014) ("We have recognized that [the education clause] contains at least two components: equity and adequacy."); Abbott v. Burke (*Abbott II*), 575 A.2d 359, 375 (N.J. 1990) (concluding that education in poor urban school districts was inequitable and inadequate); McCleary v. State (*McCleary I*), 269 P.3d 227, 252 (Wash. 2012) (noting that the tax source "implicates both the equity and the adequacy of the K–12 funding system").

3. 347 U.S. 483, 493 (1954).

4. *See* Kimberly Jenkins Robinson, *Resurrecting the Promise of* Brown: *Understanding and Remedying How the Supreme Court Reconstitutionalized Segregated Schools*, 88 N.C. L. REV. 787, 789–90, 793 (2010).

5. *See, e.g.*, Milliken v. Bradley, 418 U.S. 717, 744–45 (1974) (holding that remedy for de jure segregation could not reach beyond the school district's boundaries unless plaintiff can show schools outside those boundaries collaborated in segregation); Keyes v. School Dist. No. 1, 413 U.S. 189, 200, 208 (1973) (concluding that de facto segregation did not offend the Constitution and emphasizing that de jure segregation required a "purpose or intent to segregate").

6. Parents Involved in Cmty. Schs. v. Seattle Sch. Dist. No. 1, 551 U.S. 701, 783–87 (2007) (Kennedy, J., concurring) (explaining the heavy burden that the state would have to carry in devising a plan that considers race and satisfies strict scrutiny).

7. 411 U.S. 1, 35 (1973).

8. *Id.* at 49–51.

9. *See* Serrano v. Priest, 557 P.2d 929, 951–52 (Cal. 1976); Horton v. Meskill, 376 A.2d 359, 373–75 (Conn. 1977).

10. William S. Koski & Jesse Hahnel, *The Past, Present, and Possible Futures of Educational Finance Reform Litigation, in* HANDBOOK OF RESEARCH IN EDUCATION FINANCE AND POLICY 47 (Helen F. Ladd & Edward B. Fiske eds., 2008).

11. *Id.* at 44.

12. Elizabeth Anderson, *Fair Opportunity in Education: A Democratic Equality Perspective,* 117 ETHICS 595, 615 (2007).

13. *See, e.g.,* Montoy v. State, 102 P.3d 1160, 1164 (Kan. 2005) (concluding that the school "financing formula was not based upon actual costs to educate children" of different needs and "distorted the low enrollment, special education, vocational, bilingual education, and the at-risk student weighting factors"); Hoke Cty. Bd. of Educ. v. State, 599 S.E.2d 365, 393 (N.C. 2004) (affirming the trial court's finding that at-risk students were not receiving the remedial aid necessary to "avail themselves of [an] educational opportunity"); Washakie Cty. Sch. Dist. No. One v. Herschler, 606 P.2d 310, 336 (Wyo. 1980) ("A state formula can be devised which will weight the calculation to compensate for special needs educational cost differentials.").

14. Abbott v. Burke (*Abbott II*), 575 A.2d 359, 408 (N.J. 1990).

15. Robert Berne & Leanna Stiefel, *Concepts of School Finance Equity: 1970 to the Present, in* EQUITY AND ADEQUACY IN EDUCATION FINANCE: ISSUES AND PERSPECTIVES 7, 13 (Helen F. Ladd et al. eds., 1999).

16. James Ryan, *Schools, Race, and Money,* 109 YALE L.J. 249, 308 (1999); *see also* Derek W. Black, *Middle-Income Peers as Educational Resources and the Constitutional Right to Equal Access,* 53 B.C. L. REV. 373, 403–04 (2012).

17. Sheff v. O'Neill, 678 A.2d 1267, 1270–71 (Conn. 1996).

18. Goodwin Liu, *The Parted Paths of School Desegregation and School Finance Litigation,* 24 LAW & INEQ. 81, 106 (2006).

19. *See* Wisconsin v. Yoder, 406 U.S. 205, 232–33 (1972); Pierce v. Soc'y of the Sisters, 268 U.S. 510, 534–35 (1925); Meyer v. Nebraska, 262 U.S. 390, 400 (1923).

20. *See* Isaiah Berlin, *Two Concepts of Liberty, in* FOUR ESSAYS ON LIBERTY 118, 121–22 (1969). Negative liberty refers to "the degree to which no man or body of men interferes with my activity," a *freedom from* external interference or obstruction. *Id.* at 122. Positive liberty "consists in being one's own master," an internal *freedom to* be and do, that is, to self-direct one's life. *Id.* at 131.

21. 411 U.S. at 36.

22. *Id.* at 37.

23. CAL. CONST. art. IX, § 1; ME. CONST. art. VIII, pt. 1, § 1; MO. CONST. art. IX, § 1(a); R.I. CONST. art. XII, § 1; *accord* MASS. CONST. pt. 2, ch. V, § 2; TEX. CONST. art. VII, § 1.

24. IND. CONST. art. VIII, § 1; N.H. CONST. pt. 2, art. LXXXIII.

25. MICH. CONST. art. VIII, § 1; N.C. CONST. art. IX, § 1; ARK. CONST. art. XIV, § 1.
26. IDAHO CONST. art. IX, § 1; MINN. CONST. art. XIII, § 1; S.D. CONST. art. VIII, § 1.
27. N.D. CONST. art. VIII, § 1.
28. *See, e.g.*, Roosevelt Elementary Sch. Dist. No. 66 v. Bishop, 877 P.2d 806, 812 (Ariz. 1994); Sheff v. O'Neil, 678 A.2d 1267, 1289 (Conn. 1996); Lujan v. Colo. State Bd. of Educ., 649 P.2d 1005, 1017 (Colo. 1982); McDaniel v. Thomas, 285 S.E.2d 156, 165 (Ga. 1981); Rose v. Council for Better Educ., Inc., 790 S.W.2d 186, 206 (Ky. 1989); Hornbeck v. Somerset Cnty. Bd. of Educ., 458 A.2d 758, 785–86 (Md. 1983); McNair v. Sch. Dist. No. 1 of Cascade Cnty., 288 P. 188, 190 (Mont. 1930); Robinson v. Cahill, 303 A.2d 273, 295 (N.J. 1973); Campaign for Fiscal Equity v. State (*CFE I*), 655 N.E.2d 661 (N.Y. 1995); DeRolph v. State (*DeRolph I*), 677 N.E.2d 733, 737 (Ohio 1997); Tenn. Small Sch. Sys. v. McWherter, 851 S.W.2d 139, 150–51 (Tenn. 1993); Seattle Sch. Dist. No. 1 of King Cnty. v. State, 585 P.2d 71, 94 (Wash. 1978); Pauley v. Kelly, 255 S.E.2d 859, 877 (W. Va. 1979); Brigham v. State, 692 A.2d 384, 393 (Vt. 1997).
29. Abbott v. Burke (*Abbott IV*), 693 A.2d 417, 428 (N.J. 1997).
30. *See* IND. CONST. art. VIII, § 1; KAN. CONST. art. VI, § 1; MASS. CONST. pt. 2, ch. V, § 2; NEV. CONST. art. XI, § 1; N.H. CONST. pt. 2, art. 83; N.D. CONST. art. VIII, § 4.
31. Conn. Coal. for Justice in Educ. Funding, Inc. v. Rell, 990 A.2d 206, 253 (Conn. 2010).
32. *See* Pinto v. Ala. Coal. for Equity, 662 So. 2d 894, 896 (Ala. 1995); McDuffy v. Sec'y of the Exec. Office of Educ., 615 N.E.2d 516, 554 (Mass. 1993); Claremont Sch. Dist. v. Governor, 703 A.2d 1353, 1359 (N.H. 1997).
33. Op. of the Justices No. 338, 624 So. 2d 107, 159 (Ala. 1993) (quoting favorably Plyler v. Doe, 457 U.S. 202, 221 (1982)).
34. Pauley v. Kelly, 255 S.E.2d 859, 877 (W. Va. 1979).
35. Seattle Sch. Dist. No. 1 of King Cnty. v. State, 585 P.2d 71, 94 (Wash. 1978).
36. Rose v. Council for Better Educ., Inc., 790 S.W.2d 186, 212 (Ky. 1989); *Pinto*, 662 So. 2d at 896.
37. *Claremont*, 703 A.2d at 1359.
38. *Rose*, 790 S.W.2d at 212.
39. Scott R. Bauries, *The Education Duty*, 47 WAKE FOREST L. REV. 705, 760 (2012).
40. *See* William E. Thro, *Judicial Analysis during the Third Wave of School Finance Litigation: The Massachusetts Decision as a Model*, 35 B.C. L. REV. 597, 609 (1994).
41. *See, e.g., supra* notes 28–29 and 31–37 and accompanying text.
42. *See* Koski & Reich, *supra* note 1, at 559.
43. *See* Melissa C. Carr & Susan H. Fuhrman, *The Politics of School Finance in the 1990s, in* EQUITY AND ADEQUACY IN EDUCATION FINANCE: ISSUES AND PERSPECTIVES 147, 150 (Helen F. Ladd et al. eds., 1999).
44. Enrich, *supra* note 1, at 182.
45. *See, e.g.*, Anderson, *supra* note 12; Debra Satz, *Equality, Adequacy, and Educational Policy*, 3 EDUC. FIN. & POL'Y 424 (2008).
46. Harry Frankfurt, *Equality as a Moral Ideal*, 98 ETHICS 21, 21 (1987).

47. *See* Debra Satz, *Equality, Adequacy, and Education for Citizenship*, 117 ETHICS 623, 632, 645 (2007).
48. *See* JAMES E. RYAN, FIVE MILES AWAY, A WORLD APART: ONE CITY, TWO SCHOOLS, AND THE STORY OF EDUCATIONAL OPPORTUNITY IN MODERN AMERICA 150–51 (2010).
49. *See* James E. Ryan, *Standards, Testing, and School Finance Litigation*, 86 TEX. L. REV. 1223, 1239 (2008).
50. *See* Satz, *supra* note 45, at 434.
51. *See* Richard Briffault, *Adding Adequacy to Equity, in* SCHOOL MONEY TRIALS: THE LEGAL PURSUIT OF EDUCATIONAL ADEQUACY 25, 28 (Martin R. West & Paul E. Peterson eds., 2007) (citing, inter alia, *Abbott II*, 575 A.2d 359, 372 (N.J. 1990)).
52. Campaign for Fiscal Equity v. State (*CFE II*), 801 N.E.2d 326, 350 (N.Y. 2003).
53. Kenneth A. Strike, *Equality of Opportunity and School Finance: A Commentary on Ladd, Satz, and Brighouse and Swift*, 3 EDUC. FIN. & POL'Y 467, 476 (2008); *see* James E. Ryan & Thomas Saunders, *Foreword to Symposium on School Finance Litigation: Emerging Trends or New Dead Ends?*, 22 YALE L. & POL'Y REV. 463, 469 (2004).
54. *See* Regina R. Umpstead, *Determining Adequacy: How Courts Are Redefining State Responsibility for Educational Finance, Goals, and Accountability*, 2007 BYU EDUC. & L.J. 281, 298; *see* Briffault, *supra* note 51, at 38.
55. *See* William S. Koski, *Achieving "Adequacy" in the Classroom*, 27 B.C. THIRD WORLD L.J. 13, 21–22 (2007).
56. *See* Michael Rebell, *Professional Rigor, Public Engagement and Judicial Review: A Proposal for Enhancing the Validity of Education Adequacy Studies*, 109 TCHRS. C. REC. 1303, 1304 (2007).
57. Gannon v. State (*Gannon IV*), 390 P.3d 461, 496–501 (Kan. 2017) (per curiam).
58. Harry Brighouse & Adam Swift, *Putting Educational Equality in Its Place*, 3 EDUC. FIN. & POL'Y 444, 462 (2008).
59. *See* Lesley Jacobs, *Equality, Adequacy, and Stakes Fairness: Retrieving the Equal Opportunities in Education Approach*, 8 THEORY & RES. EDUC. 249, 253–54 (2010).
60. *See* IMMANUEL KANT, CRITIQUE OF PRACTICAL REASON (1788), *reprinted in* PRACTICAL PHILOSOPHY 133, 163–64 (Mary J. Gregor ed. & trans., 1996).
61. Koski & Reich, *supra* note 1, at 606; Strike, *supra* note 53, at 486.
62. Jennifer L. Hochschild, *The Word American Ends in "Can": The Ambiguous Promise of the American Dream*, 34 WM. & MARY L. REV. 139, 151, 161 (1992).
63. Abbott v. Burke (*Abbott II*), 575 A.2d 359, 403 (N.J. 1990).
64. Anderson, *supra* note 12, at 596.
65. *Id.* at 614–15.
66. Ryan, *supra* note 49, at 1237.
67. *See id.*; Lake View Sch. Dist. No. 25 v. Huckabee, 91 S.W.3d 472, 496 (Ark. 2002) ("[Disparities] can sustain a finding of inadequacy but also, when compared to

other schools in other districts, a finding of inequality."); Helena Elem. Sch. Dist. No. 1 v. State, 769 P.2d 684, 690 (Mont. 1989) ("[D]iscrepancies in spending as large as the ones present in Montana translate . . . into unequal educational opportunities."); Claremont Sch. Dist. v. Governor, 703 A.2d 1353, 1359 (N.H. 1997) ("A constitutionally adequate public education is not a static concept removed from the demands of an evolving world.").

68. *See* Goodwin Liu, *Education, Equality, and National Citizenship*, 116 YALE L.J. 330, 347 (2006).

69. Rob Reich, *Equality, Adequacy, and K–12 Education, in* EDUCATION, JUSTICE, AND DEMOCRACY 43, 55 (Danielle Allen & Rob Reich eds., 2013).

70. *See* Anderson, *supra* note 12, at 596–98, 616–18; Satz, *supra* note 45, at 436, 438.

71. *See* Kenneth L. Karst, *The Liberties of Equal Citizens: Groups and the Due Process Clause*, 55 UCLA L. REV. 99, 103–04 (2007).

72. *See, e.g., id.* at 133–40; Rebecca L. Brown, *Liberty, the New Equality*, 77 N.Y.U. L. REV. 1491, 1541 (2002); Laurence H. Tribe, Lawrence v. Texas: *The "Fundamental Right" That Dare Not Speak Its Name*, 117 HARV. L. REV. 1893, 1902–05 (2004).

73. R. H. TAWNEY, EQUALITY 168 (Allen & Unwin 1964); *see also* Richard B. Wilson, *The Merging Concepts of Liberty and Equality*, 12 WASH. & LEE L. REV. 182, 194 (1955).

74. Julia A. Simon-Kerr & Robynn K. Sturm, *Justiciability and the Role of Courts in Adequacy Litigation: Preserving the Constitutional Right to Education*, 6 STAN. J. C.R. & C.L. 83, 96–97 (2010).

75. *Ex parte* James, 836 So. 2d 813, 819 (Ala. 2002); Coal. for Adequacy & Fairness in Sch. Funding, Inc. v. Chiles, 680 So. 2d 400, 406–08 (Fla. 1996); Comm. for Educ. Rights v. Edgar, 672 N.E.2d 1178, 1190–93 (Ill. 1996); Neb. Coal. for Educ. Equity & Adequacy v. Heineman, 731 N.W.2d 164, 178–80 (Neb. 2007); Okla. Educ. Ass'n v. State, 158 P.3d 1058, 1065–66 (Okla. 2007); City of Pawtucket v. Sundlun, 662 A.2d 40, 58–59 (R.I. 1995).

76. Charles J. Ogletree, Jr. & Kimberly Jenkins Robinson, *Introduction, in* THE ENDURING LEGACY OF *RODRIGUEZ*: CREATING NEW PATHWAYS TO EQUAL EDUCATIONAL OPPORTUNITY 1, 12 (Charles J. Ogletree, Jr. & Kimberly Jenkins Robinson eds., 2015).

77. *See* Derek W. Black, *Averting Educational Crisis: Funding Cuts, Teacher Shortages, and the Dwindling Commitment to Public Education*, 94 WASH. U. L. REV. 423, 463 (2017).

78. *See* Scott R. Bauries, *Is There an Elephant in the Room? Judicial Review of Educational Adequacy and the Separation of Powers in State Constitutions*, 61 ALA. L. REV. 701, 742 (2010) (identifying courts in eleven states that have observed "remedial abstention").

79. *See* DeRolph v. State (*DeRolph IV*), 780 N.E.2d 529, 529–31 (Ohio 2002) (citing three prior decisions).

80. William S. Koski, *The Politics of Judicial Decision-Making in Educational Policy Reform Litigation*, 55 HASTINGS L.J. 1077, 1167 (2004).

81. *See* Bauries, *supra* note 78, at 742–43 n.225 (counting courts in seven states that have issued "policy-directive remedial orders").

82. *See* Contempt Order at 10, McCleary v. State (*McCleary II*), No. 84362-7 (Wash. Aug. 13, 2015); Continuing Contempt Order at 11, McCleary v. State (*McCleary III*), No. 84362-7 (Wash. Oct. 6, 2016); Continuing Contempt Order at 44, McCleary v. State (*McCleary IV*), No. 84362-7 (Wash. Nov. 15, 2017).

83. Black, *supra* note 77, at 463.

84. Gannon v. State (*Gannon I*), 319 P.3d 1196, 1219 (Kan. 2014).

85. *Cf.* Obergefell v. Hodges, 135 S. Ct. 2584, 2603 (2015) (recognizing the right to marry as emanating from "synergy" between equal protection and due process).

86. Tribe, *supra* note 72, at 1907.

87. *See* Mario L. Barnes & Erwin Chemerinsky, *The Once and Future Equal Protection Doctrine?*, 43 CONN. L. REV. 1059, 1076 (2011).

88. *Id.* at 1063–64.

89. *See* Enrich, *supra* note 1, at 144–55; William S. Koski, *Of Fuzzy Standards and Institutional Constraints: A Re-examination of the Jurisprudential History of Educational Finance Reform Litigation*, 43 SANTA CLARA L. REV. 1185, 1203–11 (2003).

90. Derrick Darby & Richard E. Levy, *Slaying the Inequality Villain in School Finance: Is the Right to Education the Silver Bullet?*, 20 KAN. J.L. & PUB. POL'Y 351, 360 (2011).

91. *See* Koski, *supra* note 89, at 1206.

92. *See* Aaron Y. Tang, *Broken Systems, Broken Duties: A New Theory for School Finance Litigation*, 94 MARQ. L. REV. 1195, 1205 (2011).

93. Ryan & Saunders, *supra* note 53, at 472.

94. Robert K. Toutkoushian & Robert S. Michael, *An Alternative Approach to Measuring Horizontal and Vertical Equity in School Funding*, 32 J. EDUC. FIN. 395, 397–98 (2007).

95. Derek Black, *Unlocking the Power of State Constitutions with Equal Protection: The First Step toward Education as a Federally Protected Right*, 51 WM. & MARY L. REV. 1343, 1399 (2010) (contending that federal equal protection doctrine should be applied to enforce state qualitative guarantees, although recognizing limitations with this strategy (*see infra* note 98 and accompanying text)).

96. San Antonio Indep. Sch. Dist. v. Rodriguez, 411 U.S. 1, 33 (1973).

97. *See* Liu, *supra* note 68, at 334 ("[T]he 'substantive' dimension of disadvantage—the practical importance of an absolute or relative deprivation, apart from its causal origin—has had only a shadowy presence in equal protection doctrine.").

98. *See id.* at 399.

99. *See, e.g.*, Susan H. Bitensky, *Theoretical Foundations for a Right to Education under the U.S. Constitution: A Beginning to the End of the National Education Crisis*, 86 NW. U. L. REV. 550, 579–96 & n.177 (1992).

100. *See* Meyer v. Nebraska, 262 U.S. 390, 399 (1923) ("Without doubt, [liberty] denotes not merely freedom from bodily restraint but also the right of the individual . . . to engage in any of the common occupations of life, to acquire useful knowledge.").

101. *Cf.* Plyler v. Doe, 457 U.S. 202, 221–22, 262 (1982).

102. *See* Note, *A Right to Learn? Improving Educational Outcomes through Substantive Due Process*, 120 HARV. L. REV. 1323, 1333–34 (2007) (citing DeShaney v. Winnebago Cty. Dep't of Soc. Servs., 489 U.S. 189 (1989)); *see also id.* at 1336–37 (citing Youngberg v. Romeo, 457 U.S. 307 (1982)).

103. *See, e.g.*, Areto A. Imoukhuede, *Education Rights and the New Due Process*, 47 IND. L. REV. 467, 468 (2014).

104. Obergefell v. Hodges, 135 S. Ct. 2584, 2599–2602 (2015).

105. Kenneth W. Simons, *Equality as a Comparative Right*, 65 B.U. L. REV. 387, 478 (1985).

106. *Cf.* Arthur E. Wise, *Minimum Educational Adequacy: Beyond School Finance Reform*, 1 J. EDUC. FIN. 468, 477 (1976).

107. *See* Ryan & Saunders, *supra* note 53, at 472.

108. *See* Peter Westen, *The Meaning of Equality in Law, Science, Math, and Morals: A Reply*, 81 MICH. L. REV. 604, 663 n.66 (1983).

109. *See* Pamela S. Karlan, *Equal Protection, Due Process, and the Stereoscopic Fourteenth Amendment*, 33 MCGEORGE L. REV. 473, 474 (2002).

110. *See, e.g.*, Ronald Dworkin, *What Is Equality? Part 3: The Place of Liberty*, 73 IOWA L. REV. 1, 6, 12 (1987).

Conclusion

An American Dream Deferred: A Federal Right to Education

KIMBERLY JENKINS ROBINSON

Every child must be encouraged to get as much education as he has the ability to take. We want this not only for his sake—but for the nation's sake. Nothing matters more to the future of our country: not military preparedness—for armed might is worthless if we lack the brain power to build a world of peace; not our productive economy—for we cannot sustain growth without trained manpower; not our democratic system of government—for freedom is fragile if citizens are ignorant.
—Lyndon B. Johnson, *Special Message to the Congress: Toward Full Educational Opportunity*, 1 PUB. PAPERS 25, 26 (Jan. 12, 1965)

As President Johnson's remarks to Congress proclaim, education lies at the very foundation of society in the United States. A healthy democracy demands an educated citizenry. A robust economy needs an educated workforce. National security requires a sophisticated understanding of world history and the path to peace.

Despite these enduring truths, the United States continues to harm its own interests and prosperity by tolerating widespread opportunity and achievement gaps. In this volume, authors have explored how a federal right to education could help to close these gaps and thus build a stronger nation. Through the consideration of why the United States should or should not recognize a federal right to education, how the United States could recognize such a right, and what the right should guarantee, this volume engages the ongoing debate regarding how to move education reform from tinkering at the margins to restructuring the distribution, quality, and, ultimately, the aims of education.

The need for reform is urgent and must acknowledge the national peril in which we have placed ourselves by disadvantaging so many children because of their class, race, ethnicity, or zip code. The Supreme Court has previously cautioned the nation against denials of education that impose enduring disadvantages. When the United States Supreme Court in *Plyler v. Doe* overturned a law that effectively allowed school districts to deny enrollment to children who had not legally entered the country, it noted that "education has a fundamental role in maintaining the fabric of our society. We cannot ignore the significant social costs borne by our Nation when select groups are denied the means to absorb the values and skills upon which our social order rests."[1] This denial does not only occur when we close the schoolhouse door to some children. It occurs also when schools fail to equip children with the ability to effectively contribute to our democracy and economy. In the United States, such denials are far too often accepted and commonplace.

This brief conclusion begins with a discussion of why a renewed federal commitment to excellence and equity is essential for education reform, highlights the lessons that emerge throughout the book, and concludes with an analysis of how a path forward might be forged. In considering the lessons learned, it is important to understand that many of these lessons can help to inform a variety of education reforms, even if the reforms are not focused on a federal right to education. For instance, state and local lawmakers and courts often debate what their education laws and policies should provide for children. The lessons in part 3 of this book regarding what a federal right should guarantee can inform these debates and guide state and local lawmakers and policy makers to reconsider the aims of education as well as the equity and adequacy of educational opportunities, including when they are defining a state right to education. Similarly, future reauthorizations of the Elementary and Secondary Education Act should consider the reasons that federal intervention is essential for improving the quality and outcomes of education presented in part 1 of this book. Thus, this book can guide future education reforms, even if a federal right to education is not adopted.

The Urgent Need for a Renewed Federal Commitment to Equity and Excellence

A renewed federal commitment to equity and excellence is essential because states do not provide a consistent avenue for remedying educational inequities and inadequacies. States generally have failed to demonstrate through their design and administration of education that they are committed to equity.[2] As Bowman and Martin, Boser, and their colleagues acknowledge, school funding formulas demonstrate a lack of political will for reform of funding systems, including the unwillingness of states to provide sufficient resources for low-income and minority students. Recent data confirms their concerns. A 2018 national study examined the capacity of states to reach a common student achievement outcome. The study found that "[m]ost states fall below necessary funding levels for their highest poverty children to achieve national average outcomes," with districts with high poverty concentrations in several states falling "thousands to tens of thousands of dollars short, per pupil" of the funding necessary to achieve this goal.[3] In addition, for some states, only the lowest poverty quintile of districts has sufficient funding to achieve national average achievement outcomes. This record contrasts with the mere "handful of states" that target resources to higher-poverty schools and achieve substantially higher student achievement outcomes.[4]

Other school funding research confirms that on average the highest-poverty districts receive $1,000 less per pupil in state and local funding, and districts with the highest concentration of minority students receive $1,800 less per pupil in state and local funding.[5] The aggregation of these funding disparities across classrooms, schools, and districts leads to disparities in key resources, such as effective and well-qualified teachers, classroom supplies, technology, and adequate facilities. Although a few states provide imitation-worthy exceptions,[6] state actions overall do not focus on making sure that disadvantaged students receive the resources and opportunities that they need to compete successfully with their peers.

Although some people contend that the laboratory of the states is the best venue for reforming education,[7] it is worth considering whether the successes won by the wave of adequacy litigation may be receding. The education finance litigator and scholar William Koski offers evidence that "'adequacy' finance litigation appears to be stagnating." He highlights the rejections of plaintiffs' claims in California, Colorado, and Texas, as well as long-standing battles between the courts and legislatures in Washington and Kansas, as evidence of this possibility.[8] If his assessment proves accurate, even schoolchildren in districts with a strong right to an adequate education may lack a mechanism to initiate the lengthy negotiations between the court and the legislature that follow a successful case. Moreover, even if this litigation continues to yield litigation wins, too often these protracted negotiations do not result in changes to the fundamental structure of school funding that causes the inequities.[9]

Even when states decide to make equity and excellence in education a high priority, states vary widely in their ability to pay for education.[10] Some wealthy states can invest a small share of their economic resources into education and yield a larger amount than poorer states can.[11] In contrast, some poor states lack the capacity to spend more on education.[12] The disparate capacities of states to pay for education suggests that the states alone cannot accomplish greater adequacy of educational opportunity. Nevertheless, all states possess the ability to distribute their resources equitably so that the needs of all students, including disadvantaged and diverse learners, are addressed. Yet too few do so.[13] This fact, along with the disparate capacities of states to fund education, reveals the need for a new federal impetus that drives the states toward greater equity and adequacy of educational opportunity.

Given the unwillingness and inability of states to ensure equal access to an excellent education, the United States should recognize a federal right to education. At the heart of a federal right to education lies federal leadership toward a more equitable and excellent education system. Federal leadership must highlight the numerous benefits to the nation for this reform because research confirms that reforms that help the poor most often do not succeed unless the reforms also help wealthier Americans.[14] Federal leadership also must signal that the federal government is willing to roll up its sleeves and serve as a partner with states and localities in reforming education, in contrast to its role in recent decades, in which it demands much from states while giving very little.[15]

Only the federal government possesses the capacity to help states with substantial interstate spending, resource, and achievement gaps to close these gaps, given the diverse, and sometimes limited, capacity of states to achieve this goal. In addition, a federal infusion of research, technical assistance, and financial support could expand the capacity of states to close opportunity and achievement gaps within states and undertake comprehensive reform. Federal assistance to accomplish these goals can be spread across the national tax base and draw on a strong national economy. Similarly, only the federal government can incentivize all states to remedy impactful funding inequities.[16]

A federal right to education ensures that all students possess the ability to challenge and seek a remedy for inequitable and inadequate educational opportunities. The piecemeal approach of the states leaves far too many children without recourse when their states neglect their education. The absence of any accountability for state lawmakers is one of the key reasons that the substandard education of disadvantaged students persists generation after generation. In addition, with only a few exceptions, states pay for education through systems that are not related to how much it costs to enable students to learn the content of state standards or to meet the needs of diverse learners.[17] This finding from the bipartisan panel of experts on the United States Department of Education's Equity and Excellence Commission reveals a need for federal accountability that insists that states reexamine their education systems. Research also establishes the need for federal attention to state funding of education because these systems far too often provide less funding to districts with high concentrations of disadvantaged students, offer low funding levels, and lack effective oversight to ensure that money is spent wisely and efficiently.[18] A federal right to education would create much-needed accountability for remedying these shortcomings.

A federal right to education also would accomplish the long overdue shift in the balance of education federalism that I and others have called for.[19] Through a federal right to education, the federal government would serve as the final guarantor of the quality of educational opportunity, thereby reducing—and hopefully one day eliminating—the long-standing connections between a child's class, race, ethnicity, and zip code and his or her educational opportunities.[20] The federal government can only empower states to undertake comprehensive reform if it commits additional resources and expertise to this task. This substantial commitment would signal a new approach to education federalism that is needed to empower the states to achieve the aims of a federal right to education.

Ultimately, a renewed federal commitment to reshaping educational opportunity is consistent with the nation's belief in equal opportunity and its need for an engaged democracy. Americans overwhelmingly support equal opportunity as an American value.[21] Yet long-standing class and race gaps in educational opportunities betray this value. A federal right to education would help to ensure that schoolchildren receive an equal opportunity to attend an excellent school and that they leave school with the tools that they need for successful democratic engagement.[22]

Lessons Learned

The authors in this volume agree that the United States should address the opportunity and achievement gaps that exist along lines of class, race, ethnicity, and zip code. They document the persistence of disparities in funding, quality teachers, and other resources throughout this volume. For instance, Jason P. Nance quantifies both the funding and achievement gaps, while Kevin R. Johnson highlights the particular inequities experienced by Latina/o students, who are part of the largest minority group in the nation. Linda Darling-Hammond explicates the dimensions of teacher inequality by noting that "[i]n the United States, teachers are the most inequitably distributed school resource. By every measure of qualifications—certification, subject-matter background, pedagogical training, selectivity of college attended, test scores, or experience—less qualified teachers are found in schools serving greater numbers of low-income and minority students." The authors also explain that the opportunity and achievement gaps documented in this book are enduring and impactful.

Consensus also exists regarding the need to engage in new systemic reform to remedy these gaps. The need for new reforms arises from the unwillingness of states to address these gaps. Kristine L. Bowman's case study on Michigan reveals the refusal of that state and others to remedy opportunity and achievement gaps despite repeated calls for reform. Carmel Martin, Ulrich Boser, and their colleagues underscore the infrequency with which all three branches of state government coalesce to advance systemic school finance reform, as well as the grave consequences of long-standing failures to enact and implement meaningful reform. Joshua E. Weishart and Martin, Boser, and their colleagues document specific examples of how some judiciaries have ordered remedies but have not sparked effective legislative reform, while other states have enjoyed greater success. Several authors, including the Southern Education Foundation, Darling-Hammond, and Martin, Boser, and their colleagues, also highlight the fallacy of even asking states to resolve a problem that transcends state lines, given that the largest disparities in funding exist between states.

The federal government can and should provide new and important contributions to much-needed reform, according to the authors in this volume. Nance makes the case that prior federal education reforms have fallen short of the aim of ensuring that all children receive access to a quality education and that "[t]he time has come for a much-stronger response by the federal government." Indeed, Nance, Darling-Hammond, Johnson, and Rachel F. Moran note that some federal efforts have exacerbated existing challenges.

Most of the authors in this volume, including myself, also emphasize the importance of federal intervention that moves beyond tinkering at the margins of reform and recommend a federal right to education among the array of potential interventions. My chapter contends that Congress can restructure education federalism through a federal right to education in ways that would reshape education governance and make the federal government the ultimate guarantor of equal access to an excellent education. In addition, the authors in part 3 tackle the challenging questions regarding what a federal right to education should guarantee. Moran and Weishart reject the false dichotomy of providing only equity or adequacy. Instead, the authors recommend both a higher quality of and greater equity in funding, teachers, and opportunities to learn.

The authors also offer a variety of aims for a federal right to education. Authors emphasize the need for reallocating and raising the quality of inputs while reframing the aims of education. For example, Moran contends that each child should receive the opportunity to compete and that "the opportunity to compete requires that low-income students in schools with limited resources have a meaningful chance to approximate the achievements of affluent students in better-supported institutions." Similarly, Weishart states that "we owe [students] an effective, meaningful chance of educational success—one that approximates equal chances by diminishing the positional returns that the advantaged hold over the disadvantaged in the competition for higher education and high-quality jobs. To do so, we can equitably distribute and financially incentivize quality teachers, integrate schools, and target resources to improve academic growth, close achievement gaps, raise graduation rates, reduce class size, enhance the curriculum, and improve school facilities and access to technology. All of that is within our reach." These authors understand that attention to inputs is not sufficient if it does not reform the outcomes of the nation's education system.

Several of the authors in this volume highlight the advantages that a federal forum would provide over state courts in litigating a federal right to education. Indeed, Derek W. Black contends that "[t]he primary benefit, if any, of a federal equal protection claim would be venue. Litigating education claims in federal court might lead to more effective enforcement because federal judges are not subject to election, nor are they constrained by the separation-of-powers limits that dissuade state courts." Although Eloise Pasachoff ultimately recommends against a federal right to education, she also acknowledges the benefits of a federal forum in noting that "[t]hey can serve as neutral arbiters of justice rather than as politicians beholden to voters whose support they need for reelection." Federal courts have the unique authority to issue rulings that can benefit all children in the United States and thereby transcend state and district lines. This vast authority warrants proceeding with care and caution when invoking this federal authority but should not prevent reformers from tapping into federal authority where the laboratory of the states fails to provide equitable and high-quality schools.

Finally, and perhaps most importantly, the authors in this volume overwhelmingly agree that a just society demands equal access to a high-quality education. Peggy Cooper Davis captures this conviction well: "The history of indenture, slavery, and emancipation in the United States . . . exposes the link between education and personal, political, and economic liberty. It shows that education was denied—and even prohibited—for the express purpose of inhibiting liberty, of binding men and women to forced and uncompensated labor and preventing them from exercising agency to improve their conditions and determine the course of their lives. Contemporary deprivations of quality education have similar, if less extreme, effects, for they lock the undereducated within low-wage labor markets and limit their potential for civic agency." Similarly, Moran notes that "[t]he constitution of opportunity in the public schools may not guarantee perfect equality, but neither can it tolerate inequalities so profound that they estrange the nation's most vulnerable students from the American dream." These and other authors place education as the bedrock of a just society founded on democratic ideals. Without this foundation, we forge a path toward our own failure.

The Path Forward

A federal right to education and its accompanying expansion of the federal role in education undoubtedly stands at odds with the current political sentiment that successfully rolled back the federal role in education in the Every Student Succeeds Act.[23] Therefore, rather than presenting a possible reform for the next few years, this volume marks a pathway for a future time when a consensus reemerges that greater federal leadership is needed to improve educational opportunities and outcomes, just as such a consensus emerged when Republican President George W. Bush urged and secured passage of the No Child Left Behind Act. The current aspirational nature of a federal right to education should not dissuade the nation from engaging in a serious dialogue about the injustices of the current system and the benefits of a better one. Such a debate must precede any real reform and requires federal attention for the debate to be sustained and inclusive.[24]

A recent event suggests that the states are becoming more open to advancing equity. In 2017, a gathering of state education chiefs under the leadership of the Council of Chief State School Officers and the Aspen Institute issued a statement in which state chiefs committed to a set of recommendations regarding equity.[25] Such a statement could signal a new willingness to privilege equity over some competing education interests or, at minimum, to include equity among state goals.[26] The convergence of a social movement and greater state receptivity and commitment to equity can bring the United States closer to serious contemplation of protecting every child's right to an excellent education. Furthermore, the efforts to enact a federal right to education could bring about beneficial reforms that may not occur if the efforts are never undertaken.[27]

This book explores three strategies for recognizing a federal right to education in the United States. There is much to be said for undertaking multiple strategies to recognize such a right. Those who secured rights for African Americans pursued a wide variety of strategies, including constitutional amendments, federal legislation, Supreme Court victories, and executive action. Pursuing recognition of a federal right to education also might require pursuit of multiple strategies before progress is achieved.[28]

The example of the struggle of African Americans for equal rights also reminds us that a battle for a new right is likely to be long and arduous and ultimately may prove incomplete.[29] Reform will take significant time, but it is no less worthy for undertaking it simply because reforms do not produce a quick fix. The length of the battle must not dissuade the United States from recommitting itself to the instantiation of equal opportunity that lies at the heart of the American dream. Furthermore, a federal right to education should aim to achieve meaningful and sustained transformation of the distribution and quality of educational opportunities.

A federal right to education warrants serious consideration among the array of options that the United States considers when it engages in education reform. The enduring opportunity and achievement gaps demand nothing less than such a comprehensive reform. We must take up the mantle of reform to advance equity and excellence. We owe it to the present and future generations to forge a path forward.

NOTES

1. 457 U.S. 202, 221 (1982).
2. Cynthia G. Brown, *From ESEA to ESSA: Progress or Regress?*, *in* THE EVERY STUDENT SUCCEEDS ACT: WHAT IT MEANS FOR SCHOOLS, SYSTEMS AND STATES 153, 165 (Frederick M. Hess & Max Eden eds., 2017).
3. BRUCE D. BAKER ET AL., THE REAL SHAME OF THE NATION: THE CAUSES AND CONSEQUENCES OF INTERSTATE INEQUITY IN PUBLIC SCHOOL INVESTMENTS 38–39 (2018).
4. *Id.* at 39.
5. IVY MORGAN & ARY AMERIKANER, EDUC. TR., FUNDING GAPS 2018: AN ANALYSIS OF FUNDING EQUITY ACROSS THE U.S. AND WITHIN EACH STATE 6–7, 10 (2018).
6. For instance, New Jersey has reformed its funding system to address the diverse learning needs in the state. *See* David G. Sciarra & Danielle Farrie, *From Rodriguez to Abbott: New Jersey's Standards-Linked Funding Reform*, *in* THE ENDURING LEGACY OF *RODRIGUEZ*: CREATING NEW PATHWAYS TO EQUAL EDUCA-

TIONAL OPPORTUNITY 119, 125–133 (Charles J. Ogletree, Jr. & Kimberly Jenkins Robinson eds., 2015). Massachusetts also provides an effective model for offering disadvantaged students the resources they need to succeed. *See* BAKER ET AL., *supra* note 3, at 2, 32.

7. *See, e.g.*, JEFFREY S. SUTTON, 51 IMPERFECT SOLUTIONS: STATES AND THE MAKING OF AMERICAN CONSTITUTIONAL LAW 40 (2018) ("All else being equal, the States, I suspect, are more likely to address these problems effectively through sustained and engaged legislative and executive branch initiatives that balance the benefits of centralization with the benefits of local control. . . . [T]he policy issues underlying *Rodriguez* seem more amendable to fifty imperfect solutions than one imperfect solution, particularly if (as I suggest) a one-solution approach would have faced so many remedy-limiting constraints.").

8. William S. Koski, *Beyond Dollars? The Promises and Pitfalls of the Next Generation of Educational Rights Litigation*, 117 COLUM. L. REV. 1897, 1899, 1907–15 (2017).

9. JAMES E. RYAN, FIVE MILES AWAY, A WORLD APART: ONE CITY, TWO SCHOOLS, AND THE STORY OF EDUCATIONAL OPPORTUNITY IN MODERN AMERICA 153 (2010).

10. *See* BAKER ET AL., *supra* note 3, at 2, 39.

11. *See* BRUCE D. BAKER, DANIELLE FARRIE & DAVID SCIARRA, EDUC. LAW CTR., IS SCHOOL FUNDING FAIR? A NATIONAL REPORT CARD 15–16 (7th ed. 2018).

12. *See* BAKER ET AL., *supra* note 3, at 24, 39. For a fuller analysis of why interstate inequalities exist, *see generally id.*

13. *See* BAKER, FARRIE & SCIARRA, *supra* note 11, at 11; Brown, *supra* note 2, at 165.

14. DAVID K. COHEN & SUSAN L. MOFFITT, THE ORDEAL OF EQUALITY: DID FEDERAL REGULATION FIX THE SCHOOLS? 9 (2009). *See also generally* THE PRICE WE PAY: ECONOMIC AND SOCIAL CONSEQUENCES OF INADEQUATE EDUCATION (Clive R. Belfield & Henry M. Levin eds., 2007) (analyzing the costs of inadequate education to the United States).

15. Kimberly Jenkins Robinson, *Disrupting Education Federalism*, 92 WASH. U. L. REV. 959, 987 (2015).

16. *See* BAKER ET AL., *supra* note 3, at 39–40; Robinson, *supra* note 15, at 994–1000.

17. US DEP'T OF EDUC., EQUITY & EXCELLENCE COMM'N, FOR EACH AND EVERY CHILD: A STRATEGY FOR EDUCATION EQUITY AND EXCELLENCE 17 (2013).

18. For research summarizing the shortcomings of school funding systems, *see* Kimberly Jenkins Robinson, *No Quick Fix for Funding Equity and Excellence: The Virtues of Incremental Shifts in Education Federalism*, 27 STAN. L. & POL'Y REV. 201, 210–20 (2016).

19. For a discussion of why and how the United States should embrace a transformation of education federalism, *see* Robinson, *supra* note 15, at 972–83. *See also* Kristi L. Bowman, *The Failure of Education Federalism*, 51 U. MICH. J.L. REFORM 1, 16, 40 (2017); JACK JENNINGS, PRESIDENTS, CONGRESS, AND THE PUBLIC

SCHOOLS: THE POLITICS OF EDUCATION REFORM 185–217 (2015); Goodwin Liu, *Education, Equality, and National Citizenship*, 116 YALE L.J. 330, 399 (2006); MICHAEL A. REBELL & JESSICA R. WOLFF, MOVING EVERY CHILD AHEAD: FROM NCLB HYPE TO MEANINGFUL EDUCATIONAL OPPORTUNITY 145–51 (2008).

20. *See* Robinson, *supra* note 15, at 1002–05.
21. JENNIFER HOCHSCHILD & NATHAN SCOVRONICK, THE AMERICAN DREAM AND THE PUBLIC SCHOOLS 10 (2003).
22. ANNE NEWMAN, REALIZING EDUCATIONAL RIGHTS: ADVANCING SCHOOL REFORM THROUGH COURTS AND COMMUNITIES 116 (2013).
23. Robinson, *supra* note 18, at 242–47.
24. *See* Robinson, *supra* note 15, at 986–88.
25. ASPEN EDUC. & SOC'Y PROGRAM AND THE COUNCIL OF CHIEF STATE SCH. OFFICERS, LEADING FOR EQUITY: OPPORTUNITIES FOR STATE EDUCATION CHIEFS (2017), www.ccsso.org; Daarel Burnette II, *State Chiefs at Conference Tout Equity Policies in ESSA Plans*, EDUC. WK.: STATE EDWATCH (Feb. 16, 2018), https://blogs.edweek.org.
26. *See* Brown, *supra* note 2, at 165.
27. *See generally* ROGER C. HARTLEY, HOW FAILED ATTEMPTS TO AMEND THE CONSTITUTION MOBILIZE POLITICAL CHANGE (2017).
28. JENNINGS, *supra* note 19, at 206.
29. *See, e.g.*, MICHELLE ALEXANDER, THE NEW JIM CROW: MASS INCARCERATION IN THE AGE OF COLORBLINDNESS (2010).

CONGRESSMAN ROBERT C. "BOBBY" SCOTT OF VIRGINIA

More than sixty years have passed since the promise of educational equity for students of color was enshrined in the seminal 1954 ruling in *Brown v. Board of Education*. While the ruling marked a turning point, the Supreme Court's holding stopped short of creating a federal right to education—rendering the decision a dream deferred for too many Americans. The Warren Court challenged a legally segregated nation to make educational equity a national priority but affirmed realization of such equity to be a state responsibility by noting in dicta "where the state has undertaken to provide it, [education] is a right which must be made available to all on equal terms."[1]

The ensuing Massive Resistance to educational integration by states unwilling to provide the right of education "to all on equal terms" prompted civil unrest and racial violence that erupted across the US landscape. In Congress, Congressman Adam Clayton Powell repeatedly blocked federal aid to racially segregated schools. Civil rights groups employed a litigation strategy to drive the federal courts to enforce the mandate of *Brown* in the formerly legally segregated US South, as well as in other regions in the country where de facto segregation reigned. Federal investment, coupled with aggressive federal enforcement of *Brown*'s integration mandate, contributed to the rising test scores and narrowing of gaps in the decades immediately following *Brown*. Public backlash to such enforcement roiled the nation despite the 1965 passage and promise of the Elementary and Secondary Education Act (ESEA), the nation's cornerstone developmental education funding law intended to target federal resources to high-poverty communities. Ultimately, the resistance to the full integration of public education was assisted by a more conservative High Court, which narrowly held, in *San Antonio Independent School District v. Rodriguez*, that there was no federal right to an education.

There has been no shortage of federal policy making intended to improve delivery of public education and equity for underserved students since 1954. Following the 1983 publication of *A Nation at Risk* and calls for more acute action to close persistent achievement gaps, Congress moved through subsequent reauthorizations of ESEA to place more equity-focused mandates on state educational systems. However, the federal investment in general K–12 education steadily decreased in real dollars. This was made dramatically clear when Congress passed in 2001 the No Child Left Behind Act (NCLB) to increase accountability for student learning but failed to match the law with the requisite funding. As a result, NCLB was poorly implemented, and backlash to the unfunded mandates of the law led to a shrinkage of the federal role via administrative waivers from core requirements of the federal law in 2010.

In 2015, Congress sought a middle ground between state flexibility under administrative waivers and federal mandates of NCLB with the enactment of the Every Student Succeeds Act (ESSA). It is undeniably true that student learning in 2018 far surpasses that of 1965, but achievement and equity gaps persist. According to a 2016 analysis from the Government Accountability Office, students are more likely to attend schools isolated by race and income now than in the past.[2] What is more, schools with high concentrations of poverty and racial minorities are underresourced and overdisciplined, with students more likely to enter the school-to-prison pipeline than to graduate from high school and enroll in college.

Without an enforceable federal right to an education, Congress crafts and enacts legislation using authority derived from the Spending and General Welfare Clauses to incentivize states to accomplish equal educational opportunity. Although helpful, it has become clear that such authority is ineffective in guaranteeing equitable access to educational opportunity. Enactment of the ESEA was an attempt to step into the breach and provide funding to improve K–12 education. Allocating ESEA dollars on the basis of poverty does reach lower-income racial groups and some other poor students; but political resistance to improve equity through Spending Clause authority has reduced and undermined the role the federal government should play to enforce equity-focused educational mandates. Due to the limitations of Spending Clause authority, the most meaningful tool in the US Department of Education's enforcement toolbox is to withhold federal dollars for lack of compliance with federal education law. Yet withholding federal dollars from the most underresourced communities as retribution for a state system's lack of commitment to equity starves the neediest communities of vital educational resources. At best, it is counterproductive.

As federal enforcement of the integration mandate waned, so did the test scores that had risen and achievement gaps that had narrowed through the mid-1980s. Additionally, a string of Supreme Court rulings that were hostile to educational integration and deferential to local control stymied progress. For students of color, after the apex of federal enforcement of educational integration into the mid-1980s, stagnation in student achievement correlates highly with the subsequent retreat of such federal enforcement. School districts under consent decrees are mindful of the judiciary's and federal government's retreat from enforcement. In short, presidential commitment to equity in education is vital—and that is exemplified by the aggressive civil rights enforcement of the United States Departments of Justice and Education.

Despite this truism, the Trump administration and the US Department of Education's Office for Civil Rights are limiting the use of systematic review when investigating potential cases of disparate treatment impeding equal access to educational opportunity. This development is discouraging when considered in light of the Supreme Court's 2001 ruling in *Alexander v. Sandoval* that limits to the sole authority of the federal government the enforcement of the federal disparate-impact regulations under Title VI of the Civil Rights Act. This context makes the analysis and thought leadership put forward in this publication especially timely.

Bold and creative congressional action is needed to improve educational equity and to restore the private right of action to remedy the harm that results from policies and practices that cement inequity in education. The most well-intentioned federal education law cannot anticipate changes on the ground in every school district. Dedication to full funding and the eradication of inequities based on race and class must not take a back seat to the resurgence in popularity of "local control." Whether it is by way of a right secured through constitutional amendment or through legislation to mandate federal scrutiny of failing state or local systems, this nation cannot shirk its responsibility to address institutionalized inequity in all of its forms to fully realize *Brown*'s promise of equal educational opportunity.

NOTES

1. Brown v. Board of Education of Topeka, 347 U.S. 483, 493 (1954).
2. US GOV'T ACCOUNTABILITY OFFICE, GAO-16-345, BETTER USE OF INFORMATION COULD HELP AGENCIES IDENTIFY DISPARITIES AND AD-DRESS RACIAL DISCRIMINATION 12 (2016).

ACKNOWLEDGMENTS

I am grateful for the leadership and insights of Charles J. Ogletree, Jr. Charles and I conceptualized this project together, and he remains deeply committed to progressive scholarship on issues of equal educational opportunity. He is, and always will be, an enduring inspiration for my work. I also am indebted to Thomas Dorsey for his exceptional and dedicated research assistance. His steadfast hard work and feedback have contributed greatly to this book. In addition, I am grateful for the outstanding research assistance of Judson Peverall, Samantha Thoma, and Rebecca Thompson. Anna Rennich, Michael Gibbons, and Carly Wasserman also provided excellent research and editorial support for this book. First-rate library assistance was provided by Joyce Janto of the University of Richmond School of Law Library and Kate Boudouris, Kristin Glover, Kent Olson, John Roper, and Amy Wharton of the University of Virginia School of Law Library. Finally, my scholarship would not be possible without the enduring and enthusiastic support of my family—Gerard, Sienna, Naomi, and Kamaria Robinson.

ABOUT THE EDITOR

Kimberly Jenkins Robinson is Professor of Law and Executive Director of the Education Rights Institute at the University of Virginia School of Law. She is coeditor, with Charles Ogletree, Jr., of *The Enduring Legacy of* Rodriguez: *Creating New Pathways to Equal Educational Opportunity*. She is a national expert who speaks widely about educational equity, equal educational opportunity, civil rights, and the federal role in education. Prior to joining the UVA Law faculty in summer 2019, she was the Austin Owen Research Scholar at the University of Richmond School of Law. She served as cochair of the University of Richmond Faculty Senate's Sexual Assault Response and Prevention Committee, where she led the drafting of recommendations for strengthening the university's sexual assault policy, including many recommendations that were incorporated into a revised sexual assault policy. Robinson also served as chair of the law school's Diversity Committee and cochair of a university-wide faculty learning community on reducing implicit bias in teaching. She also is a Senior Fellow at the Learning Policy Institute.

Robinson's article "Disrupting Education Federalism," which was published in the *Washington University Law Review*, won the 2016 Steven S. Goldberg Award for distinguished scholarship in education law from the Education Law Association. This article argues that the United States should reconstruct its understanding of education federalism to support a national effort to ensure equal access to an excellent education. Her scholarship has appeared in the *Harvard Law Review, Stanford Law and Policy Review, University of Chicago Law Review, Boston College Law Review,* and *William and Mary Law Review,* among other venues.

Prior to joining the Richmond Law faculty in 2010, Robinson was Associate Professor at Emory University School of Law and a Visiting Fellow at George Washington University Law School. She also served in the General Counsel's Office of the US Department of Education, where she helped draft federal policy on issues of race, sex, and disability discrimination. In addition, Robinson represented school districts in school finance and constitutional law litigation as an associate with Hogan & Hartson (now Hogan Lovells). She received her JD from Harvard Law School (cum laude) and her BA from the University of Virginia.

ABOUT THE CONTRIBUTORS

Derek W. Black is Professor of Law at the University of South Carolina School of Law. His areas of expertise include education law and policy, constitutional law, civil rights, evidence, and torts. The focus of his current scholarship is the intersection of constitutional law and public education, particularly as it pertains to educational equality and fairness for disadvantaged students. He is the author of a leading education law casebook, a scholarly book with NYU Press, and over twenty-five full-length law review articles and essays, appearing in journals such as the *Yale Law Journal, Stanford Law Review, NYU Law Review, California Law Review, Northwestern University Law Review, Vanderbilt Law Review, Washington University Law Review, Minnesota Law Review*, and *Boston University Law Review*. His work has been cited in the US Circuit Courts of Appeals and by several briefs before the US Supreme Court. He has also served as an expert witness in federal education cases. He earned his JD from the University of North Carolina and his BA from the University of Tennessee.

Ulrich Boser is the founder of the Learning Agency and a Senior Fellow at the Center for American Progress. He is also the founding director of the Center for American Progress's science of learning initiative. Boser is the author of three books including the recently released *Learn Better*, which Amazon called one of the best books of the year. Before American Progress, Boser worked as a contributing editor for *U.S. News and World Report* and a researcher for the newspaper *Education Week*. Boser's articles have appeared in a variety of publications including the *New York Times*, the *Wall Street Journal*, and the *Washington Post*. He has also been an Arthur F. Burns fellow and an adviser to the Bill & Melinda Gates Foundation and has been featured on CNN, NPR, and *NBC Nightly News*. He earned his BA from Dartmouth College with honors.

Kristine L. Bowman is Professor of Law and affiliated faculty in the Education Policy Center, Michigan State University. Her research focuses on issues of liberty and equality in K–12 education law and policy. She is the editor of the forthcoming *Oxford Handbook on US K–12 Education Law*, a coauthor of the fifth edition of *Educational Policy and the Law* (2012), and the author of numerous other publications on a range of education law topics. She is an elected member of the American Law Institute and a fellow of the American Bar Foundation; in 2010, she received the Education Law Association's Steven S. Goldberg Award for Distinguished Scholarship in Education Law. Prior to teaching, Bowman practiced at Franczek Sullivan, P.C. (now Franczek P.C.), in Chicago, where she represented school districts. During law school, she worked at the United States Department of Education, Office for Civil Rights. She earned her JD and MA from Duke University and her BA from Drake University.

Linda Darling-Hammond is the Charles E. Ducommun Professor of Education Emeritus at Stanford University and President of the Learning Policy Institute, which conducts and communicates independent, high-quality research to improve education policy and practice. She previously served as Director of the RAND Corporation's education program and as an endowed professor at Columbia University, Teachers College. Darling-Hammond is past president of the American Educational Research Association and recipient of its awards for Distinguished Contributions to Research, Lifetime Achievement, and Research-to-Policy. She is also a member of the American Association of Arts and Sciences and of the National Academy of Education. From 1994 to 2001, she was Executive Director of the National Commission on Teaching and America's Future, whose 1996 report *What Matters Most: Teaching for America's Future* was named one of the most influential reports affecting US education in that decade. In 2006, Darling-Hammond was named one of the nation's ten most influential people affecting educational policy. Among her more than six hundred publications are a number of award-winning books, including *The Right to Learn, Teaching as the Learning Profession, Preparing Teachers for a Changing World*, and *The Flat World and Education: How America's Commitment to Equity Will Determine Our Future*. She received an EdD from Temple University (with highest distinction) and a BA from Yale University (magna cum laude).

Peggy Cooper Davis is the John S. R. Shad Professor of Lawyering and Ethics at New York University School of Law. Her scholarly work has been influential in the areas of child welfare, constitutional rights of families, and interdisciplinary analysis of legal pedagogy and process. Davis's 1997 book, *Neglected Stories: The Constitution and Family Values*, illuminates the importance of antislavery traditions as guides to the meaning of the Fourteenth Amendment. Her recent book, *Enacting Pleasure*, is a collection of essays exploring the social, cultural, psychological, and political implications of Carol Gilligan's relational psychology. She also has published more than fifty articles and book chapters, most notably in the journals of Harvard, Yale, NYU, and Michigan law schools. She earned her JD from Harvard Law School and her BA cum laude from the Western College for Women.

Kevin R. Johnson is Dean, Mabie-Apallas Professor of Public Interest Law, and Professor of Chicana/o Studies at the University of California, Davis. He joined the UC Davis law faculty in 1989 and was named Associate Dean for Academic Affairs in 1998. Johnson became Dean in 2008. He has taught a wide array of classes, including immigration law, civil procedure, complex litigation, Latinos and Latinas and the law, and critical race theory. His book *How Did You Get to Be Mexican? A White/Brown Man's Search for Identity* was nominated for the 2000 Robert F. Kennedy Book Award. Johnson's book *Immigration Law and the US-Mexico Border* (2011) received the Latino Literacy Now's International Latino Book Awards—Best Reference Book. He earned his JD magna cum laude from Harvard Law School and his AB from the University of California, Berkeley.

Carmel Martin is Managing Director, State and Local Partnerships, at the Emerson Collective. She is a Distinguished Senior Fellow at American Progress. Martin was formerly Executive Vice President for Policy at American Progress, managing the organization's policy teams, shaping organizational strategy, and serving as a key member of American Progress's executive team. Martin also served as Assistant Secretary for Policy and Budget at the US Department of Education. Prior to her appointment by former president Barack Obama, Martin worked in the United States Senate for almost a decade, including as general counsel and deputy staff director for the late Senator Edward Kennedy (D-MA). Early in Martin's career, she worked as a trial attorney for the Civil Rights Division at the US Department of Justice and as a member of Hogan and Hartson's (now Hogan Lovells) education practice. Martin has appeared on PBS, NBC, CNN, and Fox. She has been published in and cited in publications including the New York Times and the *Washington Post.*

Martha Minow is the 300th Anniversary University Professor at Harvard University. She previously served as the Morgan and Helen Chu Dean and Professor at Harvard Law School (2009–17), where she has taught since 1981. Besides her many scholarly articles published in journals of law, history, and philosophy, her books include *In* Brown's *Wake: Legacies of America's Constitutional Landmark* (2010), *Just Schools: Pursuing Equality in Societies of Difference* (coedited), and *Engaging Cultural Differences: The Multicultural Challenge in Liberal Democracies* (coedited, 2002). An expert in human rights, civil rights, and constitutional law, she is Vice Chair of the Legal Services Corporation, the bipartisan, government-sponsored organization that provides civil legal assistance to low-income Americans. She served as policy director for a collaboration between the US Department of Education and the Center for Applied Special Technology designed to enable curricular access for students with disabilities. Her honors include the Sacks-Freund Award for Excellence in Teaching at Harvard Law School, the Sargent Shriver Equal Justice Award, the Joseph B. and Toby Gittler Price Award from Brandeis University, and nine honorary degrees from schools in three countries, to name a few. Her current activities include service on the board of the MacArthur Foundation and chairing the selection committee for the Profiles in Courage Award of the JKF Presidential Library and Museum. After completing her undergraduate studies at the University of Michigan, Minow received a master's degree in education from Harvard and her law degree from Yale.

Rachel F. Moran is Dean Emerita and Michael J. Connell Distinguished Professor of Law at UCLA. Before that, she was the Robert D. and Leslie-Kay Raven Professor of Law at UC Berkeley and received that campus's Distinguished Teaching Award in 1995. At Berkeley, she served as Chair of the Chicano/Latino Policy Project from 1993 to 1996 as well as Director of the Institute for the Study of Social Change from 2003 to 2008. From 2008 to 2010, she was a founding faculty member at the UC Irvine Law School. Moran is a prolific scholar. Her numerous publications include *Educational Policy and the Law* (with Mark G. Yudof, Betsy Levin, James E. Ryan, and Kristi L. Bowman, 5th ed., 2012); *Race Law Stories* (with Devon Carbado, 2008), and *Interracial Intimacy: The Regulation of Race and Romance* (2001). In addition, she has published over sixty articles and book chapters on equity and access in elementary and secondary education, affirmative action and diversity in higher education, and Latino-related law and policy issues. Her most recent work focuses on the impact of growing inequality on educational opportunity as well as on the findings from an American Bar Foundation project called "The Future of Latinos in the United States: Law, Opportunity, and Mobility," which she is codirecting with Robert L. Nelson. Moran received her AB in psychology from Stanford University with honors and with distinction and was elected to Phi Beta Kappa her junior year. She obtained her JD from Yale Law School.

Jason P. Nance is Associate Dean for Academic Affairs and Professor of Law at the University of Florida Levin College of Law. He also serves as Associate Director for Education Law and Policy at UF's Center on Children and Families. He teaches education law, remedies, torts, and introduction to the legal profession. He focuses his research and writing on racial inequalities in public education, cognitive biases and their effects on education systems, the intersection of criminal justice and public education, students' legal rights, and the legal profession. His scholarship has been published in the *Washington University Law Review*, *Emory Law Journal*, and *Wisconsin Law Review*, among several other journals. His research has been featured in many major media outlets and cited by several courts, party and amicus briefs, law journals, books, treatises, and education and other social science journals. Nance also served as the reporter for the American Bar Association's Joint Task Force on Reversing the School-to-Prison Pipeline, where he coauthored a report and proposed resolutions for the ABA to adopt to help dismantle the school-to-prison pipeline nationwide. In addition to earning a JD at the University of Pennsylvania Law School, Nance has a PhD in education administration from the Ohio State University, where he focused on empirical methodology. Before attending graduate school and law school, Nance was a public school math teacher in a large, metropolitan school district.

Eloise Pasachoff is Professor of Law, Agnes N. Williams Research Professor, and Associate Dean for Career Planning at the Georgetown University Law Center, where she teaches and writes in education law and administrative law. Her scholarship has received national awards in both of those fields, including the American Bar Association's award for scholarship in administrative law in 2017 and the Education Law Association's Steven S. Goldberg Award for Distinguished Scholarship in 2012. A former middle school and high school teacher, Pasachoff won Georgetown Law's Frank F. Flegal Excellence in Teaching Award in 2017. She earned an AB, MPA, and JD from Harvard University and an MA from Yale University.

Southern Education Foundation's mission is to advance creative solutions to ensure equity and excellence in education for low-income students and students of color in the South. Lynn Huntley was President of the Southern Education Foundation when she wrote "No Time to Lose: Why America Needs an Education Amendment to the Constitution." This work was revised to become the chapter "Why America Needs an Education Amendment to the US Constitution." Huntley came to SEF in 1995 from the Ford Foundation and directed the Comparative Human Relations Initiative, which examined strategies for improving race relations in Brazil, South Africa, and the United States. She was SEF's first female president and built on a number of important initiatives that included Still Striving, Miles to Go, New Majority, and the Southern Education Leadership Initiative.

Joshua E. Weishart is Professor of Law and Policy with a joint appointment at the West Virginia University College of Law and John D. Rockefeller IV School of Policy and Politics. His research is centered on K–12 education law and policy with a particular focus on education rights and the constitutional demands of adequacy and equity. Weishart's scholarship has been published in the Stanford Law Review and William & Mary Law Review, among other law journals, and a forthcoming chapter will appear in the *Oxford Handbook on US Education Law*. In the Rockefeller School, he conducts policy research and administers the *WV ED Law Blog*. Weishart is the recipient of multiple teaching and scholarship awards. He earned his JD from the University of California, Berkeley School of Law, an MPhil from the University of Cambridge, and a BA from West Virginia University.

ADDITIONAL CONTRIBUTORS

Perpetual Baffour is a data analyst at the School District of Philadelphia, where her work focuses on strategic analytics and the use of high-quality data tools to inform policy decision-making. Previously, Baffour was a research associate at the Center for American Progress. Her work focused on policy reform in educational innovation, standards, and fiscal equity. Baffour also served as an Emerson Fellow of National Policy for the Netter Center for Community Partnerships, housed at the Institute of Educational Leadership in Washington, DC. She earned her BA from the University of Pennsylvania.

Meg Benner is a senior consultant for the Center for American Progress and an independent consultant for various education policy organizations. Previously, she worked as Senior Director at Leadership for Educational Equity. Benner worked on Capitol Hill on education, disability, and labor policies for the House Committee on Education and the Workforce, Senator Richard Blumenthal (D-CT), and Senator Christopher Dodd (D-CT). She started her career teaching first and second grade in the Bronx. Benner received her undergraduate degree in American studies from Georgetown University and a master's degree of science in teaching from Pace University.

INDEX

Abbott v. Burke: achievement gap and, 297; adequacy and, 14, 288–89, 297

accountability frameworks: ESSA and, 295; finance reform and, 284, 290–92, 294–95; school report cards in, 295; weighted student funding and, 292, 294–95. *See also* test-based accountability

A.C. ex rel. Waithe v. Raimondo: curriculum quality and, 301n77; Fourteenth Amendment and, 17–18; fundamental right to education and, 18

achievement gap, 1–2, 189, 262, 327, 330–36; *Abbott v. Burke* and, 297; African Americans and, 7–9, 37, 115, 117, 248; Alon and Tienda on, 39; Asians and, 8–9; class and, 7–9, 30n50, 36–37, 57n18, 272–73, 340; college graduation rates and, 272–73; curriculum quality and, 248–51; excellence gap as, 272, 282n106; Hispanics and, 7–9, 37; Latina/os and, 115–17, 248; Michigan and, 70–71; parent's education and, 243; principal turnover and, 246; Putnam on, 272–73; race and, 7–9, 36–37, 57n18, 115, 117, 243, 248, 340–41; Reardon on, 37, 272; Sharkey on, 47–48; teacher quality impact on, 242–45; teacher turnover and, 245; tracking and, 248–50; Wagner on, 249; whites and, 7–8, 115

Act to Establish Free Schools, 173

Adams, Abigail, xiii

Adams, John, vii

adequacy, x–xi; *Abbott v. Burke* and, 288–89, 297; *A.C. ex rel. Waithe v. Raimondo* and, 17–18, 301n77; adequacy model for Edu-cation Amendment and, 227; business community concern for, 262; *Campaign for Fiscal Equity v. State of New York* and, 270–71, 281n88; *Connecticut Coalition for Justice in Education Funding v. Rell* on, 290; democratic equality and, 310, 313; equal liberty and, 311–15, 320; equal pro-tection and, 140, 316–20; equity versus, 24–25, 261–62, 265–69, 285–86, 303–4, 310, 316, 333; ESSA and, 144, 238; formal equality and, 317; fundamental right to education and, 143–45, 153–55; *Hancock v. Commissioner of Education* and, 289; Idaho Supreme Court on, 296; Kansas Supreme Court and, 316; Kentucky Su-preme Court and, 309; Koski on, 329–30; liberty, impairment of, requiring, 143–44; literacy and, 145; *McDuffy v. Secretary of the Executive Office of Education* and, 289; Michigan and, 145; New York and, 311; North Carolina Supreme Court and, 271; *Plyler v. Doe* and, 154–55; Ratner on, 143; right to education, implied, and, 143–45, 153–55; *Rodriguez* and, 11–12, 238–39, 266–67, 289–90; *Rose v. Council for Better Education* and, 271; *Serrano v. Priest* and, 266–67, 270; South Dakota Supreme Court and, 271; state finance litigation and, 12–13, 139, 218–20, 268–69, 285, 288–90, 329–30; stigma and, 145; substantive due process and, 144–45, 318–20; Supreme Court on, 135; test-based accountability and, 219; Washington Supreme Court and, 271–72; *Youngberg v. Romero* and, 143–45

Milton Keynes UK
Ingram Content Group UK Ltd.
UKHW012132160823
426985UK00007B/165